Judges on Judging

Views from the Bench

Third Edition

Collected and edited by

David M. O'Brien
University of Virginia

A Division of SAGE
Washington, D.C.

CQ Press
2300 N Street, NW, Suite 800
Washington, DC 20037

Phone: 202-729-1900; toll-free, 1-866-4CQ-PRESS (1-866-427-7737)

Web: www.cqpress.com

Copyright © 2009 by CQ Press, a division of SAGE. CQ Press is a registered trademark of Congressional Quarterly Inc.

All rights reserved. No part of this publication may be reproduced or transmitted in any form or by any means, electronic or mechanical, including photocopy, recording, or any information storage and retrieval system, without permission in writing from the publisher.

Cover design: Mike Grove, MG Design, Sykesville, MD
Cover image: istockphoto.com
Composition: PerfecType, Nashville, TN

♾ The paper used in this publication exceeds the requirements of the American National Standard for Information Sciences—Permanence of Paper for Printed Library Materials, ANSI Z39.48-1992.

Printed and bound in the United States of America

12 11 10 09 08 1 2 3 4 5

Library of Congress Cataloging-in-Publication Data

Judges on judging : views from the bench / collected and edited by David M. O'Brien. — 3rd ed.
p. cm.
Includes bibliographical references.
ISBN 978-0-87289-951-3 (pbk. : alk. paper)
1. Judges—United States. 2. Judicial process—United States. 3. Political questions and judicial power—United States. I. O'Brien, David M.
KF8775.A75J82 2008
347.73'14—dc22

2008036393

Contents

Preface

THE FIRST EDITION of this collection of judges' speeches and writings originated while I was working as a judicial fellow in the Office of the Administrative Assistant to the Chief Justice at the Supreme Court of the United States. I remain grateful for the opportunities that Chief Justice Warren E. Burger and Mark Cannon afforded me, along with the support of Edward Artinian and of reviewers and colleagues, particularly Henry J. Abraham. That first edition received the American Bar Association's Certificate of Merit for contributing to the public's understanding of law and courts. Like the first edition, the second edition has been well received and used in a range of courses. Those who teach and study judicial processes and judicial policymaking have found the breadth of coverage useful in presenting the contrasting views and experiences of state and federal judges, especially the differing experiences of trial and appellate court judges, as well as those who have served or are serving on the Supreme Court. Others find the chapters presenting competing judicial philosophies and approaches to interpreting the Constitution and Bill of Rights especially useful in courses on constitutional law, jurisprudence, and judicial politics. University of California–Berkeley scholar Martin Shapiro's comment on an earlier edition perhaps expressed it best: "Imagine the fun of teaching a course in which you ask students to compare opinions of particular judges with their off-the-bench writings on judging. What a great supplement to a regular constitutional law course."

In this third edition, the introductory essays have been thoroughly revised and updated. They highlight through a historical perspective the increasing frequency of and controversies over current judges' and justices' off-the-bench commentaries. Several new chapters have also been added. Two chapters present excerpts from classic works by Judge Jerome Frank and Justice Benjamin N. Cardozo. Two other new chapters include excerpts from contemporary judges and justices: one by federal district court Judge D. Brock Hornby on the changing work of trial court judges, and the other by Chief Justice John G. Roberts Jr. on the state of the federal judiciary. In addition, in light of the recent controversy on and off the bench over the Supreme Court's reliance on foreign judicial decisions and law, there is a chapter on the topic by Chief Justice Aharon Barak of the Supreme Court of Israel. This third edition also includes two new appendices: Article III of the U.S. Constitution, establishing the basis for the federal courts, and Alexander Hamilton's *Federalist* essay No. 78 on the role of the federal judiciary and the power of constitutional interpretation. This edition also incurred still more debts. I appreciate the permission to incorporate these materials and the suggestions of the following reviewers: Elizabeth Beaumont, University of Minnesota; Christopher Bonneau, University of Pittsburgh; Russell Fowler, University of Tennessee–Chattanooga; Banks Miller, Ohio State University; Patrick Schmidt, Southern Methodist University; and Kim Seckler, New Mexico State University. I also appreciate the support and work of Charisse Kiino and Allie McKay at CQ Press.

As with earlier editions, hopefully, students will find these revisions and new additions useful in understanding judicial processes, as well as the work and problems confronting courts. It is also hoped that the collection will continue to engage them in the contemporary and enduring debates over competing judicial philosophies and approaches to constitutional interpretation, judging, and the role of courts in a democracy.

David M. O'Brien
May 2008

Introduction

To a reporter's question whether the average American understands the judicial process, former congressman and later federal Court of Appeals judge Abner J. Mikva responded, "No. In a sense [people] know less about the courts than they do about the Congress. They may have a lot of mistaken views about Congress, but the problem with the courts is that they are so mysterious. I worry about that a great deal. Some of my colleagues on the bench think that is why the judicial branch is given a great deal of respect, that it isn't as well known as the other two branches. I hate to think that we're only beloved in ignorance."[1] Courts and the judicial process are generally open and accessible, though particular aspects may be closed or open only to professional observers. Whatever mystery surrounds the judiciary undoubtedly stems from what Judge Jerome Frank called "the cult of the robe"[2] and Justice Felix Frankfurter felicitously described as "judicial lockjaw."[3]

In recent years, however, the "tradition" of judicial lockjaw has been increasingly honored more often in rhetoric than in practice. Consider, for instance, the justices' off-the-bench comments regarding their controversial decision in *Bush v. Gore* (2000),[4] which reversed the Florida state supreme court's order for a recount of ballots in that state's presidential election in 2000. The Court split 7–2 in finding a constitutional violation in the voting procedure but then voted 5–4 in deciding that there was no remedy available and thus effectively secured the selection of Republican presidential candidate George W. Bush in the Electoral College. The bare majority in *Bush v. Gore*—Chief Justice William H. Rehnquist and Justices Sandra Day O'Connor, Antonin Scalia, and Clarence Thomas—were all appointed by Republican presidents Ronald Reagan and George H. W. Bush. The four dissenters—Justice John Paul Stevens, an appointee of Republican president Gerald R. Ford; Justice David H. Souter, a Bush appointee; and Justices Ruth Bader Ginsburg and Stephen Breyer, appointees of Democratic president Bill Clinton—each issued bitter dissenting opinions that reinforced charges that the ruling was simply partisan and ideological.[5] Not content to rest with the ruling, though, Justice Clarence Thomas, in a televised appearance on C-SPAN the day after *Bush v. Gore* was handed down, dismissed charges that the justices are political. "The members of the Court don't pair off," he declared. "There aren't these [conservative and liberal] cliques." Later that day, when a reporter relayed Thomas's remarks, Chief Justice Rehnquist responded, "Absolutely, absolutely."[6] By contrast, in a subsequent public lecture, though without repeating the stinging criticisms in her dissent in *Bush v. Gore,* Justice Ruth Bader Ginsburg offered the decision as an example of "how important—and difficult—it is for judges to do what is legally right, no matter what 'the home crowd' wants," and said the final assessment of *Bush v. Gore* "awaits history's judgment."[7] But in 2008, defending the ruling in *Bush v. Gore* in response to a question, Justice Scalia told students at Princeton University: "Oh, get over it! It's eight years ago.... By a five–four vote we decided enough was enough and put an end to it and I think the vast majority of the country were grateful that we did that."[8]

Justice Scalia, in particular, has ignited controversies over his off-the-bench remarks criticizing recent rulings of the Supreme Court and lower federal courts. Over his bitter dissent in *Lawrence v. Texas* (2003), a majority struck down Texas's law criminalizing homosexual sodomy. Subsequently in a lecture to the Intercollegiate Studies Institute, a conservative educational organization, he described the ruling as having "held to be a constitutional right what had been a criminal offense at the time of the founding and for nearly 200 years thereafter." A champion of basing constitutional interpretation on the Founders' "original intent," he lamented, "Most of today's experts on the Constitution think the document written in Philadelphia in 1787 was simply an early attempt at the construction of what is called a liberal political order" and ridiculed the idea that "all that the person interpreting or applying that document has to do is to read up on the latest academic understanding of liberal political theory and interpolate these constitutional understandings into the constitutional text."[9] On another occasion he criticized the ruling of the Court of Appeals for the Ninth Circuit holding that the phrase "one nation, under God" in the Pledge of Allegiance violated the First Amendment. That decision was a mistaken attempt, in his words, to "exclude God from the public forums and from political life."[10] When the Supreme Court later granted review of that decision, Michael A. Newdow, who had brought the suit, *Elk Grove Unified School District v. Newdow* (2004), asked that Justice Scalia recuse himself from the case and forced Scalia not to participate in the decision because of his off-the-bench remarks. But subsequently, after a public uproar over his going duck hunting with Vice President Dick Cheney, Justice Scalia refused to recuse himself from *Cheney v. U.S. District Court* (2004), a suit over access to the records of a White House energy task force headed by Cheney. In an extraordinary twenty-one-page memorandum, Scalia justified his decision on the ground that mere friendship was not a basis for recusal and rebutted newspaper editorials calling for his recusal. Later, when addressing a University of Connecticut Law School audience, Scalia again rebuffed criticisms of a potential conflict of interest in the case, remarking, "For Pete's sake, if you can't trust your Supreme Court justice more than that, get a life."[11] Justice Scalia has been outspoken in defending his off-the-bench positions on other matters, including defending the Court's continued exclusion of cameras in the courtroom during oral arguments, disagreeing with the Court's citation of foreign judicial decisions in its opinions, and dismissing European criticism of the impeachment of President Bill Clinton and the treatment of enemy combatants in Guantánamo Bay, Cuba.[12]

Chief Justice John G. Roberts Jr. has been more open to the media than his predecessors, Chief Justices Warren E. Burger and William H. Rehnquist. Like his predecessors he has given numerous lectures to law schools and bar associations, but he has also given interviews and appeared on ABC's *Nightline.*[13] Nor is Chief Justice Roberts alone in offering more off-the-bench comments and access. Indeed, Chief Justice Roberts and seven other justices—all except Justice Souter—provided videotaped interviews on their experiences and observations on legal writing and oral advocacy; the videotaped interviews are available on LawProse's Web site at www.lawprose.org. Like Justice Scalia, Justices Stevens, Kennedy, Ginsburg, and Breyer have been generally open to interviews and frequently delivered public lectures and published them as articles and in books.[14] Justice Ginsburg has also posted her speeches on the Supreme Court's Web site, at www.supremecourtus.gov/publicinfo/speeches. By contrast Justices Souter, Thomas, and Alito are more reticent, typically only speaking before small groups and bar associations.

Despite such contemporary justices' and judges' off-the-bench observations,[15] the tradition of judicial lockjaw evolved originally because of a number of institutional, political, and historical considerations. Article III of the Constitution, which vests the judicial power in one Supreme Court and in such lower federal courts as Congress may establish, provides that the judiciary shall decide only actual cases or controversies. From the earliest days, federal courts have therefore refused to render advisory opinions or advice on abstract and hypothetical issues.[16] Intimately related to the view that advisory opinions would violate the principle of separation of powers and compromise judicial independence, justices and judges contend that they should not offer off-the-bench commentaries on their decisions and opinions. As Justice William J. Brennan Jr. once recounted:

> A great Chief Justice [Arthur T. Vanderbilt] of my home State [New Jersey] was asked by a reporter to tell him what was meant by a passage in an opinion which has excited much lay comment. Replied the Chief Justice, "Sir, we write opinions, we don't explain them." This wasn't arrogance—it was his picturesque, if blunt, way of reminding the reporter that the reasons behind the social policy

> fostering an independent judiciary also require that the opinions by which judges support decisions must stand on their own merits without embellishment or comment from the judges who write or join them.[17]

Explanations of judicial opinions have also been thought to be ill-advised for more prudential reasons: Justice Hugo L. Black, among others, felt that off-the-bench remarks might prejudge issues that could come before the courts;[18] and Justice Harlan F. Stone counseled that such public discussions might actually invite litigation.[19]

Judicial opinions, whether those of trial or appellate judges, of course do not purport to describe the decision-making process. They are intended to justify the decision in a particular case, and they therefore reveal merely the surface of the judicial process. As Justice Frankfurter once noted: "The compromises that an opinion may embody, the collaborative effort that it may represent, the inarticulate considerations that may have influenced the grounds on which the case went off, the shifts in position that may precede final adjudication—these and like factors cannot, contemporaneously at all events, be brought to the surface."[20]

The constraints of judges' "self-denying ordinance,"[21] by which Justice Benjamin N. Cardozo abided throughout his tenure on the high bench, further inhibit disclosures about the deliberative and decision-making processes. Justices' revelations inevitably prove modest given the institutional and political realities of judicial decision making. Unlike legislative decisions, judicial decisions, particularly in the Supreme Court and multijudge appellate courts, are collegial and reached in an atmosphere that Justice Lewis F. Powell has described as one of "the last citadels of jealously preserved individualism."[22] Off-the-bench remarks about the deliberative process are therefore controlled by self-imposed standards of propriety that appear necessary to preserving the confidentiality—institutionally and personally—required of life-tenured judges who must sit together and collegially decide cases. For as Chief Justice Earl Warren recollected, "when you are going to serve on a court of that kind for the rest of your productive days, you accustom yourself to the institution like you do to the institution of marriage, and you realize that you can't be in a brawl every day and still get any satisfaction out of life."[23]

The lessons of history have also inclined members of the judiciary to refrain from voicing their views not only on matters pertaining to the judicial process and law but also on politics more generally. During the founding period, judges in fact engaged in intensely partisan debates over differing views of constitutional principles. Chief Justice John Jay ran for the governorship of New York but did not campaign, as did Justice William Cushing in running for that office in Massachusetts; and Justice Samuel Chase campaigned for the election of John Adams as president.[24] By the late 1840s and 1850s, however, there emerged considerable opposition to judges'—and specifically Justice John McLean's—active participation in partisan politics.[25] Still, throughout the late nineteenth and twentieth centuries, justices and judges continued to undertake some extrajudicial roles and activities, such as arbitrating boundary disputes and heading special commissions. Charles Evans Hughes resigned from the bench to run for the presidency against Woodrow Wilson in 1916, and Chief Justice William Howard Taft advised the Republican Party on a range of matters; Justices Frankfurter and Louis Brandeis had long, close relationships with President Franklin Roosevelt. Members of the Court have also, in extraordinary circumstances, accepted extrajudicial assignments; notably, Justice Owen Roberts headed a presidential commission to investigate Pearl Harbor, and Justice Robert Jackson served as chief prosecutor of Nazi leaders at the Nuremberg trials. Chief Justice Earl Warren reluctantly headed an investigation of the assassination of President John F. Kennedy. More recently, as constitutionally required, Chief Justice Rehnquist presided over the Senate's impeachment trial of Democratic president Bill Clinton.

During the early part of the nineteenth century, the principal forum for judges' pronouncements on judicial and political issues was provided by Congress's requirement that justices of the Supreme Court travel to the various circuits and sit on cases as well as deliver charges to grand juries there. Although most members of the Court confined their grand jury charges to discussions of their views of constitutional principles or newly enacted legislation, others used the occasion to issue political broadsides and thus enter into the heated debates raging between Federalists and Jeffersonian Republicans. This practice culminated in 1805 in the impeachment and trial of Justice Samuel Chase for "disregarding the duties and dignity of his judicial character." Specifically, the eighth article of impeachment charged the justice with "pervert[ing] his official right and duty to address the grand jury ... on matters coming within the province of the said jury, for the purpose of delivering to the said grand jury an intemperate and inflammatory political harangue,... a conduct highly censurable in any, but peculiarly indecent and unbecoming in a judge of the supreme court of the United States."[26]

A more typical, less objectionable, and still prevalent form of off-the-bench commentary may be found in various justices' and judges' works on the Constitution and public law. Among his numerous treatises, Justice Joseph Story's *Commentaries on the Constitution of the United States*[27] became a classic; it was required reading for generations of lawyers, judges, and court watchers.[28] Justices James Wilson[29] and Henry Baldwin[30] also wrote major works in the early nineteenth century, as did Justices Samuel Miller[31] and Benjamin Curtis[32] in the latter part of the century. In the twentieth century, comparable works tend to place the Court in a more political context, and to emphasize individual justices' avowed judicial and political philosophies. Justice Robert Jackson's two books[33] are representative of justices' and judges' recognition of the expressly political role of courts in our system of free government.[34] Justices Hugo Black,[35] William O. Douglas,[36] Wiley Rutledge,[37] and Chief Justice Rehnquist wrote several books.[38] Justices Scalia and Breyer have also advanced their respective judicial philosophies in books.[39] Justice O'Connor published a collection of her speeches and essays in *The Majesty of the Law,*[40] and an autobiography of her life prior to joining the Court, as has Justice Thomas.[41]

Despite these institutional, political, and historical considerations, off-the-bench commentaries are the prominent tradition and norm. There have been, to be sure, some especially reclusive judges: Chief Justices Roger Taney, Morrison Waite, Edward White, and Harlan Fiske Stone, as well as Justices Cardozo and Thurgood Marshall, rarely ventured forth after they assumed their seats on the bench. Still, even those judges—notably Justice Frankfurter—professing "judicial lockjaw" often publicly addressed a wide range of judicial and extrajudicial matters.[42]

While justices and judges, like other political actors, reserve their most personal observations for private correspondence, they communicate their views and insights in numerous and diverse forums: from university and law school commencements to celebrations, annual meetings of law-related organizations, and bar association conventions; with newspaper, magazine, and broadcast interviews; and in articles and books. Occasionally, judges have also written to members of Congress and testified before Congress on pressing issues confronting the courts and the country;[43] in addition, Chief Justice Burger began an annual practice of issuing a year-end report on the federal judiciary, in order to highlight judicial reforms and the impact on the judiciary of pending legislation.

The topics addressed by justices and judges are no less numerous and diverse; they range from rather rare comments about specific decisions to more frequent observations about the operation of the judiciary and the administration of justice. Despite the self-imposed credo that members of the bench "should not talk about contemporaneous decisions,"[44] judges have occasionally sought to clarify, explain, or defend their rulings. Chief Justice John Marshall, writing to a newspaper under the pseudonym "A Friend to the Union," defended his landmark decision in *McCulloch v. Maryland* (1819);[45] and in 1979 five justices sought to explain their ruling in a controversial case involving public access to judicial proceedings.[46] More typically, judges who publicly address matters of public law—such as the constitutional protection afforded private property,[47] the meaning of the First Amendment,[48] or the evolution of administrative law and regulatory politics[49]—do so from a historical and doctrinal perspective.[50] There are, however, some matters, such as judicial administration and legislation affecting the courts, on which, as Judge Irving Kaufman has said, "judges must speak out."[51] Indeed, in recent years not only the chief justice, who has responsibility for overseeing the federal judiciary, but an increasing number of state and federal judges have voiced their views on rising caseloads, the operation of the judicial process, and the administration of justice.

The value of off-the-bench commentaries depends on what they reveal about how judges think and what they think is important in understanding the judicial process. Their value in part turns on the relationship between judges' rhetoric and the reality of the judicial process and behavior. Judges, like other political actors, are neither always in the best position to describe their role nor possessed of the critical detachment necessary to assess their presuppositions and the ways in which their policy orientations affect their decisions and the judicial process. Moreover, the tradition of judicial lockjaw and the operation of the judicial system provide judges with fewer opportunities than those of other political actors to explain their decision-making role. Judges' descriptions of the deliberative process, for example, tend to be rather inhibited and formal in emphasizing the rule-bound nature of the process. Their explanations are therefore only partial, and they must be supplemented with what we learn from social science, history, and philosophy. What judges say remains nonetheless crucial for understanding the judicial process and the role of courts in American politics. This is so precisely because the Constitution structures the political process, and judges occupy a unique position and vantage point within our system of governance. Off-the-bench commentaries, no less than judicial opinions, may thus prove instructive about the governmental process, public policy, and enduring political principles.

Still, as noted earlier, off-the-bench commentaries have recently become more frequent and more widely publicized, and, in turn, debate over judicial lockjaw has grown and intensified. That is in part because some judges, such as Court of Appeals for the Seventh Circuit Judges Richard A. Posner and Frank H. Easterbrook, are prolific in contributing articles and books addressing jurisprudential concerns relating to constitutional and statutory interpretation. Others, such as Court of Appeals for the Second Circuit Judge Roger J. Miner (see Chapter 3), have been outspoken in criticizing the other political branches over such matters as the contemporary process of federal judicial selection. Nor is Judge Miner alone in this regard; another appointee of President Ronald Reagan, Court of Appeals for the District of Columbia Circuit Judge Laurence H. Silberman, among others, has sharply criticized the role of the American Bar Association in the process of federal judicial appointments.[52] Still other judges have sharply attacked the more conservative directions taken by the Rehnquist Court. Ninth Circuit Court of Appeals judge John T. Noonan, also a Reagan appointee, lamented the Rehnquist Court's rulings expediting the implementation of capital punishment and even suggested that the Court's rulings compel lower federal courts to commit "treason to the Constitution."[53] Another appellate judge on the Ninth Circuit castigated "Supreme Court decisions [for] subordinating individual liberties to the less-than-compelling interests of the state and stripping lower federal courts of the ability to protect individual rights."[54] Such off-the-bench comments were, in turn, denounced by Senior Judge Arthur L. Alarcon, who also sits on the U.S. Court of Appeals for the Ninth Circuit: "Public attacks on Supreme Court decisions by federal judges may incite unstable members of society to engage in civil disobedience and to defy the decisions of our nation's highest court, or worse, to commit acts of violence against its members."[55] Likewise, others have expressed their concerns about the range and propriety of judges' off-the-bench commentaries.[56] Yet an appointee of Democratic president Jimmy Carter, Ninth Circuit Court of Appeals judge Stephen Reinhardt, vigorously defends off-the-bench comments:

> In recent years there has been a noticeable trend toward more judicial speech; at the same time, there remains a firmly entrenched view within the federal judiciary that judges should remain wholly "above the fray" and avoid revealing any of their beliefs or fundamental values to the public, except to the extent that they are necessarily disclosed in published opinions. It is this concept of judicial abstinence that needs careful examination—and ultimately puncturing.
>
> I have a more generous view than many of my colleagues regarding the issues on which judges may speak and the fora in which they may properly present their views. I think that we have an obligation to help educate not just the legal community but the public at large about matters concerning which we have particular knowledge or experience. I also believe that we have a duty to be open and forthcoming with the public, and, correlatively, to subject ourselves to criticism just like all the other members of a democratic society. . . .
>
> It is, of course, impossible to draw clear lines between what speech is appropriate and what is not. Like the many other categories we invent in legal decision making, the boundaries are unclear and imprecise—perhaps more so. Almost all judges agree that we may talk to the public about the Constitution and the Bill of Rights in the abstract—discussions that often amount to little more than self-congratulatory flag-waving. There is also a general belief that we should not provide specific or detailed public answers to previously unresolved questions regarding those rights, because we may be faced with deciding those very questions in subsequent judicial proceedings. What is controversial is what lies "in between" the acceptable platitudes and the forbidden particularities. . . .
>
> I believe that judges should venture boldly into this in-between area—that we should speak forthrightly about the role of courts in American society, about the relationship between law and justice, about the true meaning of the Constitution and some of its principal provisions, and about our own personal visions of justice and judging. We should do so in specific as well as general terms. We should not hesitate to tell the American people what the consequences are when a president fails to make judicial appointments to an overburdened judicial system or

> consistently appoints judges with a grudging or narrow vision of federal jurisdiction and individual liberties. We should reveal to the American public how the courts handle death penalty cases and just what the impact is on the judicial system. We should be willing to acknowledge that the Fourth Amendment is being sacrificed in our eagerness to fight the war against drugs, and that such a sacrifice is inconsistent with our constitutional heritage.... These are controversial issues indeed. But I do not think that we should shy away from speaking about them for that reason. In fact, I think it is precisely because these issues are controversial and difficult that we should share our special knowledge and experience with the public.[57]

This collection presents the views of leading justices and judges on the judicial process, the function of judging, and the role of courts—particularly the Supreme Court—in our litigious society. It provides a unique view of the judicial process, the dilemmas of deliberation and decision making, and other matters about which court watchers and the general public may otherwise only speculate. No less important than the insights they offer about the operations of and the problems confronting courts, the selections make accessible justices' and judges' thinking about judicial activism and self-restraint as well as the role of courts in the political process.

This volume is intended to contribute to the ongoing debate over off-the-bench commentaries and to encourage readers to think about the qualities of judges—their temperament, character, judicial philosophies, and political views—as well as the role of courts in American politics.

Notes

1. "Q. and A.: Abner J. Mikva: On Leaving Capitol Hill for the Bench," *New York Times* B8 (May 12, 1983).
2. Jerome Frank, "The Cult of the Robe," 28 *Saturday Review* 12 (October 13, 1945).
3. Felix Frankfurter, "Personal Ambitions of Judges: Should a Judge 'Think Beyond the Judicial'?" 34 *American Bar Association Journal* 656 (1948).
4. *Bush v. Gore,* 531 U.S. 98 (2000).
5. See, e.g., Alan M. Dershowitz, *Supreme Injustice: How the High Court Hijacked Election 2000* (New York: Oxford University Press, 2001); Vincent Bugliosi, *The Betrayal of America: How the Supreme Court Undermined the Constitution and Chose Our President* (New York: Thunder's Mouth Press, 2001); and E.J. Dionne and William Kristol, eds., Bush v. Gore: *The Court Cases and the Commentary* (Washington, D.C.: Brookings Institution, 2001).
6. Quoted in Associated Press, "Rehnquist Hopes Courts Can Avoid Election Fights," *Washington Post* A2 (January 1, 2001).
7. Quoted in Charles Lane, "Ginsburg Critical on *Bush v. Gore,*" *Washington Post* A2 (February 3, 2001).

8. Quoted in Chris Newmarker, "Scalia, in Princeton Speech Defends 2000 Election Decision," Associated Press (March 7, 2008).
9. Quoted in "Scalia Ridicules Court's Gay Sex Ruling," Associated Press (October 23, 2003).
10. Quoted in Charles Lane, "High Court to Consider Pledge in Schools," *Washington Post* A9 (15 October 2003).
11. Quoted in Stephanie Reitz, "Scalia Proud He Stayed on Cheney Case," Associated Press (April 12, 2006).
12. See, e.g., Charles Lane, "Once Again, Scalia's the Talk of the Town: Justice Renders Frank Out-of-Court Opinions on 2000 Presidential Election, 'Sicilian' Gesture," *Washington Post* A2 (April 15, 2006); and Tony Mauro, "Scalia Tells Congress to Stay Out of High Court Business," *Legal Times* 1 (May 19, 2006).
13. See, e.g., Robert Barnes, "Court Was Once Cloistered; Now Its Chief Does 'Nightline,'" *Washington Post,* A3 (January 6, 2007).
14. See, e.g., Jeffrey Rosen, "The Dissenter," *New York Times Magazine* 50 (September 23, 2007); and Claire Cushman, "Rookie on the Bench: The Role of the Junior Justice," 32 *Journal of Supreme Court History* 282 (2007).
15. See, e.g., Adam Liptak, "Public Comments by Justices Veer Toward the Political," *New York Times* A3 (March 19, 2006); Dahlia Lithwick, "Why Are the Justices Popping Up All Over the Tube," *The American Lawyer* 12 (February 28, 2007); and Charles Lane, "The High Court Looks Abroad: As Congress Backs Bush Foreign Policy, Justices Voice Qualms," *Washington Post* A5 (November 12, 2005).
16. In 1793, the Supreme Court refused to answer a set of questions submitted to Secretary of State Thomas Jefferson, on behalf of President George Washington, concerning the interpretation of treaties with Britain and France. See Charles Warren, *The Supreme Court in United States History,* Vol. I, 110–111 (Boston: Little, Brown, 1922). See also *Muskrat v. United States,* 219 U.S. 346 (1911).
17. William J. Brennan Jr., Address, Student Legal Forum, University of Virginia, Charlottesville, Va. (February 17, 1959).
18. See Hugo L. Black, Address, 13 *Missouri Bar Journal* 173 (1943).
19. See Harlan Fiske Stone, "Fifty Years' Work of the Supreme Court of the United States," 14 *American Bar Association Journal* 428 (1928).
20. Felix Frankfurter, "'The Administrative Side' of Chief Justice Hughes," 63 *Harvard Law Review* 1, 1 (1949).
21. Quoted by George S. Hellman in *Benjamin N. Cardozo: American Judge* 271 (New York: McGraw-Hill, 1940).
22. Lewis F. Powell, "What the Justices Are Saying . . . ," 62 *American Bar Association Journal* 1454 (1976).
23. Earl Warren, "A Conversation with Earl Warren," WGBH-TV Educational Foundation (1972).
24. See Charles Warren, *The Supreme Court in United States History,* Vol. I, at 269–276.
25. See Alan F. Westin, ed., *An Autobiography of the Supreme Court* 6–10 (New York: Macmillan, 1963). See also Alan F. Westin, "Out of Court Commentary by United States Supreme Court Justices, 1790–1962: Of Free Speech and Judicial Lockjaw," 62

Columbia Law Review 633 (1962); and Russell Wheeler, "Extrajudicial Activities of the Early Supreme Court," 1973 *Supreme Court Review* 123.

26. Quoted in Westin, *Autobiography,* at 18–19.
27. Joseph Story, *Commentaries on the Constitution of the United States,* 3 vols. (Boston: Little, Brown, 1833).
28. No less important in the late nineteenth century was Judge Thomas Cooley's *A Treatise on the Constitutional Limitations* (Boston: Little, Brown, 1868).
29. James Wilson, Lectures, "Of the Judicial Department," in *The Works of James Wilson,* Vol. 2 (Chicago: Callaghan, 1896).
30. Henry Baldwin, *A General View of the Origin and Nature of the Constitution and Government of the United States* (Philadelphia: J. C. Clark, 1837).
31. Samuel Miller, *Lectures on the Constitution* (Washington: Morrison, 1880).
32. Benjamin Curtis, *Jurisdiction, Practice, and Peculiar Jurisdiction of the Courts of the United States* (Boston: Little, Brown, 1880).
33. Robert Jackson, *The Struggle for Judicial Supremacy* (New York: Knopf, 1941); and *The Supreme Court in the American System of Government* (Cambridge: Harvard University Press, 1955).
34. See also, from a different perspective, Judge Richard Neely, *How Courts Govern America* (New Haven: Yale University Press, 1981).
35. Hugo Black, *A Constitutional Faith* (New York: Knopf, 1969).
36. William O. Douglas, *We the Judges* (Garden City, N.Y.: Doubleday, 1956).
37. Wiley Rutledge, *A Declaration of Legal Faith* (Lawrence: University Press of Kansas, 1947).
38. William H. Rehnquist, *The Supreme Court: How It Was, How It Is* (New York: Morrow, 1987, 2001); *Grand Inquests: The Historic Impeachments of Justice Samuel Chase and President Andrew Johnson* (New York: Morrow, 1992); *All the Laws but One: Civil Liberties in Wartime* (New York: Knopf, 1998).
39. See Antonin Scalia, *A Matter of Interpretation: Federal Courts and the Law* (Princeton: Princeton University Press, 1997); and Stephen J. Breyer, *Active Liberty: Interpreting Our Democratic Constitution* (New York: Knopf, 2005).
40. Sandra Day O'Connor, *The Majesty of the Law* (New York: Random House, 2003).
41. Sandra Day O'Connor, *The Lazy B* (New York: Modern Library, 2005); and Clarence Thomas, *My Grandfather's Son: A Memoir* (New York: Harper, 2007).
42. See Russell Wheeler, "Of Standards for Extra-Judicial Behavior," 81 *Michigan Law Review* (1983) (book review).
43. See, e.g., the testimony of Justice Willis Van Devanter on the passage of the Judges' Bill of 1925 in U.S. Congress, 68th Cong., 2nd Sess., H.R. Committee on the Judiciary, *Hearings on the Jurisdiction of Circuit Courts of Appeals and of the Supreme Court of the United States* (Washington, D.C.: Government Printing Office, 1925); Letter of Chief Justice Charles Evans Hughes to Senator Burton Wheeler on proposed reorganization of the federal judiciary, reprinted in U.S. Congress, 75th Cong., 1st Sess., Senate Committee on the Judiciary, *Hearings on the Reorganization of the Federal Judiciary*, S. Rept. No. 711, at 38 (Washington, D.C.: Government Printing Office, 1937).
44. Felix Frankfurter, *Proceedings in Honor of Mr. Justice Frankfurter and Distinguished Alumni* 11, Occasional Pamphlet No. 3 (Cambridge: Harvard University Press, 1960).

45. See *Philadelphia Union* (28 April, 1 May 1810) (New York Historical Library Collection), and discussed by Alan Westin in *Autobiography,* at 19.
46. "Brennan Assails Media Criticisms of Court Decisions," *Washington Post* A12, col. 1 (October 18, 1979); "Justice Marshall Hits Colleagues on Rights," *Seattle Post-Intelligencer* B2 (June 3, 1979); John Paul Stevens, "Some Thoughts on a General Rule," 21 *Arizona Law Review* 599 (1979); and *New York Times* A14, col. 1 (September 9, 1979) (quoting Justice Stevens's view that "members of the general public, including the press, could not assert rights guaranteed to the accused by the Sixth Amendment"); *New York Times* A17, col. 1 (August 9, 1979) (quoting Chief Justice Burger "that the opinion referred to pretrial proceedings only"); *New York Times* A13, col. 1 (August 14, 1979) (reporting Justice Powell's address to a panel at the annual meeting of the American Bar Association and explanation that *Gannett* was based only on the Sixth Amendment); and *New York Times* A15, col. 1 (September 4, 1979) (reporting Justice Blackmun's view that after *Gannett v. DePasquale* [1979] closure of trials is permissible).
47. See, e.g., David J. Brewer, "Protection of Private Property from Public Attack," 10 *Railway and Corporation Law Journal* 281 (1891).
48. See, e.g., William Brennan, Address, 32 *Rutgers Law Review* 173 (1979); Potter Stewart, "Or of the Press," 26 *Hastings Law Journal* 631 (1975); John Paul Stevens, "Some Thoughts about a General Rule," 21 *Arizona Law Review* 599 (1979).
49. See, e.g., Harold Leventhal, "Principled Fairness and Regulatory Urgency," 25 *Case Western Reserve Law Review* 66 (1974); and "Environmental Decisionmaking and the Role of the Courts," 122 *University of Pennsylvania Law Review* 509 (1974); J. Skelly Wright, "Rulemaking and Judicial Review," 30 *Administrative Law Review* 461 (1978); and David L. Bazelon, "The Impact of Courts on Public Administration," 52 *Indiana Law Journal* 101 (1976).
50. See, e.g., citations to Justice Frankfurter's writings in Appendix A: Selected Bibliography in this volume.
51. Irving Kaufman, "Judges Must Speak Out," *New York Times* A23 (January 30, 1982).
52. Laurence H. Silberman, "The American Bar Association and Judicial Nominations," 59 *George Washington Law Review* 1092 (1991).
53. John T. Noonan, "Should State Executions Run on Schedule?" *New York Times* A17 (April 27, 1992).
54. Stephen Reinhardt, "The Supreme Court, the Death Penalty, and the Harris Case," 102 *Yale Law Journal* 205 (1992).
55. Arthur L. Alarcon, "Off-the-Bench Criticism of Supreme Court Decisions by Judges Fosters Disrespect for the Rule of Law and Politicizes Our System of Justice," 28 *Loyola of Los Angeles Law Review* 795 (1995).
56. See, e.g., "Limits on Judges' Learning, Speaking, and Acting: Part II Speaking and Part III Acting," 20 *Dayton Law Review* 1 (1994).
57. Stephen Reinhardt, "Judicial Speech and the Open Judiciary," 28 *Loyola of Los Angeles Law Review* 805 (1995).

PART I

Judicial Review and American Politics

Historical and Political Perspectives

JUDICIAL REVIEW WAS NOT fully comprehended during the founding period, and it remains controversial in American politics. The U.S. Constitution, in Article III (reprinted in Appendix A), vests the judicial power in one Supreme Court and in any lower courts that Congress may establish, yet neither the nature nor the scope of that power is defined. Instead, Chief Justice John Marshall in *Marbury v. Madison* established the power of judicial review—the power to strike down laws enacted by Congress or the states and to declare official government action unconstitutional. The historical background, the political drama, and the enduring significance of that decision is eloquently described in chapter 1 by Chief Justice Warren E. Burger. After *Marbury* the Court did not invalidate another act of Congress, and thereby invite national political controversy, until 1857 in *Dred Scott v. Sandford*—a decision Chief Justice Charles Evans Hughes in the 1930s characterized as a "self-inflicted wound." The Court nonetheless struck down some forty state and local laws prior to the Civil War, thus legitimating the role of the national government and the power of judicial review.

Subject to the constitutional restriction in Article III that the Court decide only actual cases or controversies, the justices are not self-starters—they must await an appeal in an actual case or controversy in a properly framed lawsuit. But whereas the president and Congress are restrained by the ballot box and the processes of democratic government, as well as by judicial review, Chief Justice Harlan Fiske Stone pointed out, "the only check on [the justices'] exercise of power is [their] own sense of self-restraint." [1] Chief Justice Stone was only partially correct, for the Court depends upon the cooperation of other branches of government and compliance by the people; as an irate President Andrew Jackson reportedly declared: "John Marshall has made his decision, now let him enforce it." [2] Accordingly, the Court evolved other, self-imposed rules governing its power. As Justice Tom Clark summarized these self-imposed constraints:

> The case or controversy presented must be a genuine dispute [with real and adverse litigants], raising a substantial question. The Court does not deal in advisory opinions [or abstract or hypothetical questions], moot questions [already resolved by changing circumstances], or political issues [more appropriately resolved by the President or Congress, or which the Court is incapable of resolving]. Traditionally it shies away from deciding constitutional questions; not rendering such a decision unless it is absolutely necessary to the disposition of the case. Even though a substantial constitutional issue is presented it will not be passed upon if the case can be disposed of on a non-constitutional ground. An appeal from the highest state court is dismissed if that court's judgment can be sustained on an independent state ground [i.e., if the decision is based on the state's constitution, the Court will defer to the state supreme court in recognition of the principle of comity]. A statute is not construed unless the complaining party shows that he is substantially injured by its enforcement. An attack on an act of Congress on constitutional grounds is by-passed in the event a construction of the statute is fairly possible by which the constitutional question may be avoided.[3]

The power and prestige of the Court fundamentally lie with the justices' recognition of the responsibility imposed by judicial independence under the Constitution and in a system of free government. The Constitution provides for judicial independence with the selection and appointment, as provided in Article II, of members of the federal judiciary by the president with the advice and consent of the Senate (further discussed in Chapter 3). Presidential appointment and senatorial confirmation are the principal means by which democratic values are infused into the judiciary.

The selection and appointment of state court judges varies from state to state, according to each state's constitutional provisions. The methods of appointment include popular—partisan or nonpartisan—election in twenty-one states; selection by governors in three and by legislatures in two states; eleven employ some combination of both methods; and another thirteen states, along with the District of Columbia, use a so-called merit system—under which a commission provides a list of nominees from which the governor makes an appointment and then, after one year of service, the judge's name is placed on a ballot, with voters deciding whether the judge should be retained or not, for either a specified or unspecified term.[4] All federal judges hold their offices during good behavior subject to impeachment (provided for in Article II) for high crimes and misdemeanors (only eleven judges have been impeached and only seven of those convicted). Federal judges enjoy essentially life tenure. The fourth chief justice, John Marshall, served for thirty-four years, and Justice John Paul Stevens has served for thirty-three years; both, though, were surpassed by Justice William O. Douglas's record of thirty-six years and seven months.

Judicial independence, though constitutionally provided for, was actually secured by Chief Justice Marshall. As Chief Justice Earl Warren observed:

> Insistence upon the independence of the judiciary in the early days of our nation was perhaps John Marshall's greatest contribution to constitutional law. He aptly stated the controlling principle when, in speaking of the Court during his tenure, he said that he had "never sought to enlarge the judicial power beyond its proper bounds, nor feared to carry it to the fullest extent that duty required." That is precisely the obligation of the judiciary today.[5]

The essence of judicial independence, Judge Irving Kaufman similarly notes, "is the preservation of a separate institution of government that can adjudicate cases or controversies with impartiality."[6] The history of the judiciary is replete with examples of judges' assertions of independence. Justice Tom Clark, for instance, proved a bitter disappointment for Democratic president Harry Truman, who elevated Clark from his position as attorney general to the Court. As attorney general, Clark had advised Truman that he had the power to seize the steel mills in order to avert a nationwide strike that might threaten the country's war effort in Korea. But on the bench, Clark voted against Truman in the "Steel Seizure Case," *Youngstown Sheet & Tube Co. v. Sawyer* (1952). And Chief Justice Burger, appointed to the Court by Republican President Richard Nixon, wrote for a unanimous court in *United States v. Nixon* (1974) denying the president's generalized claim to executive privilege as a shield against turning over the so-called Watergate tapes, a decision which contributed to Nixon's resigning from office.

Despite the fact that courts are not self-starters, their self-imposed limitations on judicial review, and the tradition of judicial independence, the judiciary has proven to be neither the least dangerous branch, as Alexander Hamilton envisioned in *The Federalist* No. 78 (reprinted in Appendix B), nor quiescent "under the chains of the Constitution,"[7] as Thomas Jefferson hoped. The Supreme Court and the judiciary loom large in American politics in part because, as Alexis de Tocqueville observed: "Scarcely any political question arises in the United States that is not resolved, sooner or later, into a judicial question."[8] Justice Felix Frankfurter likewise commented, "almost every question in the history of the United States is ultimately shaped for adjudication by the Supreme Court."[9] Justice Robert H. Jackson proclaimed more boldly: "This is government by lawsuit. These constitutional lawsuits are the stuff of power politics in America."[10] The overwhelming work of state and federal courts actually involves rather mundane civil, criminal, and regulatory matters—disputes over contracts, personal injuries, government benefits, labor relations, and the regulation of businesses, public utilities, and health and safety services. The judiciary is nevertheless drawn into political conflicts precisely because the Constitution's separation of powers among the three branches of government amounts to a prescription for political struggle. The doctrine of separation of powers, Justice Louis Brandeis pointed out, "was not to promote efficiency but to preclude the exercise of arbitrary power. The purpose was not to avoid friction but, by means of the inevitable friction incident to the distribution of the governmental powers among three departments, to save the people from autocracy."[11]

The Supreme Court provides a forum for resolving political conflicts, but it is a forum of last resort. Recourse to the Court, James Madison explained, "must necessarily be deemed last in relation to the authorities of the other departments of government, not in relation to the rights of the parties to the constitutional compact, from which the judicial, as well as the other departments hold their delegated trusts."[12] The Court provides an "auxiliary precaution," not the primary check on political passions and conflicts. Denied the power of both the sword and the purse, the Court depends on the cooperation of the coequal branches of government and ultimately public acceptance. In a system of free government, Chief Justice William Howard Taft, the only member of the Court to serve previously as president, observed: "The fact is that the judiciary, quite as much as Congress and the Executive, is dependent on the cooperation of the other two, that government may go on."[13] As a political institution and unit of government sharing power, Justice Jackson explains in Chapter 2, the Court confronts vexatious disputes between the president and Congress and over the exercise of federal and state powers and from the competition among the states, as well as arising from persistent and perennial demands to balance majoritarian democracy with the rights of individuals and minorities.

As a guardian of the Constitution and the symbols and instruments of free government, the Supreme Court was destined for controversy. The exercise of judicial review inevitably proves problematic for, as Justice Jackson observed, the judiciary "is an institution of distinctive characteristics which were intended to give it independence and detachment, but which also tend to make it antidemocratic." There is no "evading the basic inconsistency between popular government and judicial supremacy."[14] Nor is the Court "saved from being oligarchic because it professes to act in the service of humane ends." As Justice Frankfurter reminded us: "The powers exercised by this Court are inherently oligarchic."[15]

The power and prestige of the Court rest on a paradox. The power of judicial review is at once antidemocratic and countermajoritarian, yet that power, in Chief Justice Edward White's words, "rest[s] solely upon the approval of a free people."[16] Judicial review cannot be reconciled with democratic governance.

However, the Constitution prescribes not a democracy pure and simple but a republic—a mixed form of government—in which political power is diffused among institutions that remain dependent on and accountable to the people in a variety of ways. In a system of free government, majorities are constantly in flux and constrained by constitutional checks and balances. As Madison argued, "[a] dependence on the people is ... the primary control on the government."[17] The judiciary fulfills an important albeit limited role as an auxiliary precaution against both the abuse of governmental power by a tyrannical minority and the excesses of majoritarian democracy. Far from being antithetical, judicial review is essential to the promise and performance of free government.

Notes

1. *United States v. Butler*, 297 U.S. 1, 79 (1936) (Stone, J., dis. op.).
2. Quoted by Edward Samuel Corwin, *The Doctrine of Judicial Review: Its Legal and Historical Basis and Other Essays* 22 (New Haven: Yale University Press, 1914).
3. Thomas C. Clark, "Random Thoughts on the Court's Interpretation of Individual Rights," 1 *Houston Law Review* 75, 78 (1963).
4. For further discussion, see Christopher P. Banks and David M. O'Brien, *Courts and Judicial Policymaking,* at 118–126 (Upper Saddle River, N.J.: Prentice-Hall, 2008).
5. Earl Warren, Address, American Law Institute, 20 (May 20, 1959).
6. Irving R. Kaufman, "The Essence of Judicial Independence," 80 *Columbia Law Review* 671, 688 (1980). See also Peter H. Russell and David M. O'Brien, eds., *Judicial Independence in the Age of Democracy: Critical Perspectives from Around the World* (Charlottesville, Va.: University Press of Virginia, 2001).
7. Thomas Jefferson, "Resolutions Relative to the Alien and Sedition Laws," in *The Writings of Thomas Jefferson,* Vol. 17, 389, ed. Andrew A. Lipscomb and Albert Ellery Bergh (Washington, D.C.: N.p., 1904–1905).
8. Alexis de Tocqueville, *Democracy in America* 151, ed. Phillips Bradley (New York: Doubleday, 1945).
9. Felix Frankfurter, *Proceedings in Honor of Mr. Justice Frankfurter and Distinguished Alumni* 8, Occasional Pamphlet No. 3 (Cambridge: Harvard Law School, 1960).
10. Robert H. Jackson, *The Struggle for Judicial Supremacy* 287 (New York: Knopf, 1941).
11. *Meyers v. United States,* 272 U.S. 52, 293 (1926) (Brandeis, J., dis. op.).
12. Quoted by Corwin, *The Doctrine of Judicial Review* 22.
13. *Ex parte Grossman,* 267 U.S. 87, 119–120 (1925).
14. Jackson, supra note 11, at vii and 311.
15. *AFL v. American Sash & Door Co.,* 335 U.S. 538, 555–556 (1949) (footnotes omitted).
16. Edward Douglass White, "The Supreme Court of the United States," 7 *American Bar Association Journal* 341 (1921).
17. James Madison, *The Federalist,* No. 51, supra note 2, at 322.

CHAPTER 1

The Doctrine of Judicial Review

Mr. Marshall, Mr. Jefferson, and Mr. Marbury

Warren E. Burger

Chief Justice, Supreme Court of the United States (1969–1986) and Judge, U.S. Court of Appeals, District of Columbia (1956–1969)

LORD BRYCE ONCE OBSERVED:

> No feature of the government of the United States has awakened so much curiosity in the European mind, caused so much discussion, received so much admiration, and been more frequently misunderstood, than the duties assigned to the Supreme Court and the functions which it discharges in guarding the Ark of the Constitution.[1]

I should add that in some quarters, the Supreme Court's guardianship of that Ark probably has received more guarded praise than in distant places where its impact is purely theoretical.

Lord Bryce, of course, had reference to the doctrine of judicial review, sometimes described as the doctrine of judicial supremacy, in the interpretation of constitutional terms and principles....

It is helpful to an understanding of this subject to examine it in the setting in which *Marbury v. Madison* was decided in 1803 with all its momentous consequences for our country and to suggest to you that this great case had its antecedents in our colonial experience, and its taproots in the declarations of fundamental rights of Englishmen back to Magna Carta.

Acknowledgment to Chief Justice Warren E. Burger for excerpts from his Presidential Address, delivered to the Bentham Club, University College, London (February 2, 1972).

Marbury v. Madison: Act 1, The Setting

Very early in the history of our country the colonial experience of living under a parliamentary system with no check on the legislative or executive branch, except that of popular will in a limited way, led our Founding Fathers to feel strongly the need for limitations on all branches of government. The intellectual spadework for the system ultimately adopted for our federal government had been done, of course, by such seventeenth- and eighteenth-century political theorists as Hobbes and Locke.[2] As we know, the great rationalist Montesquieu contributed the notion of a separation of powers within the government itself, in order that each branch might act as a sort of brake upon the others.[3] As the system works today, one of the checks exercised by the Supreme Court involves measuring executive or legislative action against the Constitution whenever a challenge to such action is first properly brought within the framework of a "case" or "controversy,"[4] and then properly brought within the "appellate jurisdiction"[5] of the Supreme Court.

It has been suggested from time to time that the subject of judicial review of Congressional Acts was not in the minds of the delegates to the Constitutional Convention in 1787. However, such an obviously important question could not have entirely eluded their attention. Some of the delegates, without doubt, looked to an independent judiciary with fixed tenure as a means of protecting the states against the powers of the new national government, whose scope was as yet unseen and unknown and therefore feared. Others, particularly the propertied classes, probably regarded a Supreme Court and an independent Federal Judiciary as a source of protection against the egalitarian popular government advocated by Jefferson. They could not fail to be aware that the exercise of such powers by the judiciary must in some way involve limitations on legislative and executive action.

Some residual controversy remains as to the exercise of judicial review today, but it is largely as to scope, not basic power. It is now accepted that the original assertion of the power was not judicial usurpation as Jefferson considered it.[6] Needless to say, the major challenges to the power have occurred during those periods when, for whatever reason, the Supreme Court has been under attack for its role in contemporary affairs.

As an example, many polemics as well as some of the most thoughtful and scholarly challenges were written during the 1930s when, to many of its critics, the Supreme Court represented the dead hand of the past impeding legitimate experimentation and innovation in trying to cope with a crisis. At present, it is fair to say that, absent some unforeseeable convulsion of great magnitude, the doctrine of judicial review, as announced by Chief Justice John Marshall in 1803 in *Marbury v. Madison*,[7] is likely to remain part of the American system.

It is often assumed that the doctrine was the invention of Chief Justice Marshall in that most famous of all his opinions. It is true, of course, that Chief Justice Marshall first announced this keystone doctrine of our constitutional law in the *Marbury* case; and it is also true that our written Constitution makes no reference to the theory in defining judicial power.[8] But Marshall was not and never claimed to be the originator of the doctrine since he was well aware of a growing acceptance of the idea that constitutional adjudication was inherent in the very nature of a written constitution. This is not to disparage Marshall, for he was the one who recognized the need to enunciate the doctrine as part of Federal jurisprudence and seized—some might say forced—the first opportunity to assert the power of the Court to measure an act of Congress by the yardstick of the Constitution.

But this takes me ahead of my story, and I must turn back to 1776, the very year of the Declaration of Independence. In that year the people of the town of Concord, Massachusetts, held a Town Meeting and adopted a resolution that "a Constitution alterable by the Supreme Legislative is no security at all to the subject, against encroachment of the Governing Part on any or on all their rights and privileges." Earlier, when the Colony of Massachusetts Bay was under British Colonial rule, the sturdy farm people of Berkshire County refused to let the Colonial courts sit from 1775 to 1780 until the people of Massachusetts adopted a Constitution with a Bill of Rights enforceable by judges.

Notice the premise in these events, 25 years before *Marbury*, that a written constitution would govern the acts of a legislature and protect fundamental liberties. And notice also the tacit assumption that the judicial branch was the appropriate vehicle for providing that protection.

In 1793, ten years before Marshall's decision in *Marbury v. Madison*, Spencer Roane, a great judge of the Virginia Court and an intimate of Thomas Jefferson, said, in the case of *Kamper v. Hawkins*,

> If the legislature may infringe this Constitution [of Virginia], it is no longer fixed; ... and the liberties of the people are wholly at the mercy of the legislature.[9]

To be sure, Judge Roane was speaking to the power of the state courts to strike down legislative acts contrary to the Virginia Constitution, but conceptually the doctrine is indistinguishable from *Marbury*. In 1793 the Commonwealth of Virginia, of course, regarded itself as a sovereign at least equal to the new National Government. Some lawyers, including very good ones of that day, would later hesitate and ponder before taking the final step to make the doctrine equally applicable to a Federal Constitution and a Federal Legislature, but very quickly their strong sense of the rights of the states, that were widely viewed as sovereign in the eighteenth and early nineteenth centuries, would impel them to accept such a restraint on the federal legislative body. Their hesitation was no more than that of thoughtful men chary of granting open-ended power to anyone.

Although I attributed a certain uniqueness to the American doctrine of judicial review as formally articulated in *Marbury v. Madison*, it is quite clear that this, like almost all else in our law, has its roots in English legal thought.

Magna Carta, of course, was primarily intended by the Barons as a limitation on King John; but it has come to stand for a limitation on princes and parliaments alike. In one of the very early opinions of the Supreme Court of the United States,[10] one of many containing references to Magna Carta, it was said:

> ... after volumes spoken and written [about the guarantees of Magna Carta], the good sense of mankind has at length settled down to this: *that they were intended to secure the individual from the arbitrary exercise of the powers of government....* (Emphasis supplied.)

Another thread of influence originates with the struggle between Lord Coke and the Stuart kings. Coke's writings and Reports were well known to the American colonists, and even though the dictum in *Dr. Bonham's Case* has never been very closely followed in England, it has been seminal in our law. In that case Coke asserted that

> ... in many cases, the common law will controul Acts of Parliament, and sometimes adjudge them to be utterly void: for when an Act of Parliament is against common right and reason, or repugnant, or impossible to be performed, the common law will controul it, and adjudge such Act to be void.[11]

And even that super authoritarian, Cromwell, said, 150 years before *Marbury v. Madison*:

> In every government, there must be something fundamental, somewhat like a Magna Carta which would be unalterable....[12]

I doubt that the stern Mr. Cromwell intended to propound the idea that a judicial body like our Supreme Court, independent of both the executive and legislative branches, should be empowered to act as a sort of umpire, but obviously he was concerned about unbridled legislative power.

A very important point of departure from England's jurisprudence was the American insistence on written guarantees that would be definite and would narrow the area for interpretation. Each of the thirteen original states of the Union had a written constitution, giving tangible expression to what the farmers of Concord and Berkshire, Massachusetts, demanded as early as 1775. Having said that the idea of written guarantees in a constitution departed in a sense from England's precedents, I am bound to note that even this idea traces directly back to Magna Carta and to the written charters of the colonies.

An important function of a constitution is its organic allocation of powers of government, and in this area alone the authority must reside somewhere for a binding pronouncement that, for example, treaty-making power is shared by the Executive and the Senate, that the veto power is exclusively for the Executive, the overriding power exclusively in the Congress. More than a decade before *Marbury*, Justices of the Supreme Court sitting on circuit held that state laws contrary to the Federal Constitution were invalid, and this was confirmed in *Van Horne Lessee v. Dorrance.*[13] In his opinion in that case Justice Paterson, sitting on circuit, asserted aptly:

> I take it to be a clear position; that if a legislative act oppugns a constitutional principle, the former must give way, and ... it will be the duty of the Court to adhere to the Constitution, and to declare the act null and void.[14]

We see, therefore, that long before *Marbury* American political leaders, including many of the most distinguished lawyers and judges in the Colonies and in the original thirteen states, accepted it as fundamental that a written Constitution was a restraint on every part of the federal government. It does not disparage John Marshall's greatness as a judge or a statesman to say that when he wrote the opinion in *Marbury* he was doing little more than declaring what was widely accepted by so many of the best legal minds of his day—at least when they could divorce politics from reason! If it had not come in *Marbury*, it would have come later, but John Marshall was not a man to wait for perfect opportunities if a plausible one offered itself. It had to be said, and *Marbury* was the fortuitous circumstance that made it possible to establish this great principle early in our history.

The setting in which this great case developed is important. The incumbent President Adams was defeated by Thomas Jefferson in the election of November 1800. But between the time of the election and the following March when Jefferson actually took office, Adams remained in control of the government and in control of what we call a "lame duck" Congress.[15] One of the first things he did after his defeat was to encourage the ailing Chief Justice Ellsworth to resign. The Federalist Adams was, of course, deeply concerned about the future of the country, and undoubtedly about the future of the Supreme Court in the hands of Jefferson and his Republicans....

An interesting footnote to history, often overlooked in the appropriate recognition of John Marshall and the wisdom of John Adams in appointing him, emerges from the circumstance that Marshall was not Adams' first choice for

Chief Justice after Ellsworth resigned. John Jay, who had served as the first Chief Justice of the United States by appointment of George Washington, resigned as Chief Justice in 1795 to become Governor of New York State. Adams wrote to Jay urging him to return to his old position as Chief Justice but he declined. Interestingly, Jay refused because, as he put it, "I left the [Supreme] Bench perfectly convinced that under a system so defective, it would not obtain the energy, weight and dignity which are essential to its affording due support to the National Government, nor acquire the public confidence and respect which, as the last resort of the justice of the nation, it should possess."[16] His decision not to return to the Court in that frame of mind, thus opening the way for Marshall, was one of the most fortuitous events in the two centuries of our history.

Whatever Jay may have thought of the office, you may be sure that Jefferson was anything but overjoyed at the eleventh hour appointment of John Marshall, who was his distant kinsman but not a friend.

Jefferson's deep and bitter hostility toward John Marshall is one of the unplumbed mysteries of this complex man. Some historians explain it in terms of his opposition to Marshall's judicial philosophy, but other explanations are also suggested.[17]

Jefferson's choice for Chief Justice, had Marshall not been appointed, was Spencer Roane, an able Virginia judge. Yet Judge Roane, described by Professor Charles Warren[18] as "an ardent strict constructionist of the Constitution," showed his basic agreement with Marshall in an opinion for the Virginia court in 1793, stating:

> It is the province of the judiciary to expound the laws.... It may say too, that an act of assembly has not changed the Constitution [of Virginia], though its words are expressly to that effect.... [I]t is conceived, for the reasons above mentioned, that the legislature have not power to change the fundamental laws.... [W]ould you have them [judges] to shut their eyes against that law which is of the highest authority of any...?[19]

From the day Jefferson took office as President on 4 March 1801, those who were even slightly aware of his hostility toward the Supreme Court, the Federal Judicial Branch as a whole, and John Marshall in particular, could sense that these events foreshadowed a collision of two strong men who had quite different views as to how the United States could best fulfill its destiny.

Underlying the impending conflict was a very fundamental difference between the Federalist belief that a strong national government was the key to the future of the new nation and the opposing belief of the Jeffersonian radical Republicans who feared all centralized power and wanted to keep the states the strong and indeed the dominant political power. When he took office Jefferson still looked with considerable favor on the French Revolution, notwithstanding its later excesses and horrors. Jefferson had been largely aloof from the hardships of our war of rebellion; he lacked the firsthand experience that Washington, Hamilton, and even Marshall, as a junior officer, shared in a war in which thirteen quarrelsome and disunited colony-states, functioning through an impotent confederation and a parochial Congress, fumbled and almost failed in raising, equipping, and maintaining armies. Jefferson's lifelong passion for minimal government had never been subjected to the acid test of trying to conduct a war with a truly "minimal" government.

Jefferson's remarkable political instincts enabled him to see, far ahead of his contemporaries, that the latent power of the National Judiciary, and especially the Supreme Court, could be a major obstacle to his dream of a simple, loose-jointed, national confederation, linking but not binding the several states.[20] But Jefferson was at heart a majoritarian. What the People wanted, the People would have.

Whatever his earlier beliefs, by 1800 Jefferson's distrust of and opposition to the federal judiciary had hardened. From 1800 onward, Jefferson did not waver in this attitude, and in 1820 we find him declaring that

> to consider the judges as the ultimate arbiters of all constitutional questions ... would place us under the despotism of an oligarchy.[21]

Similarly, in a letter to a friend dated 18 August 1821, Jefferson wrote—some would say, prophetically—

> It has long ... been my opinion, and I have never shrunk from its expression ... that the germ of dissolution of our federal government is in the Constitution of the federal judiciary; an irresponsible body (for impeachment is scarcely a scarecrow), working like gravity by night and by day, gaining a little today and a little tomorrow, and advancing its noiseless step like a thief, over the field of jurisdiction, until all shall be usurped from the States, and the government of all be consolidated into one. To this I am opposed; because when all government, domestic and foreign, in little as in great things, shall be drawn to Washington as the centre of all power, it will render powerless the checks provided of one government on another, and will become as venal and oppressive as the government from which we separated.[22]

From the time he was President to the end of his life, Jefferson did not alter his hostility either to strong central government or to the federal judiciary, and the Supreme Court, in particular, was the target of repeated bitter comments. Of course, in the United States we judges have had to learn to accept philosophically all manner of "slings and arrows," and by modern standards Jefferson's characterization of Federal judges as "thieves" is a fairly moderate comment. If he ever recognized that the unsound pronouncements of the Supreme Court could be "reversed" through the constitutional amending process by the People he trusted so much, I have not discovered evidence of it. However, Jefferson would also well understand difficulties of the amending process.

Marbury v. Madison: The Second Act

So much for the setting. We now come to the final act.

As sometimes is true of great events in history, *Marbury v. Madison* was an accident. But it was an accident which the solid, steady, and resourceful Marshall exploited to the fullest. The accident of fortuitous combination was the coincidence of a need, an opportunity, and a man—a man with the foresight, the wit, and the courage to make the most of his chance.

Adams, as I have noted, was a "lame duck" President after November 1800, with a "lame duck" Congress on hand for five months after the election. Naturally he made as many appointments as possible. Persuading Ellsworth to resign to make way for Marshall as Chief Justice was one step. The appointment of a goodly number of Federal judges was another. But the far lesser post of Justice of the Peace was the grist of Marbury's case.

The story is too well known to be chronicled in detail. Marbury was one of those whose commission as a Justice of the Peace was signed by President Adams and sealed by Marshall (who was still acting as President Adams' Secretary of State even after being appointed Chief Justice and confirmed by the Senate). But Marbury's commission was not delivered. Legend, supported by letters, tells us this was because of Marshall's careless error as he hastened to complete his duties as Secretary of State and don his robe as Chief Justice before 4 March 1801.

The minor office of Justice of the Peace was hardly worth a lawsuit, but Marbury was a spunky fellow and he sought a direct mandamus in the Supreme Court against Madison, Jefferson's Secretary of State, to compel what Marbury rightly claimed was the purely ministerial act of delivering the commissions that Madison's predecessor Marshall, as Secretary of State, had forgotten to mail out. In the Supreme Court it can be assumed that the first reaction was, "of course," since the Judiciary Act provided that precise remedy—mandamus by an original action in the Supreme Court.

Marshall saw it otherwise. If mandamus was issued and Jefferson's Administration ignored it—as was likely—the first confrontation between court and Executive would be lost—and all of it over a Justice of the Peace commission! The court could stand hard blows, but not ridicule, and the ale houses would rock with hilarious laughter. If the court simply refused to issue mandamus in the face of the very explicit authority of the Federalist-drafted Judiciary Act of 1789, this, too, would be an ignominious retreat by the court—a court fearing to act because it would not be obeyed.

But if, as no one had even remotely suspected up to that time, Congress could not vest original jurisdiction in the Supreme Court in any cases except those specifically recited in Article III, then the court could say, "Yes, Marbury was duly confirmed"; and "Yes, the Commission was duly signed and sealed"; and "Yes, this court may examine into the manner in which the Executive conducts its own affairs"; and "Yes, delivery is a purely ministerial act," and "Yes, it is shameful that the new administration will not perform the simple, ministerial act of delivery"; but the court could also say, "However, this court has no power under the Constitution to entertain any original action except those specified in Article III, and hence section 13 of the Judiciary Act of 1789[23] purporting to give the Supreme Court such authority is invalid and, sadly, this action to compel the Executive to do its duty cannot be entertained here as an original action."

And this is precisely what Marshall persuaded the court to do in a straight-faced, long-winded opinion that exhaustively, and exhaustingly, explored every possible alternative. After doing so, he sadly concluded that the Federalist Congress of 1789 had passed, and the Federalist President, George Washington, had signed, an Act—drafted by no less than Ellsworth, Marshall's distinguished predecessor—that everyone had thought excellent for 13 years, but section 13 of which was void because it conflicted with Article III of the Constitution.

Jefferson's Secretary of State, Madison, had won the battle; Marbury, the Federalist, had lost, and the real war, the great war over the supremacy of the Supreme Court in constitutional adjudication, had been won by Marshall—and by the United States.

Because it was a small case—almost a joke—few people cared. But Jefferson the lawyer and politician saw that he had been outmaneuvered by the holding of the court near the time of an election—1803—when it would be very difficult to make an issue of a case decided in his favor and against Marbury, his political opponent. Not even a Pyrrhic Victory! Small wonder he likened the federal judiciary to thieves in the night!

For salt and vinegar in Jefferson's wounds, in the same Term the Supreme Court announced in solemn tones with respect to another section of the same Judiciary Act of 1789 (as to which its section 13 had now been declared void) that

> practice and acquiescence under it [the Act of 1789] for a period of several years [13 years!], commencing with the organization of the judicial system ... has ... fixed the construction ... [and] is too strong ... to be shaken ... is at rest, and ought not now to be disturbed.

Marshall is spared the charge of judicial hypocrisy for, having sat as the trial judge on circuit, he took no part in the case in which this was said, *Stuart v. Laird.*[24]

Not for 54 years after *Marbury* did the court hold another Act of Congress unconstitutional.[25] In another irony of history, the court decided in 1857 that Congress had no power to ban slavery in the Louisiana Territory under an 1820 Act known as the Missouri Compromise. This case was the infamous *Dred Scott* decision[26] that added fuel to the fires leading to our Civil War.

Another interesting footnote to Mr. Marbury's case is that after 10,000 words, more or less, Marshall held that the court had no jurisdiction on the case since the statute purporting to create jurisdiction was void. So we have, perhaps, the most important single opinion of the court in nearly 200 years pronounced in the context of a holding that the court had no jurisdiction at all! From this, of course, we authoritatively conclude that the court always has jurisdiction to decide its own jurisdiction!

As with so many great conceptions, the idea of judicial review of legislation now seems simple and inevitable in the perspective of history. People, not governments, delegated certain powers to the national government and placed limits on those powers by specific and general reservations. The people having flatly stated certain guarantees relating to religious freedom, to speech, to searches, seizures, and arrests, would it be reasonable to think that legislative action could alter those rights? The very explicit procedures for constitutional amendments, standing alone, negate the idea that a written constitution could be altered by legislative or executive action.

The language of Article III vesting judicial power "in one Supreme Court" for "all Cases, in Law and Equity, arising under this Constitution, the Laws of the United States, and Treaties . . ." would be sterile indeed if the Supreme Court would not exercise that judicial power by deciding conflicts between the Constitution, federal laws and treaties on the one hand, and Acts of Congress, the Executive or States on the other.

Epilogue

To speak of the doctrine of judicial review and of *Marbury*, and fail to add at least a few more words on Marshall, would be to serve a great claret without letting it breathe and in a thick porcelain mug.

When one speaks of the "Great Chief Justice" . . .every literate person knows the reference is to John Marshall. It does not disparage his unique qualities but rather emphasizes his unparalleled gifts to note that he had no formal education and read law at William and Mary College for a mere few weeks before he was admitted to practice. This becomes more important when we remember that his contemporaries included Alexander Hamilton, Thomas Jefferson, James Madison, and Aaron Burr, who were all highly educated in the classics, all deeply read and trained in law.

There are several other factors, all relating to the political climate of the day, that may help to understand Marshall and his place in history. Going back to the appointment of the first court in 1790, we must recall that there were no political parties and it was then devoutly hoped that none would evolve. But men who risk all to conduct a revolution must be passionate believers, and our Founding Fathers were just that.

It is not at all surprising, therefore, that when the newly created Supreme Judicial Court of the United States[27] met for the first time on 1 February 1790, it was composed of men who tended to reflect the views of George Washington and his administration. In short, they were all federalists—the word was not uniformly capitalized then—and they were firm believers in the need for a strong federal or national government as a condition of survival. The Federalists remained in power until Jefferson defeated them in 1800—over 12 years. Quite naturally, then, when Marshall came to the Supreme Court every one of its members shared his political and judicial philosophy.

Since the court had delivered opinions in only a handful of cases when John Marshall was appointed, there could hardly be a more propitious moment for a judge of great intellectual capacity and remarkable qualities of statesmanship to ascend the highest court in the country. He had every advantage in his favor: he was very literally writing on a clean slate, with the support of five colleagues who shared his basic philosophy, and he had the wit and courage to make the most of his opportunity. As a soldier in the Continental Army, he had learned the need for a unified and strong national government to ensure the cohesiveness essential to survival of a new nation composed of three million highly individualistic and scattered people. As a political leader of Virginia, a member of its legislature, a member of the national Congress, and a Secretary of State, he understood government. Moreover, as one of the leaders in the Virginia struggle to secure adoption of the new Constitution over the vigorous opposition of men of such stature as Thomas Jefferson and Patrick Henry, he knew how fragile were the ties that held the former colonies together.

Thus the everlasting benefit of a country begotten in revolution and weaned in confusion and conflict, the United States of America was to be tutored in constitutional law for 34 formative years by a man who knew precisely what was needed to make a strong nation.

Small wonder, then, that John Adams in 1823, looking back, saw his appointment of John Marshall to the Supreme Court of the United States as one of his greatest contributions to his country. How indeed could there have been a greater one?

Notes

1. J. Bryce, *The American Commonwealth,* Vol. I, 242 (New York: Macmillan, 1931).
2. Thomas Jefferson, in writing the Declaration of Independence, relied heavily upon Locke's *Second Treatise on Government,* almost to the point of plagiarism.
3. Montesquieu's *L'Esprit des Lois* contains the clearest expression of the principle.
4. "The judicial Power shall extend to ... Cases ... [and] Controversies...." U.S. Const. Art. III, §2, cl. 1.
5. "[T]he supreme Court shall have appellate Jurisdiction both as to Law and Fact, with such Exceptions, and under such Regulations as the Congress shall make." U.S. Const. Art. III, §2, cl. 2.
6. Although most scholars agree that Art. III (granting the judicial power and extending it to "Cases ...arising under this Constitution, [and] the Laws of the United States .. .") coupled with the Supremacy Clause in Art. VI, cl. 2, necessarily includes the power to disregard state or federal statutes found to be unconstitutional, several major efforts to lay a scholarly basis for the contrary conclusion have been made. See, e.g., L. Boudin, *Government by Judiciary* (New York: Godwin, 1932); and W. Crosskey, *Politics and the Constitution in the History of the United States* (Chicago: University of Chicago Press, 1953). However, the understanding of the Constitutional Convention seems to have been quite clearly in favor of such a power; see, e.g., M. Farrand, *The Framing of the Constitution* (New Haven: Yale University Press, 1913); and C. Warren, *The Making of the Constitution* (Chicago: University of Chicago Press, 1937 ed.). See generally H.M. Hart and H. Wechsler, *The Federal Courts and the Federal System* 7–37 (Mineola, N.Y.: Foundation Press, 1973).
7. 1 Cranch 137 (1803).
8. The reasons for not writing it into the Constitution are speculative at best. Perhaps it would have been too controversial for some; it could have delayed the final draft; others may have thought it part of the warp and woof of a system of delegated and divided power. In any event, since our Constitution is a document to divide and assign powers and governing functions, the choice of the "one supreme Court" to construe and enforce "the supreme Law of the Land" seems simple, and the grant of power a necessary corollary of that choice. Thus the omission of any reference to the theory may have been due to an unwillingness to elucidate the obvious.
9. *Kamper v. Hawkins*, 1 Virginia Cases 20, 38 (1793). This is by no means the only state case in which state legislative acts were declared unconstitutional by state courts or in which the principle of judicial review was announced. In addition to Virginia, a number of states had each either announced the principle or strongly hinted at it. Among them were Maryland (*Whittington v. Polk*, 1 Harris & Johnson 236, 241 [1802]), South Carolina (*Lindsay v. Comm'rs.*, 2 Bay 38, 61–62 [1796]); also *Bowman v. Middleton*, 1 Bay 252, 254 (1792), a conspicuous case in which the court declared an act void because it was against "common right" and "magna charta", North Carolina (*State v.,* 1 Haywood 28, 29, 40 [1794]), Kentucky (*Stidger v. Rogers*, 2 Kentucky 52 [1801]), New Jersey (*State v. Parkhurst,* 4 Halstead 427 [1802]), and Pennsylvania (*Austin v. University of Pennsylvania*, 1 Yeates 260 [1793]). For further detail and a

more complete list of early state cases, see R. McLaughlin, *A Constitutional History of the United States* 312, n. 34 (New York: Appleton, 1935).

10. *Bank of Columbia v. Okley*, 4 Wheat. 235, 244 (1819).
11. (1610) 8 Co. 113b, 118a, 77 E.R. 646, 652. For a more complete discussion, see C. Haines, *The American Doctrine of Judicial Supremacy* 29–43 (New York: Russell & Russell, 1959).
12. O. Cromwell, *Letters and Speeches*, ed. by T. Carlyle (New York: AMS Press, 1974), Part 7, Speech 3 (12 September 1654).
13. 2 Dallas 304 (1795). S. 25 of the Judiciary Act of 1789 in terms granted federal appellate jurisdiction to review judgments of state courts concerning the validity of a treaty or statute of the United States under the Federal Constitution. S. 1, Statutes at Large 85.
14. Ibid., at 309.
15. In Marshall's time, the old Congress met in December after the November elections, and the newly elected Members did not take their seats until the following March. Since some of the old Members had been voted out of office, the December to March sitting came to be called a "lame duck Congress." The problem has been solved by the 20th Amendment which shortens the delay between the time a Member is elected and the time he takes his seat.
16. C. Warren, supra note 6, at 173.
17. S.E. Morison, *The Oxford History of the American People* (New York: Oxford University Press, 1965), at 362 states: "Toward Marshall his kinsman Jefferson entertained an implacable hatred because he [Marshall] had shown him up and broken the sentimental … bubble in the XYZ affair."
18. C. Warren, *Congress, The Constitution and the Supreme Court* 58–59 (Boston: Little Brown, 1935 ed.).
19. *Kamper v. Hawkins*, 1 Virginia Cases 20, 38 (1793).
20. Somewhere along the line in the development of his political philosophy, Jefferson had lost trust in the belief, expressed in a letter to a friend in 1798, that "the laws of the land, administered by upright judges, would protect you from any exercise of power unauthorized by the Constitution of the United States." Jefferson to Rowan, 26 September 1798: Ford ed., *Writings*, Vol. VIII, 448 (New York: Putnam's, 1892–1898).
21. Jefferson to Jarvis, 28 September 1820: Ford ed., *Writings*, Vol. XII, 162.
22. H.A. Washington, ed., *The Writings of Thomas Jefferson*, Vol. VII, 216 (New York: H. W. Derby, 1861).
23. S. 13 of the First Judiciary Act provided: "The Supreme Court … shall have power to issue writs of … mandamus … to any courts appointed, or persons holding office … of the United States." 1 Stat. 81.
24. 1 Cranch 299, 309 (1803).
25. However, in *Martin v. Hunter's Lessee*, 1 Wheaton 304 (1816), Justice Story for the Court firmly asserted the power of the Supreme Court to invalidate a state statute contrary to the Federal Constitution.
26. *Dred Scott v. Sandford*, 19 Howard 393 (1857).
27. The Journal of the Court used this title for the Court until the February 1791 session.

CHAPTER 2

The Supreme Court in the American System of Government

Robert H. Jackson

Justice, Supreme Court of the United States (1941–1954)

No sound assessment of our Supreme Court can treat it as an isolated, self-sustaining, or self-sufficient institution. It is a unit of a complex, interdependent scheme of government from which it cannot be severed. Nor can it be regarded merely as another law court. The Court's place in the combination was determined by principles drawn from a philosophy broader than mere law.

Our foundations were quarried not only from the legal ideas but also from the political, social, philosophical, scientific, and theological learnings of the eighteenth century, "the silver age of the Renaissance." All these were dominated by a belief in "the laws of nature and of nature's God." Faith in a "higher law," which had achieved a venerable place in the history of ideas through the speculations of jurists, monks, and scholars, burst forth toward the end of the eighteenth century into a fanatical creed that took over French and American liberal thinking and led in each case to a violent revolution.

Our judicial, executive, and legislative branches all were grounded in a belief that they were bound by the authority of a clear and universally acceptable natural law, revealed by man's reason and always and everywhere the same. Its fundamentals were proclaimed self-evident truths, as indisputable as the axioms of geometry, which needed only to be declared to be acknowledged as right and just by the opinion of

---

Acknowledgment to Harvard University Press for excerpts from The Supreme Court in the American System of Government *by Robert H. Jackson, Cambridge, Mass.: Harvard University Press,* *© 1955 by William Eldred Jackson and G. Bowdoin Craighill Jr., Executors, © 1983 by William Eldred Jackson.*

mankind. These truths of natural law to that age stood as the ultimate sanction of liberty and justice, equality and toleration. The whole constitutional philosophy of the time was based on a system of values in which the highest was the freedom of the individual from interference by officialdom—the rights of man. To supplement this natural order, little man-made government was thought to be needed, and the less the better.

To make certain that these natural rights should have some man-made sanctions, the forefathers added ten Amendments to the original instrument, translating their version of the rights of man into legal limitations on the new government. They did not stop, as the French did, at reciting these in a preamble to the Constitution, where they served as an admonition only to a parliament that was all-powerful because there could be no judicial review of its legislation. On the contrary, the forefathers established a Bill of Rights which conferred as a matter of law, enforceable in court, certain immunities and rights upon citizens which correspondingly limited the power of the majority duly expressed through governmental action....

Against this background a study of the Supreme Court can hardly fail to be instructive....

The Supreme Court as a Unit of Government

We ought first to inquire what kind of institution the Supreme Court really is, the degree of its independence, the nature of its power, and the limitations on its capacity and effectiveness.

The Supreme Court of the United States was created in a different manner from most high courts. In Europe, most judiciaries evolved as subordinates to the King, who delegated to them some of his functions....

The status of the Court as a unit of the Government, not as an institution subordinate to it, no doubt has given it prestige, for the people do not regard the Justices as employees of the Government of the day or as civil servants, as in continental Europe. Also, federal judges enjoy two bulwarks of independence—life tenure (except for impeachable misbehavior) and irreducible salaries (except by taxation and inflation).

Nonetheless, the Constitution-makers left the Court in vital respects a dependent body. The political branches nominate and confirm the Justices, a control of the Court's composition which results in a somewhat lagging political influence over its trend of decision, and any party that prevails in the Federal Government through several presidential terms will gradually tend to impress its political philosophy on the Court. The political branches also from time to time may alter the number of Justices, and that power was used to influence the course of decision several times before it was again proposed by President Roosevelt.

The Court also is dependent on the political branches for its powers in other vital respects. Its only irrevocable jurisdiction is original, and that reaches only cases affecting Ambassadors, public Ministers, or Consuls, or cases in which a state is a party. In all other cases it has appellate jurisdiction, but "with such exceptions and under such regulations as Congress shall make."

The Court also is dependent upon the political branches for the execution of its mandates, for it has no physical force at its command. The story is traditional that President Jackson once withheld enforcement, saying, "John Marshall has made his decision—*now let him enforce it!*" Also, the Court, of course, depends upon Congress for the appropriation of funds with which to operate. These all add up to a fairly formidable political power over the Supreme Court, if there were a disposition to exert it.

But perhaps the most significant and least comprehended limitation upon the judicial power is that this power extends only to cases and controversies. We know that this restriction was deliberate, for it was proposed in the Convention that the Supreme Court be made part of a Council of Revision with a kind of veto power, and this was rejected.

The result of the limitation is that the Court's only power is to decide lawsuits between adversary litigants with real interests at stake, and its only method of proceeding is by the conventional judicial, as distinguished from legislative or administrative, process. This precludes the rendering of advisory opinions even at the request of the nation's President and every form of pronouncement on abstract, contingent, or hypothetical issues. It prevents acceptance for judicial settlement of issues in which the interests and questions involved are political in character.

It also precludes imposition on federal constitutional courts of nonjudicial duties. Recent trends to empower judges to grant or deny wiretapping rights to a prosecutor or to approve a waiver of prosecution in order to force a witness to give self-incriminating testimony raise interesting and dubious questions. A federal court can perform but one function—that of deciding litigations—and can proceed in no manner except by the judicial process....

The judicial power of the Supreme Court, however, does extend to all cases arising under the Constitution, to controversies to which the United States is a party, and to those between two or more states. Thus, the Court must face political questions in legal form, for surely a controversy between two separately organized political societies does present a political question, even if waged with the formalities of a lawsuit. And any decision which confirms, allocates, or shifts power as between different branches of the Federal Government or between it and a constituent state is equally political, no matter whether the decision be reached by a legislative or a judicial process.

Our Constitution was the product and expression of a virile political philosophy held by those who wrote it. Controversies over its meaning often spring from political motives, for the object of politics always is to obtain power. Such controversies have to be solved either by consideration of the experiences and statements of the framers [themselves] which indicate the original will, or by reference to some relevant subsequent events and currents of opinion deemed controlling. And all constitutional interpretations have political consequences.

We must not forget that, at bottom, the Civil War was fought over constitutional doctrine. It oversimplifies that tragedy to say that it was a war over slavery, an institution which many southern leaders had come to deplore and one which Mr. Lincoln did not propose to abolish in the states where it existed.

The controversy was over the power of the Federal Government to control the spread of slavery into new territory, and over the voluntary or compulsory character of the federal compact. These, like most other questions which have deeply agitated our people, found their way to the Supreme Court in the guise of private controversies between litigating parties....

Executive v. Legislative

It is hard to conceive a task more fundamentally political than to maintain amidst changing conditions the balance between the executive and legislative branches of our federal system. The Supreme Court often is required to arbitrate between the two because litigation in one form or another raises questions as to the legitimacy of the acts of one branch or the other under the doctrine of separation of powers. In such cases the Court has found no precedent from any other country or in the judicial interpretation of any similar written instrument, and it has had to devise its own doctrine from time to time.

The Court, both before and after the Roosevelt influence was felt in its appointments, has tended strongly to support the power of the President in matters involving foreign affairs. On the other hand, where only internal affairs are involved, the Court has been more inclined to restrict executive power. It halted a presidential effort indirectly to control the policies of the administrative agencies by removal of a Federal Trade Commissioner. In the cases striking down the NIRA [the National Industrial Recovery Act], the Court refused to sanction the congressional practice of delegating power to the President to make codes for industry that would be the equivalent of new laws.

The Court has kept the Executive from usurping the adjudicative function through military trials of offenders by holding such trials illegal in *Ex parte Milligan*, after, however, they had been running riot for a number of years.

In the more recent Steel Seizure case the Court refused to sanction a presidential seizure of private property without congressional authorization, holding that the President has no such inherent power under the Constitution. But I felt constrained in that case to point out the inadequacies of judicial power to appraise or control the realistic balance of power between Congress and the President. This is because of the gap that exists between the President's paper powers and his actual powers. The real potency of the Executive office does not show on the face of the Constitution. The relative influence of the President and of the Congress has fluctuated widely, depending on the personal and political strength of the particular President as compared with that of the congressional leadership. A Congress stampeded by a powerful leader like Thaddeus Stevens may cripple a President who is politically vulnerable, and a senatorial coalition may break the foreign policy of even an able and strong President like Wilson. On the other hand, a White House tenant who is a skillful manipulator of his extralegal influences may force an unwelcome program through Congress.

What are these sources of presidential strength? First, the Executive power is concentrated in a single head in whose choice the whole nation has a part, making him the focus of public hopes and expectations. No collection of local representatives can rival him in prestige. None can gain such ready and effective access to the modern means of communication with the masses or exert such influence on public opinion; this is one of his most effective leverages upon those in Congress who are supposed to balance his power. As the nation's activities have spread, the President wields the power of appointment and promotion over a vast multitude of our people. He is not merely the Chief Magistrate of the Republic; he is the titular and usually the actual head of the prevailing political party, whose loyalties and interest enable him to win as political leader what he could not command under the Constitution. Woodrow Wilson summed it all up in the observation that "if he rightly interpret the national thought and boldly insist upon it, he is irresistible.... His office is anything he has the sagacity and force to make it."

Yet it depends not upon the President alone but upon his sagacity and force measured against that of the Congress as manifested in its leadership. If Congress forfeits the respect of the country, it will not be able to balance the power of the Executive. No matter what the Supreme Court opines, only Congress itself can keep its power from slipping through its fingers.

Federal Power v. State Power

It is the maintenance of the constitutional equilibrium between the states and the Federal Government that has brought the most vexatious questions to the Supreme Court. That it was the duty of the Court, within its own constitutional functions, to preserve this balance has been asserted by the Court many times; that the Constitution is vague and ambiguous on this subject is shown by the history preceding our Civil War. It is undeniable that ever since that war ended we have been in a cycle of rapid centralization, and Court opinions have sanctioned a considerable concentration of power in the Federal Government with a corresponding diminution in the authority and prestige of state governments.

Here again the principal causes of this concentration have not been within judicial control. Improved methods of transportation and communication; the increasing importance of foreign affairs and of interstate commerce; the absorption of revenue sources by the nation with the consequent appeal by distressed localities directly to Washington for relief and work projects, bypassing the state entirely; the direct election of Senators; and various other factors—all have contributed to move the center of gravity from the state capital to that of the nation.

I think it is a mistake to lump all states' rights together as is done so frequently in political discussions.... It was early perceived that to allow the Federal Government to spend money for internal improvements would aggrandize its powers as against those of the states. It was not until the famous decision holding the Social Security Act constitutional that this controversy over the federal power to tax and spend for the general welfare was settled, and settled in favor of the existence of that power in the Federal Government. I believe that this controversy was rightly settled, but there is no denying that the power is vast and, uncontrolled, leads to the invasion of sources of revenue and builds up the Federal Government by creating organizations to make the expenditures. But here we are dealing with powers granted to the Federal Government, if not entirely without ambiguity, at least in language which fairly admits of the construction given it and which fairly warned those who adopted the Constitution that such results might follow.

Considerations of a different nature arise from interferences with states' rights under the vague and ambiguous mandate of the Fourteenth Amendment. The legislative history of that Amendment is not enlightening, and the history of its ratification is not edifying. I shall not go into the controversy as to whether the Fourteenth Amendment, by a process of incorporation or impregnation, directs against the states prohibitions found in the earlier Amendments. Whether it does or not, I think the Fourteenth Amendment has been considerably abused.

For more than half a century the Supreme Court found in the Fourteenth Amendment authority for striking down various social experiments by the states. The history of judicial nullification of state social and economic legislation is too well known to justify repetition here. It came to its culmination when the Court wound up the October 1935 Term by declaring that there was no power in either state or nation to enact a minimum wage law, a position repudiated within a few months by the conventions of both political parties and retracted by the Court itself with some haste. That retraction probably brought an end to the use of the Fourteenth Amendment to prevent experiments by the states with economic and social and labor legislation....

Today, however, we have a different application of the Fourteenth Amendment. Today it is being used not to restrain state legislatures but to set aside the acts of state courts, particularly in criminal matters.

It is a difficult question and always will remain a debatable question where, in particular instances, federal due process should step into state court proceedings and set them aside. When the state courts render harsh or unconsidered judgments, they invite this power to be used. But I think in the long run the transgressions of liberty by the Federal Government, with its all-powerful organization, are much more to be feared than those of the several states, which have a greater capacity for self-correction.

State v. State

Another clearly political type of litigation is that of state against state. It was logical that in a federation the different units should have some arbiter to settle their differences. Congress was made a supervisor of their separate compacts or agreements. The Supreme Court was made the arbiter of their controversies.

To what source may the Court look for law to govern such controversies? The actual practice perhaps is well illustrated in Mr. Justice Cardozo's opinion in *New Jersey v. Delaware*. His search carried him through many ancient documents, which he interpreted according to the common law of property, and he compared the claims of the two states in the light of that body of learning. But this was inadequate for the solution of the case and resort was had to international law. He traced international law through the Court's own decisions and through all of the conventional authorities, American and foreign. He found international law inconclusive and no positive law applicable. He declared that "international law, or the law that governs between states, has at times, like the common law within states, a twilight existence during which it is hardly distinguishable from morality or justice, till at length the *imprimatur* of a court attests its jural quality." He concluded that in these circumstances it was within the power of the judicial process to develop and apply a formula consonant with justice and with the political and social needs of the interstate or international legal system. Reduced to its simplest terms, what the Court seemed to be saying in that case was that it found no controlling law and was obliged to declare some, in the light of the experience and learning of the law in similar situations. The Court has no escape in many cases of this character from the undesirable alternatives of refusing to obey its duty to decide the case or of devising some rule of decision which has no precedent or positive law authority.

I know that it is now regarded as more or less provincial and reactionary to cite the Tenth Amendment, which reserves to the states and the people the powers not delegated to the Federal Government. That Amendment is rarely mentioned in judicial opinions, rarely cited in argument. But our forefathers made it a part of the Bill of Rights in order to retain in the localities certain powers and not to allow them to drift into centralized hands

Majority v. Individual

Perhaps the most delicate, difficult and shifting of all balances which the Court is expected to maintain is that between liberty and authority. It is not so easy as some people believe to determine what serves liberty best by way of restriction of authority. For example, the removal of the Japanese from the West Coast during the War, which seemed to me plainly unconstitutional as applied to citizens, was rationalized as a service to ultimate liberty. And I suppose no one would be more likely than Abraham Lincoln to win recognition by common vote as the greatest servant of freedom; yet President Lincoln, at the outset of his administration, suspended the writ of habeas corpus and resorted to wholesale arrest without warrant, detention without trial, and imprisonment without judicial conviction. Private mail was opened, and Cabinet officers simply sent telegrams ordering persons to be arrested and held without communication or counsel. The power was given to generals of various of the northern states to suppress newspapers and suspend the writ. President Lincoln, in his famous letter to Erastus Corning and others, defended his conduct, saying all that ever could be said and what always will be said in favor of such policies in time of emergency. Those policies were sharply but unavailingly condemned in May of 1861 by the aged Chief Justice Taney, and he has said all that can be said on the other side. Had Mr. Lincoln scrupulously observed the Taney policy, I do not know whether we would have had any liberty, and had the Chief Justice adopted Mr. Lincoln's philosophy as the philosophy of the law, I again do not know whether we would have had any liberty.

Lord Acton has said that liberty is a term of 200 definitions. About all I am sure of is that it is something never established for the future, but something which each age must provide for itself. I think we are given the rough outlines of a free society by our Bill of Rights. Liberty is not the mere absence of restraint, it is not a spontaneous product of majority rule, it is not achieved merely by lifting underprivileged classes to power, nor is it the inevitable by-product of technological expansion. It is achieved only by a rule of law....

The Supreme Court, in the exercise of its power, has repeatedly come into collision with the strong executives of the nation. Jefferson, Jackson, Lincoln, and Franklin Roosevelt have been in open conflict with it. The clash has occurred where the Court was believed to be entering political realms through the passageway of private litigation. It would serve no purpose to review the merits of the conflict here, but in almost every instance it has occurred in such form as really to raise the question of minority and individual rights against majority rule; in each instance the President has been the representative of a powerful, popular majority. This is one of the great dilemmas of judicial power and one most avoided in discussion of the subject. So far as I can see, nothing has been accomplished in any of the controversies to settle or put at rest the questions which cause them. Judicial power to nullify a law duly passed by the representative process is a restriction upon the power of the majority to govern the country. Unrestricted majority rule leaves the individual in the minority unprotected. This is the dilemma and you have to take your choice. The Constitution makers made their choice in favor of a limited majority rule.

PART II

The Dynamics of the Judicial Process

"WE ARE VERY QUIET here, but it is the quiet of a storm centre."[1] Courts—particularly the Supreme Court, as Justice Oliver Wendell Holmes observed—are indeed a storm center—facing the panoply of human problems, crowded dockets, and unrelenting work schedules. Moreover, in Justice Benjamin Cardozo's memorable words, "the great tides and currents which engulf the rest of men, do not turn aside in their course, and pass judges by."[2] The political nature of courts and judges inexorably poses tensions and influences the process of judgment. Judges are political actors, and not surprisingly, their political presuppositions and policy orientations affect their decisions and the process of decision making.

Moreover, the dynamics of judicial politics begin prior to judges' ascending the bench. Indeed, judicial politics and policymaking reflects in no small part the politics of judicial selection and appointment. Under Article II of the U.S. Constitution, the president nominates and, with the "advice and consent of the Senate," appoints all federal judges. In contrast, state judges are appointed through a variety of methods. The methods of judicial selection in the states include (1) popular—partisan and nonpartisan—election; (2) appointment by governors or legislatures; and (3) some combination of both methods, or so-called merit and hybrid (combining both merit and election) systems. In the merit or hybrid systems, a nonpartisan commission provides lists of potential nominees from which the governor or legislature makes appointments; then, after one year of service, the judges have their names placed on a ballot and voters decide whether they should be retained; subsequently, the judges may be subject to further retention elections.

With a growing appreciation for how judges have made law throughout the twentieth century—from the rise of the academic writings of the American Legal Realists to controversial Court rulings on school desegregation, in *Brown v. Board of Education of Topeka, Kansas* (1954); abortion, in *Roe v. Wade* (1973) and

Planned Parenthood of Southeastern Pennsylvania v. Casey (1992); and discrimination against homosexuals in *Roemer v. Evans* (1996) and *Lawrence v. Texas* (2003). Among other contested Bill of Rights decisions came ongoing debates over the role of courts, the methods of interpretation, and the politics of judicial selection and appointment. The appointment of federal judges, no less than the election of state judges, in turn, have become more hotly contested over the last thirty years. In chapter 3 Judge Roger J. Miner, an appointee of President Ronald Reagan to the Court of Appeals for the Second Circuit, surveys the history and politics of appointing federal judges and, against that background, considers some trends in federal judicial selection. Notably, he is critical of the greater role of staff, employed both by the White House and the Senate Judiciary Committee, in screening potential nominees, as well as the premium placed on nominees' political ideology in winning Senate confirmation and achieving a seat on the federal bench.

The experience of appointment to the bench and the challenge of serving vary from judge to judge. Justice Lewis Powell recalled that his appointment to the Court, even though he had turned down earlier offers of a nomination, was "like being struck by lightning." [3] Chief Justice Earl Warren reminisced that "perhaps the most lonesome day I ever had in my life was the day I arrived at the Supreme Court":

> [O]n Monday morning, I walked in about ten o'clock in the morning, and the Court didn't convene then until noon, and so I walked into the office of the Chief Justice and there was Mrs. McHugh who had been the secretary for Chief Justice Vinson ... and there were three law clerks, ... [and] two old messengers. ... And that was my staff, that's all there was, and here I came on four days notice, with no preparation and no knowledge of [the cases] in the Court at that time ... [T]o make the adjustment to the Supreme Court from [the governorship of California], was really an adjustment.[4]

The adjustment to the bench usually takes some time. There is a kind of "freshman effect" on new appointees. Justice Tom Clark suggested as much when recounting a conversation with Justice Robert Jackson, whom he had asked: "'How long did it take you to get acclimated here, Bob?' And he said, 'You know I asked Chief Justice Hughes that.' And I said, 'What did the Chief Justice say?' 'He said it would take about three years.' So I said, 'What do you think?' He said, 'Oh I'd say it's nearer to five.'" [5] In recent speeches, Justice Clarence Thomas has likewise said that it took him five years—or what he termed his "rookie year"—to come up to speed on the high court.[6]

The experiences of judges and the dynamics of the judicial process are significantly different in trial and appellate courts. Former Court of Appeals Judge

Thurman Arnold explained that he resigned because he found the work of a judge much duller than that of an advocate; he "might have liked the trial court but on the appellate court we sat in groups of three and all we did was to listen to argument and write opinions."[7] At the trial level, the central function of the judge, sitting alone, is to oversee the adversarial process and umpire the factual determination of legal culpability. At the federal appellate level, judges, usually sitting in groups of three or more, review the records of lower courts' decisions for procedural errors or misapplication of the law. The trial judge, in other words, is primarily "a trier of facts"; whereas appellate judges clarify and "declare the law" in written opinions. This functional distinction represents a basic allocation of judicial power with important public policy consequences.

Trial Judges and the Adversarial Process

The role and responsibilities of trial judges are often underestimated or neglected, perhaps because trial courts are but the first tier in the judicial system or because of an "upper court bias." We read and hear more about appellate courts, especially the Supreme Court. Still, as U. S. district court judge Charles Wyzanski points out:

> The task of writing opinions is as nothing compared with the duty of so conducting a trial, particularly a jury trial, that the jurors, the parties, the witnesses, the counsel, and the spectators not only follow the red threads of fact and of law but leave the courtroom persuaded of the fairness of the procedure and the high responsibility of courts of justice in advancing the values we cherish most deeply.[8]

Trial judges in both the federal and state systems, in fact, handle the bulk of judicial business. Moreover, the caseloads of state and federal courts have exploded in recent decades. Although in 1950 they faced just over 90,000 new filings each year, by 2007 they confronted more than 300,000 new cases each year—257,500 in district courts and a little more than 58,000 in appellate courts. (Those numbers, though, are dwarfed by the millions of cases handled by state courts.) A substantial number of federal criminal defendants either do not go to trial or plead guilty, often as a result of plea bargaining, and a small percentage (about 14 percent) of those criminal cases that do go to trial are subsequently appealed. As one federal judge observed: "Justice stops in the district. They either get it here or they can't get it at all."[9] In most instances, trial courts, especially state trial courts, are courts of first and last resort. The discretion exercised by trial judges therefore is a crucial feature of our judicial system. As Second Circuit Court of Appeals judge Henry J. Friendly emphasized, "In some instances the trial court is accorded broad, virtually unreviewable discretion, as is the case with criminal sentencing in the federal system. In others, the trial judge's discretion is accorded no deference beyond its persuasive power."[10]

Because lower court judges preside over trials (other duties include management of case processing, approval of plea bargains, supervision of the settlement process, and monitoring remedial decrees),[11] to a greater degree than appellate judges they experience the drama of the adversary process. A pioneering American Legal Realist and federal appellate judge, Jerome Frank, eloquently argued in his classic *Courts on Trial* (1949), excerpted in Chapter 4, that the adversary system is based not on a "theory of truth" but on a "'fight' theory, a theory which derives from the origin of trials as substitutes for private out-of-court battles."

The spectacle of partisan justice uniquely replayed in each trial inevitably influences judicial decision making and behavior. A judge is not a mechanical scale or computer, in Judge Frank's words: "Trial judges, being human, vary in their respective qualities of intelligence, perceptiveness, and attentiveness—and other mental and emotional characteristics operative while they are listening to, and observing witnesses." After presiding over a trial and reflecting on the evidence and law, the judge "experiences a gestalt"[12] on which he renders a final decision and then rationalizes in a written opinion. Judge Marvin E. Frankel, in Chapter 5, describes the work of a judge presiding over trials. He underscores the tensions between the role of a judge as an impartial arbitrator and the frustrating realities of the adversary process—a process some judges describe as legalized gambling based on a sporting theory of justice. The adversary system has long been criticized for its excesses, abusive treatment of witnesses, procedural delays, and high financial costs. However, in Chapter 6 federal district court judge D. Brock Hornby points out that in the late twentieth and early twenty-first centuries trials have declined, and lower federal court judges spend more time involved in pre-trial negotiations, plea bargaining, and caseload management.

Appellate Judges and the "Caseload Crisis"

"No judge writes on a wholly clean slate,"[13] especially appellate court judges who review the decisions of lower courts and administrative agencies. In chapter 7, Ninth Circuit Court of Appeals judge Alex Kozinski, an appointee of President Reagan, provides a perspective on decision making from the appellate bench. Notably, he emphasizes the constraints on appellate judges arising from their necessary reliance on law clerks, the collegial nature of appellate court decision making, the obligation to follow precedents laid down by higher courts, and the pressures of the political system. The collegial nature of appellate decision making should be emphasized and contrasted to the individualized decision making of trial judges. Federal appellate judges, for instance, sit in rotating panels of three.

Occasionally, on especially important or divisive cases, the entire court sits as a panel, or *en banc*. The dynamics of decision making therefore varies with the rotation of judges and the number of judges sitting *en banc*.

In response to the rising number of appeals during the past few decades, Congress increased the number of appellate judges, and in 1981 the Fifth Circuit was reorganized and split into a new Fifth Circuit and a new Eleventh Circuit. Given the collegial nature of appellate decision making, the number, rotation, and location of judges in a circuit directly affects decision making. Chief Judge John Godbold, who served on the Eleventh Circuit, explains some of the dimensions and problems of appellate decision making:

> I came on the former Fifth [Circuit] when there were twelve judges. We went to thirteen, then to fifteen, and finally to twenty-six. On the former Fifth, we had either thirty-five or thirty-six, counting the senior judges, at one time. That number gave more than seven thousand different possible combinations of judges sitting in panels of three.... [Moreover] as the [court] grew in size to twenty-six, it tended to fragment into several groups. I don't mean just in opinion writing, but also in differing views of the law.... A smaller *en banc* court performs the process of adjudication in the traditional manner. Usually, there is one view in one direction and an opposing view, with debate back and forth, and maybe people change their minds, but ultimately the court concludes with probably two views and maybe three once in a while.... In contrast the twenty-six-person *en banc* performed somewhat like a legislative body. It divided up into groups, with judges seeking accommodation on some ground that, while maybe not ideal for everybody, was at least agreeable to a majority. Its function became almost legislative and, therefore, antithetical to the way that appellate courts normally operate.[14]

The growing numbers of appeals and appellate judges strain working relationships and threaten the stability and continuity of law: more cases, more judges, and more opinions. In the Fifth, Eighth, and Eleventh Circuits, for instance, a judge trying to keep abreast of case law developments faced reading more than 2,000 new opinions each year. One appellate judge, Eighth Circuit judge Donald Lay, for example, once described his frustration: "A few months ago I was reading an opinion from our court; after reading several pages on a certain point, I wondered who wrote it. I was amazed to find that I had authored the opinion some 10 years before. The point is we read so much that we can no longer even recognize—let alone remember—our own opinions."[15]

In order to handle expanding caseloads, the number of law clerks assigned to a federal judge rose from one to two to three (and, at the Supreme Court, to four).[16] There are also more staff attorneys and other office personnel. Whether the increased number of law clerks and support staff will indeed prove to be the "carcinoma of the federal judiciary" [17] and turn courts into "opinion writing bureaus" [18] depends on the personalities and qualities of judges as well as the extent to which they actually relinquish their responsibilities to clerks or become preoccupied with supervising their staffs. "I don't think people are shocked any longer to learn that an appellate judge receives a draft of a proposed opinion from a law clerk." So remarked Chief Justice William H. Rehnquist, adding: "I think they would be shocked, and properly shocked, to learn that an appellate judge simply 'signed off' on such a draft without fully understanding its import and in all probability making some changes in it. The line between having law clerks help one with one's work, and supervising subordinates in the performance of *their* work, may be a hazy one, but it is at the heart ... [of] the fundamental concept of 'judging.'" [19] Some judges dismiss the threat of "bureaucratic justice," [20] while others warn of its dangers—too many, too long, too footnoted, law review-type, patchwork opinions.[21] There is no denying that the greater role and importance of law clerks in the judicial process has changed dramatically.

The increasing role of law clerks and support staff is not the only problem facing the federal judiciary. The sheer growth in caseloads has resulted in an expansion of the size of the federal bench; between 1950 and 2008, for example, the number of lower federal court judges more than tripled. The rising caseloads and number of federal judges reflects Congress's enactment of federal legislation, particularly in its "wars" on crime, drugs, and terrorism, as well as its expansion of the jurisdiction of federal courts, along with some of the federal judiciary's own rulings.

A growing concern of a number of federal judges is the increasing size of the federal judiciary. Justice Antonin Scalia, for one, has worried that "the best and the brightest" will become discouraged from accepting judgeships because of the workload and the predominance of intellectually uninteresting cases, such as those involving Social Security disability payments. Other lower federal court judges, including appellate judges Jon O. Newman of the Ninth Circuit and J. Harvie Wilkinson of the Fourth Circuit, have lamented the growth in federal judgeships because of its adverse effects on the judicial process as well as on federalism and federal–state court relations. Judge Newman thus proposed limiting the number of federal judges to no more than 1,000.

By contrast, in chapter 8, appellate judge Stephen Reinhardt of the Ninth Circuit, an appointee of Democratic president Jimmy Carter, argues rather provocatively that the size of the federal bench should be doubled, not limited.

The Supreme Court and the Judicial Process

The Supreme Court is often depicted as the most secretive, inaccessible institution in government. Yet as Justices Lewis J. Powell Jr. and William H. Rehnquist explain in chapters 9 and 10, except for the justices' conferences and deliberations prior to handing down a ruling, "the Marble Temple" is open to public view. Briefs for cases are available from the offices of the clerk and public information officer, and members of the public and media may listen to oral arguments and the "handing down" of decisions as well as obtain copies of final published opinions. Notably, since April 2000 the Supreme Court has maintained its own Web site (at *www.supremecourtus.gov)* that makes available transcripts of oral arguments and the full text of its decisions, orders, and opinions.

Life at the Supreme Court—once described as "unremitting toil"—is in fact much less glamorous than popularly imagined and largely centers in the chambers of the justices. Justice John Harlan Jr. characterized the justices' chambers as "nine little law firms"—an apt description if one notes that law firms rarely work together; rather, they move in different if not opposite directions. "As much as 90 percent of our total time," Justice Powell similarly observed, "we function as nine small, independent law firms":

> I emphasize the words *small and independent*. There is the equivalent of one partner in each chamber, three or four law clerks [seven of the justices each use four clerks; the Chief Justice employs an additional assistant as well; while Justices William Rehnquist and John Paul Stevens rely on three and two, respectively], two secretaries, and a messenger. The informal interchange between chambers is minimal, with most exchanges of views being by correspondence or memoranda. Indeed, a justice may go through an entire term without being once in the chambers of all of the other eight members of the Court.[22]

Justice Powell added the caveat that in other respects a modern law firm and the Supreme Court are light years apart. For one thing, he noted, he averaged sixty hours per week at the Court: "This is considerably more than my chargeable hours ever were at the peak of a large and demanding law practice."[23] Similarly, Justice Harlan cautioned that "decisions of the Court are not the product of an institutional approach, as with a professional decision of a law firm or policy determination of a business enterprise. They are the result merely of a tally of individual votes cast after the illuminating influences of collective debate. The rule of ultimate individual responsibility is the respected and jealously guarded tradition of the Court."[24] The traditions and processes of decision making at the Supreme Court are indeed unlike those in law firms. But like the heads of law firms, the justices are shrewd, strong-willed individuals—in Justice Harry Blackmun's words, "all prima donnas."[25]

The business of the Supreme Court, like that of other federal courts, continues to grow: from a bare 565 cases on the docket in 1920 to over 1,300 in 1950, over 2,300 in 1960, and over 10,000 cases in 2007–2008. Unlike other courts, the modern Supreme Court's docket is largely discretionary. Therefore, to a considerable degree, the justices may determine their own agenda. The cornerstone of the Court's operations, Justice Harlan once remarked, "is the control it possesses over the amount and character of its business."[26]

The Court must give full, plenary consideration to cases that come either under its original jurisdiction, as specified by the Constitution, or as mandatory rights of appeal, as provided by Congress. Until 1925 the Court was required to hear and decide the merits of every case, except for a small number in which it exercised discretionary jurisdiction after the creation of Circuit Courts of Appeals in 1891. Because of the expanding number of cases arising from the Industrial Revolution and increased government regulation at the turn of the century, the Court eventually could not keep abreast of its docket. Congress, passing the Judges' Act in 1925, temporarily alleviated the Court's problem by largely replacing mandatory rights of appeal with petitions for *writs of certiorari*—petitions requesting the Court to exercise its discretion to hear the merits of cases, thus giving the Court power to refuse plenary consideration and enabling it to control its agenda.

Prior to 1925, 80 percent of the Court's docket was on mandatory appeal and 20 percent on *certiorari.* Congress subsequently incrementally expanded the Court's discretionary jurisdiction by eliminating other mandatory appeals and replacing them with *certiorari* petitions. Finally, in 1988 Congress enacted the Act to Improve the Administration of Justice, which eliminated virtually all of the Court's nondiscretionary jurisdiction, except for appeals in reapportionment cases, suits under the Civil Rights and Voting Rights acts, antitrust laws, and the Presidential Election Campaign Fund Act. As a result, today approximately 99 percent of all filings are on *certiorari.* Deciding what to decide, therefore, is one of the most important steps in the Court's decision-making process. The review of "*cert.*" petitions, Justice Harlan Stone once claimed, is very laborious.[27] But as Justice Harlan underscored:

> The *certiorari* system affords the Court opportunities for more mature deliberation in the decision of cases than would otherwise be possible. For a large volume of unfinished business is bound to have an unfortunate impact on the decisional process, in that a court working under the compulsion of keeping its docket reasonably current inevitably has to deny itself the opportunity for unhurried reflection which is so indispensable to sound decision in all but the perfunctory type of case.[28]

Still, as Justice Byron White once queried, if the Court gave plenary consideration to less than 2 percent of the cases on its docket, for the overwhelming number of cases is it not a matter of petition denied, justice denied?[29] Justice Hugo Black provided a partial response to that question:

> I don't think it can fairly be said that we give no consideration to all who apply. I think we do. You can't decide the case, you can't write long opinions, but when we meet, we take up the cases that are on our docket that have been brought up since we adjourned. Frequently I'll mark up at the top [of a petition] 'Denied—not of sufficient importance,' 'No dispute among the circuits,' or something else. And I'll go in and vote to deny it. Well, I've considered it to that extent. And every judge does that same thing in [our] conference.[30]

As Justice Black suggested, every case is given some consideration and of course no case is entitled to "unlimited" review. In obviously doubtful, difficult, and important *cert.* petitions, two justices may be assigned independently to write full memoranda on the issues presented, prior to the justices' voting on whether to grant review. No less crucial but often overlooked is the fact that the vast majority of the cases on the Court's docket do not appear to merit review or are frivolous. Testifying before Congress in 1937, Chief Justice Charles Evans Hughes observed:

> I think that it is safe to say that almost 60 percent of the applications for *certiorari* are wholly without merit and ought never to have been made. There are probably about 20 percent or so in addition which have a fair degree of plausibility, but which fail to survive critical examination. The remainder, falling short, I believe, of 20 percent, show substantial grounds and are granted.[31]

Even prior to the introduction of the *certiorari* system, which encouraged the filing of questionable cases, Justice John Clarke in 1922 expressed his "surprise at the great number of cases finding their way into [the] court which are of entirely negligible importance, whether considered from the point of view of the principles of law or of the property involved in them. That impression has been intensified as time has passed, for their number constantly increases."[32] Similarly, Justice Harlan estimated that "more than one-half [of all appeals are] so untenable that they never should have been filed."[33]

The number of frivolous cases, in particular frivolous *cert.* petitions, largely stems from the Court's *in forma pauperis* (in the form of a pauper) practice—a congressionally established practice that gives every citizen the right to file without payment of fees upon an oath of indigency. *In forma pauperis* petitions (IFPs) have steadily increased from 22 in 1930, to over 1,000 in 1960, to well over half of the Court's present docket. Justice Harlan, among others, concluded that "more than nine-tenths of the [IFP] petitions [are] so insubstantial that they never should have been filed."[34] Individuals, without the cost of attorneys or payment of filing fees, thus may petition the Court with absolutely gratuitous claims. Clarence Brummett, for one, repeatedly asked the Court to assist him in a war of extermination he had vowed against Turkey.[35] Justice William Brennan gave as illustration some of the frivolous petitions that arrive:

> "Are Negroes in fact Indians and therefore entitled to Indians' exemptions from federal income taxes?" "Are the federal income tax laws unconstitutional insofar as they do not provide a deduction for depletion of the human body?" "Is the 16th Amendment unconstitutional as violative of the 14th Amendment?" and ... "Does a ban on drivers turning right on a red light constitute an unreasonable burden on interstate commerce?"[36]

Growing numbers of IFPs—the largest category—come from "jailhouse lawyers," indigent prisoners claiming some constitutional violation or deprivation. "The claims made are often fantastic, surpassing credulity," commented Justice William O. Douglas.[37] Although "98 or 99 of them are frivolous," he added, "we read them all because they produce classic situations like *Gideon* and *Miranda* and so on."[38] Even after a case has been granted review, after further deliberations, the justices may still dismiss a case as improvidently granted.

Deciding what to decide occurs during the Court's conferences. Conferences are held during the last week of September to consider the more than 2,000 petitions that were carried over from the prior term or that came in over the summer and, thereafter, when the Court is in session, on Wednesdays and Fridays to consider both petitions and cases on which oral argument was presented earlier in the week. Summoned by a buzzer five minutes before the hour, only the justices are present in the conference room, an oak-paneled chamber lined with books from floor to ceiling, located directly behind the courtroom. Over the mantel of an exquisite marble fireplace at one end hangs a portrait of Chief Justice John Marshall. Next to the fireplace stands a large rectangular table where the justices sit, surrounded by carts full of petitions, briefs, and other books. The chief justice sits at the east end and the senior associate justice at the west end. Along the right-hand side of Chief Justice Roberts, next to the fireplace, sit Justices Antonin Scalia, Anthony Kennedy, and David Souter; on the left-hand side, Clarence Thomas, Ruth Bader Ginsburg, Stephen Breyer, and Samuel Alito. Sitting closest to the outside door, the junior justice by tradition receives and sends messages that come and go via knocks on the door—a tradition about which Justice Tom Clark wryly commented: "For five years I was the highest-paid doorkeeper in the world."[39]

The conferences, for obvious reasons, are conducted in absolute secrecy. (Prior to 1910, when a leak was suspected, two page boys were also present to run errands for the justices.) Like Chief Justice Rehnquist (in chapter 10), Justice Brennan emphasized: "But the secrecy is as to our deliberations. There is no secrecy as to how we operate at the conference."[40] Each conference and oral argument session begins with the justices' customary shaking of hands—a custom begun by Chief Justice Melville Fuller, which reminded Justice James Byrnes of "the usual instruction of the referee in the prize ring."[41] A typical conference begins, according to Chief Justice Warren E. Burger, "with a discussion of the applications for review in this court; and then we move to a consideration of which opinions are ready for announcement; and from that we go to a discussion of the argued cases."[42]

The role of the chief justice in opening discussions of cases is crucial, for it provides the opportunity to fix the relative import of a case within the context of the Court's entire deliberations, and perhaps to suggest (if not determine) the amount of time to be spent on each case during the more than forty conferences each term. Chief Justice Charles Evans Hughes, a respected task leader, reportedly strove to limit discussion of *cert.* petitions to three and a half minutes and was largely successful for, as Justice Owen Roberts recalls, "[s]o complete were his summaries that in many cases nothing needed to be added by any of his associates."[43] Given the number of petitions to consider at each Friday conference, Chief Justice Earl Warren observed: "It may be fairly said that a majority of the time of our conferences is devoted to this purpose."[44]

Because the chief justice presides over the conference and is the executive officer for the Court, he also has an equally important role as a social leader—a role that in fact dovetails with that of task leader. Accomplishing the work of the Court requires cooperation among the justices, but that may prove at times difficult among strong-willed individuals with their own habits, prejudices, and philosophies. For example, Justice James McReynolds, an avowed antisemite, refused even to talk to newly appointed Justice Brandeis for three years. Chief Justice Edward D. White was apparently unsuccessful in easing the situation, whereas the amiable Chief Justice William Howard Taft had somewhat greater success. The chief justice's role as social leader may thus prove vexing, for he cannot command collegiality or good feelings among the justices.

During the conferences, the chief justice's skills as a task and social leader are especially crucial to avoiding open conflict and promoting teamwork and cohesion. The responsibilities are particularly vexatious given crowded dockets and the limited time available for discussion of each case on the Court's agenda. Some chief justices are more successful than others in fulfilling their roles as task and social leaders. Chief Justice Hughes was largely successful in both roles—in Justice Felix Frankfurter's words, "he made others feel his moral superiority, they merely felt a fact ... all who served with him recognized [his] extraordinary qualities.... To see him preside was like [seeing] Toscanini leading an orchestra."[45] In contrast, Harlan Fiske Stone's elevation from associate to chief justice led to severe tension and serious conflict, in part because he was unable to control the conference process and cut off debate or to mediate conflicts when they arose. When a chief justice is unable to fulfill one or the other of these two important functions, it usually falls to one of the associate justices to take the initiative, or, alternatively, there emerges a competition among the justices for influence. Chief Justices Frederick M. Vinson and Burger were not very effective, and sometimes divisive; by contrast Chief Justices Warren and Rehnquist eased tensions even with those who disagreed with them. Chief Justice John Roberts has emphasized in interviews that "the chief's ability to get the Court to do something is really quite restrained." Unlike his predecessor, Justice Roberts has pressed for more unanimous or near unanimous decisions because "every justice should be worried about the Court acting as a Court and functioning as a Court, and they should all be worried, when they're writing separately, about the effect on the Court as an institution."[46] Yet, in Roberts's first several terms as chief justice, the number of separate concurring and dissenting opinions continued to outnumber opinions for the entire Court, and about a third of the decisions came down on a five to four vote.

As a decisional rule for granting *cert.* petitions review, the justices vote on the basis of an informal Rule of Four. That is, at least four justices must agree that a case is certworthy and hence merits oral argument and plenary review. The rule, like other practices and traditions at the Court, emerged incrementally in response to changing caseload demands. As the rule became established, it was occasionally breached if three or even two justices felt particularly strongly about hearing a case. During his tenure as chief justice, Hughes explained the liberal application of the rule: "*certiorari* is always granted if four justices think it should be, and, not infrequently, when three, or even two, justices strongly urge the grant."[47] Justice John Paul Stevens in chapter 11 further discusses the history and operation of the Rule of Four. Notably, he also suggests that in view of the Court's growing docket, the rule should be revised to grant *cert.* on the basis of a majority vote, but with the Court's changing composition in the 1990s and the decline in the number of cases granted—a decline from about 180 cases in the 1980s to only about 80 cases per term in the late 1990s and 2000s—he no longer supports abandoning the Rule of Four.

The Rule of Four ostensibly has no bearing on the merits of a case or the lower court decision. Though Justice Robert Jackson contended that denial of *cert.* carries tacit approval of the lower court ruling, most justices maintain that "a denial nowise implies agreement" on the merits. Rather, it implies that, for at least six members, "the issue was either not ripe enough or too moribund for adjudication; that the question had better wait for the perspective of time or that time would bury the question or, for one reason or another, it was desirable to wait and see; or that the constitutional issue was entangled with nonconstitutional issues that raised doubt whether the constitutional issue could be effectively isolated; or for various other reasons not related to the merits."[48] The chapter by Justice Stevens also draws attention to some of the changes that occurred, due to increasing caseloads, in the process of preparing for conference and deciding what to decide. Given the steady increase in IFPs since Chief Justice Hughes's time, Justice Stevens points out, the chief justice assumed the task of circulating a so-called dead list identifying the cases he deemed unworthy of conference discussion. It was also the practice for some chief justices to prepare an outline of the issues presented by each *cert.* petition and to distribute it to the other justices prior to their Friday conference.

Current practice is for the chief justice to circulate a *discuss list*—a list of appeals and the *cert.* petitions he deems worthy of discussion, to which the other justices may add cases they think worth discussing. Moreover, eight of the justices—Chief Justice Roberts and Justices Scalia, Kennedy, Souter, Thomas, Ginsburg, Breyer, and Alito—rely on *cert.* pool memos, which are two- or three-page memos each prepared by one of their clerks and circulated among the justices, explaining the facts and issues and recommending whether to grant or deny a petition. Justice Stevens is the only one not participating in the *cert.* pool system and he has his own law clerks screen 100 or more petitions each week. Although Stevens does not participate in the *cert.* pool, he explained that it was "necessary to delegate a great deal of responsibility in the review of certiorari petitions to my law clerks. They examine them all and select a small minority that they believe I should read myself. As a result, I do not even look at the papers in over 80 percent of the cases that are filed."[49]

Given crowded dockets, the justices necessarily rely on their law clerks (and on several research librarians, as well as, since 1975, two legal officers at the Court, for assistance with cases on original jurisdiction or involving extraordinary remedies or requiring expedition—as with motions to stay the execution of a death penalty pending an appeal—and the like). Speculations about the Court's screening process are perhaps inevitable. Chief Justice Hughes, among others, dispelled the myth that petitions are distributed to the justices according to their circuit assignments—each justice is assigned to one or more circuits to hear special appeals (particularly in death penalty cases), a practice that dates from the Founding when the justices literally "rode" circuit and sat with district court judges to comprise an appellate court. When deciding what to decide, the justices do not operate via committees or panels. Another suspicion, Justice Jackson reported, is that clerks "constitute a kind of junior court which decides the fate of *certiorari* petitions."[50] There is no denying that the *cert.* pool now plays an important screening function, and Justice Stevens has observed that the pool is too adverse to recommending the granting of cases. But every justice ultimately decides and votes on whether to grant or deny based on an understanding of the issues, familiarity with other pending cases, and their own experience. Reminiscent of Judge Frank's description of a trial judge's decision, Justice Harlan observed: "Frequently the question whether a case is 'certworthy' is more a matter of 'feel' than of precisely ascertainable rules."[51]

Immediately after conference, the present practice is for the junior justice to report to the clerk of the Court which cases have been granted and which denied. (The chief justice also tallies the votes, and every justice has a docket book in which he or she may note votes and discussions for personal records.) The clerk then notifies both sides in a case granted review, as well as other individuals or organizations permitted to file *amicus curiae* (friend of the court) briefs, that they have thirty days to file supporting briefs. Briefs may run up to fifty pages, but most of the justices prefer shorter briefs. As Chief Justice Roberts observed: "I have yet to put down a brief and say 'I wish that it had been longer.'" Justice Thomas agrees, wanting "simplicity and clarity." Likewise, Justice Breyer has said: "If I see 50 pages, it can be 50 pages, but I am already going to groan.... If I see 30 pages, I think, well he has really got the law on his side because he only took up 30." Most justices dislike "legalese" in briefs and typographical mistakes. As Justice Scalia admonished: "My goodness, if you can't even proofread your brief, how careful can I assume you are" in citing cases and precedents. But the justices do differ about some matters of legal writing and advocacy. For Justice Scalia the tradition of beginning a brief with a summary of the argument is a waste: "I mean, why would I read the summary if I am going to read the brief? Can you tell me why I should read it?" By contrast, Justice Thomas finds the summary section useful, because its "like giving you, you know, what's going to be on TV next week." All of the justices, though, would probably agree with Justice Kennedy's advice about the hallmarks of legal writing and advocacy: "Lucid. Cogent. Succinct. Interesting. Informative. Convincing."[52]

Once all briefs have been submitted, both in print and electronically, the clerk schedules the case for oral argument. The Burger Court's oral argument calendar grew to approximately 180 cases each term—far more than some justices felt advisable given the complexity of the cases on the Court's agenda and the necessity for reflection and collegial deliberation. The calendar did so because the justices agreed to cut oral argument time to one hour per case; each side is now given thirty minutes. "As a rule of thumb," Justice White, for one, said, "the Court should not be expected to produce more than 150 opinions per term in argued cases, including *per curiam* opinions in such cases."[53] A half-century ago, when the Court was reviewing fewer cases and handing down fewer opinions, Justice Frankfurter complained that the Court's "schedule crowds the mind and thereby tends to force us toward premature judgments. There is such a thing as an intellectual traffic jam." However, following Chief Justice Burger's retirement in 1986 and the elevation of Justice William H. Rehnquist to the center chair, the Court gradually, then sharply, reduced the number of cases granted oral arguments and plenary consideration. Under Chief Justices Rehnquist and Roberts, only about eighty cases receive oral arguments each term, with the result that the Court annually reviews less than one percent of the cases on its docket. Chief

Justice Roberts has defended the Court's shrinking plenary docket and attributed it to "[t]he relative lack of major legislation in recent years."[54]

The opportunity to argue a case before the Supreme Court, Justice Harlan reputedly said, is an opportunity to lose, not win, a case. Justice Harlan in chapter 12 further discusses the value of oral argument, but it is worth noting Justice Wiley Rutledge's observation that the function of oral presentation is controlled by two factors: "One is its brevity. The other is the preparation with which the judge comes to it."[55]

The importance of providing a concise bird's-eye view of the central facts and controlling issues in a case is underscored by the Court's strictly enforced time limits. Until about 1846 there was unlimited argument of each case before the Court, but as the docket became more crowded, the length of time permitted became more limited, thus requiring more brevity from counsel. During Chief Justice Edward White's tenure the summary docket was invented; if an appeal could not be dismissed or a writ denied and the Court did not deem the case meriting unlimited argument time, each side was allowed thirty minutes. After the Judges' Act of 1925 enlarged the Court's discretion as to which cases it would hear, Chief Justice Taft established another practice that further relieved the Court of the burden of hearing full argument in questionable cases. If the petitioner's opening argument failed to sustain his contention, he would announce that it would not hear the respondent. Noted for his rigorous enforcement of the rules governing oral argument, Chief Justice Hughes reportedly called time on an attorney in the middle of uttering the word "if." During Chief Justice Warren's tenure the time allotted per side was reduced from two hours to one hour, and the Court heard arguments only three days a week. Since 1972, the Court allows only one half-hour per side (though exceptions may be made, particularly under Chief Justice Roberts).

Naturally, justices differ in the premium they place on oral argument. Justice Douglas insisted that "oral arguments win or lose the case,"[56] whereas Chief Justice Warren found oral arguments "not highly persuasive."[57] Accordingly, preparation for oral arguments varies among the justices. Most justices currently come prepared with "bench memos" identifying central facts, issues, and possible questions. Justice Holmes, however, rarely found oral argument influential, often taking catnaps while on the bench. Instead, he relied primarily on lower court records and to some extent the briefs. Justice Frankfurter, who claimed never to read the briefs, would consume large segments of an attorney's time—sometimes exasperating both counsel and other justices. In one instance, Justice Frankfurter interrupted counsel ninety-three times during a 120-minute oral argument.[58] On another occasion of Frankfurter's interrogations, Justice Douglas intervened to help counsel with a useful answer, whereupon Justice Frankfurter asked the attorney, "I thought you were arguing the case?" The attorney responded, "I am, but

I can use all the help I can get."[59] More recently, Chief Justice Roberts observed that there has been a reemergence of a Supreme Court bar—lawyers who specialize in arguing cases before the high bench—and that has contributed to improving oral argument sessions.[60] He also has recalled, having argued thirty-nine cases before the Court prior to his appointment to the high bench, that he "once literally had more than 100 questions [posed by the justices] in a half an hour.... It is easier to ask the questions than answer them.[61] In Justice Thomas's view, for most cases the "argument is settled in the brief," but he added that the great thing about oral arguments is the opportunity they give "people to get to the final institution and 'say their piece.'" Chief Justice Roberts agrees that "the briefs are more important" than oral arguments, which are just "the tip of the iceberg."[62] Oral argument provides the justices with an opportunity to probe the factual basis and limits of the logic of counsel's arguments, and to exchange views with each other. On the current Court all the justices, with the exceptions of Justices Thomas and Alito, are active participants during oral arguments. In Justice Thomas's view, in most cases the "argument is settled in the brief."

During the Wednesday and Friday conferences (as Justices Powell and Rehnquist note in their chapters), the chief justice by tradition begins the discussion of cases on which the Court has heard oral argument earlier in the week. As Chief Justice Burger explained the procedure, which Chief Justices Rehnquist and Roberts have followed:

> The Chief Justice gives a brief summary of what the case is about, as he sees it, what the issues are, and perhaps in some of them indicating his view of the matter; that is not always the case because as the discussion goes around the table then, from the Chief Justice to the senior [Associate] Justice and in seniority, it is not uncommon for a Justice to say he would like to hear the full discussion before he comes to a conclusion. This might mean that he waits until the junior Justice has expressed his views, and then a general discussion may take place.[63]

There was a good deal of give and take during the Burger Court years (1969–1986), and Justice White observed, "by the time that everyone has had his say, the vote is usually quite clear; but, if not, it will be formally taken."[64] However, after becoming chief justice, Rehnquist persuaded the others not to interrupt each other until each had voted and expressed his or her position. Chief Justice Roberts has tried to maintain that practice. As a result, there is much less conference discussion, and Justice Scalia has said that it is something of a misnomer to refer to conferences as "collective deliberations."

The traditional manner of voting used to be that the justices voted in ascending order of their seniority, with the chief justice voting last. Justice Tom Clark, for one, explained the rationale for this manner of voting: "Ever since Chief Justice

John Marshall's day the formal vote begins with the junior Justice and moves up through the ranks of seniority, the Chief Justice voting last. Hence the juniors are not influenced by the vote of their elders."[65] But that procedure has not been followed in over fifty years. As Justice Blackmun explained, "we vote by seniority, as you know, despite [the fact] that some texts say we vote by juniority."[66] He echoed Justice Black's admonition that it is "a fiction that everybody always waits for the youngest man to express himself, or vote, as they say. Well that's fiction."[67] Furthermore, as Justice Harlan stressed, by "common consent all conference votes are tentative."[68] "The books on voting are never closed until the decision actually comes down. Until then any member of the Court is perfectly free to change his vote, and it is not an unheard-of occurrence for a persuasive minority opinion to eventuate as the prevailing opinion."[69]

The tentative nature of initial conference votes underscores the important role of the chief justice in assigning the Court's opinion when he is in the majority. If the chief justice is not in the majority, then the senior justice who is in the majority, by tradition, may either draft the opinion or assign it to another. Occasionally, at the initial conference a clear majority inclined toward disposing of a case in a particular way does not emerge, and thus the case may be carried over to another conference. Chief Justice Warren reported that *Brown v. Board of Education* was carried over week after week. Indeed, the arguments in that case were held in the middle of November, but the Court did not vote until the middle of February, after two prior conferences devoted to simply discussing the issues in that watershed decision.[70] In such situations, Chief Justice Burger recounted:

> The practice has grown up of assigning ... one Justice to simply prepare a memorandum about the case, and at that time all other Justices are invited if they want to submit a memorandum; and then out of that memorandum usually a consensus is formed and someone is identified who can write an opinion that will command a majority of the Court.[71]

The responsibility for opinion assignments presents the chief justice with several strategic options and considerations that may enhance or frustrate the working relationships among the justices. The assignment of opinions is made after each two-week session of oral arguments and conferences, unlike the prior practice of assigning cases the day after each conference. Hence, the chief justice has flexibility in distributing the workload relatively evenly among the justices, while weighing in the selection, for example, how a particular justice views precedents and policy bearing on a particular case. The chief justice may assign an opinion to a justice in the majority whose views are closer to those of the minority in order perhaps to accommodate the other justices' views and thereby achieve a larger consensus if not a unanimous opinion. Of course, in unanimous decisions and those so-called landmark or watershed cases in which the chief justice is in the majority, he may choose to write the Court's opinion—as did Chief Justices Warren in *Brown* and Burger in *United States v. Nixon*. Chief Justice Rehnquist wrote some of the most important decisions during his time in the center chair but tried to equalize the assignment of cases, depending upon other justices' productivity and the Court's schedule. Chief Justice Roberts has tried to do likewise and commented, "I can't take all the good ones for myself, and I have to take my share of the dogs."[72]

The drafting of opinions occurs in each of the justices' chambers, with the justices and their law clerks collaborating for long hours. It is usually weeks before an acceptable initial draft is circulated to other justices. In the average case an opinion requires three weeks of work in preparation before it is circulated to each of the justices: "Then the fur begins to fly."[73] The circulation of draft opinions is pivotal in the justices' deliberative and decision-making process, providing opportunities for shifting votes and either further coalition-building or fragmentation within the Court. As Justice Brennan explained:

> I have converted more than one proposed majority opinion into a dissent before the final decision was announced. I have also, however, had the more satisfying experience of rewriting a dissent as a majority opinion for the Court. Before everyone has finally made up his mind a constant interchange among us by memoranda, by telephone, at the lunch table, continues while we hammer out the final form of the opinion. I had one case ... in which I circulated 10 printed drafts before one was approved as the Court opinion.[74]

The circulation of numerous drafts is the norm, and the switching of votes—even the conversion of a majority into a dissenting opinion, or vice versa—is not uncommon.

Although all votes are tentative until a decision is finally handed down, the psychological pressures on a justice assigned an opinion are complex, and they are an important dimension of the Court's decision-making process. The justice assigned the task of formulating the position registered by a majority must carefully craft an opinion persuasive to a majority, and, if possible, not occasion separate, concurring, or, worse yet, dissenting opinions. Each justice copes differently with the psychological pressures of this responsibility—and assumes a particular style and approach; each may as well employ various strategies for marshaling the other justices. In Justice Holmes's view, drafting an opinion requires that a "judge can dance the sword dance; that is, he can justify an obvious result without stepping on either blade of opposing fallacies."[75] Drafting an opinion requires delicate balancing of opposing views, persuasive argumentation, and often subtle or not so subtle negotiation and bargaining. In one instance, Justice Stone candidly told Justice Frankfurter: "If you wish to write [the opinion] placing the case on the ground which I think tenable and desirable, I shall cheerfully join you. If not, I will add a few observations for myself."[76] On another occasion, Justice James C. McReynolds gently appealed to Justice Stone: "All of us get into a fog now and then, as I know so well from my own experience. Won't you 'Stop, Look, and Listen'?"[77] For Justice Holmes, the task of writing the Court's opinion proved to be especially vexing; he complained: "The boys generally cut one of the genitals out of mine, in the form of some expression that they think too free."[78] Since the 1930s the justices have become increasingly divisive and published more concurring, dissenting, and separate opinions (those concurring and dissenting in part), disagreeing with the opinion for the Court.[79] Chief Justice Roberts initially pressed for more consensus but admitted that "we haven't made a lot of progress moving beyond fairly sharp decisions."[80]

The author of a concurring or dissenting opinion, by comparison, does not carry the burden of speaking for the Court. Comparatively speaking, the dissenter, in Justice Cardozo's words, "is irresponsible. The spokesman of the Court is cautious, timid, fearful of the vivid word, the heightened phrase.... Not so the dissenter.... For the moment he is the gladiator making a last stand against the lions."[81] Dissenting opinions, in the view of Hughes, a justice who rarely wrote dissents, appeal "to the brooding spirit of the law, to the intelligence of a future day, when a later decision may possibly correct the error into which the dissenting judge believes the court to have been betrayed."[82] A dissenting opinion is a way of undercutting the majority's opinion, but it is also a potentially useful tactic in negotiating with other justices, for the threat of dissent may persuade the majority to narrow its holding or tone down the language of its opinion. Some cases, of course, are "small fish," and a justice may choose not to write a dissent in the hope of persuading the case-author to side with him in some future case. Justice Pierce Butler, for instance, once wrote to his colleague: "I voted to reverse. While this sustains your conclusion to affirm, I still think reversal would be better. But I shall in silence acquiesce. Dissents seldom aid in the right development of the law. They often do harm. For myself I say: 'I lead us not into temptation.'"[83]

The drafting and circulation of opinions is therefore central to, if not the hallmark of, the contemporary Supreme Court's deliberative process. The circulation of drafts permits the refinement of ideas and promotes negotiation and reflection prior to the handing down of a case on Opinion Day (which until the mid–1960s was only on Mondays, but now is on any day the Court is in session), when the justices either read verbatim or, more often, summarize their ruling and opinions.

Notably, no less than liberal Justice Brennan,[84] conservative Justice Antonin Scalia has staunchly defended the practice of filing dissenting and concurring opinions. In an address to the Supreme Court Historical Society, he quoted a couplet of Thomas à Becket in T.S. Eliot's *Murder in the Cathedral,* when Becket is tempted by the devil to resist Henry II and he rebuffs him with the retort: "That would be greatest treason / To do the right deed for the wrong reason." And that same principle, Justice Scalia claimed, applies to judicial opinions: "to get the reasons wrong is to get it all wrong, and that is worth a dissent, even if the dissent is called a concurrence." Justice Scalia praises separate opinions for their internal and external consequences: "The most important internal effect of a system permitting dissents and concurrences is to improve the majority opinion." The prospect of a dissent, he emphasized, may make the majority's opinion writer receptive to suggested changes, and a draft dissent "often causes the majority to refine its opinion, eliminating the more vulnerable assertions." Also, he added, "a system of separate opinions renders the profession of a judge—and I think even the profession of a lawyer—more enjoyable" and contended that "dissents augment rather than diminish the prestige of the Court. When history demonstrates that one of the Court's decisions has been a truly horrendous mistake, it is comforting—and conducive of respect for the Court—to look back and realize that at least some of the Justices saw the danger clearly, and gave voice, often eloquent voice, to their concern." "A second external consequence of a concurring or dissenting opinion is that it can help change the law," as well as "inform the public in general, and the bar in particular, about the state of the Court's collective mind." In addition, Justice Scalia stressed that "by enabling, indeed compelling, the Justices of the Court, through their personally signed majority, dissenting and concurring opinions, to set forth clear and consistent positions on both sides of the major legal issues of the day, it has kept the Court in the forefront of the intellectual development of the law.... The Court itself is not just the central organ of legal *judgment;* it is center stage for significant legal *debate.*"[85]

Justice Ginsburg has likewise emphasized the importance of dissenting opinions for the Court's decision making. In her words:

> On the utility of dissenting opinions, I will mention first their in-house impact. My experience teaches that there is nothing better than an impressive dissent to improve an opinion for the Court. A well reasoned dissent will lead the author of the majority opinion to refine and clarify her initial circulation. An illustration: I wrote for the Court in the Virginia Military Institute case, which held that VMI's denial of admission to women violated the Equal Protection Clause. The published opinion was ever so much better than my first draft, thanks to Justice Scalia's attention-grabbing dissent.[86]

Justice Ginsburg also noted the potential external impact of dissenting opinions, such as prompting congressional reaction and legislation.

Finally, Chapter 13 excerpts Chief Justice Roberts's Year-End Report on the Federal Judiciary (2007). Chief Justice Burger began issuing such annual reports on each January 1, a practice that has continued under Chief Justices Rehnquist and Roberts. They typically review caseload trends and spotlight proposals for judicial reforms and the impact on the judiciary of pending legislation. Chief Justice Roberts, as in his first report, focuses on the importance of increasing the salaries of federal judges.

Notes

1. Oliver W. Holmes, "Law and the Court," in *Collected Legal Papers* 292 (New York: Harcourt, Brace, 1921).
2. Benjamin N. Cardozo, *The Nature of the Judicial Process* 168 (New Haven: Yale University Press, 1921).
3. Lewis F. Powell Jr., "Supreme Court Film," transcript at 1 (film shown to visitors of the Supreme Court of the United States, Washington, D.C., in the mid–1980s).
4. Earl Warren, "A Conversation with Earl Warren," Brandeis Television Recollections, WGBH-TV, Boston, transcript at 1–2 (Boston: WGBH Educational Foundation, 1972).
5. Thomas C. Clark, "Supreme Court Film" transcript, at 8.
6. For further discussion of junior justices, see Clare Cushman, "Rookie on the Bench: The Role of Junior Justices," 32 *Journal of Supreme Court History,* 282–296 (2007) (containing an interview with Justice Stephen Breyer).
7. Thurman Arnold, *Selections from the Letters and Legal Papers of Thurman Arnold,* 3 (Washington, D.C.: Merkle Press, 1961).
8. Charles E. Wyzanski, *Whereas—A Judge's Premises,* 4 (Boston: Little, Brown, 1964).
9. Quoted by Robert Carp and Russell Wheeler, "Sink or Swim: The Socialization of a Federal District Judge," 21 *Journal of Politics* 359, 361 (1972).
10. Henry J. Friendly, "Indiscretion about Discretion," 31 *Emory Law Journal* 747 (1982).
11. See, generally, Robert F. Peckham, "The Federal Judge as a Case Manager: The New Role in Guiding a Case from Filing to Disposition," 69 *California Law Review* 770 (1981); W. Homan, "Plea Bargaining and the Role of Judges," 53 *Federal Rules Decisions* 499 (1971); and Hubert L. Will, Robert R. Merhige Jr., and Alvin B. Rubin, *The Role of the Judge in the Settlement Process* (Washington, D.C.: Federal Judicial Center, 1977).
12. Ibid., at 153 and 171.
13. Felix Frankfurter, *The Commerce Clause under Marshall, Taney, and Waite* 12 (Raleigh: University of North Carolina, 1937).
14. John Godbold, "Interview," 15 *The Third Branch* 1, 2 (July 1983).
15. Donald P. Lay, "Will the Proposed National Court of Appeals Create More Problems Than It Solves?" 66 *Judicature* 437 (1983).
16. For two excellent studies of the changing and increasing role of law clerks at the Supreme Court, see Artemus Ward and David Weiden, *Sorcerers' Apprentices: 100*

Years of Law Clerks at the United States Supreme Court (New York: New York University Press, 2006); and Todd C. Peppers, *Courtiers of the Marble Palace: The Rise and Influence of the Supreme Court Law Clerk* (Stanford: Stanford University Press, 2006).

17. See Patrick E. Higginbotham, "Bureaucracy—The Carcinoma of the Federal Judiciary," 31 *Alabama Law Review* 261 (1980); and Wade McCree Jr., "Bureaucratic Justice: An Early Warning," 129 *University of Pennsylvania Law Review* 777 (1981).
18. William H. Rehnquist, "Are the Old Times Dead?" MacSwinford Lecture, University of Kentucky (23 September 1983).
19. William H. Rehnquist, Remarks, Ninth Circuit Conference, Coronado, California, at 24 (27 July 1982).
20. See McCree, "Bureaucratic Justice."
21. See Harry T. Edwards, "A Judge's View on Justice, Bureaucracy, and Legal Method," 80 *Michigan Law Review* 259 (1981).
22. Lewis F. Powell, "What the Justices Are Saying . . . ," 62 *American Bar Association Journal* 1454 (1976).
23. Lewis F. Powell, Address, Eleventh Circuit Conference, at 4 (8 May 1983).
24. John M. Harlan II, "A Glimpse of the Supreme Court at Work," 11 *University of Chicago Law School Record* 1 (1963).
25. Harry Blackmun, "A Justice Speaks Out: A Conversation with Harry A. Blackmun," Cable News Network, Inc., Transcript at 4 (4 December 1982).
26. Harlan, "A Glimpse of the Supreme Court," at 4.
27. Harlan Fiske Stone, "Fifty Years' Work of the United States Supreme Court," 14 *American Bar Association Journal* 428, 436 (1928).
28. John M. Harlan II, "Some Aspects of the Judicial Process in the Supreme Court of the United States," 33 *Australian Law Journal* 108 (1959).
29. See, e.g., Byron F. White, "The Case for the National Court of Appeals," 23 *Federal Bar News* 134, 140 (1976).
30. Hugo L. Black, "Justice Black and the Bill of Rights," *CBS News Special,* Transcript at 5 (New York: CBS News, 3 December 1968).
31. Letter to Senator Burton Wheeler, reprinted in U.S. Congress, Senate, Committee on the Judiciary, *Hearings on the Reorganization of the Federal Judiciary,* S. Rept. No. 711, 75th Cong., 1st Sess., at 40 (Washington, D.C.: Government Printing Office, 1937).
32. John H. Clarke, "Observations and Reflections on Practice in the Supreme Court," 8 *American Bar Association Journal* 263 (1922).
33. John M. Harlan II, "Manning the Dikes," 13 *Record of the New York City Bar Association* 541, 546 (1958).
34. Ibid., at 547.
35. See *Ex parte Brummett,* 295 U.S. 719 (1935); 299 U.S. 514 (1936); 302 U.S. 644 (1937); 303 U.S. 570 (1938); 306 U.S. 615 (1939); 309 U.S. 625 (1940); *Ex parte Brummett,* 304 U.S. 545 (1938); 311 U.S. 614 (1940); 313 U.S. 548 (1941); and 314 U.S. 585 (1941).
36. William J. Brennan Jr., "The National Court of Appeals: Another Dissent," 40 *University of Chicago Law Review* 473 (1973).

37. William O. Douglas, "The Supreme Court and Its Case Load," 45 *Cornell Law Quarterly* 401, 407 (1960).
38. William O. Douglas, "Mr. Justice Douglas," *CBS Reports,* Transcript at 12 (New York: CBS News, 6 September 1972).
39. Quoted in "The Supreme Court: How It Operates in Private Chambers Outside Courtroom," *Smithsonian* (Washington, D.C.: Smithsonian Institution, 1976).
40. William J. Brennan Jr., "State Court Decisions and the Supreme Court," 31 *Pennsylvania Bar Association Quarterly* 393, 403 (1960).
41. James F. Byrnes, *All in One Lifetime* 154 (New York: Harper & Bros., 1958).
42. Warren E. Burger, "Supreme Court Film," supra note 4, at 11.
43. Owen Roberts, Address, Meeting of the Association of the Bar of the City of New York and the New York County Lawyers' Association (12 December 1946).
44. Earl Warren, Remarks, American Law Institute, at 7 (Washington, D.C.: American Law Institute, 1956).
45. Felix Frankfurter, *Of Law and Men* 133, 148 (New York: Harcourt, Brace, 1956).
46. Quoted in Jeffrey Rosen, "Roberts's Rules," *The Atlantic Monthly* 95 (January/February, 2007).
47. Charles Evans Hughes, "Reason as Opposed to the Tyranny of Force," Speech delivered to the American Law Institute (6 May 1937), and reprinted in *Vital Speeches of the Day* 458, 459 (1937).
48. Brennan, "State Court Decisions," at 402–403.
49. John Paul Stevens, "Some Thoughts on Judicial Restraint," 66 *Judicature* 177, 179 (1982).
50. Quoted by Thomas C. Clark in, "Internal Operation of the United States Supreme Court," 43 *Journal of the American Judicature Society* 45, 48 (1959).
51. Quoted in ibid.
52. All quotes are from interviews with the justices posted on LawProse's Web site, available at www.lawprose.org.
53. Byron White, "The Work of the Supreme Court: A Nuts and Bolts Description," 54 *New York State Bar Journal* 346, 383 (1982).
54. Speech at Northwestern University School of Law, quoted in Robert Barnes, "Roberts Supports Court's Shrinking Docket," *Washington Post* A6 (February 2, 2007); see also David M. O'Brien, "A Diminished Plenary Docket: A Legacy of the Rehnquist Court," 89 *Judicature* 134–138 (November–December, 2005).
55. Wiley Rutledge, "The Appellate Brief," 28 *American Bar Association Journal* 251 (1942). See also John C. Godbold, "Twenty Pages and Twenty Minutes—Effective Advocacy on Appeal," 30 *Southwestern Law Journal* 801 (1976); and Irving R. Kaufman, "Advocacy as Craft—There Is More to Law Schools than a 'Paper Chase,'" 28 *Southwestern Law Journal* 495 (1974).
56. Quoted in the *Philadelphia Inquirer* (9 April 1963), and by Henry J. Abraham, *The Judicial Process* 203 (New York: Oxford University Press, 1980).
57. Earl Warren, "Seminar with Mr. Chief Justice Warren," University of Virginia Legal Forum, at 9 (25 April 1973).
58. See Jerome Frank, *The Marble Palace* 104–105 (New York: Knopf, 1958).

59. As reported by Anthony Lewis, "The Justices' Supreme Job," *New York Times Magazine* (June, 11, 1961)(emphasis added).
60. John G. Roberts, "Oral Advocacy and the Re-emergence of a Supreme Court Bar," 30 *Journal of Supreme Court History* 68–81 (2005).
61. Quoted in Robert Barnes, "For High School Students, Some Justice," *Washington Post* A20 (March 6, 2008).
62. Interviews with Chief Justice Roberts and Justice Thomas posted on LawProse's web site at www.lawprose.org.
63. Burger, "Supreme Court Film," at 12.
64. White, "The Work of the Supreme Court,", at 383.
65. Clark, "Internal Operation," at 50.
66. Blackmun, "A Justice Speaks Out," at 21.
67. Black, "Justice Black and the Bill of Rights," at 5.
68. Harlan, "Some Aspects," at 21.
69. Harlan, "A Glimpse of the Supreme Court," at 7.
70. Warren, "A Conversation," at 12.
71. Burger, "Supreme Court Film," at 12.
72. Quoted in Barnes, "For High School Students."
73. Clark, "Internal Operation," at 51.
74. Brennan, "State Court Decisions," at 405.
75. Quoted by Alpheus T. Mason, book review of *The Holmes–Einstein Letters,* in *New York Review of Books* 60 (November, 22, 1964).
76. Quoted by Alpheus T. Mason, *Harlan Fiske Stone: Pillar of the Law* 501 (New York: Viking Press, 1956).
77. Quoted by Alpheus T. Mason, *The Supreme Court from Taft to Burger* 65 (Baton Rouge: Louisiana State University Press, 3d ed., 1979).
78. Quoted by David M. O'Brien, *The Public's Right to Know: The Supreme Court and the First Amendment* 75 (New York: Praeger, 1981).
79. For further discussion see David M. O'Brien, *Storm Center: The Supreme Court in American Politics,* Chapter 5 (New York: W. W. Norton, 8th ed., 2008).
80. Quoted in Barnes, "For High School Students."
81. Quoted by Thomas C. Clark, "Some Thoughts on Supreme Court Practice," Address, University of Minnesota Law School (April 13, 1959).
82. Charles Evans Hughes, *The Supreme Court of the United States* 68 (New York: Columbia University Press, 1928).
83. Quoted by Abraham, *The Judicial Process,* at 227.
84. William J. Brennan Jr., "In Defense of Dissents," 37 *Hastings Constitutional Law Review* 427 (1986).
85. Antonin Scalia, "Dissenting Opinions," *Journal of Supreme Court History* 1994 333–344.
86. Ruth Bader Ginsburg, "The 20th Annual Leo and Berry Eizenstat Memorial Lecture: The Role of Dissenting Opinions" (October 21, 2007), available at www.supremecourtus.gov/publicinfo/speeches/sp_10-21-07.html.

CHAPTER 3

Advice and Consent in Theory and Practice

Roger J. Miner

Judge, U.S. Court of Appeals, Second Circuit (1985–1997) and U.S. District Court (1981–1985)

ARTICLE II, SECTION 2 of the Constitution requires that the President of the United States nominate and, by and with the advice and consent of the Senate, appoint the federal judges who will exercise the judicial power conferred under the authority of Article III of the Constitution. Today, that constitutional command is all but ignored. The President has abdicated his duty to nominate, the Senate provides no advice whatsoever, and the function of senatorial consent is a mere formality in most instances. As regards the appointment of federal judges, the Constitution simply is not working as the Framers intended. That this should be so at a time when the appointment process is in the hands of those who profess a blind adherence to the doctrine of original intent is strange indeed. The difficulty of discerning the original intent of the Framers has been expounded upon at great length and need not be reexamined. I do pause to note that former Senator Eugene McCarthy recently spoke of his support for the constitutional right of the citizenry to bear arms, as long as the arms are of the type in use when the Constitution was written.[1] So much for originalism as a general proposition.

We know that the constitutional provision came about through compromise. Listen to the debates, summarized as follows in the records of the Constitutional Convention:

Acknowledgment to Judge Roger J. Miner for permission to reprint his speech given at the annual dinner of the American University Law Review *(April 4, 1992), which appears in 41* American University Law Review *1075 (1992).*

> Mr. L. Martin was strenuous for an appt. by the 2d. branch [of the Natl. Legislature]. Being taken from all the States it wd. be best informed of characters & most capable of making a fit choice.[2]
>
> Mr. Sherman concurred in the observations of Mr. Martin, adding that the Judges ought to be diffused, which would be more likely to be attended to by the [Senate] than by the Executive.[3]
>
> Mr. Govr. Morris [spoke as follows:]
>
> It had been said the Executive would be uninformed of characters. The reverse was ye truth. The Senate will be so. They must take the character of candidates from the flattering pictures drawn by their friends. The Executive in the necessary intercourse with every part of the U.S. required by the nature of his administration, will or may have the best possible information.[4]
>
> Mr. Madison disliked the election of the Judges by the Legislature or any numerous body. Besides, the danger of intrigue and partiality, many of the members were not judges of the requisite qualifications. The Legislative talents which were very different from those of a Judge, commonly recommended men to the favor of Legislative Assemblies. It was known too that the accidental circumstances of presence and absence, of being a member or not a member, had a very undue influence on the appointment. On the other hand He was not satisfied with referring the appointment to the Executive. He rather inclined to give it to the Senatorial branch. . . . [5]
>
> Docr. Franklin observed that two modes of chusing the Judges had been mentioned, to wit, by the Legislature and by the Executive. He wished such other modes to be suggested as might occur to other gentlemen; it being a point of great moment. He would mention (one which) he had understood was practiced in Scotland. He then in a brief and entertaining manner related a Scotch mode, in which the nomination proceeded from the Lawyers, who always selected the ablest of the profession in order to get rid of him, and share his practice (among themselves).[6]

How prescient they were! Consider this entry in the record under the name of Mr. Ghorum:

> As the Executive will be responsible in point of character at least, for a judicious and faithful discharge of his trust, he will be careful to look through all the States for proper characters. The Senators will be as likely to form their attachments at the Seat of Govt where they reside, as the Executive. If they can not get the man of the particular State to which they may respectively belong, they will be indifferent to the rest.[7]

Actually, Mr. Ghorum only had it half right. Presidents also have formed their attachments at the seat of government. The geographical origins of the following

Supreme Court nominees of recent years are illustrative: Burger, Scalia, Bork, Ginsburg, and Thomas from the D.C. Circuit; Marshall, White, and Rehnquist from Department of Justice headquarters. Long before there was a Washington, D.C., and long before there was a Beltway, the Founding Fathers warned of the myopic vision that would attend residence at the seat of government.

What Luther Martin, that doughty Anti-Federalist, said about Senators also applies now to Congressmen and even the President:

> If he has a family, he will take his family with him to the place where the government shall be fixed, that will become his home, and there is every reason to expect, that his future views and prospects will centre in the favours and emoluments either of the general government, or of the government of that State where the seat of empire is established: In either case, he is lost to his own State.[8]

It is rare indeed to find a former Member of Congress who does not continue to reside in Washington, D.C., in a new incarnation. Senator Warren B. Rudman of New Hampshire recently announced that he would not be a candidate for reelection. He indicated that he was not inclined to return to the practice of law, although he was sure that "the offers would be stupendous."[9] There certainly is a great lure for those who leave office to remain in Washington. It goes by the name of wealth. According to Senator Rudman, there is no challenge left in serving in a government that is "not functioning"[10]—this from the man who said that his "warmest memory" of the Senate was his support for David H. Souter for the Supreme Court.[11]

The fact remains that a compromise was reached and that the Senate was given a role to play in the appointment of federal judges. The *Federalist Papers*, the greatest public relations job in the history of the Republic, confirms this notion. The media market gurus of today just cannot compare to the folks who wrote the *Federalist Papers*, in my opinion. Of course, the Papers were designed to reach a literate audience, which is difficult to find in the last decade of the 20th century. In *Federalist* No. 76, Hamilton put forth an extraordinary effort to sell the citizenry the compromise worked out at the Constitutional Convention. He aimed some persuasive language at those who preferred appointment by the Executive alone and some equally persuasive language at those who preferred appointment by the Senate alone. He referred to the cooperative function to be performed by the Senate in the appointment process and described the purpose of that function in the following words:

> To what purpose then require the co-operation of the Senate? I answer that the necessity of their concurrence would have a powerful, though in general a silent operation. It would be an excellent check upon a spirit of favoritism in the

> President, and would tend greatly to preventing the appointment of unfit characters from State prejudice, from family connection, from personal attachment, or from a view to popularity.[12]

If the cooperation function of the Senate is to be performed, the constitutional imperative of senatorial advice must be fulfilled. "Advice" means the same thing today as it did when the Constitution was written. I have a dictionary almost 175 years old, and it defines "advice" as "counsel" and "instruction."[13] A more modern dictionary defines advice as "an opinion or recommendation offered as a guide to action, conduct, etc."[14] It seems clear to me that the Senate cannot fulfill the advice requirement unless it has input in the nomination itself. That has not happened for many years. It did happen with excellent effect when Herbert Hoover was looking for a successor to Oliver Wendell Holmes. Although Hoover sought a noncontroversial midwestern Republican for political reasons, heavy advice from the Senate impelled him to name Benjamin N. Cardozo of New York. The nomination was made despite the fact that there were already two New Yorkers on the bench—Stone and Hughes—and one Jew, Brandeis. There is a well-known story that Hoover showed his list of proposed nominees, with Cardozo at the bottom, to Senator William E. Borah of Idaho. Borah is reported to have said, "Your list is all right, but you handed it to me upside down."[15] Cardozo was easily confirmed, supported as he was by business, labor, liberals, conservatives, academics, and the entire legal community. As to the religion question, Senator Borah told Hoover: "[A]nyone who raises the question ... is unfit to advise you concerning so important a matter."[16] Hoover, of course, was the only Republican President ever to appoint a person of the Jewish faith to the United States Supreme Court,[17] and he was not too wild about it, either.

The Cardozo appointment was a real case of merit selection. The Framers of the Constitution really thought that merit would prevail in judicial appointments. How wrong they were! Listen once again to Hamilton, this time in *Federalist* No. 78:

> The records of those [legal] precedents must unavoidably swell to a very considerable bulk, and must demand long and laborious study to acquire a competent knowledge of them. Hence it is that there can be but few men in the society, who will have sufficient skill in the laws to qualify them for the stations of judges. And making the proper deductions for the ordinary depravity of human nature, the number must be still smaller of those who unite the requisite integrity with the requisite knowledge.[18]

Hamilton was sure that the Senate would advise and consent only on the basis of merit. He wrote: "it could hardly happen that the majority of the senate would feel any other complacency towards the object of an appointment, than such, as the appearances of merit, might inspire, and the proofs of the want of it, destroy." [19]

How does one define merit for purposes of federal judicial service? I think that Professor Henry Abraham, a great Supreme Court scholar, had it right when he said that it could be defined in terms of six components: demonstrated judicial temperament; professional expertise and competence; absolute personal as well as professional integrity; an able, agile, lucid mind; appropriate professional background or training; and the ability to communicate clearly, both orally and in writing.[20]

Objective merit no longer is the lodestar of federal judicial appointments. It probably never was, entirely. Even in the beginning, when there were no political parties, the Federalists seemed to get the nod over the Anti-Federalists. The Federalists still get the nod, as I shall demonstrate shortly. Professor Abraham has identified three other bases for presidential nominations to the Supreme Court: personal friendship; the balancing of representation or representativeness on the Court; and real political and ideological compatibility.[21] These factors, singly or in combination, have formed the basis for judicial selection over the years in the Supreme Court and in the lower courts as well. To these, I would add another factor that has surfaced in recent years—confirmability, that is, the ability not to create too great a stir when an indolent Senate undertakes its consent function. Indeed, it is the ideological factor (concealed and obfuscated to the greatest extent possible) and the confirmability factor that have most occupied the Chief Executives in recent years.[22] Merit has been more or less consigned to the back seat. In that connection, I think that it can safely be said that the President's characterization of [Clarence Thomas] as "the best person for this position" [23] did not find unanimous acceptance in the legal community.

It seems that the center of all activity relating to judicial appointments at present is centered in the office of the Counsel to the President, Mr. C. Boyden Gray.[24] It is there that the hot flame of ideology burns brightly, tended by those who consider themselves the descendants of the original Federalists but who indeed are not. Just as the original Federalists dissembled in the use of their name to gain political ascendancy, so do the Federalists of today. The originals of course wanted to strengthen the new nation and to build a strong central government at the expense of the states. However, they adopted a name that was indicative of just the opposite. Luther Martin opposed ratification of the Constitution and railed against being labelled an Anti-Federalist. He wrote that those "who advocate the system [of national government established in the Constitution], pretend to call themselves federalists, [but] in convention the distinction was quite the reverse; those who opposed the system, were there considered and styled the federal party, those who advocated it, the antifederal." [25] Despite the carping of Luther Martin, those who supported the Constitution made the label stick, and history ever will know them as Federalists.

Those who call themselves Federalists today are hardly of the same order. They are extremely conservative and see little good in a strong central government.[26] For some reason, they do believe in a strong Executive, but consistency is not their strong suit. Those who seek to maintain the modern Federalist label are entitled to one or more liberal thoughts. To them is attached the label "libertarian" Federalists.[27] The modern movement started among some law students in the 1980s. These students perceived a clear and present danger in the concept of the Constitution as a living document and organized as a protest against the liberal law professors who they accused of advocating a too-expansive reading of the Charter and of ignoring original intent.[28] They tended to cluster around such academics as Bork and Scalia.[29] The force of history and attachment to the coattails of political winners have catapulted them to positions of power, first as law clerks, then as movers and shakers in the office of the Attorney General and now in the office of the President. This has been accomplished not by acquiring political power but by co-opting it. Lee Liberman, a founder of the new Federalists and now Assistant Counsel to the President, examines all candidates for federal judgeships for ideological purity.[30] It is well known that no federal judicial appointment is made without her imprimatur. A recent dispatch in the *New York Law Journal* reports the President's nomination of a judge to my court, the nominee being described as a litigator in a New York City law firm and as "a director of the local chapter of the Federalist Society."[31]

And so the center of power for the appointment of federal judges has shifted away from Presidents and Senators to staff. In the case of district judges, Senators of the President's party still are afforded the right in the first instance to submit the names of proposed nominees for approval by the Presidential staff.[32] This process should be known as nomination by a Senator and advice and consent by the Presidential staff. The incumbent President is known to have no interest in the process. In former administrations, the Attorney General played a large role in judicial selection. During the regime of Attorney General Thornburgh, one Murray Dickman, a political operative and a nonlawyer who came to Washington from Pennsylvania with his boss, was the Attorney General's "point man" on judicial nominations.[33] Obviously, he deferred to Ms. Liberman.[34] The present Attorney General seems to be little more than a conservative adjunct of the White House Counsel's office.[35]

While a candidate for any federal court appointment must pass muster by the Attorney General, the American Bar Association (which is known to cave in whenever the administration threatens to disregard it), the FBI, and the IRS, the most important muster point is the office of the Counsel to the President. Staff is the key, just as staff is the key in all of government. If one desires response from a Congressman, a Senator, a Justice, the Secretary of a Department, or an agency head, one must go to staff. It is no different in the judicial selection process. It is becoming no different in the adjudicatory process itself.

With no input from the President and no advice from the Senate (except perhaps the right of first refusal in district court appointments), the next step in the appointment of federal judges is Senate confirmation. Again, there is the intervention of staff. The confirmation hearings make that clear, as staffers are seen passing notes to the Senators during the proceedings. Staffers also are known to leak confidential information received by the Senate regarding nominees.[36] Do these hearings serve any purpose? In the vast majority, they do not. The questions are mostly pro forma in the case of district and circuit judge confirmations. During my confirmation hearing for the Circuit Court, Senator Thurmond asked me whether I understood that it was the duty of a judge to interpret the law and not make the law. I said that I did. From the other side of the aisle, Senator Simon asked if I understood that it might not always be the case that a judge should interpret the law and not make the law. I said that I understood that too. That was about the size of my hearing, except for a unanimous confirmation vote in executive session. The Senate seems to turn its attention briefly to the confirmation process only in the case of Supreme Court Justices. While it is true that a number of nominees to the Supreme Court have been rejected, the reasons for rejection today would seem to depend solely on the polls taken by the Senators and general public reaction to the nominee.

It is interesting that no nominee for the Supreme Court made a personal appearance before the Judiciary Committee until 1925, when Harlan Fiske Stone appeared. Despite hostile questioning, it is said that "he came through with flying colors in a performance marked by strength, dignity, and articulateness."[37] Recent Supreme Court nominees have shown little of these qualities in appearances before the Senate Judiciary Committee. Of course, neither have those who asked the questions. We are now treated to what is in effect a staged, albeit bumbling, performance on both sides. The nominee, aided by public relations experts, Justice Department briefers, and those on the other side of the table who support confirmation, try to say as little as possible, using the old dodge: "I may have to decide that matter."

Robert Bork, for all his faults, including his desire to attend an intellectual feast when he had not yet been invited to eat, may have been the last of the straight shooters. He answered honestly, directly, without guile and with some intellect, all the questions put to him. His answers scared the hell out of everybody, and he was not confirmed. He accurately predicted that direct answers would never again be the norm, because nominees would be selected from those who have not written or spoken about important issues.[38] Those who followed him have studiously avoided any controversial responses to questions put to them, in one case even ignoring what the nominee himself had said and written previously. The hearings have become an exercise in futility because of the failure to ask proper questions and get proper answers.[39] These public spectacles should be eliminated unless they can be rendered meaningful. Perhaps counsel should do the questioning. Perhaps the nominees should be required to appear immediately upon nomination without being given time to prepare evasive answers. Perhaps it should not profit the President's staff to seek out "trackless" nominees rather than certified intellectuals like Bork. Of course, intellectual distinction has no political constituency. Perhaps staff shouldn't be involved at all—Senatorial staff or Presidential staff.

If I were a Senator, I would not tolerate evasion or stonewalling in answering my questions. While a nominee may not disclose how he or she would decide a particular case, there are a number of questions that he or she should be required to answer—questions respecting an understanding of history; questions about important prior decisions of the Court; questions designed to elicit an understanding of the current issues confronting the Court; questions of approach to judging, of philosophy, of adherence to stare decisis. I would not accept an answer that obviously is untrue, such as one that denies having taken any position on a controversial issue before the Court that is under discussion by the entire nation. If I could not get the answers I wanted, I would vote "no." I do not think that there is anything out of bounds about requiring answers to questions about financial, sexual, or other misdeeds. Because of the importance of the federal judiciary in our nation, one who aspires to membership in it must demonstrate excellence in all things. That excellence should be demonstrated to the personal satisfaction of the President and the personal satisfaction of each and every member of the Senate.

Excellence! What a wonderful and rare thing it is! Yet, it is the cornerstone of all human achievement and is found in every vocation. James Bryant Conant said: "Each honest calling, each walk of life, has its own elite, its own aristocracy, based on excellence of performance."[40] It seems to me that the ability to recognize legal excellence is one of the most important benefits you have gained from your legal education and from your participation in the Law Review. Aristotle tells us that "[w]ith regard to excellence, it is not enough to know [it], but we must try to have and use it."[41] Although we all should strive to excel, as Aristotle urges, not everyone can acquire excellence. What everyone can and should acquire, however, is the ability to appreciate excellence in others. To have such an appreciation, we must understand that people have different abilities, just as they have different qualities and talents. All are not equal when it comes to excellence. There are but a few who have that surpassing ability to achieve exceptional performance in the law. As lawyers, you should strive to identify and acknowledge superior legal talent and ability and to insist, as the bar did in that shining hour when Cardozo was appointed, that only the best among you be selected to serve on the Supreme Court and on the lower federal courts.[42] The process of nomination and advice and consent may have broken down for now and may not be functioning as the Framers intended,[43] but the political process can make it work again. That is the beauty of our system. And that is where you come in and where I, as a federal judge, cannot go.

Notes

1. T. Kelleher, "Punchlines," *New York Newsday* 85 (14 April 1992).
2. M. Farrand, ed., *The Records of the Federal Convention of* 1787 41 (New Haven: Yale University Press, rev. ed. 1966).
3. Ibid.
4. Ibid., at 82.
5. Ibid., Vol. 1, at 120.
6. Ibid., at 118–120.
7. Ibid., Vol. 2, at 42.
8. L. Martin, "The Genuine Information Delivered to the Legislature of the State of Maryland Relative to the Proceedings of the General Convention Lately Held at Philadelphia," reprinted in H. J. Storing, ed., 2 *The Complete Anti-Federalist* 46–47 (Chicago: University of Chicago Press, 1981).
9. A. Clymer, "Rudman, Irked by the Senate, Is Retiring," *New York Times* A14 (25 March 1992).
10. Ibid.
11. Ibid.
12. A. Hamilton, *The Federalist*, No. 76.
13. *Walker's Dictionary* 12 (1819).
14. *The Random House College Dictionary* 20–21 (rev. ed. 1980).
15. H. J. Abraham, *Justices and Presidents: A Political History of Appointments to the Supreme Court* 203 (New York: Oxford University, 2d ed. 1985).
16. Ibid.
17. The appointments were: Louis D. Brandeis (by President Wilson, a Democrat, in 1916); Benjamin N. Cardozo (by President Hoover, a Republican, in 1932); Felix Frankfurter (by President Roosevelt, a Democrat, in 1939); Arthur J. Goldberg (by President Kennedy, a Democrat, in 1962); and Abe Fortas (by President Johnson, a Democrat, in 1965). See ibid., at 389–391. [Democratic President Bill Clinton subsequently appointed two Jewish Justices, Ruth Bader Ginsburg and Stephen Breyer in 1993 and 1994, respectively.]
18. Hamilton, *The Federalist*, No. 78.
19. Hamilton, *The Federalist*, No. 66.
20. Abraham, supra note 15, at 4.
21. Ibid., at 5.
22. See, generally, H. Schwartz, *Packing the Courts: The Conservative Campaign to Rewrite the Constitution* xiv (1988) (discussing historical background and recent developments in "ideological judge-picking").
23. G. Gibbons, "Bush Names Thomas to Succeed Marshall on Supreme Court," Reuters (1 July 1991), available in LexisNexis Library, Wires File.

24. M. Wines, "A Counsel with Sway over Policy," *New York Times* A16 (25 November 1991).
25. Martin, supra note 8, at 47.
26. See, generally, J. Abramson, "Right Place at the Right Time," *American Lawyer* 99 (June 1986).
27. "Judge Scalia's Cheerleaders," *New York Times* B6 (23 July 1986).
28. See M. Rust, "Our Forefathers, Ourselves," *Student Lawyer* 36–38 (March 1987).
29. A. Kamen, "Federalist Society Quickly Comes of Age," *Washington Post* A3 (1 February 1987).
30. W. John Moore, "The White House Lawyer Nobody Knows," 23 *National Law Journal* 1357 (1991).
31. Update Section, *New York Law Journal* 1 (26 March 1992).
32. A Friend of the Constitution (Pseudonym), "Congress, the President, and Judicial Selection: Lessons from the Reagan Years," in *Judicial Selection: Merit, Ideology, and Politics* 49, 54–55 (1990); S. Goldman, "The Bush Imprint on the Judiciary: Carrying on a Tradition," 74 *Judicature* 294, 297 (1991).
33. Goldman, supra note 32, at 296–297.
34. See Moore, supra note 30, at 1357.
35. D. Johnston, "New Attorney General Shifts Department's Focus," *New York Times* A17 (3 March 1992); A. Lewis, "The Attorney Corporal," *New York Times* A27 (5 March 1992).
36. H. Dewar, "Senate Effort to Find Source of Leaks May Become Trip to a Bottomless Pit," *Washington Post* A5 (9 February 1992) (discussing investigation by independent counsel of Senate leaks relating to Anita Hill's accusation of sexual harassment by Clarence Thomas).
37. Abraham, supra note 15, at 194.
38. R. J. Bork, *The Tempting of America* 347 (New York: Free Press, 1990).
39. F. L. Bailey, "Where Was the Crucible? The Cross-Examination That Wasn't," *A.B.A. Journal* 46 (January 1992); S. Taylor Jr., "Confirmation Process Flawed ... by Senate Cowardice," *New Jersey Law Journal* 18 (21 November 1991).
40. J. B. Conant, "Our Fighting Faith" (baccalaureate sermon, 16 June 1940). The title is taken from a statement in an address by James A. Garfield, *The Future of the Republic: Its Dangers and Its Hopes* (1873).
41. Aristotle, *The Nicomachean Ethics*, Bk. 10, Ch. 9, reprinted in J. Bartlett, *Bartlett's Familiar Quotations* 87:25 (Emily Morison Beck, ed., 15th ed., Boston: Little, Brown, 1980).
42. H. J. Abraham, "'A Bench Happily Filled': Some Historical Reflections on the Supreme Court Appointment Process," 66 *Judicature* 282, 288–290 (1983).
43. A. P. Melone, et al., "Too Little Advice, Senatorial Responsibility, and Confirmation Politics," 75 *Judicature* 187, 187–188 (1992).

CHAPTER 4

The "Fight" Theory versus the "Truth" Theory

Jerome Frank
Judge, U.S. Court of Appeals, Second Circuit (1941–1957)

WHEN WE SAY THAT present-day trial methods are "rational," presumably we mean this: The men who compose our trial courts, judges and juries, in each lawsuit conduct an intelligent inquiry into all the practically available evidence, in order to ascertain, as near as may be, the truth about the facts of that suit. That might be called the "investigatory" or "truth" method of trying cases. Such a method can yield no more than a guess, nevertheless an educated guess.

The success of such a method is conditioned by at least these two factors: (1) The judicial inquirers, trial judges or juries, may not obtain all the important evidence or; (2) The judicial inquirers may not be competent to conduct such an inquiry. Let us, for the time being, assume that the second condition is met—i.e., that we have competent inquirers—and ask whether we so conduct trials as to satisfy the first condition, i.e., the procuring of all the practically available important evidence.

The answer to that question casts doubt on whether our trial courts do use the "investigatory" or "truth" method. Our mode of trials is commonly known as "contentious" or "adversary." It is based on what I would call the "fight" theory, a theory which derives from the origin of trials as substitutes for private out-of-court brawls.

Many lawyers maintain that the "fight" theory and the "truth" theory coincide. They think that the best way for a court to discover the facts in a suit is to have each side strive as hard as it can, in a keenly partisan spirit, to bring to the court's

---

Acknowledgment to Princeton University Press for excerpts from Jerome Frank, Courts on Trial, *Princeton, N.J.: Princeton University Press, © 1949.*

attention the evidence favorable to that side. Macaulay said that we obtain the fairest decision "when two men argue, as unfairly as possible, on opposite sides," for then "it is certain that no important consideration will altogether escape notice."

Unquestionably that view contains a core of good sense. The zealously partisan lawyers sometimes bring into court evidence which, in a dispassionate inquiry, might be overlooked. Apart from the fact element of the case, the opposed lawyers also illuminate for the court niceties of the rules which the judge might otherwise not perceive. The "fight" theory, therefore, has invaluable qualities with which we cannot afford to dispense.

But frequently the partisanship of the opposing lawyers blocks the uncovering of vital evidence or leads to a presentation of vital testimony in a way that distorts it. I shall attempt to show you that we have the fighting spirit to become dangerously excessive.

This is perhaps most obvious in the handling of witnesses. Suppose a trial were fundamentally a truth-inquiry. Then, recognizing the inherent fallibilities of witnesses, we would do all we could to remove the causes of their errors when testifying. Recognizing also the importance of witnesses' demeanor as clues to their reliability, we would do our best to make sure that they testify in circumstances most conducive to a revealing observation of that demeanor by the trial judge or jury. In our contentious trial practice, we do almost the exact opposite.

No businessman, before deciding to build a new plant, no general before launching an attack, would think of obtaining information on which to base his judgment by putting his informants through the bewildering experience of witnesses at a trial. "The novelty of the situation," wrote a judge, "the agitation and hurry which accompanies it, the cajolery or intimidation to which the witness may be subjected, the want of questions calculated to excite those recollections which might clear up every difficulty, and the confusion of cross-examination ... may give rise to important errors and omissions." "In the court they stand as strangers," wrote another judges of witnesses, "surrounded with unfamiliar circumstances giving rise to an embarrassment known only to themselves...."

What is the role of the lawyers in bringing the evidence before the trial court? As you may learn by reading any one of a dozen or more handbooks on how to try a lawsuit, an experienced lawyer uses all sorts of stratagems to minimize the effect on the judge or jury of testimony disadvantageous to his client, even when the lawyer has no doubt of the accuracy and honesty of that testimony. The lawyer considers it his duty to create a false impression, if he can, of any witness who gives such testimony. If such a witness happens to be timid, frightened by the unfamiliarity of court-room ways, the lawyer, in his cross-examination, plays on that weakness, in order to confuse the witness and make it appear that he is concealing significant facts....

The lawyer not only seeks to discredit adverse witnesses but also to hide the defects of witnesses who testify favorably to his client. If, when interviewing such a witness before trial, the lawyer notes that the witness has mannerisms, demeanor-traits, which might discredit him, the lawyer teaches him how to cover up those traits when testifying: He educates the irritable witness to conceal his irritability, the cocksure witness to subdue his cocksureness. In that way, the trial court is denied the benefit of observing the witness's actual normal demeanor, and thus prevented from sizing up the witness accurately.

Lawyers freely boast of their success with these tactics. They boast also of such devices as these: If an "adverse," honest witness, on cross-examination, makes seemingly inconsistent statements, the cross-examiner tries to keep the witness from explaining away the apparent inconsistencies....

Nor, usually, will a lawyer concede the existence of any facts if they are inimical to his client and he thinks they cannot be proved by his adversary. If, to the lawyer's knowledge, a witness has testified inaccurately but favorably to the lawyer's client, the lawyer will attempt to hinder cross-examination that would expose inaccuracy. He puts in testimony which surprises his adversary who, caught unawares, has not time to seek out, interview, and summon witnesses who would rebut the surprise testimony....

These, and other like techniques, you will find unashamedly described in the many manuals on trial tactics written by and for eminently reputable trial lawyers. The purpose of these tactics—often effective—is to prevent the trial judge or jury from correctly evaluating the trustworthiness of witnesses and to shut out evidence the trial court ought to receive in order approximate the truth.

In short, the lawyer aims at victory, at winning in the fight, not at aiding the court to discover the facts. He does not want the trial court to reach a sound educated guess, if it is likely to be contrary to his client's interests. Our present trial method is thus the equivalent of throwing pepper in the eyes of a surgeon when he is performing an operation.

However unpleasant all this may appear, do not blame trial lawyers for using techniques I have described. If there is to be criticism, it should be directed at the system that virtually compels their use, a system which treats a lawsuit as a battle of wits and wiles.... These tricks of the trade are today the legitimate and accepted corollary of our fight theory....

Our contentious trial method, I have said, has it roots in the origin of court trials as substitutes for private brawls....

"Classical" laissez-faire economic theory assumed that, when each individual, as an "economic man," strives rationally, in the competitive economic struggle or "fight," to promote his own self-interest, we attain public welfare through the wisest use of resources and the most socially desirable distribution of economic goods. The "fight" theory of justice is a sort of legal laissez-faire. It assumes a "litigious man." It assumes that, in a law suit, each litigious man, in the court-room competitive strife, will, through his lawyer, intelligently and energetically try to use the evidential resources to bring out the evidence favorable to him and unfavorable to his court-room competitor; that thereby the trial court will obtain all the available relevant evidence; and that thus, in a socially beneficial way, the court will apply the social policies embodied in the legal rules to the actual facts, avoiding the application of those rules to a mistaken version of the facts. Legal laissez-faire theory therefore assumes that the government can safely rely on the "individual enterprise" of individual litigants to ensure that court-orders will be grounded on all the practically attainable relevant facts....

No one can doubt that the invention of the courts, which preserve the peace by settling disputes, marked a great step forward in human progress. But are we to be satisfied with this forward step that we will rest content with it? Should not a modern civilized society ask more its courts than that they stop peace-disrupting brawls? The basic aim of the courts in our society should, I think, be the just settlement of particular disputes, the just decision of specific law-suits.

The just settlement of disputes demands a legal system in which the courts can and do strive tirelessly to get as close as is humanly possible to the actual facts of specific court-room controversies. Courthouse justice is, I repeat, done at retail, not wholesale. The trial court's job of fact-finding in each particular case therefore looms up as one of the most important jobs in modern court-house government. With no lack of deep admiration and respect for our many able trial judges, I must say that that job is not as well done as it could and should be....

CHAPTER 5

The Adversary Judge
The Experience of the Trial Judge

Marvin E. Frankel
Judge, U.S. District Court, Southern District of New York (1965–1978)

The Role as Written

THERE IS AN UNHAPPILY wide consensus that excellent trial judges are not in long supply. Among the causes are (*a*) the difficulty of knowing in advance who will turn out to be a good judge, (*b*) disagreement concerning the most effective means of selection, and (*c*) given our ambivalence on this as on other subjects, our lack of steady determination to do the things necessary—for example, to stop using judgeships for patronage—to select the people most likely to be most suitable.

While we fail too regularly to people the bench ideally, the ideal is not itself very uncertain. We can state with a substantial consensus the qualities we desire in our trial judges. The trial judge ought to be neutral, detached, kindly, benign, reasonably learned in the law, firm but fair, wise, knowledgeable about human behavior, and, in lesser respects as well, somewhat superhuman. Here and throughout, especially as the discussion grows more concrete and specific, the vision I have in mind is the judge presiding over the trial by jury of serious criminal cases, which is perhaps the crucible model and the one in which our failures are most frequent and notable. Responding to our tradition of judges as variable individuals—contrasting

Acknowledgment to Judge Marvin E. Frankel for excerpts from the Third Annual Tom Sealy Law and Free Society Lecture at the University of Texas School of Law (November 20, 1975), which appears in 54 Texas Law Review *465 (1976).*

with the European continental goal of the standard, uniform, more predictable but perhaps less colorful judge—Judge Bernard L. Shientag, in a well-known lecture, defined the qualities in terms of "the personality" of the trial judge. He listed, and enlarged upon, the eight "virtues" of independence, courtesy and patience, dignity (but not excluding humor), open-mindedness, impartiality, thoroughness and decisiveness, an understanding heart, and social consciousness.[1] Others, judges and more objective observers, have compiled similar lists.[2] The consensus is not complete; both the list of requisites and the ranking of agreed qualities vary among people seemingly qualified to address the subject.[3]

Whatever the variations, a central core of agreed standards defines the trial judge as the neutral, impartial, calm, noncontentious umpire standing between the adversary parties, seeing that they observe the rules of the adversary game. The bedrock premise is that the adversary contest is the ideal way to achieve truth and a just result rested upon the truth.[4]

The idea of the judge solely, or even primarily, as "umpire" is not universally accepted. August pronouncements define the role more grandly. It is said that the trial judge—perhaps most especially in the federal court—has a more robust part. He may comment upon the evidence, perhaps direct somewhat, or at least guide, the course of the proceedings. I have given elsewhere my opinion that the judge as director or commentator, in a criminal case tried [by] a jury, is likely to be either ineffectual or dangerous.[5] But the disagreements about that are not vitally important at the moment.

What should go without saying is that the essence of the judicial role, active or passive, is impartiality and detachment, both felt and exhibited. In the quest for truth through the clash of contradictions, which is, of course, the only reason in theory for having trials, the judge does not care where the chips may fall. Concerned only that the right is done, the judge "should be patient, dignified, and courteous to litigants, jurors, witnesses, lawyers, and others"[6] as he presides over the contentious strivings toward that end.

These are banalities. Like many fundamental propositions, they are thought to be self-evident. Nevertheless, the fact is that these professed ideals, like others, seem not to be designed, under our practice, for consistently effective pursuit. The tension between the ideals and some insistent realities triggers the conflicts, or potentials for conflict, that constitute my central theme.

The Adversary Performance

Much of the time, the script, cues, and setting of the courtroom drama support the judge in performing his role as impartial arbiter between the parties and faithful guide of the jury toward the truth. The prescribed role has been learned by the judge during a (usually) long course of training and observation in the lists.

The professed expectations of all the other participants, which are basic determinants of the role to begin with, support the prescription. The standard doctrine, respected for its own sake and as a weapon in the hands of higher courts, is a potent force. The ceremonial business is also a congruent pressure. The two sides, in the well, are physically equal. The judge sits between them, usually on a raised bench, and is called upon to reaffirm more than once the equality of the contestants before the law. The jurors are enjoined, over and over again, to be impartial, and the judge is both their mentor and their colleague in this effort. The usual pressures to conform encourage and drive the judge to be neutral.

But there are contradictions, powerful pressures in a different direction, that constitute the focus of this essay. The pressures may be of several kinds. I mean to consider only those that may be called systemic, inherent in the trial process as we conduct it. This excludes, among other things, an array of possible obstacles to impartiality that vary with cases, litigants, and judges—matters like legal or ideological preconceptions, biases touching people or groups, and things still more sinister and, it is hoped, more rare. The exclusions leave enough, I think, to warrant our concern.

The very nature of our accepted trial procedures generates forces that work against the judge's efforts to be neutral and detached. All of the several conditions and circumstances I plan to identify under this heading have in common a tendency to embroil the judge in the battle, to enlist him as an ally or to identify him as an enemy. Upon some reflection, however, I find these factors subdividing into two categories: those that cause the judge to take on combative qualities and those that serve to frustrate or impede or visibly depreciate his duty of leadership toward the truth. It seems convenient at any rate to divide the topic in this way.

The Judge Embattled

The supreme concern of the parties on trial, and therefore of counsel, is to win. Of course, the battle should be fought by the rules, but the goal is victory—not the triumph of "justice" viewed in detachment, but triumph. The high objective of the defense lawyer on trial is acquittal—not an acquittal because the client is innocent, just an acquittal. To be reminded of the cliché about criminal defense lawyers who say they could not bear the responsibility of representing an innocent man is amusing, not startling. We know that the great (and desired, and expensive) defense lawyers are those believed to be most likely to achieve vindication for clients who are not innocent. The following passage exaggerates somewhat, but makes the point:

> Because trial lawyers identify closely with their clients, they enjoy their practice only when they win, and nobody wins all the time. Recalling his own days as

> Steuer's assistant, a now prominent New York lawyer said recently that "there's grown to be a legend that none of Steuer's clients was convicted. That's nonsense, and no honor to Max. A good half of them were convicted—but nearly all of them were guilty...."[7]

The preeminence of the concern for victory is less total for the prosecutor, but it is not a subordinate matter either. Prosecutors seek convictions. Under the rules, which seem increasingly to be obeyed, they have other, broader obligations. But their goal on trial is a guilty verdict, and their behavior in court is oriented accordingly.

With partisan counsel fighting to win, and with the judge as umpire to enforce the rules of the fight, there might seem a priori no reason in the nature of the contest why the judge should himself be, or seem to be, or perceive himself as being drawn into the fray. The trial judge, likely to have moved to the bench from the ranks of advocates, may not start out wholly indisposed or unused to combat, but that progression is not unusual; all kinds of umpires are former contestants. The adversary trial, however, happens to be a game in which the role of umpire includes unorthodox features. Although it has no instant replays of particular events, its participants have a large stake in increasing the probability that the whole game may have to be replayed. This possibility depends largely, of course, on whether the judicial umpire himself commits fouls—"errors," as we say—in the regulating of the contest. And this element is liable to cause the detachment of the trial judge to be tested, threatened, and sometimes impaired, if not entirely lost.

The "big cases," heavily populated with lawyers, heighten the tension. When the crucial question has been asked, or almost asked, the courtroom explodes as people spring up at the several tables shouting objections, usually loudly because they are in some haste and heat to cut off forbidden answers. All perhaps look somehow menacing from combined effects of tension, hostility to the questioner, and anticipated conflict. Viewed from the bench, the rising warriors sometimes have an assaultive look, which is surely a fantasy, but a palpable one to be not, I think, experienced exclusively by judicial paranoids. Whatever the individual emotional impact, the occasion is a testing time for the judge. It may be an easy chance or a hard one. If the latter, the sense of being challenged and opposed by the demand for a ruling is a recurrent experience.

Nobody doubts the range of adversary implications in our description of the judge as being "on trial." Among the more explicit references to trying the judge are the usually proper things lawyers must do or say "for the record." But propriety or no, the statement may have a cutting edge. When the lawyer says, "Just for the record, judge," depending upon the degree of the judge's self-confidence, the phrase may seem to mean simply "to preserve our rights." Or, perhaps it means, "This is too much for you, judge, but it is to be your undoing above." And the lawyer may in fact intend that it be heard either way. Judge-baiting, if not one of the approved techniques, is, after all, not an utter rarity, although perhaps less common than some judges perceive it to be.

In viewing the judge as a probable adversary, the defendant manifests an attitude, and continues a tradition, that is ancient and far from dishonorable with us. Along with the prestige often attached to the office, along with the rituals of deference, we view trial judges with a deep strain of mistrust and hostility. We remember more trial judges in history as notorious than as notable. The hardy survival of the jury with us, as distinguished from its tendency to atrophy elsewhere, reflects a fundamental skepticism about judges. The Constitution itself teaches the lesson, commanding in effect that the fact findings of a jury be less vulnerable than a judge's.[8] The low pay of judges, in a society prone to estimate people in dollars, is part of the same story.

The Judge Discomforted

Apart from the threats to his detachment and neutrality, the adversary battle before the jury is frequently conducted under conditions that entail a potential sense of frustration, even stultification, for the presiding judge. Each of the contestants seeks to win. For either or both, in part or in whole, the goal of victory may be inconsistent with the quest for truth, which represents the public goal the judge is commissioned to pursue. "The very premise of our adversary system of criminal justice is that partisan advocacy on both sides of a case will best promote the ultimate objective that the guilty be convicted and the innocent go free."[9] If premises could be vindicated by reiteration, that one would by now have overwhelmed the skepticism it tends on its face to inspire. Whatever the case, the trial judge spends a good deal of his time solemnly watching clear, deliberate, entirely proper efforts by skilled professionals to block the attainment of "the ultimate objective."

When I say efforts are "clear" and "deliberate," I mean nothing less. This is not a jaundiced hunch; it is an open and shared professional understanding, concealed only from the jury. Often, the judge has been made explicitly aware before trial that the prosecution's assertions, though they will be contested at every step, are true. Less often, but often enough, the concession is made after trial, at sentencing or some other point when confession seems prudent or advantageous.

A whole class of examples arises in courts where plea bargaining is practiced. The bargaining, in which the judge frequently participates, starts from an understanding that the defendant has done approximately the wrong with which he is charged. In many cases, however, no deal is made. The defendant goes to trial. In the trial, the defense, by cross-examination and otherwise, fights to prevent demonstration of facts that were conceded before trial and are thus, in a sufficient and meaningful sense, known by the judge and counsel to be true.

Every trial judge could add illustrations from his own experience. I tender one here, perhaps more dramatic than routine, but apposite, I think, for our theme. A trial about two years ago involved a group of defendants charged with major dealings (multi-kilogram, hundreds of thousands of dollars) in heroin and cocaine. Important for both conspiracy and substantive counts was a suitcase that had been opened in a Toledo railroad baggage room and found to contain over five kilograms of heroin and a kilogram of cocaine.

Three of the defendants moved before trial to suppress this evidence as the product of an unlawful search and seizure. Their claim of a possessory interest giving them standing to seek suppression was resisted by the prosecution. It was concluded that the issue should go to an evidentiary hearing. The three defendant-movants took the stand for this purpose, protected by the prohibition against later use of their testimony as evidence at their trial, and proceeded to recount how they were indeed in the narcotics business, how they had bought the suitcase and packaged the heroin and cocaine for shipment to a Toledo customer, how their emissary had carried it from New York to the Toledo baggage room, delivering the claim check to the customer, and how they had retained "title" to the shipment pending receipt of payment in full.

The motion was eventually denied, both because the quaint claim of retained title proved defective and because the Toledo search was held in any event to have been reasonable.[10] But the points of particular interest here came later.

After other evidentiary hearings on pretrial motions adding to a total of 11 court days, we proceeded to a 19-day trial. While defendants did not take the stand, the considerable talents of numerous defense counsel were bent for four weeks on destroying any suggestion by any witness that would place their clients within miles at any time of any narcotics, including, of course, the Toledo shipment. Counsel for one of the erstwhile movants opened with the observation to the jury that there would "not be a shred of credible evidence," but only incredible assertions from "individuals who are the scum of the earth." A chemist who offered the opinion, novel only to the jury, that the substances in the Toledo suitcase were heroin and cocaine was raked by cross-examination for some three hours, his experience tested, his veracity and motives questioned, the modesty of his academic rank (and the fact that he was a mere Ph.D., not an M.D.) being duly brought to his attention when it became apparent he had a tendency to irascibility.[11]

Altogether, a total of 49 witnesses appeared. The jury heard over six hours of summation and a charge requiring (or at least lasting) nearly two hours. In deliberations extending over three days, including two nights of sequestration in a hotel, the jury called for testimony and exhibits reflecting questions, *inter alia*, that the movant-defendants had answered adversely to themselves, under oath, many weeks before. In the end, the defendants were convicted.

The purposes of and justifications for that four-week trial are familiar and (mostly) precious. The prosecution bears the burden of proof. Only lawful evidence is allowed. Defendants are presumed to be innocent. Jurors are to search out the truth, but doubts are to be resolved in favor of the defense. Granted all that and more, our immediate subject is role strain. How does it all look and feel to the impartial judge, regulating the contest, waiting to see whether the jury arrives at findings he knows to be correct or is successfully kept from doing so? Judges vary, of course, so there is no single answer, not even for any single judge.

My own survey—much self-analysis plus amateur polling—discloses several:

1. Trial judges are, preponderantly, ex-trial lawyers. The game is still fascinating. Participating, even as a referee, is still fun.
2. The broad interests protected by the trial process are vital in themselves, and their furtherance day in and day out is a worthy form of service. The result in any single case is a matter of relatively lesser consequence.
3. It is galling to stand by helplessly while facts are obscured and distorted as part of the professional contribution to truth-seeking. The judicial role in such an enterprise is a sterile kind of umpiring. A quality of unreality haunts a process of bitterly contesting assertions that have been admitted (or sworn) to be true by the contestant in the very courtroom where the conflict now rages. The satisfactions of the cases involving genuine, good-faith contests are nullified by such travesties.
4. The judge's role as teacher, along with the citizen-juror's role in the administration of justice, is warped and diminished when the jurors become the unwitting butt of a joke, launched on a chancy hunt after answers known to all the participants except themselves. Every trial is a drama. "Each case [is] a work of art,"[12] and it is entirely acceptable that there be felt in the courtroom the "faint magic of the theater...."[13] But the play alone cannot be sufficient when the question is the doing of justice in real life. The jurors, who should leave the courthouse more appreciative than they were of themselves and the laws they helped vindicate, too often receive an unedifying demonstration that trickery and low cunning may be permitted to defeat the ends of justice.

Notes

1. B. Sheintag, *The Personality of the Judge* (New York: The Association of the Bar of the City of New York, 1944).

2. See, e.g., B. Botein, *Trial Judge* (New York: Simon and Schuster, 1952); H. Jones, "The Trial Judge—Role Analysis and Profile," in *The Courts, the Public, and the Law Explosion* 24 (Englewood Cliffs, N.J.: Prentice Hall, 1965); H. Lummus, *The Trial Judge* (Chicago: Foundation Press, 1937); C. Wyzanski, "A Trial Judge's Freedom and Responsibility," 65 *Harvard Law Review* 1281 (1952).
3. See M. Rosenberg, "The Qualities of Justices—Are They Sustainable?" 44 *Texas Law Review* 1063 (1966).
4. See, e.g., *Herring v. New York,* 422 U.S. 853 (1975).
5. See M. Frankel, "The Search for Truth: An Umperial View," 123 *University of Pennsylvania Law Review* 1031, 1041–1045 (1975).
6. The quoted words are from the *Code of Judicial Conduct,* Canon 3, Rule A(3). See also Canon 2, Rule A.
7. M. Mayer, *The Lawyers* 34 (New York: Harper & Row, 1967).
8. "In Suits at common law, where the value in controversy shall exceed twenty dollars, the right of trial by jury shall be preserved, and no fact tried by a jury, shall otherwise be reexamined in any Court of the United States, than according to the rules of the common law." U.S. Constitution, Amendment VII.
9. *Herring v. New York,* 422 U.S. 853, 862 (1975).
10. *United States v. Capra,* 372 F. Supp. 603 (S.D.N.Y., 1973), *aff'd.* in part, *rev'd.* in part, 501 F.2d 267 (2d Cir. 1974), *cert. denied,* 420 U.S. 990 (1975).
11. Consider for edifying cross-examination:

    Q. And what was the title of your professorship?
    A. It is assistant professor in pediatrics.
    Q. You were an assistant professor, right?
    A. Right, at Children's Hospital.
    Q. And the next grade above that is what, associate professor?
    A. That's right.
    Q. And then there is another grade above that?
    A. That's right.
    Q. And that is called professor?
    A. That's right. That's right.
    Q. So that the lowest form of professorship is assistant professor?
    A. That is not true.
    Q. Is there something below that?
    A. Yes. Instructor, research associate, there are teaching assistants that are involved with teaching. Now, we are getting into the definition of professor. This addition to professor is teacher—
    Q. Doctor, if I may cut you off for a second, my question to you is that the lowest grade of professor is assistant professor, is that correct?
    A. And my answer is: not correct.
    Q. Oh, you say that instructor is a lower grade of professor?
    A. Yes, and you also have a research—
    Q. Do they call these instructors professors or instructors?
    A. Yes, they can call them instructor professor, they could also be called—there are other forms called research assistant professor.

Q. Now, down in Washington, D.C., at the Children's Hospital, you worked presumably with children, is that correct?

A. Would you like to define what is children?

Transcript of trial testimony at 1956–57, *United States v. Capra*, 372 F. Supp. 603 (S.D.N.Y. 1973).

12. C. Bok, *I, Too, Nicodemus* 329 (New York: Knopf, 1946).
13. Ibid., at 324.

CHAPTER 6

The Business of the U.S. District Courts

D. Brock Hornby

Judge, U.S. District Court, District of Maine (1990) and Associate Justice, Maine Supreme Judicial Court (1988–1990)

UNITED STATES DISTRICT COURTS are the nation's federal trial courts. The traditional assumption has been that their primary business is umpiring trials and imposing sentences. With little public awareness, however, that business has changed dramatically over time: now, federal judges conduct fewer and fewer trials, and their sentencing authority has diminished greatly. But the volume of civil lawsuits and criminal prosecutions continues. What has the business of the federal "trial" courts become in the twenty-first century? What should be our contemporary image of a federal district judge at work?

The late management pioneer, Peter F. Drucker, offered business and nonprofit organizations a critical insight: look outside to determine your mission and measure your effectiveness. According to Drucker, "any serious attempt to state 'what our business is' must start with the customer's realities, his situation, his behavior, his expectations, and his values."[1] The organization does not get to define its business. "It is defined by the want the customer satisfies" in obtaining the product or service. Value to the customer differs from value to the organization. Quality is "not what the supplier puts in. It is what the customer gets out and is willing to pay for."

This insistence upon customer focus may be an unfamiliar perspective for thinking about federal courts, whose "customers" are lawyers, litigants, the American public, and Congress (I shall call them users and stakeholders). But as the

---

Acknowledgment to Judge D. Brock Hornby for excerpts from "The Business of the U.S. District Courts," appearing in 10 Green Bag *2d 453–468 (2007).*

following exposition demonstrates, the perspective affords instructive insights into what federal "trial" courts' business has become....

Civil Lawsuits

The numbers reveal that many federal court users no longer obtain civil trials. The percentage of these lawsuits reaching trial fell from 11.5% in 1962 to 6.1% in 1982 to 1.8% in 2002. The absolute number of civil trials has fallen 60% since the mid-1980s. The figures demonstrate either a market shift or a weakening of federal courts' competence in delivering dispute resolution by trial, or both. But as trial numbers fell, case filings grew dramatically until 1985, before leveling off. Since then, they have moved modestly higher, peaking at 281,338 in 2004.[2] The statistics do not reveal why filings persist while trials decrease. I suggest the following.

Often, plaintiffs and their lawyers still want a federal jury verdict or the threat of one, or at least the full disclosure of their opponents' case that federal rules compel. They continue to file federal lawsuits accordingly. But the desire to control costs (among insurers in particular) and a fear of jury unpredictability or break-the-company verdicts provoke greater defense willingness to mediate, arbitrate, or settle rather than bear the risk and extraordinary expense of trial. Fear of public access to confidential or damaging information also plays a part in trial avoidance. In 1998, Congress actually encouraged diversion of federal cases from trial by ordering courts to establish court-annexed programs for alternatives such as mediation.

Another source of continued federal filings is defendants who, facing difficult lawsuits in state court, remove their cases to federal court. Removals from state court have trended upward over the past twenty-five years, moving somewhat erratically in the last decade. Defendants without local ties, who fear favoritism toward their in-state opponent in a state court, prefer a federal judicial officer who does not face retention or reelection campaigns. In complicated cases, they may conclude that federal courts can better manage the case and grapple with the issues, because federal courts have greater access to legal research, law clerks, and library materials, more time to deal with complicated issues, and greater experience with such cases. These defendants sometimes believe that they have a better chance in federal court at getting disclosure of their opponents' case (usually federal magistrate judges supervise and enforce discovery) and ultimately judgment without trial, avoiding the feared jury verdict. They may also believe that a federal court's generally wider geographic jury pool improves their bargaining position in mediation and settlement efforts short of trial....

Congress regularly gives federal district courts new business. A recent example: unhappy with state courts' treatment of class actions, Congress enacted the

Class Action Fairness Act of 2005 so that additional categories of class actions go to federal rather than state courts. Whenever Congress sees something bothersome enough to pass a law, it generally provides that federal district courts will hear the resulting disputes. Any new federal statutory remedy yields new federal case filings, whether or not trials result.

Congressional lawmaking carries a particular implication for federal courts' work. When Congress drafts a statute, it cannot possibly foresee all the disputes it will encompass or engender. As a result, statutory language often turns out ambiguous for particular circumstances. Sometimes, to submerge disagreement so as to get the law enacted, Congress intentionally chooses ambiguous language. Either way, users ask federal courts to expound upon what the new law means and the circumstances to which it applies. America's laws continue to multiply (about 1,900 pages of new statutes per session in the 1950s, 6,750 pages per session in the 1990s; about 14,477 new Federal Register pages in 1960, 80,322 in 2002) and, with them, insatiable demand for authoritative interpretation. The demand comes from individual users. It comes also from user segments, such as American business (e.g., trade association lawsuits), consumers, and the public (e.g., environmental groups). Alternative dispute resolution (mediation and arbitration) does not provide this authoritative interpretation; only courts do.

Now you might legitimately observe, "Law interpretation is the business of the Supreme Court and the appellate courts. What makes you think that users and stakeholders ask district courts to play an increased role here?" Four reasons.

First, law interpretation has always been district courts' business, but district judges used to deal with it primarily in jury instructions. Increasingly, litigants ask district courts to make discrete legal rulings before or instead of trial. As a result, "trial" courts now produce a multitude of written decisions that look very much like appellate opinions, expounding upon the law for the parties and the future. A large component of this shift from jury instructions to written opinions results from users—mostly defendants—asking more and more for summary judgment because, they say, the significant facts are undisputed. This quest for summary judgment usually reflects defendants trying to avoid the risk of a jury verdict and erecting expensive procedural obstacles to a plaintiff's effort to reach verdict or settlement. But sometimes litigants and lawyers simply cannot agree on what a new, complex, or ambiguous law means in particular circumstances. Thus, although the underlying facts may be not all that uncertain, they need an authoritative legal exposition. Whatever the cause, the resulting district court written opinions are more prominent and durable than jury instructions ever were.

Second, Congress has given district courts a quasi-appellate role in disputes such as social security disability and special education benefit entitlement. In those cases, facts are established mostly before an administrative law judge; the district court determines whether legal principles have been applied correctly, a law exposition function.

Third, Congress, Federal Rules drafters, and appellate courts increasingly instruct district courts to give detailed explanations for their decisions, explanations generally provided most effectively in writing. Congress requires that written decisions be available on the Web. Computerized legal research makes them easy for lawyers to find and cite as precedent. Subject-matter blogs, legal or nonlegal, find and discuss them. Thus, federal district courts' role in law exposition grows ever more visible.

Fourth, litigants generally cannot reach an appellate court or the Supreme Court except through a district court. If litigants obtain a clear statement of applicable law from the district court, they may decide to resolve their case without an appeal's added expense and delay (the Supreme Court has a small, discretionary docket; immigration and sentencing appeals swamp appellate courts). So the district court's written opinion may be the final decision. At the very least, its written analysis informs any appeal and, through publication, perhaps decisions in other cases.

Federal judicial officers increasingly are asked to step outside their traditionally passive umpire role. Scores of articles have recognized the aggressive case management responsibilities that Congress and Federal Rules drafters assigned, and district courts assumed, in the twentieth century's closing decades. These changes inserted federal judicial officers into what used to be exclusively lawyers' decisions on how to prepare cases. Starting with scheduling orders establishing deadlines for every important event, continuing through discovery management and final pretrial conferences, encouraging settlement or alternative resolution, judges and magistrate judges now play central roles in determining and limiting how lawsuits progress. (The discovery process generates a particular set of user demands, lawyers asking magistrate judges to protect clients from expensive, burdensome discovery—especially electronically stored data or messages—or compelling opponents to produce what they hope will be helpful information.) Court documents now are filed online over the internet. Federal judges and their administrative staff ("case managers") track their caseload's progress electronically and intervene as needed to keep each case moving. Law professors debate the advisability of this active management, but Congress, the parties, and most lawyers seem to want it.

Consider the additional mandate to district judges in class actions: determining whether there is a structure and process by which hundreds or millions of people, sometimes nationwide or beyond, can obtain reimbursement for some injury-producing conduct. These cases often involve complex scientific or economic issues, and they carry tremendous administrative responsibilities. Congress, plaintiffs' lawyers, and defendants ask federal district judges to perform that task. Almost all class action disputes end in dismissal or settlement without trial. So it is the judge's role first in helping structure the dispute and then in declaring applicable law that is critical. Indeed, in the class action context, the judge is asked to assume fiduciary responsibility (even farther from an umpire) for the aggrieved class, in determining whether a proposed settlement can end the lawsuit. If money is left over because some class members do not claim their shares, the judge may be called upon to act as a kind of grants manager, determining what charities receive the excess and ensuring that they use the funds properly.

Users increasingly ask district courts to engage in what I call "fact sorting." Even if the law is not uncertain, there is a perennial dispute over whether a "genuine issue of material fact" exists, the standard for determining whether the judge can order judgment without trial. Lawyers regularly joust over who can prove what, and whether their opponents' version of the facts, if accurate, justifies their legal position (in a harassment case, for example, whether particular comments, if uttered, are enough for liability). In cases involving experts' opinions, they debate whether the underlying science or knowledge is valid (or "junk science") and whether the expert has applied it appropriately. They demand that the judicial officer decide who has complied with or broken the procedural rules in presenting factual assertions or denials, and whether the opposition ultimately has admissible evidence, expert or otherwise, to back up its claimed facts. Typically, they present all this information electronically, through the courts' electronic case filing system. The district judge or magistrate judge sorts these electronically-provided facts, determines which are undisputed and which facts matter, thus discarding other facts, whether the outcome is judgment or trial. Disputes over experts require fact-finding on the adequacy of the expert's credentials, the status of the science or technical knowledge, how tests were conducted, what other experts do, and whether the expert's opinion fits the underlying facts, all affecting admissibility of evidence on important issues like causation. Sometimes, lawyers present live testimony on these expert issues in open court. The complexity of many federal cases makes this process both time-consuming and hugely expensive....

Many district judges think that the primary value they provide is the availability of a well-run trial in a public courtroom, following on the heels of effective case management and open discovery. In that context, they may consider their legal rulings as mostly incidental to the underlying goal of successfully shaping a difficult case for a jury's comprehension. Meanwhile, what have users and stakeholders been seeking? Plaintiffs who file federal lawsuits still seek the threat of a jury verdict, the leverage of federal litigation's cost, and federal discovery. Defendants who remove their lawsuits from state courts still want the federal courts' greater resources, the larger jury pool, perhaps better discovery, a realistic threat of summary judgment, and judicial officers who do not confront reelection. What has changed, I suggest, is that users increasingly do not expect or even want a trial. Congress likewise doesn't particularly want trials; it wants judges to manage the caseload (prisoner grievances, student loan collections, and class actions, for starters), and it depends upon judges to clarify legislative ambiguities. Users' and stakeholders' primary demands have become authoritative law exposition, assistance in structuring disputes, organizing and managing litigation, controlling discovery, and fact sorting. Once litigants satisfy these demands, they resolve any remaining disputes. It is difficult to say even that they settle the disputes in light of likely trial outcomes, since they have fewer and fewer such outcomes to assess, and the likelihood of trial has become so small.

So how might reality television portray a federal "trial" judge in civil lawsuit garb? In an office setting without the robe, using a computer and court administrative staff to monitor the entire caseload and individual case progress; conferring with lawyers (often by telephone or videoconference) in individual cases to set dates or limits; in that same office at a computer, poring over a particular lawsuit's "facts," submitted electronically as affidavits, documents, depositions, and interrogatory answers; structuring and organizing those facts, rejecting some or many of them; finally, researching the law (at the computer, not a library) and writing (at the computer) explanations of the law for parties and lawyers in light of the sorted facts. For federal civil cases, the black-robed figure up on the bench, presiding publicly over trials and instructing juries, has become an endangered species, replaced by a person in business attire at an office desk surrounded by electronic assistants.

Criminal Prosecutions

For the criminal business of federal courts, the data reveal unequivocally that users mostly avoid trials. There still are showcase trials, recently Martha Stewart, Kenneth Lay, and Jeffrey Skilling, important public morality plays. But a severely declining fraction of federal criminal cases reaches trial (15% in 1962, 5% in 2002, the absolute number of trials falling 30%). At the same time, the number of federal prosecutions holds steady or trends upward. From 2001 to 2004, criminal case filings grew 13%[3] (although in the past two years they have declined).[4]

What do users and stakeholders seek instead of criminal trials? Prosecutors want guilty plea adjudications; they are cheaper and more certain. Defendants would like the chance of a jury acquittal. But they do not want to face a substantially higher sentence if the jury convicts. Under federal Sentencing Guidelines, a trial virtually guarantees a convicted defendant significantly more prison time. Therefore, most defendants now join prosecutors in wanting no trial if they face a serious risk of conviction, because they can reduce their sentences by pleading guilty. Presumably, the American public wants a judicial process that keeps prosecutors and defense lawyers honest, where the innocent are set free, the guilty are punished, and the process acts as a deterrent to criminal conduct. To that end, the public depends upon federal judges' careful supervision at guilty plea proceedings, ensuring that pleas are voluntary, informed, and factually supported—together with the alternative availability of a jury trial, where the Constitution requires procedural protections and proof beyond a reasonable doubt—to maintain the integrity of the process and reduce the likelihood that innocent defendants will plead guilty.

Federal judges' sentencing role has changed drastically. Perceiving disparities in nationwide sentencing practices, Congress ordered creation of Sentencing Guidelines in the Sentencing Reform Act of 1984 to restrict judges' sentencing discretion. In 2005, the Supreme Court declared the Guidelines "advisory,"[5] but left standing the requirement that judges perform the Guidelines analysis as part of the sentencing determination. The Guidelines remain highly influential, and judges who sentence outside them must provide written explanations for appellate review.

The Guidelines increased dramatically the time that federal judges devote to sentencing. Presentence reports are detailed and lengthy. Probation Officers propose factual findings (e.g., the defendant's role as leader or follower, quantity of drugs/dollars involved, previous criminal convictions). If there is a dispute, the judge must find the facts, perhaps after a trial-type hearing. Those findings produce numerical scores determining, from a published grid, the prison time and fine range. The Guidelines are a complex Code, with commentary, drafting history, and thousands of appellate opinions interpreting them. They change almost annually because of Sentencing Commission or congressional action. More and more judicial time is devoted to studying, then expounding upon, this complicated law's application to particular factual circumstances.

Federal prosecutors decide which defendants to prosecute, which charges to press, which defendants to leave solely to state prosecutors, and whether to request a sentence below the Guideline range. Those under-the-radar decisions, subject to no judicial review and no public examination, hugely affect sentence length. Offenders and their lawyers try to persuade a judge that they are different from other offenders and deserve more mercy at sentencing. If they strike a favorable deal with the prosecutor, they try to prevent the probation officer or judge from undoing their bargain.

Sentencing demonstrates separation of powers in microcosm. Congress legislates the penalty range, sets some of the criteria and requires use of Guidelines. The executive branch, through the prosecutor, determines whom to charge and how, thereby creating sentencing limits. But in the end, the judge imposes the sentence. In an environment of wide prosecutorial discretion, that constitutional judicial role gains new significance: not just determining the sentence within limits set by Congress and prosecutors and with appropriate attention to the Guidelines, but also holding prosecutors to statutory and constitutional values, calling public attention to failures or unfairness in the prosecutorial process, in appropriate cases refusing to endorse them, and ensuring that defense lawyers have provided adequate representation. Federal judges have lost free rein in sentencing, but the American public as stakeholder depends upon them to articulate publicly the principles that control a sentence, to monitor and expose prosecutorial failure to fulfill congressional goals such as proportionality and equality, and to ensure that defense lawyers fulfill their responsibilities....

Our new image of a federal "trial" judge for criminal cases ("Law and Order" and "Shark" take notice) still should be a black-robed person regularly up on the bench in a public courtroom, but far less frequently presiding at trials, and far more often taking guilty pleas, sentencing, and cajoling or disciplining offenders who misbehave after prison. There is still abundant public courtroom time because, as the number of trials has declined, sentencing proceedings have lengthened, and supervised release revocation hearings have been added to the judge's courtroom duties....

Conclusion

So, what is the federal district courts' "business" in the twenty-first century? "Equal Justice Under Law," a ringing phrase, is too broad a mission statement. Drucker said that a hospital's mission is not to provide health care, as hospital administrators profess, but narrower, to take care of illness. Likewise, the district courts' mission never has been the general maintenance of equal justice. Federal judges care intensely about equal justice, but that is not the courts' mission.

Instead, it is and always has been their mission to interpret and clarify laws, adjudicate and protect rights, maintain fair processes, and punish. But the method of carrying out that mission has changed. Federal judges accomplish these goals less through trials, sentencing discretion is drastically curtailed, and the traditional role of passive umpire has shifted in obvious and subtle ways.

Law professors and judges should stop bemoaning disappearing trials. Trials have gone the way of landline telephones—useful backups, not the instruments primarily relied upon, if ever they were. Dramatists enjoy trials. District judges enjoy trials. Some lawyers enjoy trials. Except as bystanders, ordinary people and businesses don't enjoy trials, because of the unacceptable risk and expense.

In the twenty-first century, the federal district courts' primary roles in civil cases have become law exposition, fact sorting, and case management—office tasks—not umpiring trials. In criminal cases, the judge's work remains courtroom-centered but, instead of trials, it has become law elaboration and fact finding at sentencing, supervising federal offenders after prison, and safeguarding the integrity of a criminal process that sends defendants to prison without trial. In 2007, that is the federal district courts' business. Trials as we have known them, and unfettered sentencing discretion, are not coming back.

Notes

1. Peter Drucker, *The Essential Drucker* 12, 42, 24 (New York: Collins Business, 2001).
2. Table 8-7 in 1997, 2001, 2005, 2006 *Judicial Business of the United States Courts* (Washington, D.C.: U.S. Government Printing Office, 1998, 2002, 2006, 2007); Table S-4 in 1992 *Judicial Business of the United States Courts* (Washington, D.C.: U.S. Government Printing Office, 1993); Table S-8 in 1988 *Judicial Business of the United States Courts* (Washington, D.C.: U.S. Government Printing Office, 1989).
3. 2004 *Business of the United States Courts,* supra, at 21.
4. 2006 *Judicial Business of the United States Courts,* supra, at 21.
5. *United States v. Booker,* 543 U.S. 220 (2005).

CHAPTER 7

What I Ate for Breakfast and Other Mysteries of Judicial Decision Making

Alex Kozinski
Judge, U.S. Court of Appeals, Ninth Circuit (1985)

It is popular in some circles to suppose that judicial decision making can be explained largely by frivolous factors, perhaps for example the relationship between what judges eat and what they decide. Answering questions about such relationships is quite simple—it is like being asked to write a scholarly essay on the snakes of Ireland: There are none.

But as far back as I can remember in law school, the notion was advanced with some vigor that judicial decision making is a farce. Under this theory, what judges do is glance at a case and decide who should win—and they do this on the basis of their digestion (or how they slept the night before or some other variety of personal factors). If the judge has a good breakfast and a good night's sleep, he might feel lenient and jolly, and sympathize with the downtrodden. If he had indigestion or a bad night's sleep, he might be a grouch and take it out on the litigants. Of course, even judges can't make both sides lose; I know, I've tried. So a grouchy mood, the theory went, is likely to cause the judge to take it out on the litigant he least identifies with, usually the guy who got run over by the railroad or is being foreclosed on by the bank. This theory immodestly called itself Legal Realism.

Just to prove that even the silliest idea can be pursued to its illogical conclusion, Legal Realism spawned Critical Legal Studies. As I understand this so-called

Acknowledgment to Judge Alex Kozinski for his speech at the Symposium on the California Judiciary, Loyola Law School, Los Angeles, appearing in 26 Loyola of Los Angeles Law Review *993 (1993).*

theory, the notion is that because legal rules don't mean much anyway, and judges can reach any result they wish by invoking the right incantation, they should engraft their own political philosophy onto the decision-making process and use their power to change the way our society works. So, if you accept that what a judge has for breakfast affects his decisions that day, judges should be encouraged to have a consistent diet so their decisions will consistently favor one set of litigants over the other.

I am here to tell you that this is all horse manure. And, like all horse manure, it contains little seeds of truth from which tiny birds can take intellectual nourishment. The little truths are these: Under our law judges do in fact have considerable discretion in certain of their decisions: making findings of fact, interpreting language in the Constitution, statutes and regulations; determining whether officials of the executive branch have abused their discretion; and fashioning remedies for violations of the law, including fairly sweeping powers to grant injunctive relief. The larger reality, however, is that judges exercise their powers subject to very significant constraints. They simply can't do anything they well please.

These constraints come in many forms, some subtle, some quite obvious. I want to focus here only on three that I believe are among the most important. The first, and to my mind the most significant, is internal: the judge's own self-respect. Cynics and academics (a redundancy) tend to belittle this if they consider it at all. Don't make that mistake. Judges have to look in the mirror at least once a day, just like everyone else; they have to like what they see. Heaven knows, we don't do it for the money; if you can't have your self-respect, you might as well make megabucks doing leveraged buyouts.

More concretely, the job is just too big to be done by one person alone. You are surrounded by eager young law clerks far too smart to be fooled by nonsense. I know of no judge who will tell his law clerks: "I want to reach this result, write me an opinion to get me there." You have to give them reasons, and those reasons better be pretty good—any law clerk worth his salt will argue with you if the reasons you give are unconvincing. Should you choose to abandon principle to reach a result, you will not be able to fool yourself into believing you're just following the law. It will have to be a deliberate choice, and it's a choice that, by and large, judges tend not to make. As Senator Thurmond said at my investiture as Chief Judge of the Claims Court in 1982, "You are in a different world when you put a robe on. It is something that just makes you feel that you have got to do what is right, whether you want to or not. I think the moment you put on that robe, you enter this ultra-world." A little corny, perhaps, but true.

The second important constraint comes from your colleagues. If you're a district judge, your decisions are subject to review by three judges of the court of appeals. If you are a circuit judge, you have to persuade at least one other colleague, preferably two, to join your opinion. Even then, litigants petition for rehearing and *en banc* review with annoying regularity. Your shortcuts, errors and oversights are mercilessly paraded before the entire court and, often enough, someone will call for an *en banc* vote.

If you survive that, judges who strongly disagree with your approach will file a dissent from the denial of *en banc* rehearing. If powerful enough, or if joined by enough judges, it will make your opinion subject to close scrutiny by the Supreme Court, vastly increasing the chances that certiorari will be granted. Even Supreme Court Justices are subject to the constraints of colleagues and the judgments of a later Court.

Now, don't get me wrong, just about any judge can get away with cutting a corner here or there. There are too many cases and too little time to catch all the errors, deliberate or unintentional. But what you absolutely cannot get away with is abandoning legal principles in favor of results on a consistent basis. Any judge who tries to do this cuts deeply into his credibility and becomes suspect among his colleagues. There are, from time to time, district judges whose decisions come to the court of appeals with a presumption of reversibility. I have heard lawyers say, with good reason, that they dread winning before those judges because it becomes very difficult to defend their judgments on appeal. Circuit judges who break the rules too often become especially vulnerable to *en banc* calls and ultimately to reversal by the Supreme Court....

The third important constraint on judicial excesses lies in the political system, a constraint often overlooked but awesome nonetheless. By its nature, the political process seldom reacts to specific cases, although it does so from time to time. The passage of the Civil Rights Act of 1991 was exclusively a response to five Supreme Court decisions from the recent terms; Congress believed the Court had misread civil rights legislation and moved swiftly and decisively to overrule the decisions by statute.

But the political process occasionally operates in even blunter ways. Examples of these from the past are FDR's plan to pack the Supreme Court and proposals to clip the federal courts' jurisdiction over sensitive matters.

A more recent example is the removal of three justices of the California Supreme Court by the voters. There are many explanations for why the justices were removed, and I'm sure that some of the other speakers today know much more about the situation than I do. My own impression is that the electorate was persuaded—rightly or wrongly—that these three justices simply were not playing fair: They were using the power of their office to engraft a political agenda onto the law.

Now, there is an unspoken premise to what I have said, namely that there are more or less objective principles by which the law operates, principles that dictate the reasoning and often the result in most cases. I know you are taught to doubt this in law school, as I was; it is nevertheless true. Now, these principles are not followed by every judge in every case, and even when followed, there is frequently some room for the exercise of personal judgment.

But none of this means principles don't exist or that judges can use them interchangeably or ignore them altogether. Let me give you an example of one principle I think is extremely important: Language has meaning. This doesn't mean every word is as precisely defined as every other word, or that words always have a single, immutable meaning. What it does mean is that language used in statutes, regulations, contracts and the Constitution place an objective constraint on our conduct. The precise line may be debatable at times, but at the very least the language used sets an outer boundary that those interpreting and applying the law must respect. When the language is narrowly drawn, the constraints are fairly strict; when it is drawn loosely they're more generous, but in either case they do exist. Let me illustrate.

An example of a Constitutional provision that is very strict is contained in Article II, Section 1, Clause 5: "No person except a natural born Citizen, or a Citizen of the United States, at the time of the Adoption of this Constitution, shall be eligible to the Office of the President...." This language allows little or no room for interpretation. While there could possibly be some debate as to whether someone born of American parents abroad would be considered a natural born citizen, there is absolutely no room to argue that someone like me, who was born outside the United States to foreign parents, is eligible to be President. Language here, indeed, provides a firm and meaningful constraint on conduct.

Obviously not all clauses of the Constitution are as narrowly drawn as this provision. For example, the Fourth Amendment prohibits unreasonable searches and seizures. What is unreasonable is subject to judgment. But it is not a judgment made in a vacuum. It must be made in light of almost two centuries of interpretation and our shared notions of individual privacy and personal autonomy. I submit that, regardless of what any particular judge may subjectively think, a warrantless nighttime search of every house on a particular block would not be reasonable. Again, marginal cases may present difficult line-drawing problems, but this doesn't negate the fact that the language of the Constitution does provide a meaningful constraint for the large majority of cases.

Another very important principle is that judges must deal squarely with precedent. They may not ignore it or distinguish it on an insubstantial or trivial basis. Few of us write on a truly clean slate and what has gone before provides an important constraint on what we can do in cases now before us. Precedent, like language, frequently leaves room for judgment. But there is a difference between judgment and dishonesty, between distinguishing precedent and burying it. Judges get incensed when lawyers fail to cite controlling authority or when they misstate the holdings of cases they cannot distinguish in a principled fashion.

When judges do this, it is doubly shameful, because the results are far more damaging. I've heard lawyers complain, with good reason, that within the same circuit there will be two lines of authority on the very same subject. The two lines go off in different directions without acknowledging each other's existence, like ships passing in the night. In such circumstances lawyers have much difficulty in advising clients how to conduct their affairs, the rule of law depending on who the judges in their case happen to be.

Let me give you a final principle that's not frequently recognized as such, but is, in my view, extremely important. We all view reality from our own peculiar perspective; we all have biases, interests, leanings, instincts. These are important. Frequently, something will bother you about a case that you can't quite put into words, will cause you to doubt the apparently obvious result. It is important to follow those instincts, because they can lead to a crucial issue that turns out to make a difference. But it is even more important to doubt your own leanings, to be skeptical of your instincts. It is frequently very difficult to tell the difference between how you think a case should be decided and how you hope it will come out. It is very easy to take sides in a case and subtly shade the decision-making process in favor of the party you favor, much like the Legal Realists predict. My prescription is not, however, to yield to these impulses with abandon, but to fight them. If you, as a judge, find yourself too happy with the result in a case, stop and think. Is that result justified by the law, fairly and honestly applied to the facts? Or is it merely a bit of self-indulgence?

Judging is a job where self-indulgence is a serious occupational hazard. One must struggle against it constantly if one is to do the job right. I guess what I ultimately object to in the teachings of the Legal Realists and their modern day disciples is that they play on judges' already inflated egos by telling them that they can follow their leanings with abandon and everything will be all right. Everything will not be all right. There are awesome forces in our society that extract a heavy price for judicial self-indulgence. Judges have traditionally held a special place in the public's mind as arbiters of our disputes and protectors of our individual freedoms. But judges can only do that job if they are trusted. In standing up for our Constitution, judges are frequently called upon to make decisions that are highly unpopular: releasing convicted criminals, striking down legislation that has wide public support, and letting Nazis march in neighborhoods populated with survivors of Auschwitz. By and large, the public has been willing to accept decisions like these because they trust judges when they say that the Constitution requires this, believing that the unpopular result serves a higher principle that protects all of us.

Woe be to us when that trust in the judiciary is lost. If the public should become convinced—as many academicians apparently are—that judges are reaching results not based on principle but to serve a political agenda, unpopular decisions will become not merely points of dissatisfaction but the impetus for far-reaching changes that will affect our way of life for years to come, perhaps permanently.

The signs are on the horizon and ought not be ignored. Throwing judges out of office because of how they voted on cases, rather than reservations about qualifications or personal integrity, seems to me a very serious cause for alarm. Also highly alarming are the recent battles in the Senate over the appointment of the Chief Justice, Judge Bork, Justice Thomas and some of the judges of the lower federal courts. Judicial appointment and tenure has suddenly become a political football in a way that has serious implications for our way of life. It will not stop there. I predict that if the current climate continues, we'll see further attempts to fiddle with the jurisdiction of the federal courts, or to limit the scope of judicial review or to circumscribe the appointment or removal process. The independence of the judiciary will be undermined or lost, and with it will go the important functions it performs in our constitutional scheme of government....

CHAPTER 8

Whose Federal Judiciary Is It Anyway?

Stephen Reinhardt
Judge, U.S. Court of Appeals, Ninth Circuit (1979–)

A MAJOR BATTLE is underway over the future of the federal judiciary. So far, it has been waged behind closed doors. Soon, it will move into the open. Its outcome will affect all young lawyers, and more important, all Americans with legal problems, civil and criminal.

The struggle is over the heart and soul of our federal judicial system. Whose courts are they? What is the purpose of federal courts? Are they there to serve the judges or the people? All the people or just the few? The battle is taking place in the form of a struggle over the size of the federal courts. Will they grow so that they can serve the needs of an expanding population with expanding rights, or will they be frozen in size and the number of judges capped at the number now serving? If those favoring a freeze on the number of judges prevail, the end result will be a drastic limitation on the number of cases that can be litigated in the federal courts.

We hear much about the problem of increasing delay in our federal courts. We hear complaints that litigants are frequently denied oral argument, that the size of briefs is being limited unreasonably, that written opinions are being replaced by inadequate informal memorandum dispositions. All these charges are true, all these complaints are justified, and all result from a single cause. We do not have enough federal judges to do all the work that is necessary to provide first-class justice to all.

Acknowledgment to Judge Stephen Reinhardt for excerpts from his 1993 address at Loyola Law School's St. Thomas More Law Honor Society Medallion Award Banquet, appearing in 27 Loyola of Los Angeles Law Review *1 (1993).*

The solution is simple. There are only 170 federal appellate court judges in a country of 240 million people. Yet except for the 100 odd cases a year the Supreme Court hears, courts of appeals are the courts of last resort in all federal cases. Why only 170 judges, sitting in panels of three—meaning only roughly fifty-five panels—to hear all the federal appeals affecting two to three hundred million people? No reason at all. But the opposition to growth is fierce—and stems from an odd mixture of motives.

Let me first give you a practical example of the consequence of the movement to stop growth in the federal courts. The Judicial Conference, consisting of the leadership of the federal judiciary, sponsors bills to add federal judges when, under a complex formula, the number of cases warrant it. This year the Judicial Conference, in an unprecedented move, refused to approve the ten new judgeships to which the Ninth Circuit is entitled, tabling the proposal pending a September report by its Long Range Planning Committee on the future size of the federal judiciary. As a result, Ninth Circuit judges must continue to handle a rapidly growing caseload with less than three-fourths of the judges that are needed—even under the highly conservative formula employed by the Judicial Conference. The result will be more delay, more work by judges that falls short of the quality we are capable of providing, and more frustrated litigants and lawyers.

The proposal to freeze the number of federal judges has gained considerable support in the federal judiciary. It is the subject of a soon-to-be released study by the Federal Judicial Center. Recently one committee of the Judicial Conference even went so far as to recommend reducing the number of federal appellate court judges to 120—a reduction of almost one-third. Were this proposal to be adopted, the limitation on access to the court by people deserving of a federal hearing would be immense.

The freeze movement serves the philosophical objectives of Chief Justice Rehnquist and Justice Scalia. These justices have for years sought to limit access to the federal courts, principally through a series of rulings on arcane procedural subjects such as standing, ripeness, and mootness. These indirect limitations have taken their toll, especially in public interest areas. In cases ranging from *Los Angeles v. Lyons*,[1] the chokehold case, to *Lujan v. Defenders of Wildlife*,[2] the latest environmental case, the Supreme Court has turned back the requests of those who seek to limit arbitrary or unlawful governmental action on the ground that their cases do not qualify for a federal court hearing under the Rehnquist Court's new procedural rules. These justices have a different vision of the role of the federal courts—a far different one—from Earl Warren or William Brennan, for example, from William O. Douglas or Thurgood Marshall. Justice Scalia has frankly and openly stated his views on the proper limits of federal court jurisdiction. He believes that the courts should be reserved for "important cases" and disdains those involving mundane matters, such as claims of employment discrimination on the basis of race or gender, unfair denials of desperately needed benefits in disability and social security cases, and arbitrary governmental actions in deportation proceedings even though the issue, ultimately, may be one of life or death. There would be no better way to rid the federal courts of these "unimportant" cases involving serious injuries to the rights of individuals than to limit drastically the number of cases that can be heard.

At the heart of the freeze movement is judicial elitism. It is the view that federal courts and federal judges are too important for routine matters that only affect ordinary persons. Conservative judges, such as former Judge Bork and his intellectual allies, have long urged that the federal court system be preserved as a small jewel, to resolve major disputes with significant economic consequences. In short, the elitists think that the federal courts exist primarily in order to resolve cases involving large business interests—to decide "big buck" cases, cases that interest them. Problems incurred by real people, human problems, are simply beneath these judges. Human problems can be handled in the state courts or by administrative agencies, they believe.

The essential flaw in the approach of the judicial elitists is that they believe the courts are there to satisfy their intellectual desires, to provide them with intellectual stimulation—rather than to serve the needs of the public, to promote the public welfare.

Surprisingly, it is not only conservative judges who wish to freeze the size of the federal courts. Among the leaders of the movement are a number of liberal and moderate judges who are comfortable with the way courts have always operated and fear change. They yearn for the days, long gone if they ever existed, when a federal judge could walk down the street and be recognized and greeted by an admiring populace. They have visions of sitting in their chambers ruminating on important matters of the day and issuing decisions that will gain the immediate attention of the leaders in the business and academic world who will proclaim in unison, "Well done, Follansbee," or some such plaudit. They think their first names should be Learned or Augustus or maybe that they should even be known by two, such as Oliver Wendell. These judges are simply victims of nostalgia for days they never knew.

The supporters of the freeze movement have more worthy concerns as well. They worry that restructuring of the court system may be necessary—and that may well be the case. They fear a proliferation of circuits, or the creation of mammoth courts of appeals with an attendant increase in the number of internal circuit conflicts. It is true that structural problems will require our attention, that change will be necessary, that we cannot anticipate all the difficulties that will arise, that there will be disadvantages as well as advantages. But that is a small price to pay for having a judicial system that remains fair and open, that is available to all. We will simply have to solve the problems of bigness—and we can. We have made a good start in that direction on the Ninth Circuit, and we can make a similar one in the rest of the country.

The opponents of growth also argue that bureaucratization will result, and that the quality of federal judges will decrease. Both these arguments are demonstrably wrong. Bureaucracy occurs when there are too few judges, not too many. When there are too few judges for the number of cases, we lean too heavily on staff, enact procedures that result in the arbitrary classification of cases that receive second class treatment, and then dispose of them by shortcuts taken behind closed doors.

Nothing is healthier than a full public ventilation of all of the issues in a case—through a full-scale oral argument in a public courtroom. Then, everyone knows what is going on. But that essential process is simply unavailable when there are not enough judges to hear the cases. In short, there is more danger of bureaucratization from too few judges than from too many.

As to the quality of federal judges—we are simply deluding ourselves if we think that we are the brightest and the best. There are three, four, ten, or more lawyers out there, at least as well qualified as each judge who is appointed. Nor will the quality diminish because the selection process will become "routine." There is nothing routine about the judicial selection process. The struggles for appointments will be just as fierce, the examination of qualifications by opponents just as rigorous. In the case of lower court judges, these battles take place largely out of public view anyway. There is simply no reason to believe that any change will occur in the selection process as a result of the fact that more rather than fewer judicial prizes are at stake.

So, where are we in this struggle? The freeze forces are moving rapidly within the judiciary. They have much support at the top—among the judicial establishment. Among the rank and file, the picture is less clear, but there is certainly significant support there as well. Judges are conservative by nature. They view change with skepticism—particularly institutional change. Over three-fourths of the current judiciary was appointed by Ronald Reagan or George [H.W.] Bush. Many of the rest, almost all Carter appointees, have grown weary or comfortable in office. Soon, however, there will be a fair-sized number of new judicial appointees—if the current administration ever gets around to starting the long and arduous process of filling the numerous existing vacancies. One would certainly hope for a young, vigorous group of new judges, with ideals untarnished, with concern for the rights of all—a group of judges who would understand the need for growth.

But the problem of the future of our nation's federal courts is far too important to be left to judges. It is the people and their elected representatives who must determine what the size of our courts will be, what role they will play in our system of government, whose needs they will serve, what kinds of cases can be brought in the federal courts. The battle is just beginning. Now is the time for lawyers, bar associations, law professors, deans, students, public interest groups, and others to join the fight. I urge you all to do so. Write letters and articles, speak out, introduce resolutions, work through professional and other organizations to which you belong. Get on record, get your organizations on record. If you care for your courts, fight for them. If you believe the courts should remain open to all, make your views heard.

Why is your voice so important? Because if those who oppose an elitist federal court system are to prevail, they will in all likelihood have to overcome the influence of the judicial establishment. Neither the issue nor its importance is readily apparent to the public—or even to the Congress. The debate is superficially over the number of judges to be appointed. But the behind-the-scenes agenda of many of the advocates of a freeze is to roll back the Warren-Brennan era, to return us to a time before the Congress enacted so many of the laws that serve to protect society's interests today—environmental, civil rights, and social welfare legislation. If people are deprived of the opportunity to seek remedies for the violation of those statutes, if they are denied access to the federal courts, their rights will be of little value. It is the federal courts that, since the 1950s, have kept our governments honest, have protected individual rights against arbitrary government action. Only if our courts remain healthy, vigorous, and open, only if we ensure that there are enough judges to protect individual liberties and freedom, will those rights remain safe.

I can assure you that the advocates of a minimalist federal court system—the "jewel" advocates—are well aware of the effect their proposal would have if adopted. They talk openly of forcing Congress to limit federal jurisdiction, of stopping Congress from passing new laws that can be enforced in federal courts. They sometimes suggest that their goal can be accomplished by removing other parts of our present jurisdiction, such as diversity cases or run-of-the-mill narcotics prosecutions. The first would simply be a drop in the bucket, and the second is simply not practical from a political standpoint. Congress is not going to pass any law that looks like a step backwards in its war on crime. Anyone familiar with the political process can tell you that. So, what's at stake is clearly the type of cases that Justices Rehnquist and Scalia have long targeted. Clearly what's at stake are cases affecting not large business interests, but the poor, the minorities, women, and the disadvantaged. And clearly the end result of a freeze would be to limit drastically Congress's ability to expand individual rights. The freeze would not just be on the number of judges. It would also be on our access to our courts, and thus on our liberties and freedom.

At present we have fewer than 1,000 federal judges (excluding magistrate-judges and bankruptcy judges) in the federal court system. That is far fewer than the number of judges in the state of California's judicial system. It is not much more than the number of lawyers in some of the nation's larger law firms. It is an infinitesimal number of judges for a rapidly growing nation of 240 million people—a country whose laws must grow to meet its needs. Yet it is this "magic" number of 1,000—a number totally without rhyme or reason—that the freeze advocates have seized on as their maximum. To adopt such a cap would not only be irrational, it would be disastrous.

What do we need to do? And by we, I mean those I spoke of earlier—I mean you—students, professors, lawyers. First, we must persuade Congress to look at the question of the size of the federal courts in terms of what is needed to help the courts fulfill their mission. Second, we must develop a clear definition of the role and function of the federal courts, with primary emphasis on the rights of individuals, of those who need assistance from government as well as those who need protection against arbitrary government action. Third, we must sell that position to the Congress and to the Administration. Fourth, we must press for the rejection of any freeze and instead urge a substantial increase in the size of the federal judiciary....

Finally, let me add one word about cost. Doubling the size of the judiciary will cost a small amount of money. That is true. But the price is right. The annual cost of operating the federal court system is less than the cost of building one space shuttle, only slightly more than one stealth bomber. We receive less than three-tenths of one percent of the federal budget. Doubling our size would be a drop in the bucket. And the benefits to our criminal and civil justice system would be enormous. Even in an age of deficit reduction, court expansion is a winner....

Notes

1. *Los Angeles v. Lyons,* 461 U.S. 95 (1983).
2. *Lujan v. Defenders of Wildlife,* 112 S.Ct. 2130 (1992).

CHAPTER 9

What Really Goes on at the Supreme Court

Lewis F. Powell Jr.
Justice, Supreme Court of the United States (1972–1987)

The court is a place where Justices, and their small staffs, work extremely long hours; where the work is sometimes tedious, though always intellectually demanding; where we take our responsibility with the utmost seriousness; and where there is little or no time for socializing.

The constitutional duty of the Court, as John Marshall said in *Marbury v. Madison*, is to "say what the law is." In discharging this function, the Court is the final arbiter, and therefore its role in our system of government is powerful and unique. But it is remote from the mainstream of government.

It is natural, however, to be curious about secrets. For years—perhaps throughout the history of the Court—there have been stories and gossip about secret goings-on behind the Court's closed doors. I recall an article in the *New York Times Magazine* of 16 March 1975 that described the Supreme Court as probably the most "secret society in America."

The fact is that the extent of our secrecy is greatly exaggerated. The doors of the Court are open to the public. Both the press and the public are welcome at all of our argument sessions. Our decisions in the argued cases are printed and widely disseminated.

The charge of secrecy relates only to the discussions, exchanges of views by memoranda, and the drafting that precede our judgments and published opinions. As lawyers know, we get together almost every Friday to discuss petitions by litigants

Acknowledgment to Justice Lewis F. Powell Jr. for his remarks delivered at the Southwestern Legal Foundation (May 1, 1980).

who wish us to hear their cases, and to debate and vote tentatively on the argued cases. Only Justices attend these conferences. There are no law clerks, no secretaries, and no tape recorders—at least none of which we have knowledge.

The Chief Justice, and the most junior Justice, have the responsibility of recording our votes. These votes always are tentative until the cases are finally decided and brought down. Each Justice may—and usually does—keep his own notes at Conference.

We rarely discuss cases with each other before going to Conference. After a tentative vote has been taken, the drafting of opinions is assigned to the individual Justices. When a Justice is satisfied with his draft, he circulates it to the other Chambers. Comments usually are made by exchanges of memoranda, although we feel free to visit Justices and discuss differences. There is less of this than one would like, primarily because of our heavy case load and the logistical difficulties of talking individually to eight other Justices.

The process that I have described actually may take months after a case is argued. The preparation of an opinion often requires painstaking research, drafting, and revising, and additional efforts to resolve differences among Justices to the extent this is feasible.

It is this unstructured and informal process—the making of the decision itself, from the first conference until it is handed down in open Court—that simply cannot take place in public.

The integrity of judicial decision making would be impaired seriously if we had to reach our judgments in the atmosphere of an ongoing town meeting. There must be candid discussion, a willingness to consider arguments advanced by other Justices, and a continuing examination and re-examination of one's own views. The confidentiality of this process assures that we will review carefully the soundness of our judgments. It also improves the quality of our written opinions.[1]

Our decisions concern the liberty, property, and even the lives of litigants. There can be no posturing among us, and no thought of tomorrow's headlines.

I now wish to address two of the current myths about the Court. These have been repeated so often that they have attained a life of their own. One is simply untrue; the other reflects a fundamental misconception of the Court's role.

The nine Justices often are portrayed as fighting and feuding with each other.

This is a wholly inaccurate picture of the relationships at the Court. At the personal level, there is genuine cordiality. No Justice will deny this. We lunch together frequently, visit in each other's homes, celebrate birthdays, and enjoy kidding each other during our long and demanding conferences.

It is true that over the years there have been some fascinating examples of personal animosity on the Court. There are three Justices on the present Court who were law clerks during periods when some notable rivalries existed. Justice John Paul Stevens, one of these former clerks, recently told the Richmond Bar that he had been pleasantly surprised to find no such animosity on the present Court. "Reports to the contrary," he stated, are "simply not true."[2]

The media's erroneous perception of discord on the Court perhaps is based on a failure to distinguish between personal and professional disagreement.[3] Many cases present extremely close and difficult questions of law. Often these questions are intertwined with sensitive collateral judgments or morality and social policy. Examples of such cases include those involving capital punishment, abortions, obscenity, and the vast ramifications of equal protection and civil rights.

We do indeed have strong professional differences about many of our cases. These are exposed for the public to see. Unlike, for example, the Executive Branch, we record fully our disagreements in dissenting opinions. Frequently the language of a dissent is not a model of temperate discourse. We fight hard for our professional views. But, contrary to what one may read, these differences reflect no lack of respect for the Members of the Court with whom we disagree. In the course of a given Term, I find myself more than once in sharp disagreement with every other Justice.

It is fortunate that our system, unlike that in many other countries, invites and respects the function of dissenting opinions. The very process of dissent assures a rigorous testing of the majority view within the Court itself, and reduces the chance of arbitrary decision making. Moreover, as "Court-watchers" know, the forceful dissent of today may attract a majority vote in some future year.

A more substantive misconception concerns the role of the Supreme Court and the way it functions. A national magazine, in an article last July, described the Court as "rudderless, its nine Justices still searching for a theme."[4] Other commentators have said that the Court lacks strong leadership, and has no consistent judicial or ideological philosophy. Those who write this nonsense simply do not understand the responsibilities either of the Supreme Court or of the Chief Justice.[5] In the early years of what is called the Burger Court, one often read that the new Justices would vote consistently as a conservative bloc (the "Nixon bloc") to dismantle the great decisions of the Warren Court.[6] Now that this woeful expectation has not been realized, the criticism is that we are leaderless and unpredictable.

I have wondered whether those who decry the "rudderless Court" would like to be judged by a different kind of court. If, for example, one's liberty were at stake, would he like to be judged by a Court whose members were dominated by a willful Chief Justice? And what confidence could a litigant have in a Court that decided cases according to some consistently applied philosophy or "theme," rather than on the facts of his case and the applicable law?

To be sure, sweeping constitutional phrases such as "due process" and "equal protection of the law" cannot be applied with the exactitude of the rule against perpetuities. And in cases involving these and like phrases, Justices may tend to adhere to what often are called their own "liberal" or "conservative" interpretations. But in the application of these views, judgments are made on a case-by-case basis in light of relevant precedents.

Each of us has an equal vote, and though we endeavor to harmonize our views to reach a Court judgment,[7] the members of this Court vote independently. I do not suggest, however, that we differ in this respect from our predecessors. There is a long tradition at the Court of independent decision making. Indeed, this is the sworn duty of each Justice....

Notes

1. Both litigants and the public could be harmed if total "openness" were to prevail. For example, the decision in an antitrust case may affect the market prices of securities. Unless our initial Conference votes were final, the weeks or months of the opinion-writing process would be a continuous sideshow, with investors uncertain as to what to do. Or in a capital case that involved the death penalty, the condemned defendant would agonize over each memorandum circulated among the Justices.
2. *Richmond Times Dispatch* C–14 (31 January 1980).
3. Misconception as to differences among the Justices is not confined to the media. Law clerks, who are at the Court only for a year and usually have not practiced, may take personally the professional disagreements among us. A clerk's loyalty to his or her Justice tends to be high. This sometimes may cause a clerk—disappointed by the outcome of a particular case—to think harshly of Justices who have disagreed with his or her "boss."
4. *Newsweek* 67 (23 July 1979).
5. They seem to want a court that would take every opportunity to advance some preferred moral, philosophic, or political viewpoint. This would not be a court of law. It would be a supreme legislature—appointed for life. See *Younger v. Harris*, 401 U.S. 37, 52–53 (1971).
6. There was never justification for the alarm about a monolithic "Nixon bloc." The long history of the Court happily makes clear that Justices recognize no obligation to reflect the views of the President who appointed them. Life tenure, and the strong tradition of an independent federal judiciary, have assured this.
7. The Court fairly may be criticized for the increasing number of dissenting and concurring opinions. The diversity of views expressed in some cases reflects not only independence but more often the complexity of the type of cases that now come before us. See Gerald Gunther's "The Highest Court, the Toughest Issues," *Stanford Magazine* 34, 38 (Fall/Winter 1978).

CHAPTER 10

The Supreme Court's Conference

William H. Rehnquist

Chief Justice, Supreme Court of the United States (1986–2005) and Associate Justice (1972–1986)

WHAT I WOULD LIKE to do is to describe in some detail how the Conference of the Supreme Court of the United States operates.

It has been pointed out that the Conference of the Supreme Court is "secret." It is indeed secret, or closed, since only the nine members of the Court are permitted to be present while it is in session. But in order to put the matter in perspective, I would like to point out that a good part of the Court's work is done in public sessions, and that every single case, petition, or application presented to the Court is disposed of by an order entered in the public records of the Court. Let me present a synopsis of our Court's judicial year so that it can be seen how all of this fits together.

Beginning the first week of October in each year, we commence a new Term; we begin the Term by having three days of oral arguments before the full bench, sitting in the public Court Room in the Supreme Court building in Washington. On days of oral argument, the Court generally sits from ten o'clock in the morning until noon, takes an hour for lunch, and returns to the bench at one o'clock in the afternoon and sits until three or a little after. Generally each case which we hear argued is allocated one hour of time, so that in three days we will have heard 12 cases argued. These sessions of oral argument are held in the courtroom and are completely open to the press and to the public.

As soon as we come off the bench Wednesday afternoon around three o'clock, we go into "conference" in a room adjoining the chambers of the Chief Justice.

Acknowledgment to Chief Justice William H. Rehnquist for excerpts from his remarks "The Open and Closed Nature of the U.S. Supreme Court," U.S. Information Service (October 1977).

This Conference is attended only by members of the Court, and at our Wednesday afternoon meeting we deliberate and vote on the four cases which we heard argued the preceding Monday. The Chief Justice begins the discussion of each case with a summary of the facts, his analysis of the law, and an announcement of his proposed vote (that is, whether to affirm, reverse, modify, etc.). The discussion then passes to the senior Associate Justice, who does likewise. It then goes on down the line to the junior Associate Justice. When the discussion of one case is concluded, the discussion of the next one is immediately taken up, until all the argued cases on the agenda for that particular Conference have been disposed of.

On Thursday during a week of oral argument we have neither oral arguments nor Conferences scheduled, but on the Friday of that week we begin a Conference at 9:30 in the morning, go until 12:30 in the afternoon, take 45 minutes for lunch, and return and continue our deliberations until the middle or late part of the afternoon. At this Conference we dispose of the eight cases which we heard argued on the preceding Tuesday and Wednesday, and we likewise dispose of all the petitions for certiorari (a writ from a higher court to a lower one, requesting the record of a case for review) and appeals which are before us that particular week.

Our jurisdiction to hear and decide cases on the merits is largely a discretionary one, rather than an obligatory one, and therefore the fact that we are asked to review many more cases during a particular year in the 1970s than we were in a particular year in the 1950s does not mean that we will necessarily hear and decide more cases on their merits in the more recent years. Our Friday Conference thus serves two separate purposes. First, as I have indicated, we vote and dispose of eight cases on the merits which we have heard orally argued earlier in the week. But at the same Conference we pass on what may be anywhere from 80 to 100 petitions for certiorari or appeals, usually not to decide them on their merits, but simply to decide whether we will grant plenary review and hear them argued at some later time. And while it requires a majority of the Court to dispose of a case one way or the other that has been argued on the merits, it requires only the votes of four of the nine members of the Court in order to grant a petition for certiorari in order that a case may be argued on the merits.

Thus a week of oral argument is composed of three public sessions, each lasting for about four hours, together with two closed Conferences which may together occupy anywhere from six to eight or nine hours. The Court's calendar usually puts two weeks of oral arguments such as this in a row, and at the end of such a two-week period we will have by our Conference votes tentatively decided somewhere between 20 and 24 cases on the merits. At the beginning of the week following the two-week sessions of oral arguments, the Chief Justice circulates to the other members of the Court an Assignment List, in which he assigns for the writing of a Court opinion all of the cases in which he voted with the Conference majority. Where the Chief Justice was in the minority, the senior Associate Justice voting with the majority assigns the case. This means that at the end of each two-week argument session, each member of the Court will have either two or possibly three Court opinions to write. In addition, he may well have to plan to write a dissenting or separate concurring opinion expressing the view of the minority or his own views in a particular case.

During the Recess following the two weeks of oral argument, a part of the time of the Justices and the law clerks and secretaries is devoted to preparation of the opinions which are to be written for the Court, preparation of dissenting opinions, and study of opinions circulated by other Justices. But a large amount of time during each Recess must likewise be spent in preparation for the next round of oral arguments, as well as preparation for the continued weekly Conferences dealing with the petitions for certiorari and appeals. Typically, during each Term of the Court, we schedule roughly 14 weeks of oral argument, beginning the first week in October and ending the last week in April. As the opinions in the cases heard early in the Term are written, circulated, and obtain a majority within the Court, and whatever dissenting views respecting them are likewise circulated, the Friday Conference will decide that such a case is ready to "come down." This means that immediately after we go on the bench at ten o'clock in the morning for a day of oral argument, the Justice who has written the opinion will briefly summarize the holding of the case and the Clerk of the Court will make copies of the Court opinion and dissenting opinions available to the public. Before this particular moment, all of the drafting, changing, and circularizing within the Court are regarded as absolutely confidential; the minute the opinion is handed down, it is available to the public and subscribers to a publication such as *Law Week* may obtain its full text in a matter of days.

A fair summary of the process I have described, it seems to me, is that in all of the 150 or so cases which the Court decides on the merits each Term the public is furnished not only the result reached, but each member of the Court joins one or another opinion in the case expressing his views on the questions raised. What is not available to the public is the internal deliberations which have taken place within the Court, or within each Justice's chambers, which have led to the reaching of this particular result. With respect to the decisions to grant or deny certiorari, or to summarily affirm or dismiss appeals, the result but not the reasoning is available to the public. The reason for the difference is essentially, I think, not a desire to conceal from the public the reasons for these latter dispositions, but rather the fact that because there are around 4,000 of them, as opposed to 150 decisions on the merits, there simply is not the time available to formulate statements of reasons why review is denied or appeals are affirmed or dismissed without argument.

On the basis of my experience in sitting in on these deliberations, I have no hesitation in saying that the Court's Conference is a somewhat fragile institution. It is virtually unique in my experience in government in that the nine principals whose commissions authorize them to decide the cases before them are the only persons in attendance; no law clerks, no secretaries, no marshals, clerks, messengers, or pages, are present. The result of this fact is twofold. First, it permits a remarkably candid exchange of views among the members of the Conference. This candor undoubtedly advances the purpose of the Conference in resolving the cases before it. No one feels at all inhibited by the possibility that any of his remarks will be quoted outside of the Conference Room, or that any of his half formed or ill conceived ideas, which all of us have at times, will be later held up to public ridicule. I think this fact is generally recognized, and it is, I believe, a consideration of some importance.

But the second equally important aspect of the nature of the Conference is that it forces each member of the Court to prepare himself for the Conference deliberation. All of us discuss the matters which will be coming up at Conference with our law clerks, and in the best tradition of our profession try to find good counsel from briefs, arguments, and research in the course of making up our minds. But the knowledge that once in the Conference it is our own presentation, and not that of one of our staff, which must be depended on, does make a difference in the way the Conference functions.

On a typical Friday, we will spend anywhere from five to seven hours arguing, exhorting, and at least figuratively gnashing our teeth over a series of cases that must be decided that day. As is evident from the written opinions which emanate from the Court, there are within the Court the most serious disagreements as to important constitutional principles. Yet day in and day out, week in and week out, year in and year out, a cordiality prevails among the individual members of the Court which transcends any differences there may be with respect to the decision in any particular case or group of cases.

Our ultimate dispositions of the cases we decide, and the divisions among us in making those dispositions, are of course a matter of record in the opinions which are filed. But there we have had the benefit of more careful deliberation and fine tuning, and an opportunity for second thoughts about what might have been hasty reactions to the views of our colleagues.

CHAPTER 11

Deciding What to Decide
The Docket and the Rule of Four

John Paul Stevens
Justice, Supreme Court of the United States (1975–)
and Judge, U.S. Court of Appeals, Seventh Circuit (1970–1975)

WHENEVER FOUR JUSTICES of the United States Supreme Court vote to grant a petition for a writ of certiorari, the petition is granted even though a majority of the Court votes to deny. Although the origins of this so-called Rule of Four are somewhat obscure, it was first publicly described by the justices who testified in support of the judges' bill that became the Judiciary Act of 1925.[1] That Act enabled the Supreme Court to cope with the "utterly impossible" task of deciding the merits of every case on its crowded docket.[2] The Act alleviated the Court's problem by giving it the power to refuse to hear most of the cases on its docket.[3] Since 1925, most of the cases brought to the Supreme Court have been by way of a petition for a writ of certiorari—a petition which requests the Court to exercise its discretion to hear the case on the merits—rather than by a writ of error or an appeal requiring the Court to decide the merits.

In their testimony in support of the judges' bill, members of the Court explained that they had exercised discretionary jurisdiction in a limited number of federal cases since 1891 when the Circuit Courts of Appeals were created,[4] and also in a limited number of cases arising in the state courts since 1914.[5] They described in some detail the procedures they had followed in processing their discretionary docket, and made it clear that they intended to continue to follow those practices

---

Acknowledgment to Justice John Paul Stevens for an excerpt from the James Madison Lecture, New York University School of Law (October 27,1982), which was published in 58 New York University Law Review *1 (1983).*

in managing the enlarged certiorari jurisdiction that would be created by the enactment of the judges' bill.

Several features of the Court's practice were emphasized in order to demonstrate that the discretionary docket was being processed in a responsible, nonarbitrary way.[6] These four are particularly worthy of note:(1) Copies of the printed record, as well as the briefs, were distributed to every justice;[7] (2) every justice personally examined the papers and prepared a memorandum or note indicating his view of what should be done;[8] 3) each petition was discussed by each justice at conference;[9] and (4) a vote was taken, and if four, or sometimes just three, justices thought the case should be heard on its merits, the petition was granted.[10] In his testimony, Justice Van Devanter pointed out that in the 1922 and 1923 Terms the Court had acted on 398 and 370 petitions respectively.[11] Since these figures indicate that the Court was processing only a handful of certiorari petitions each week, it is fair to infer that the practice of making an individual review and having a full conference discussion of every petition was not particularly burdensome. Indeed, at that time the number was so small that the Court was then contemplating the possibility of granting an oral hearing on every petition for certiorari.[12] Times have changed and so have the Court's practices.

In the 1947 Term, when I served as a law clerk to Justice Rutledge, the practice of discussing every certiorari petition at conference had been discontinued. It was then the practice for the Chief Justice to circulate a so-called dead list identifying the cases deemed unworthy of conference discussion. Any member of the Court could remove a case from the dead list, but unless such action was taken, the petition would be denied without even being mentioned at conference.

In the 1975 Term, when I joined the Court, I found that other significant procedural changes had occurred. The "dead list" had been replaced by a "discuss list"; now the Chief Justice circulates a list of cases that he deems worthy of discussion and each of the other members of the Court may add cases to that list. In a sense, the discuss list practice is the functional equivalent of the dead list practice, but there is a symbolic difference. In 1925, every case was discussed; in 1947, every case was discussed unless it was on the dead list; today, no case is discussed unless it is placed on a special list.

Other changes have also occurred. It is no longer true that the record in the court below is routinely filed with the certiorari petition. It is no longer true that every justice personally examines the original papers in every case. Published dissents from denials of certiorari were unknown in 1925 but are now a regular occurrence.[13] Today law clerks prepare so-called pool memos that are used by several justices in evaluating certiorari petitions. The pool memo practice may be an entirely proper response to an increase in the volume of certiorari petitions from seven or eight per week when the judges' bill was passed in 1925 to approximately

100 per week at the present time. It is nevertheless noteworthy that it is a significant departure from the practice that was explained to the Congress in 1924.

The rule that four affirmative votes are sufficient to grant certiorari has, however, survived without change. Indeed, its wisdom has seldom, if ever, been questioned.

During most of the period in which the Rule of Four was developed, the Court had more capacity than it needed to dispose of its argument docket. The existence of the rule in 1924 provided a persuasive response to the concern—expressed before the judge's bill was enacted—that the Court might not accept enough cases for review if its discretionary docket were enlarged. In my judgment, it is the opposite concern that is now dominant. For I think it is clear that the Court now takes far too many cases. Indeed, I am persuaded that throughout its history since the enactment of the judges' bill in 1925, any mismanagement of the Court's docket has been in the direction of taking too many, rather than too few, cases.

In his talk on *stare decisis* in 1944, Justice Jackson noted that the substitution of discretionary in place of mandatory jurisdiction had failed to cure the problem of overloading because judges found it so difficult to resist the temptation to correct perceived error or to take on an interesting question despite its lack of general importance.[14] In a letter written to Senator Wheeler in 1937 describing the workload of the Supreme Court, Chief Justice Hughes, after noting that less than 20 percent of the certiorari petitions raised substantial questions, stated: "I think that it is the view of the members of the Court that if any error is made in dealing with these applications it is on the side of liberality."[15] In a recent letter Paul Freund, who served as Justice Brandeis's law clerk in 1932, advised me that the Justice "believed the Court was granting review in too many cases—not only because of their relative unimportance for the development or clarification of the law but because they deprived the Court of time to pursue the really significant cases with adequate reflection and in sufficient depth."[16]

It can be demonstrated that the Rule of Four has had a significant impact on the number of cases that the Court has reviewed on their merits. A study of Justice Burton's docket book for the 1946 and 1947 Terms reveals that in each of those Terms the decision to grant certiorari was supported by no more than four votes in over 25 percent of the granted cases.[17] It is, of course, possible that in some of those cases a justice who voted to deny might have voted otherwise under a Rule of Five, but it does seem fair to infer that the Rule of Four had significant impact on the aggregate number of cases granted.

A review of my own docket sheets for the 1979, 1980, and 1981 Terms confirms this conclusion. No more than four affirmative votes resulted in granting over 23 percent of the petitions granted in the 1979 Term, over 30 percent of those granted in the 1980 Term, and about 29 percent of those granted in the 1981 Term.[18] In my judgment, these are significant percentages. If all—or even most—of those petitions had been denied, the number of cases scheduled for argument on the merits this Term would be well within the range that all justices consider acceptable.

Mere numbers, however, provide an inadequate measure of the significance of the cases that were heard because of the rule. For I am sure that some Court opinions in cases that were granted by only four votes have made a valuable contribution to the development of our jurisprudence. My experience has persuaded me, however, that such cases are exceptionally rare. I am convinced that a careful study of all of the cases that have been granted on the basis of only four votes would indicate that in a surprisingly large number the law would have fared just as well if the decision of the court of appeals or the state court had been allowed to stand.[19] To enable interested scholars to consider the validity of this judgment, I have prepared footnotes listing 26 cases granted by a mere four votes in the 1946 Term[20] and 36 such cases granted in the 1979 Term.[21]

The rule is sometimes justified by the suggestion that if four justices of the Supreme Court consider a case important enough to warrant full briefing and argument on the merits, that should be sufficient evidence of the significance of the question presented.[22] But a countervailing argument has at least equal force. Every case that is granted on the basis of four votes is a case that five members of the Court thought should not be granted.[23] For the most significant work of the Court, it is assumed that the collective judgment of its majority is more reliable than the views of the minority.[24] Arguably, therefore, deference to the minority's desire to add additional cases to the argument docket may rest on an assumption that whether the Court hears a few more or a few less cases in any term is not a matter of first importance.[25]

Notes

1. 43 Stat. 936.
2. On 18 December 1924, Justice McReynolds testified before the Committee on the Judiciary of the House of Representatives as follows: "Every year now Congress is passing many acts and every act that is passed probably sooner or later will come to us in some one or other of its aspects. The more Federal acts there are the more opportunities there are of bringing cases to us, and it has been growing and growing until it is utterly impossible for us to try every case in which there is a Federal question involved. So it must be determined whether the court will slip behind and delays will increase or whether the number of cases presented to the court shall be restricted." *Hearings on H.R. 8206 before the Committee on the Judiciary,* 68th Cong., 2d Sess., 20 (1924) (hereinafter "House Hearings").
3. "For the three terms preceding [the 1925 Act] 80 percent of the cases came to the Court

as a matter of course, regardless of the Court's judgment as to the seriousness of the questions at issue. In less than twenty percent did the Court exercise discretion in assuming jurisdiction." F. Frankfurter and J. Landis, "The Supreme Court Under the Judiciary Act of 1925," 42 *Harvard Law Review* 10–11 (1928).

4. William Howard Taft described the background of the 1891 Act as follows: "At the centenary celebration of the launching of the Federal Constitution in Philadelphia, the addresses of the Justices of the Supreme Court and of the distinguished members of the Bar contained urgent appeals to Congress to relieve the Court, which was then considerably more than three years behind. "Congress sought to remove the congestion by the Act of March 3d, 1891 [26 Stat. 826]. It created nine Circuit Courts of Appeals as intermediate courts of review.... "In the Act of 1891, Congress for the first time conferred upon the Supreme Court, in extensive classes of litigation, discretion to decline to review cases if they did not seem to the Court to be worthy of further review. In this discretionary jurisdiction the most numerous class of cases was of those which depended upon the diverse citizenship of the parties as the basis of federal jurisdiction." W. Taft, "The Jurisdiction of the Supreme Court Under the Act of February 13, 1925," 35 *Yale Law Journal* 2 (1925).
5. Justice Van Devanter testified: "Then, we have the cases coming from the State courts. For a great many years cases came from the State courts on writ of error only to the Supreme Court, the cases being those in which there were Federal questions which were decided adversely to the litigant asserting the Federal right. The statute was changed about 1914 so as to permit the Supreme Court to take cases on petitions for certiorari where the Federal question was decided in favor of the Federal right. That situation continued until 1916, when a statute was enacted which enlarged the number of cases that could come on petition for certiorari from State courts, and decreased accordingly the number that could come on writ of error." *Hearings on S.* 2060 *and* 2061 *before a Subcomm. of the Committee on the Judiciary,* 68th Cong., 1st Sess., 34 (1924) (hereinafter "Senate Hearings"). The Evarts Act, enacted in 1916, 39 Stat. 726, removed cases arising under the Federal Employers Liability Act from those which the Court was statutorily required to hear and thereby made a substantial enlargement in the Court's discretionary docket. Nevertheless, it remained true that over 80 percent of the Court's docket was obligatory rather than discretionary.
6. For example, Chief Justice Taft testified: "I heard the late Philander Knox, with whom I was on intimate terms, say either to me or to some one in my hearing, a word or two indicating that he thought the question of whether a case got in by certiorari or not was governed by the temperament, the digestion, and the good nature of the particular person in the court to whom the question was referred, that it was distributed in some way so that each member of the court had two or three certioraris that it could let in.

   "Now, the truth is, and I want to emphasize that because I think perhaps I have more to do with certioraris in one way than any other member of the court, because I have to make the first statement of the case when a certiorari comes up for disposition; I write out every case that comes up for certiorari and I read it to the court. I think the members of the court are a little impatient sometimes because I give too much detail. Perhaps that is because I am a new member or was a new member. And then having stated the case I go around and ask each member of the court, who has his memorandum, as to what view he takes. Then having discussed the case we vote on it." House Hearings, supra note 2, at 26–27.

7. Justice Van Devanter testified: "The petition and brief are required to be served on the other party, and time is given for the presentation of an opposing brief. When this has been done copies of the printed record as it came from the circuit court of appeals and of the petition and briefs are distributed among the members of the Supreme Court...." House Hearings, supra note 2, at 8.
8. Justice Van Devanter unequivocally stated that "each judge examines them and prepares a memorandum or note indicating his view of what should be done." Ibid.
9. "In conference these cases are called, each in its turn, and each judge states his views *in extenso* or briefly as he thinks proper; and when all have spoken any difference in opinion is discussed and then a vote is taken. I explain this at some length because it seems to be thought outside that the cases are referred to particular judges, as, for instance, that those coming from a particular circuit are referred to the justice assigned to that circuit, and that he reports on them, and the others accept his report. That impression is wholly at variance with what actually occurs." Chief Justice Taft elaborated on the procedure (see supra note 6).
10. Reading the legislative history in its entirety, I gain the impression that the principal emphasis in the presentation made by the justices concentrated on the individual attention given to every petition by every justice and the full discussion of every petition at conference, and that significantly less emphasis was placed on the Rule of Four. House Hearings, supra note 2, at 8.
11. House Hearings, supra note 2, at 13. In *Southern Power Co. v. North Carolina Public Service Co.*, 263 U.S. 508, 509, the Court noted that 420 petitions for certiorari had been filed during the 1922 Term. However the difference between this figure and the figures mentioned by Justice Van Devanter may be explained (possibly by a difference between filings and dispositions), it is plain that the Court was required to deal with relatively few petitions each week.
12. Shortly after the enactment of the 1925 Act, Chief Justice Taft wrote: "A question has been under consideration by the Court as to whether it would be practical to give oral hearings to applications for certioraris. The changes in the new Act will doubtless increase the number of these applications, and if the Court could be relieved by short oral statements of the burden of close examination of briefs and records, it might help its disposition of the business and at the same time give assurance to counsel of the fact, which seems sometimes to have been doubted, that the full Court seriously considers every application for a certiorari and votes upon it as a real issue to be judicially determined. If there are to be five hundred applications for certiorari a year (a conservative estimate), and ten minutes should be allowed to a side, this would consume, if all the applications were orally presented and opposed, eight weeks of the oral sessions of the Court. The Court gives about eighteen weeks to oral sessions during an annual term, so that it would take a little less than one-half of the oral sessions devoted by the Court to argument. Of course it is suggested that even if argument were permitted, advantage would not be taken in many cases in which briefs would be solely relied on. An experiment of a week or two at the beginning of the term might possibly enable the Court to judge more safely as to this. I fear, however, that the experiment would show to be

true what Senator Cummins said upon the floor of the Senate, when it was proposed to require oral hearings of certiorari applications, that we might just as well not pass the law at all." Taft, supra note 4, at 12.

13. I have previously commented on this use of the Court's scarce resources. See *Singleton v. Commissioner,* 439 U.S. 942 (Opinion of Stevens, J., respecting the denial of the petition for writ of certiorari).
14. "We once thought that substitution of discretionary in place of mandatory jurisdiction would cure overloading. It has helped greatly. But the burden of passing on petitions invoking discretion is considerable, and the temptation to judges is great to take hold of any result that strikes them as wrong or any question that is interesting, even if not of general importance. The fact is that neither the judges nor the profession have whole-heartedly and consistently accepted the implications of discretionary jurisdiction in courts of last resort." R. Jackson, "Decisional Law and Stare Decisis," 30 *American Bar Association Journal* 334 (1944).
15. Letter from Chief Justice Charles Evans Hughes to Senator Burton K. Wheeler (21 March 1937).
16. Letter from Paul A. Freund to John Paul Stevens (24 August 1982). I found that comment of particular interest because one of the points made in Justice Brandeis's criticism of the *Jensen* rule in his dissent in *Washington v. Dawson Co.,* 264 U.S., at 237—an opinion that was written while the judges' bill was under consideration—was that adherence to the *Jensen* rule would "make a serious addition to the classes of cases which this Court is required to review."
17. Harold Burton Papers, Manuscript Division, Library of Congress.
18. I am indebted to my law clerks, Carol Lee and Jeffrey Lehman, for assembling this data from Justice Burton's records and from my docket sheets, for identifying the cases listed in notes 20 and 21, infra, and for making a number of valuable criticisms of the text of these remarks. I am also indebted to my former law clerk Matthew Verschelden for valuable research assistance concerning the doctrine of *stare decisis.*
19. "It is interesting to note that the impression gained by Judge Henry J. Friendly from thumbing the volumes of 'a generation ago' is that the Court was deciding a good many cases not meriting its attention—as several Justices thought." H.J. Friendly, *Federal Jurisdiction: A General View* 51 (New York: Columbia University Press, 1973).
20. *Confederated Bands of Ute Indians v. United States, aff'd.,* 330 U.S. 169; *Albrecht v. United States, aff'd.,* 329 U.S. 599; *Land v. Dollar, aff'd.* unanimously, 330 U.S. 731; *Transparent-Wrap Mach. Corp. v. Stokes & Smith Co., rev'd.* 5–4, 329 U.S. 637; *Adams v. Commissioner, aff'd.,* 332 U.S. 752; *United States v. Standard Oil, aff'd.,* 332 U.S. 301; *Bazley v. Commissioner, aff'd.,* 331 U.S. 737; *Ellis v. Union Pacific R.R., rev'd.* 8–1, 329 U.S. 649; *Fay v. New York, aff'd.,* 332 U.S. 261; *Mexican Light & Power v. Texas Mexican R.R., aff'd.,* 331 U.S. 731; *NLRB v. Jones & Laughlin Steel, rev'd.,* 331 U.S. 416; *Penfield Co. v. SEC, aff'd.,* in part, 330 U.S. 585; *Foster v. Illinois, aff'd.,* 332 U.S. 134; *Rutherford Food v. McComb, aff'd.* 8–1, 331 U.S. 722; *United States v. Bayer,* rev'd., 331 U.S. 532; *Champion Spark Plug v. Sanders, aff'd.* 9–0, 331 U.S. 125; *Oklahoma v. United States, aff'd.* per curiam, 331 U.S. 788; *Interstate Natural Gas v. FPC, aff'd.* 6–2, 331 U.S. 682; *McCullough v. Krammerer Corp., rev'd.* 5–4, 331 U.S. 96; *Wade v. Mayo* (IFP), *rev'd.,* 334 U.S. 672; *Oyama v. California,*

rev'd., 332 U.S. 633; *Haley v. Ohio, rev'd.*, 332 U.S. 596; *Local* 2880 *v. NLRB*, dismissed voluntarily on motion; *Blumenthal v. United States, aff'd.*, 332 U.S. 539; *United States v. Fried*, dismissed voluntarily on motion; *Price v. Johnson, rev'd.*, 334 U.S. 266.

21. *Sears v. County of Los Angeles, aff'd.* by eq. div. ct.; *Walker v. Armco Steel*, 446 U.S. 740; *Nachman v. Pension Benefit Guaranty Corp.*, 446 U.S. 359; *United States v. Clarke*, 445 U.S. 253; *Roberts v. United States*, 445 U.S. 552; *Thomas v. Washington Gas Light*, 448 U.S. 261; *NY Gaslight Club v. Carey*, 447 U.S. 54; *EPA v. National Crushed Stone Assn.*, 449 U.S. 64; *Fedorenko v. United States*, 449 U.S. 490; *Firestone v. Risjord*, 449 U.S. 368; *Cuyler v. Adams*, 449 U.S. 433; *Massachusetts v. Meehan*, 445 U.S. 39; *Larocca v. United States*, 446 U.S. 398; *Andrus v. Glover*, 446 U.S. 608; *Walter v. United States*, 447 U.S. 649; *California Retail Liquor v. Midcal Alum.*, 449 U.S. 97; *Diamond v. Chakrabarty*, 447 U.S. 303; *Standefer v. United States*, 447 U.S. 10; *United States v. Sioux Nation*, 448 U.S. 371; *Dawson Chemical v. Rohm and Haas*, 448 U.S. 176; *Reeves v. Stake*, 447 U.S. 429; *Maine v. Thiboutot*, 448 U.S. 1; *Northwest Airlines v. Transport Workers Union*, 451 U.S. 77; *Minnick v. Cal. Dept. of Corrections*, 452 U.S. 105; *Michael M. v. Sup. Ct. of Sonoma Cty.*, 450 U.S. 464; *Rawlings v. Kentucky*, 448 U.S. 98; *United States v. Cortez*, 449 U.S. 411; *Memphis v. Greene*, 451 U.S. 100; *Republic Steel v. OSHA*, (dismissed pursuant to Rule 53); *Andrus v. Utah*, 446 U.S. 500; *Andrus v. Shell Oil*, 446 US. 657; *Cuyler v. Sullivan*, 446 U.S. 335; *Maher v. Gagne*, 448 U.S. 122; *United States v. Henry*, 447 U.S. 264; *Roadway Express v. Piper*, 447 U.S. 752; *Watkins v. Sowders*, 449 U.S. 341.
The fact that there may be significant cases listed above and in note 20 does not necessarily demonstrate the value of the Rule of Four, because the significant issues decided in these cases might well have come before the Court in other litigation in due course. The frequency with which an issue arises is one measure of its significance.
22. See House Hearings, supra note 2, at 8.
23. It is of interest to note that another distinguished tribunal with a comparable volume of business and comparable discretionary control over its docket follows a majority vote case selection rule. Over 5,000 petitions for review are filed in the California Supreme Court each year. I am told that that court follows a selection process of dividing the petitions into an "A" list and a "B" list, and that only the cases on one of those lists are discussed in conference. They also follow a Rule of Four, but since there are only seven justices on that court, that number represents a majority.
24. In an uncharacteristic slip during the interval between his service as an Associate Justice and his service as Chief Justice, Charles Evans Hughes inadvertently "observed that in the routine, every action of the Court is taken on the concurrence of a majority of its members." C. Hughes, *The Supreme Court of the United States* 56–57 (New York: Columbia University Press, 1928). I wonder if subconsciously the Chief Justice regarded the processing of certiorari petitions as a form of "second class work." Cf. Stevens, "Some Thoughts on Judicial Restraint," 66 *Judicature* 172 (1982).
25. A question raised in 1959 by Professor Henry M. Hart Jr. puts the problem of numbers in proper perspective: "Does a nation of 165 million realize any significant gain merely because its highest judicial tribunal succeeds in deciding 127 cases by full opinion instead of 117? 137 cases? 147 cases? Or even 157 cases? The hard fact must be

faced that the Justices of the Supreme Court of the United States can at best put their full minds to no more than a tiny handful of the trouble cases which year by year are tossed up to them out of the great sea of millions and even billions of concrete situations to which their opinions relate. When this fact is fully apprehended, it will be seen that the question whether this handful includes or excludes a dozen or so more cases is unimportant. It will be seen that what matters about Supreme Court opinions is not their quantity but their quality." H. Hart, Foreword: "The Time Chart of the Justices," 73 *Harvard Law Review* 73 (1958).

CHAPTER 12

The Role of Oral Argument

John M. Harlan II
Justice, Supreme Court of the United States (1955–1971) and Judge, U.S Court of Appeals, Second Circuit (1954–1955)

I THINK THAT there is some tendency ... to regard the oral argument as little more than a traditionally tolerated part of the appellate process. The view is widespread that when a court comes to the hard business of decision, it is the briefs, and not the oral argument, which count. I think that view is a greatly mistaken one....

First of all, judges have different work habits. There are judges who listen better than they read and who are more receptive to the spoken word than the written word.

Secondly, the first impressions that a judge gets of a case are very tenacious. They frequently persist into the conference room. And those impressions are usually gained from the oral argument, if it is an effective job. While I was on the court of appeals, I kept a sort of informal scoreboard of the cases in which I sat, so as to match up the initial reactions which I had to the cases after the close of the oral argument with the final conclusions that I had reached when it came time to vote at the conferences on the decision of those cases. I was astonished to find during the year I sat on that court how frequently—in fact, more times than not—the views which I had at the end of the day's session jibed with the final views that I formed after the more careful study of the briefs which, under our system in the Second Circuit, came in the period between the closing of the arguments and the voting at the conference.

Thirdly, the decisional process in many courts places a special burden on the oral argument. I am giving away no secrets, I am sure, when I say that in one of the

---

Acknowledgment to Cornell University Law Review *for permission to reprint portions of "The Role of Oral Argument," by Justice John M. Harlan II, from 41* Cornell Law Review *6 (1955), © Cornell University.*

courts of appeals where I was assigned to sit temporarily the voting on the cases took place each day following the close of the arguments. In the Supreme Court, our practice, as is well known, has been to hold our conferences at the end of each week of arguments. They have been on Saturdays up until now, but under a more enlightened schedule they will be on Fridays next term, because beginning October we are going to sit four days a week. Under either of those systems you can see the importance which the oral argument assumes.

Fourth, and to me this is one of the most important things, the job of courts is not merely one of an umpire in disputes between litigants. Their job is to search out the truth, both as to the facts and the law, and that is ultimately the job of the lawyers, too. And in that joint effort, the oral argument gives an opportunity for interchange between court and counsel which the briefs do not give. For my part, there is no substitute, even within the time limits afforded by the busy calendars of modern appellate courts, for the Socratic method of procedure in getting at the real heart of an issue and in finding out where the truth lies.

Now, let me turn for a moment to some of the factors which seem to me to make for effective oral arguments. The art of advocacy—and it is an art—is a purely personal effort, and as such, any oral argument is an individualistic performance. Each lawyer must proceed according to his own lights, and if he tries to cast himself in the image of another, he is likely to become uneasy, artificial, and unpersuasive. But after you make allowance for the special talents of individuals, their different methods of handling arguments, their different techniques, it seems to me that there are four characteristics which will be found in every effective oral argument, and they are these: *first*, what I would call "selectivity"; *second*, what I would designate as "simplicity"; *third*, "candor"; and *fourth*, what I would term "resiliency." Let me address myself briefly to each.

By "selectivity," I mean a lawyer's selection of the issues to be argued. There is rarely a case which lends itself to argument of all of the issues within the normal time limitations upon oral argument. On the other hand, there is hardly a case, however complicated, where, by some selection of the issues to be argued, one hour is not enough. I am not talking about the unusual type of case, which we have from time to time in all courts, where in the nature of things extra time is essential. But in most cases, I think, the skillful advocate would not want more time for oral argument than the ordinary rules of court permit. However, it often happens that lawyers who attempt to cover *all* of the issues in the case find themselves left with the uncomfortable feeling that they have failed to deal with any of the issues adequately. You will find that thoughtful selection of the issues to be argued orally is a basic technique of every good appellate advocate.

Most cases have one or only a few master issues. In planning his oral argument the wise lawyer will ferret out and limit himself to the issues which are really controlling, and will leave the less important or subordinate issues to the court's own study of the briefs. Otherwise, one is apt to get tanglefoot, and the court is left pretty much where it began.

The next thing I refer to is "simplicity." Simplicity of presentation and expression, you will find, is a characteristic of every effective oral argument. In the instances where that quality is lacking, it is usually attributable to one of two reasons—lack of preparation or poor selection of the issues to be argued. There are some issues that do not lend themselves to oral argument as well as they do to written presentation. The preparation of an oral argument is a good deal more than merely making a short form summary of the briefs. An oral argument which is no more than that really adds nothing to a lawyer's cause.

The process of preparation that the appellate advocate undergoes involves, *first*, the selection of the issues he will argue; *second*, a marshaling of the premises on which those issues depend; *third*, planning the structure of his argument; and, *fourth*, deciding how he shall express his argument. It is sometimes forgotten by a lawyer who is full of his case, that the court comes to it without the background that he has. And it is important to bear this in mind in carrying out the preparation for argument in each of its phases. Otherwise the force of some point which may seem so clear to the lawyer may be lost upon the court.

The third thing which is of the essence of good advocacy is "candor." There is rarely a case, however strong, that does not have its weak points. And I do not know any way of meeting a weak point except to face up to it. It is extraordinary the number of instances one sees where through a question from the court or the argument of one's adversary a vulnerable point is laid bare, and the wounded lawyer ducks, dodges, and twists, instead of facing up to the point four square. Attempted evasion in an oral argument is a cardinal sin. No answer to an embarrassing point is better than an evasive one. With a court, lack of candor in meeting a difficult issue of fact or of law goes far to destroying the effectiveness of a lawyer's argument, not merely as to the point of embarrassment, but often as to other points on which he should have the better of it. For if a lawyer loses the confidence of the court, he is apt to end up almost anywhere.

The fourth and final thing which I have suggested goes to the root of a good oral argument is "resiliency." For some reason that I have never been able to understand, many lawyers regard questioning by the court as a kind of subversive intrusion. And yet, when one comes to sit on the other side of the bar, he finds very quickly that the answer made to a vital question may be more persuasive in leading the court to the right result than the most eloquent of oral arguments. I think that a lawyer, instead of shunning questions by the court, should welcome them. If a court sits through an oral argument without asking any questions, it is often a pretty fair indication that the argument has been either dull or unconvincing.

I am mindful, of course, that the court's privilege of asking questions is sometimes abused, and that often the price a lawyer has to pay is some interruption in the continuity of his argument, and perhaps some discomfiture—and in extreme instances perhaps never getting through with what he had planned to say. And yet, I think that the price is well worth what the lawyer may have to pay in the loss of the smooth-flowing quality he would like his argument to have. A lawyer can make no greater mistake, I can assure you, in answering questions by the court than to attempt to preserve the continuity of his argument by saying: "Judge, I have dealt with that in my brief" or by telling the judge who asks the question that he will come to it "later"—usually he never does. Even if the lawyer does come back to the question later on, the force of his answer, if it is a good one, and often also of his argument in other aspects where he perhaps is in a stronger position, is usually lost—at least upon the judge who has asked the question.

No doubt some judges ask too many questions, and I hasten to say, again as one freshly from the trial bar, that I am one of those who believe that competent lawyers ought to be allowed to try their cases and argue their appeals in their own fashion. Where an over-enthusiastic judge exceeds the bounds of what the lawyer might consider fair interruption, the lawyer will have to handle that problem for himself. I can tell you, however, how two lawyers, one a freshman and the other a seasoned barrister, dealt with such a situation. The freshman lawyer was trying his first case, a negligence case in which his client, the plaintiff, was a lovely young lady. Of course, he called her as the first witness. After the young man had gotten his client's name, age, and address on the record, the court interrupted and started to ask questions. The young lawyer stood first on one foot and then on the other as the court's questioning continued. He finally sat down, and in due course the court came to the end of his questioning and said: "Counselor, you may now continue with the witness. Proceed." The young man arose and said: "If your Honor please, I have no more questions to ask because I think the court has covered my case very thoroughly. But," he added, "I would like to make a statement. If your Honor please, this is my first case, my first client. I have prepared my case thoroughly. I have gone back to the Year Books on the law; I have questioned all eye witnesses to the accident with the greatest care; but if your Honor wants to try this case, it is all right with me, except, for goodness' sake, don't lose it!"

The examination of the more seasoned barrister was interrupted at a sensitive point by a question which the lawyer did not care for. "Have you an objection, counselor?" said the court as the lawyer put on a remonstrative look. "Perhaps, your Honor," replied the lawyer, "but I would first like to inquire on whose behalf your Honor put that question." "What difference would that make, counselor?" asked the court. "All the difference in the world," said the lawyer, "for if your Honor is asking the question on behalf of my opponent, then of course I must object to it, but if your Honor asks the question on my behalf, then I simply withdraw it." . . .

CHAPTER 13

Year-End Report on the Federal Judiciary (2007)

John G. Roberts Jr.

Chief Justice, Supreme Court of the United States (2005–) and Judge, U.S. Court of Appeals, District of Columbia Circuit (2003–2005)

IN RECENT YEARS, even mature democracies with established traditions have modified their judicial systems to incorporate American principles and practices. For example, Great Britain, which exported its common law system to the American colonies some 400 years ago, has recently imported the distinctly American concept of separation of powers. It has transferred the House of Lords' judicial review to an independent Supreme Court. Japan has adopted trial procedures inspired by American jury practice, while South Korea is increasingly employing American-style oral advocacy in its judicial proceedings. But perhaps most important, our federal courts provide the benchmark for emerging democracies that seek to structure their judicial systems to protect basic rights that Americans have long enjoyed as the norm.

Most Americans are far too busy to spend much time pondering the role the United States judiciary—they simply and understandably expect the court system to work.... I ask a moment's reflection on how our country might look in the absence of a skilled and independent judiciary. We do not need to look far beyond our borders, or beyond the front page of any newspaper, to see what is at stake. More than two hundred years after the American Revolution, much of the world

---

Excerpted from Chief Justice John G. Roberts Jr., "2007 Year-End Report on the Federal Judiciary" (January 1, 2008), available at www.supremecourtus.gov.

remains subject to judicial systems that provide doubtful opportunities for challenging government action as contrary to law, or receiving a fair adjudication of criminal charges, or securing a fair remedy for wrongful injury, or protecting rights in property, or obtaining an impartial resolution of a commercial dispute. Many foreign judges cannot exercise independent judgment on matters of law without fear of reprisal or removal.

Americans should take enormous pride in our judicial system. But there is no cause for complacency. Our judicial system inspires the world because of the commitment of each new generation of judges who build upon the vision and accomplishments of those who came before. I am committed to continuing three of my predecessor's important but unfinished initiatives to maintain the quality of our courts.

First, I will carry on the efforts to improve communications with the Executive and Legislative Branches of government. The Constitution's provision for three separate but coordinate Branches envisions that the Branches will communicate through appropriate means on administrative matters of common concern. Each has a valuable perspective on the other. The Branches already engage in constructive dialogue through a number of familiar forums, including the Judicial Conference, congressional hearings, and advisory committee meetings. But the familiar avenues are not necessarily the only ones.

The Judiciary has a special interest, rooted in history, in improving relations with the Legislative Branch. Until 1935, the Congress and the Supreme Court were both housed in the Capitol, and it has been observed that the sharing of common space encouraged mutual understanding, respect, and collegiality even as the legislators and judges performed their distinctly different responsibilities. I am assured that my colleagues are happy in our separate building and not inclined to move back to the Capitol (even were we invited), so I have asked the Administrative Office of the United States Courts to consider other opportunities for improving inter-Branch communication and cooperation. The separate Branches may not always agree on matters of mutual interest, but each should strive, through respectful exchange of insights and ideas, to know and appreciate where the others stand.

Second, I share my predecessor's view that the Judiciary must relentlessly ensure that federal judges maintain the highest standards of integrity. Federal judges hold a position of public trust, and the public has a right to demand that they adhere to a demanding code of conduct. The overwhelming majority do. But for those who do not, the Judiciary must take appropriate action....

Finally, I am resolved to continue Chief Justice Rehnquist's twenty-year pursuit of equitable salaries for federal judges. Over the past year congressional leaders and a wide range of groups that value a capable and independent Judiciary have made progress on this matter. The House Judiciary Committee passed a bill by an overwhelming bipartisan vote of 28 to 5 that would help reverse the steady erosion of judicial salaries since 1969, the benchmark year that Congress has utilized in recent years for assessing federal pay levels....

This salary restoration legislation is vital now that the denial of annual increases over the years has left federal trial judges—the backbone of our system of justice—earning about the same as (and in some cases less than) *first-year lawyers* at firms in major cities, where many of the judges are located.

I do not need to rehearse the compelling arguments in favor of legislation. They have already been made by distinguished jurists, lawyers, and economists in congressional hearings, letters, and editorials—and seconded by a broad spectrum of commercial, governmental, and public interest organizations that appear as litigants before the courts. I simply ask once again for a moment's reflection on how America would look in the absence of a skilled and independent judiciary. Consider the critical role of our courts in preserving individual liberty, promoting commerce, protecting property, and ensuring that every person who appears in an American court can expect fair and impartial justice. The cost of this long overdue legislation—less than .004% of the annual federal budget—is miniscule in comparison to what is at stake....

Part III
The Judiciary and the Constitution

"We are under a constitution," Chief Justice Charles Evans Hughes declared, "but the Constitution is what the judges say it is."[1] The traditionally held view, in Chief Justice John Marshall's words, is that "[c]ourts are the mere instruments of law, and can will nothing."[2] Chief Justice Marshall thereby embraced the traditional view that judges have no power to make law, a view advocated by Alexander Hamilton in *The Federalist,* No. 78 (reprinted in Appendix A), and Sir William Blackstone in his *Commentaries on the Laws of England (1765–1768).*[3] Likewise, Justice Joseph Story, who served on the Court from 1812 to 1845 and also taught at Harvard Law School, in his influential *Commentaries on the Constitution of the United States* (1833), saw no need to offer a theory of constitutional interpretation, explaining that:

> The reader must not expect to find in these pages any novel views and novel construction of the Constitution. I have not the ambition to be the author of any new plan of interpreting the theory of the Constitution, or of enlarging or narrowing its powers by ingenious subtleties and learned doubts.... Upon subjects of government, it has always appeared to me, that metaphysical refinements are out of place. A constitution of government is addressed to the common sense of the people, and never was designed for trials of logical skill or visionary speculation.[4]

Justice Story assumed that "The first and fundamental rule in the interpretation of all instruments is, to construe them according to the sense of the terms and the intention of the parties." Chief Justice Roger Taney similarly held that the Constitution "speaks not only in the same words, but with the same meaning and intent with which it spoke when it came from the hands of its framers.... Any other rule of construction would abrogate the judicial character of this Court, and make it the mere reflex of popular opinion or passion of the day."[5]

That traditional view, however, was questioned in the late nineteenth and early twentieth centuries by the American Legal Realists, who challenged the view that judges are mere oracles of the law and who highlighted the indeterminacy of legal facts and rules. Perhaps the seminal essay advocating Legal Realism remains Oliver Wendell Holmes's lecture "The Path of Law," published in the 1897 *Harvard Law Review* and excerpted in Chapter 14. Delivered while Holmes was a justice on the Supreme Judicial Court of Massachusetts, before his appointment to the Supreme Court of the United States in 1902, it presaged the rise of American Legal Realism. No less influential was Benjamin N. Cardozo's *The Nature of the Judicial Process* (1921), published when he was serving on the New York Court of Appeals (1917–1932), before his service on the Supreme Court (1932–1938). Chapter 15 provides an excerpt of that work dealing with "The Judge as a Legislator." The power to declare the law, Justice Cardozo maintained, "carries with it the power, within limits the duty, to make law when none exists."[6]

The full force of American Legal Realism profoundly changed debates over constitutional interpretation. Still, not all provisions of the Constitution are unambiguous, of course. Interpretation is necessary because the nature of the Constitution, as even Chief Justice Marshall noted, "requires, that only its great outlines should be marked, its important objects designated, and the minor ingredients which compose those objects, be deduced from the nature of the objects themselves."[7] In constitutional interpretation the intent of the Founders provides a guide, but it is often difficult if not impossible to determine the extent of agreement among those who drafted and those who ratified the document in the various state constitutional conventions. Changing political circumstances, furthermore, present new problems that require judicial creativity in constitutional interpretation. Chief Justice William Howard Taft, for one, considered this to be the Court's "highest and most useful function." That "judges should interpret the exact intention of those who established the Constitution," he said, was a "theory of one who does not understand the proper administration of justice." Frequently, he continued, "new conditions arise which those who were responsible for the written law could not have had in view." Rather than "the exercise of legislative power ... [this] is the exercise of a sound judicial discretion in supplementing the provisions ... which are necessarily incomplete or lacking in detail essential to their proper application."[8]

The Supreme Court's dilemma, as Chief Justice Marshall understood so well, lies in "never forget[ting] that it is a *constitution* we are expounding ... [but] a constitution intended to endure for ages to come, and, consequently, to be adapted to the various *crises* of human affairs."[9] Central to the Court's dilemma and the problems of constitutional interpretation is the notion of a living Constitution: whether the Constitution should be construed to meet changing political circumstances, or whether the burden of the Court lies in bringing political controversies within the language, structure, and spirit of the Constitution. The notion of a living Constitution is examined by Chief Justice William Rehnquist and from a different perspective by Chief Judge William Wayne Justice in chapters 16 and 17, respectively. The exchange between Chief Justice Rehnquist and Judge Justice illuminates the relationship between the Court and the Constitution, including some of the perennial issues in constitutional interpretation.

"Do judges make law? Course they do. Made some myself," proclaimed Justice Jeremiah Smith of the New Hampshire Supreme Court.[10] "All judges exercise discretion, individualize abstract rules, make law," Judge Jerome Frank declared.[11] Judicial lawmaking on a case-by-case basis is necessary in common law—law composed of rulings on matters not expressly treated in legislation. Interpretation of federal or state statutes may require judicial legislation as well; for example, when two statutes must be reconciled or when statutory language needs clarification to guide administrative action or the application of law to particular circumstances. In such instances, Justice Holmes said, "Judges do and must legislate, but they can do so only interstitially; they are conned from the molar to molecular motions."[12]

Judicial legislation in constitutional law is another matter according to advocates of "strict constructionism" and a "jurisprudence of original intentions."[13] Judicial creativity is essential to constitutional interpretation, but as Justice Hugo Black, dissenting in *Griswold v. Connecticut*, warned, "unbounded judicial [creativity] would make of this Court's members a day-to-day constitutional convention."[14] The threshold of permissible judicial creativity is crossed, Justice Black argued, when the Court discovers and enforces values that are neither specifically enumerated in, nor fairly traceable to, some provision in the text of the Constitution. Likewise, in 1905 Justice Holmes criticized the majority in *Lochner v. New York* for becoming a superlegislature by inventing a "liberty of contract," thereby enforcing the majority's laissez-faire economic philosophy.[15] Although advocating that the judiciary has a special role in protecting discrete and insular minorities and ensuring access to the political process, Chief Justice Harlan Fiske Stone also lamented: "My more conservative brethren in the old days enacted their own economic prejudice into law. What they did placed in jeopardy a great and useful institution of government. The pendulum has now swung to the other extreme, and history is repeating itself. The Court is now in as much danger of becoming a legislative Constitution-making body, enacting into law its own predilections, as it was then."[16] Similarly, Justice Black cautioned, "when a 'political theory' embodied in our Constitution becomes outdated, it seems to me that a majority of the nine members of this Court are not only without constitutional power but are far less qualified to choose a new constitutional political theory than the people of this country."[17]

"Every Justice has been accused of legislating," Justice Robert Jackson observed, "and every one has joined in that accusation of others."[18] What nevertheless remains essential, as Justice William Brennan pointed out, is that "[t]he Justices are charged with deciding according to law.... And while the Justices may and do consult history and the other disciplines as aids to constitutional decision, the text of the Constitution and relevant precedents dealing with that text are their primary tools."[19]

In a political system based on a written constitution and with an independent judiciary, constitutional interpretation is necessary, judicial creativity important, and judicial lawmaking to some degree inevitable. But in the second Justice John Marshall Harlan's words, "the Constitution does not confer on courts blanket authority to step into every situation where the political branch may be thought to have fallen short."[20] Given the role of the judiciary in a system of free government, and the difficulty of overriding by constitutional amendment a decision of the Court, Ninth Circuit appellate court Judge J. Clifford Wallace, in chapter 18, argues that the letter and spirit of the Constitution must serve as the Court's principal guide. That guide and the self-imposed restraints on judicial review are crucial to the functioning of an independent judiciary and a system of free government. For as Justice Felix Frankfurter once observed, "constitutional law is not at all a science, but applied politics."[21]

Yet precisely because constitutional law is not "a science, but applied politics," the *methods, sources,* and *scope* of constitutional interpretation remain widely debated on and off the bench. Judge Wallace, among others, argues that "strict constructionism" and reliance on the "original intent" of the Framers of the Constitution is essential to a "jurisprudence of restraint" that, he contends, is in many ways preferable to "judicial activism." In Chapter 19, Robert H. Bork, former appellate court judge and Ronald Reagan's 1987 unsuccessful nominee to the Supreme Court, advances a different kind of argument for a "jurisprudence of original intentions," by challenging contemporary jurists' turn to principles of morality and political philosophy in constitutional interpretation and theory. In Chapter 20, however, another Reagan appointee, appellate court Judge Richard A. Posner counters that "strict constructionism" and "originalism" are not adequate methodologies for constitutional interpretation. Besides, in his words, "the Constitution does not say, 'Read me broadly' or 'Read me narrowly.'" Nevertheless, in Chapter 21 Justice Antonin Scalia champions "originalism" as "the lesser evil" in constitutional interpretation. By contrast, in an address delivered in commemoration of the U.S. Constitution's bicentennial in 1987, excerpted in Chapter 22, Justice Thurgood Marshall rejected appeals to and glorification of "original intent" in favor of viewing the Constitution and the Bill of Rights as living documents. And Chapter 23 contains Justice William J. Brennan Jr.'s observations on the Constitution and methods of constitutional interpretation.

More recently, however, there has been a reaction among justices and judges to the utility of abstract theories of constitutional interpretation—both liberal and conservative—and to broad, sweeping rulings embracing new theories. Representing that view in Chapter 24, Justice Ruth Bader Ginsburg reconsiders the basis for the Court's ruling in *Roe v. Wade,* and in Chapter 25 Justice Stephen G. Breyer argues for a pragmatic or consequentialist approach to constitutional interpretation that draws on the Constitution's democratic foundations. In Chapter 26 Judge Richard A. Posner argues against the usefulness of constitutional law theory for judges in judging and deciding cases.

Another recent controversy over constitutional interpretation has involved the Supreme Court's references to foreign courts' decisions and law in the construction of constitutional rights in cases dealing with the death penalty and discrimination against homosexuals.[22] Justices Ginsburg,[23] Breyer,[24] and Kennedy[25] have been the most outspoken in defending the use of comparative judicial decisions. By contrast, Justices Scalia and Thomas have been sharply critical of citing foreign decisions and law in the Court's opinions,[26] while justices of foreign national supreme courts have criticized the U.S. Supreme Court's failure to rely more on foreign judicial decisions and law.[27] Chapter 27 includes an excerpt from the Supreme Court of Israel Chief Justice Aharon Barak's book *The Judge in a Democracy,*[28] which discusses the importance of considering comparative law in judicial decision making and constitutional interpretation.

Finally, in Chapter 28 Judge William Wayne Justice discusses the "two faces" of judicial activism, distinguishing between judicial activism in constitutional interpretation and the construction of rights, or "jurisprudential activism" in his words, and "remedial activism"—that is, court orders to remedy the government's violation of individual rights. Notably, judicial activism in the construction of rights is neither solely a liberal nor solely a conservative enterprise: both liberal and conservative judges and justices have been charged with "jurisprudential activism." Moreover, Judge Justice argues that both forms of judicial activism are deeply rooted in the history of the judiciary's role in American politics and may be reconciled with democratic theory, depending on the particular circumstances of the case or controversy at hand and how it is viewed.

Notes

1. Charles Evans Hughes, *Addresses of Charles Evans Hughes* 185–186 (New York: Putnam's, 1916).
2. *Osborn v. Bank of the United States,* 27 U.S. (9 Wheat.) 738, 866 (1824).
3. Sir William Blackstone, *Commentaries on the Laws of England* (Chicago: University of Chicago Press, Facsimile edition, 1979).
4. Joseph Story, *Commentaries on the Constitution of the United States* vi and 135 (Durham, N.C.: Carolina Academic Press, 1987, reprint of 1833 ed.)

5. *Dred Scott v. Sandford,* 60 U.S. 393, 426 (1857).
6. Benjamin N. Cardozo, *The Nature of the Judicial Process* 124 (New Haven: Yale University Press, 1921).
7. *McCulloch v. Maryland,* 17 U.S. (4 Wheat.) 316, 407 (1819).
8. William Howard Taft, *Popular Government* 222–223 (New Haven: Yale University Press, 1913).
9. *McCulloch v. Maryland,* 17 U.S. (4 Wheat.) 316, 407, 415 (1819).
10. Quoted by Paul A. Freund, *On Understanding the Supreme Court* 3 (Boston: Little, Brown, 1949).
11. Jerome Frank, *Law and the Modern Mind* 137–138 (New York: Brentano's, 1930).
12. *Southern Pacific Co. v. Jensen,* 244 U.S. 205, 220 (1917).
13. See, e.g., J. Clifford Wallace, "The Jurisprudence of Judicial Restraint: A Return to the Moorings," 50 *George Washington Law Review* 1 (1981).
14. *Griswold v. Connecticut,* 381 U.S. 479, 520 (1965) (Black, J., dis. op.).
15. *Lochner v. New York,* 198 U.S. 45 (1905) (Holmes, J., dis. op.).
16. Harlan Fiske Stone, Letter to Irving Brant (August 25, 1945), quoted by Alpheus T. Mason, *The Supreme Court from Taft to Burger* 168 (Baton Rouge: Louisiana State University Press, 3d ed., 1979).
17. *Harper v. Virginia State Board of Elections,* 383 U.S. 663, 678 (1966) (Black, J., dis. op.).
18. Robert H. Jackson, *The Struggle Over Judicial Supremacy* 80 (New York: Knopf, 1949).
19. William J. Brennan Jr., "Inside View of the High Court," *New York Times Magazine* 35 (6 October 1963).
20. John M. Harlan Jr., Address, American Bar Center (Chicago, Ill.: 13 August 1963).
21. Felix Frankfurter, "The Zeitgeist and the Judiciary," in *Law and Politics* 6, ed. by Archibald MacLeish and E. F. Prichard (New York: Harcourt, Brace, 1939).
22. For further discussion and references to justices' opinions and off-the-bench comments regarding reliance on comparative judicial decisions and law, see David M. O'Brien, "More Smoke Than Fire: The Rehnquist Court's Use of Comparative Judicial Opinions and Law in the Construction of Constitutional Rights," 22 *Journal of Law & Politics,* 83–111 (2006).
23. See, e.g., Ruth Bader Ginsburg, "'A Decent Respect to the Opinions of [Human]kind': The Value of a Comparative Perspective in Constitutional Adjudication," Address before the Constitutional Court of South Africa (February 7, 2006), available at www.supremecourtus.gov/publicinfo/speeches/sp_02-97b-06.html; "Looking Beyond Our Borders: The Value of a Comparative in Constitutional Adjudication," 40 *Idaho Law Review* 1 (2003); "*Brown v. Board of Education* in International Context," Lecture at Columbia University School of Law (October 21, 2004), available at www.supremecourtus.gov/publicinfo/speeches/sp_10-25-04.html; and with Deborah Jones Merritt, "Affirmative Action: An International Human Rights Dialogue," 21 *Cardozo Law Review* 253 (1999).
24. See, e.g., Stephen J. Breyer, Keynote Address at the American Society of International Law Proceedings (April 2–5, 2003), in 97 *American Society of International Law Proceedings* 265 (2003).

25. See, e.g. Jeffrey Toobin, "Swing Shift: How Anthony Kennedy's Passion for Foreign Law Could Change the Supreme Court," *The New Yorker* 42 (September 12, 2005).
26. See e.g., Antonin Scalia, "Commentary," 40 *St. Louis University Law Journal* 1119 (1996); and Keynote Address, 98 *American Society for International Law Proceedings* 305 (2004).
27. See, e.g., Claire L'Heureux-Dube, "The Importance of Dialogue: Globalization and the International Impact of the Rehnquist Court," 34 *Tulsa Law Journal* 15 (1998); and Michael D. Kirby, "International Law-The Impact on National Constitutions," 21 *American University International Law Review* 327 (2006).
28. Aharon Barak, *The Judge in a Democracy* (Princeton, N.J.: Princeton University Press, 2006).

CHAPTER 14

The Path of Law

Oliver Wendell Holmes Jr.
Justice, Supreme Court of the United States (1902–1932) and Justice of Supreme Court of Massachusetts (1882–1902)

WHEN WE STUDY LAW we are not studying a mystery but a well known profession. We are studying what we shall want in order to appear before judges, or to advise people in such a way as to keep them out of court. The reason why it is a profession, why people will pay lawyers to argue for them or to advise them, is that in societies like ours the command of the public force is intrusted to the judges in certain cases, and the whole power of the state will be put forth, if necessary, to carry out their judgments and decrees. People want to know under what circumstances and how far they will run the risk of coming against what is so much stronger than themselves, and hence it becomes a business to find out when this danger is to be feared. The object of our study, then, is prediction, the prediction of the incidence of the public force through the instrumentality of the courts.

The means of the study are a body of reports, of treatises, and of statutes, in this country and in England, extending back for six hundred years, and now increasing annually by hundreds. In these sibylline leaves are gathered the scattered prophecies of the past upon the cases in which the axe will fall. These are what properly have been called the oracles of the law. Far the most important and pretty nearly the whole meaning of every new effort of legal thought is to make these prophecies more precise, and to generalize them into a thoroughly connected system. The process is one, from a lawyer's statement of a case, eliminating as it does all the dramatic elements with which his client's story has clothed it, and retaining

Acknowledgment to the Harvard Law Review Association for excerpts from Oliver Wendell Holmes's "The Path of Law," published originally in 10 Harvard Law Review *457 (1897), and in 110* Harvard Law Review *991 (1997).*

only the facts of legal import, up to the final analyses and abstract universals of theoretic jurisprudence. The reason why a lawyer does not mention that his client wore a white hat when he made a contract, while Mrs. Quickly would be sure to dwell upon it along with the parcel gilt goblet and the sea-coal fire, is that he forsees that the public force will act in the same way whatever his client had upon his head. It is to make the prophecies easier to be remembered and to be understood that the teachings of the decisions of the past are put into general propositions and gathered into text-books, or that statutes are passed in a general form. The primary rights and duties with which jurisprudence busies itself again are nothing but prophecies. One of the many evil effects of the confusion between legal and moral ideas, about which I shall have something to say in a moment, is that theory is apt to get the cart before the horse, and to consider the right or the duty as something existing apart from and independent of the consequences of its breach, to which certain sanctions are added afterward....

I wish, if I can, to lay down some first principles for the study of this body of dogma or systematized prediction which we call the law, for men who want to use it as the instrument of their business to enable them to prophesy in their turn, and, as bearing upon the study, I wish to point out an ideal which as yet our law has not attained.

The first thing for a business-like understanding of the matter is to understand its limits, and therefore I think it desirable at once to point out and dispel a confusion between morality and law, which sometimes rises to the height of conscious theory, and more often and indeed constantly is making trouble in detail without reaching the point of consciousness. You can see very plainly that a bad man has as much reason as a good one for wishing to avoid an encounter with the public force, and therefore you can see the practical importance of the distinction between morality and law. A man who cares nothing for an ethical rule which is believed and practised by his neighbors is likely nevertheless to care a good deal to avoid being made to pay money, and will want to keep out of jail if he can....

I do not say that there is not a wider point of view from which the distinction between law and morals becomes of secondary or no importance, as all mathematical distinctions vanish in presence of the infinite. But I do say that that distinction is of the first importance for the object which we are here to consider—a right study and mastery of the law as a business with well understood limits, a body of dogma enclosed within definite lines. I have just shown the practical reason for saying so. If you want to know the law and nothing else, you must look at it as a bad man, who cares only for the material consequences which such knowledge enables him to predict, not as a good one, who finds his reasons for conduct, whether inside the law or outside of it, in the vaguer sanctions of conscience. The theoretical importance of the distinction is no less, if you would reason on your subject aright. The law is full of phraseology drawn from morals, and by the mere force of language continually invites us to pass from one domain to the other without perceiving it, as we are sure to do unless we have the boundary constantly before our minds. The law talks about rights, and duties, and malice, and intent, and negligence, and so forth, and nothing is easier, or, I may say, more common in legal reasoning, than to take these words in their moral sense, at some stage of the argument, and so to drop into fallacy. For instance, when we speak of the rights of man in a moral sense, we mean to mark the limits of interference with individual freedom which we think are prescribed by conscience, or by our ideal, however reached. Yet it is certain that many laws have been enforced in the past, and it is likely that some are enforced now, which are condemned by the most enlightened opinion of the time, or which at all events pass the limit of interference as many consciences would draw it. Manifestly, therefore, nothing but confusion of thought can result from assuming that the rights of man in a moral sense are equally rights in the sense of the Constitution and the law....

The confusion with which I am dealing besets confessedly legal conceptions. Take the fundamental question, What constitutes the law? You will find some text writers telling you that it is something different from what is decided by the courts of Massachusetts or England, that it is a system of reason, that it is a deduction from principles of ethics or admitted axioms or what not, which may or may not coincide with the decisions. But if we take the view of our friend the bad man we shall find that he does not care two straws for the axioms or deductions, but that he does want to know what the Massachusetts or English courts are likely to do in fact. I am much of his mind. The prophecies of what the courts will do in fact, and nothing more pretentious, are what I mean by the law....

This is not the time to work out a theory in detail, or to answer many obvious doubts and questions which are suggested by these general views. I know of none which are not easy to answer, but what I am trying to do now is only by a series of hints to throw some light on the narrow path of legal doctrine, and upon two pitfalls which, as it seems to me, lie perilously near to it. Of the first of these I have said enough. I hope that my illustrations have shown the danger, both to speculation and to practice, of confounding morality with law, and the trap which legal language lays for us on that side of our way. For my own part, I often doubt whether it would not be a gain if every word of moral significance could be banished from the law altogether, and other words adopted which should convey legal ideas uncolored by anything outside the law. We should lose the fossil records of a good deal of history and the majesty got from ethical associations, but by ridding ourselves of an unnecessary confusion we should gain very much in the clearness of our thought.

So much for the limits of the law. The next thing which I wish to consider is what are the forces which determine its content and its growth. You may assume, with Hobbes and Bentham and Austin, that all law emanates from the sovereign, even when the first human beings to enunciate it are the judges, or you may think that law is the voice of the Zeitgeist, or what you like. It is all one to my present purpose. Even if every decision required the sanction of an emperor with despotic power and a whimsical turn of mind, we should be interested none the less, still with a view to prediction, in discovering some order, some rational explanation, and some principle of growth for the rules which he laid down. In every system there are such explanations and principles to be found. It is with regard to them that a second fallacy comes in, which I think it important to expose.

The fallacy to which I refer is the notion that the only force at work in the development of the law is logic. In the broadest sense, indeed, that notion would be true. The postulate on which we think about the universe is that there is a fixed quantitative relation between every phenomenon and its antecedents and consequents. If there is such a thing as a phenomenon without these fixed quantitative relations, it is a miracle. It is outside the law of cause and effect, and as such transcends our power of thought, or at least is something to or from which we cannot reason. The condition of our thinking about the universe is that it is capable of being thought about rationally, or, in other words, that every part of it is effect and cause in the same sense in which those parts are with which we are most familiar. So in the broadest sense it is true that the law is a logical development, like everything else. The danger of which I speak is not the admission that the principles governing other phenomena also govern the law, but the notion that a given system, ours, for instance, can be worked out like mathematics from some general axioms of conduct. This is the natural error of the schools, but it is not confined to them. I once heard a very eminent judge say that he never let a decision go until he was absolutely sure that it was right. So judicial dissent often is blamed, as if it meant simply that one side or the other were not doing their sums right, and, if they would take more trouble, agreement inevitably would come.

This mode of thinking is entirely natural. The training of lawyers is a training in logic. The processes of analogy, discrimination, and deduction are those in which they are most at home. The language of judicial decision is mainly the language of logic. And the logical method and form flatter that longing for certainty and for repose which is in every human mind. But certainty generally is illusion, and repose is not the destiny of man. Behind the logical form lies a judgment as to the relative worth and importance of competing legislative grounds, often an inarticulate and unconscious judgment, it is true, and yet the very root and nerve of the whole proceeding. You can give any conclusion a logical form. You always can imply a condition in a contract. But why do you imply it? It is because of some belief as to the practice of the community or of a class, or because of some opinion as to policy, or, in short, because of some attitude of yours upon a matter not capable of exact quantitative measurement, and therefore not capable of founding exact logical conclusions. Such matters really are battle grounds where the means do not exist for determinations that shall be good for all time, and where the decision can do no more than embody the preference of a given body in a given time and place. We do not realize how large a part of our law is open to reconsideration upon a slight change in the habit of the public mind. No concrete proposition is self-evident, no matter how ready we may be to accept it, not even Mr. Herbert Spencer's "Every man has a right to do what he wills, provided he interferes not with a like right on the part of his neighbors." ...

I think that the judges themselves have failed adequately to recognize their duty of weighing considerations of social advantage. The duty is inevitable, and the result of the often proclaimed judicial aversion to deal with such considerations is simply to leave the very ground and foundation of judgments inarticulate, and often unconscious, as I have said. When socialism first began to be talked about, the comfortable classes of the community were a good deal frightened. I suspect that this fear has influenced judicial action both here and in England, yet it is certain that it is not a conscious factor in the decisions to which I refer. I think that something similar has led people who no longer hope to control the legislatures to look to the courts as expounders of the Constitutions, and that in some courts new principles have been discovered outside the bodies of those instruments, which may be generalized into acceptance of the economic doctrines which prevailed about fifty years ago, and a wholesale prohibition of what a tribunal of lawyers does not think about right. I cannot but believe that if the training of lawyers led them habitually to consider more definitely and explicitly the social advantage on which the rule they lay down must be justified, they sometimes would hesitate where now they are confident, and see that really they were taking sides upon debatable and often burning questions.

So much for the fallacy of logical form. Now let us consider the present condition of the law as a subject for study, and the ideal toward which it tends. We still are far from the point of view which I desire to see reached. No one has reached it or can reach it as yet. We are only at the beginning of a philosophical reaction, and of a reconsideration of the worth of doctrines which for the most part still are taken for granted without any deliberate, conscious, and systematic questioning of their grounds. The development of our law has gone on for nearly a thousand years, like the development of a plant, each generation taking the inevitable next step, mind, like matter, simply obeying a law of spontaneous growth. It is perfectly natural and right that it should have been so.... Most of the things we do, we do for no better reason than that our fathers have done them or that our neighbors do them, and the same is true of a larger part than we suspect of what we think. The reason is a good one, because our short life gives us no time for a better, but it is not the best. It does not follow, because we all are compelled to take on faith at second hand most of the rules on which we base our action and our thought, that each of us may not try to set some corner of his world in the order of reason, or that all of us collectively should not aspire to carry reason as far as it will go throughout the whole domain. In regard to the law, it is true, no doubt, that an evolutionist will hesitate to affirm universal validity for his social ideals, or for the principles which he thinks should be embodied in legislation. He is content if he can prove them best for here and now. He may be ready to admit that he knows nothing about an absolute best in the cosmos, and even that he knows next to nothing about a permanent best for men. Still it is true that a body of law is more rational and more civilized when every rule it contains is referred articulately and definitely to an end which it subserves, and when the grounds for desiring that end are stated or are ready to be stated in words....

I trust that no one will understand me to be speaking with disrespect of the law, because I criticise it so freely. I venerate the law, and especially our system of law, as one of the vastest products of the human mind. No one knows better than I do the countless number of great intellects that have spent themselves in making some addition or improvement, the greatest of which is trifling when compared with the mighty whole. It has the final title to respect that it exists, that it is not a Hegelian dream, but a part of the lives of men. But one may criticise even what one reveres. Law is the business to which my life is devoted, and I should show less than devotion if I did not do what in me lies to improve it, and, when I perceive what seems to me the ideal of its future, if I hesitated to point it out and to press toward it with all my heart....

There is another study which sometimes is undervalued by the practical minded, for which I wish to say a good word, although I think a good deal of pretty poor stuff goes under that name. I mean the study of what is called jurisprudence. Jurisprudence, as I look at it, is simply law in its most generalized part. Every effort to reduce a case to a rule is an effort of jurisprudence, although the name as used in English is confined to the broadest rules and most fundamental conceptions. One mark of a great lawyer is that he sees the application of the broadest rules....

I have been speaking about the study of the law, and I have said next to nothing of what commonly is talked about in that connection—text-books and the case system, and all the machinery with which a student comes most immediately in contact. Nor shall I say anything about them. Theory is my subject, not practical details. The modes of teaching have been improved since my time, no doubt, but ability and industry will master the raw material with any mode. Theory is the most important part of the dogma of the law, as the architect is the most important man who takes part in the building of a house. The most important improvements of the last twenty-five years are improvements in theory. It is not to be feared as unpractical, for, to the competent, it simply means going to the bottom of the subject. For the incompetent, it sometimes is true, as has been said, that an interest in general ideas means an absence of particular knowledge. I remember in army days reading of a youth who, being examined for the lowest grade and being asked a question about squadron drill, answered that he never had considered the evolutions of less than ten thousand men. But the weak and foolish must be left to their folly. The danger is that the able and practical minded should look with indifference or distrust upon ideas the connection of which with their business is remote. I heard a story, the other day, of a man who had a valet to whom he paid high wages, subject to deduction for faults. One of his deductions was, "For lack of imagination, five dollars." The lack is not confined to valets. The object of ambition, power, generally presents itself nowadays in the form of money alone. Money is the most immediate form, and is a proper object of desire. "The fortune," said Rachel, "is the measure of the intelligence." That is a good text to waken people out of a fool's paradise. But, as Hegel says, "It is in the end not the appetite, but the opinion, which has to be satisfied." To an imagination of any scope the most far-reaching form of power is not money, it is the command of ideas. . . . We cannot all be Descartes or Kant, but we all want happiness. And happiness, I am sure from having known many successful men, cannot be won simply by being counsel for great corporations and having an income of fifty thousand dollars. An intellect great enough to win the prize needs other food beside success. The remoter and more general aspects of the law are those which give it universal interest. It is through them that you not only become a great master in your calling, but connect your subject with the universe and catch an echo of the infinite, a glimpse of its unfathomable process, a hint of the universal law.

CHAPTER 15

The Judge as a Legislator

Benjamin N. Cardozo
Justice, Supreme Court of the United States (1932–1938) and Justice, New York Court of Appeals (1917–1932)

FEW RULES IN OUR TIME are so well established that they may not be called upon any day to justify their existence as means adapted to an end. If they do not function, they are diseased. If they are diseased, they must not propagate their kind. Sometimes they are cut out and extirpated altogether. Sometimes they are left with the shadow of continued life, but sterilized, truncated, impotent for harm....

Rules derived by a process of logical deduction from pre-established conceptions of contract and obligation have broken down before the slow and steady and erosive action of utility and justice....

Not the origin, but the goal, is the main thing. There can be no wisdom in the choice of a path unless we know where it will lead. The teleological conception of his function must be ever in the judge's mind. This means, of course, that the juristic philosophy of the common law is at bottom the philosophy of pragmatism. Its truth is relative, not absolute. The rule that functions well produces a title deed to recognition. Only in determining how it functions we must not view it too narrowly. We must not sacrifice the general to the particular. We must not throw to the winds the advantages of consistency and uniformity to do justice in the instance. We must keep within those interstitial limits which precedent and custom and the long and silent and almost indefinable practice of other judges through the centuries of the common law have set to judge-made innovations. But within the limits thus set, within the range over which choice moves, the final principle of selection for judges, as for legislators, is one of fitness to the end.... We do not pick

Acknowledgment to Yale University Press for excerpts from The Nature of the Judicial Process *by Benjamin N. Cardozo, copyright New Haven, Conn.: Yale University Press, 1921.*

our rules of law full-blossomed from the trees. Every judge consulting his own experience must be conscious of times when a free exercise of will, directed of set purpose to the furtherance of the common good, determined the form and tendency of a rule which at that moment took its origin in one creative act....

Law is, indeed, an historical growth, for it is an expression of customary morality which develops silently and unconsciously from one age to another.... But law is also a conscious or proposed growth, for the expression of customary morality will be false unless the mind of the judge is directed to the attainment of the moral end and its embodiment in legal forms. Nothing less than conscious effort will be adequate if the end in view is to prevail. The standards or patterns of utility and morals will be found by the judge in the life of the community. They will be found in the same way as by the legislator. That does not mean, however, that the work of the one any more than that of the other is a replica of nature's forms....

The truth, indeed, is, as I have said, that the distinction between the subjective or individual and the objective or general conscience, in the field where the judge is not limited by established rules, is shadowy and evanescent, and tends to become one of words and little more. For the casuist and the philosopher, it has its speculative interest. In the practical administration of justice, it will seldom be decisive for the judge.... The perception of objective right takes the color of the subjective mind. The conclusions of the subjective mind take the color of customary practices and objectified beliefs. There is constant and subtle interaction between what is without and what is within.... The personal and the general mind and will are inseparably united. The difference, as one theory of judicial duty or the other prevails, involves at most a little change of emphasis, or of the method of approach, of the point of view, the angle, from which problems are envisaged. Only dimly and by the force of an influence subconscious, or nearly so, will the difference be reflected in the decisions of courts.

My analysis of the judicial process comes then to this, and little more: logic, and history, and custom, and utility, and the accepted standards of right conduct, are the forces which singly or in combination shape the progress of the law. Which of these forces shall dominate in any case must depend largely upon the comparative importance or value of the social interests that will be thereby promoted or impaired. One of the most fundamental social interests is that law shall be uniform and impartial. There must be nothing in its action that savors of prejudice or favor or even arbitrary whim or fitfulness. Therefore in the main there shall be adherence to precedent. There shall be symmetrical development, consistently with history or custom when history or custom has been the motive force, or the chief one, in giving shape to existing rules, and with logic or philosophy when the motive power has been theirs. But symmetrical development may be bought at too high a price. Uniformity ceases to be a good when it becomes uniformity of oppression. The social interest served by symmetry or certainty must then be balanced against the social interest served by equity and fairness or other elements of social welfare. These may enjoin upon the judge the duty of drawing the line at another angle, of staking the path along new courses, of marking a new point of departure from which others who come after him will set out upon their journey.

If you ask how he is to know when one interest outweighs another, I can only answer that he must get his knowledge just as the legislator gets it, from experience and study and reflection; in brief, from life itself. Here, indeed, is the point of contact between the legislator's work and his. The choice of methods, the appraisement of values, must in the end be guided by the like considerations for the one as for the other. Each indeed is legislating within the limits of his competence. No doubt the limits for the judge are narrower. He legislates only between gaps. He fills the open spaces in the law. How far he may go without traveling beyond the wall of interstices cannot be staked out for him upon a chart. He must learn it for himself as gains the sense of fitness and proportion that comes with years of habitude in the practice of an art. Even within the gaps, restrictions not easy to define, but felt, however impalpable they may be, by every judge and lawyer, hedge and circumscribe his action. They are established by the traditions of the centuries, by the example of other judges, his predecessors and his colleagues, by the collective judgment of the profession, and by the duty of adherence to the pervading spirit of the law.... None the less, within the confines of these open spaces and those of precedent and tradition, choice moves with a freedom which stamps its action as creative. The law which is the resulting product is not found, but made. The process being legislative, demands the legislator's wisdom.

There is in truth nothing revolutionary or even novel in this view of the judicial function. It is the way that courts have gone about their business for centuries in the development of the common law. The difference from age to age is not so much in the recognition of the need that law shall conform itself to an end. It is rather in the nature of the end to which there has been need to conform. There have been periods when uniformity, even rigidity, the elimination of the personal element, were felt to be the paramount needs. By a sort of paradox, the end was best served by disregarding it and thinking only of the means. Gradually the need of a more flexible system asserted itself. Often the gap between the old rule and the new was bridged by the pious fraud of a fiction. The thing which concerns us here is that it was bridged whenever the importance of the end was dominant. Today the use of fictions has declined; and the springs of action are disclosed where once they were concealed....

You may say that there is no assurance that judges will interpret the *mores* of their day more wisely and truly than other men. I am not disposed to deny this, but in my view it is quite beside the point. The point is rather that this power of interpretation must be lodged somewhere, and the custom of the constitution has lodged it in the judges. If they are to fulfill their function as judges, it could hardly be lodged elsewhere. Their conclusions must, indeed, be subject to constant testing and retesting, revision and readjustment; but if they act with conscience and intelligence, they ought to attain in their conclusions a fair average of truth and wisdom. The recognition of this power and duty to shape the law in conformity with the customary morality is something far removed from the destruction of all rules and the substitution in every instance of the individual sense of justice. . . .

CHAPTER 16

The Notion of a Living Constitution

William H. Rehnquist

Chief Justice, Supreme Court of the United States (1986–2005) and Associate Justice, Supreme Court of the United States (1972–1986)

AT LEAST ONE of the more than half-dozen persons nominated during the past decade to be an Associate Justice of the Supreme Court of the United States has been asked by the Senate Judiciary Committee at his confirmation hearings whether he believed in a living Constitution.[1] It is not an easy question to answer; the phrase "living Constitution" has about it a teasing imprecision that makes it a coat of many colors.

One's first reaction tends to be along the lines of public relations or ideological sex appeal, I suppose. At first blush it seems certain that a *living* Constitution is better than what must be its counterpart, a *dead* Constitution. It would seem that only a necrophile could disagree. If we could get one of the major public opinion research firms in the country to sample public opinion concerning whether the United States Constitution should be *living* or *dead*, the overwhelming majority of the responses doubtless would favor a *living* Constitution.

The phrase is really a shorthand expression that is susceptible of at least two quite different meanings. The first meaning was expressed over a half-century ago by Mr. Justice Holmes in *Missouri v. Holland*[2] with his customary felicity when he said:

> ... When we are dealing with words that also are a constituent act, like the Constitution of the United States, we must realize that they have called into life a being

---

Acknowledgment to Chief Justice William H. Rehnquist for the Ninth Annual Will E. Orgain Lecture at the University of Texas School of Law (May 12, 1976), which also appears in 54 Texas Law Review *693 (1976).*

> the development of which could not have been foreseen completely by the most gifted of its begetters. It was enough for them to realize or to hope that they had created an organism; it has taken a century and has cost their successors much sweat and blood to prove that they created a nation.[3]

I shall refer to this interpretation of the phrase "living Constitution," with which scarcely anyone would disagree, as the Holmes version.

The framers of the Constitution wisely spoke in general language and left to succeeding generations the task of applying that language to the unceasingly changing environment in which they would live. Those who framed, adopted, and ratified the Civil War amendments[4] to the Constitution likewise used what have been aptly described as "majestic generalities"[5] in composing the Fourteenth Amendment. Merely because a particular activity may not have existed when the Constitution was adopted, or because the framers could not have conceived of a particular method of transacting affairs, cannot mean that general language in the Constitution may not be applied to such a course of conduct. Where the framers of the Constitution have used general language, they have given latitude to those who would later interpret the instrument to make that language applicable to cases that the framers might not have foreseen.

In my reading and travels I have sensed a second connotation of the phrase "living Constitution," however, one quite different from what I have described as the Holmes version, but which certainly has gained acceptance among some parts of the legal profession. Embodied in its most naked form, it recently came to my attention in some language from a brief that had been filed in a United States District Court on behalf of state prisoners asserting that the conditions of their confinement offended the United States Constitution.

The brief urged:

> We are asking a great deal of the Court because other branches of government have abdicated their responsibility.... Prisoners are like other "discrete and insular" minorities for whom the Court must spread its protective umbrella because no other branch of government will do so.... This Court, as the voice and conscience of contemporary society, as the measure of the modern conception of human dignity, must declare that the [named prison] and all it represents offends the Constitution of the United States and will not be tolerated.

Here we have a living Constitution with a vengeance. Although the substitution of some other set of values for those which may be derived from the language and intent of the framers is not urged in so many words, that is surely the thrust of the message. Under this brief writer's version of the living Constitution, nonelected members of the federal judiciary may address themselves to a social problem simply because other branches of government have failed or refused to do so. These same judges, responsible to no constituency whatever, are nonetheless acclaimed as "the voice and conscience of contemporary society."

If we were merely talking about a slogan that was being used to elect some candidate to office or to persuade the voters to ratify a constitutional amendment, elaborate dissection of a phrase such as "living Constitution" would probably not be warranted. What we are talking about, however, is a suggested philosophical approach to be used by the federal judiciary, and perhaps state judiciaries, in exercising the very delicate responsibility of judicial review. Under the familiar principle of judicial review, the courts in construing the Constitution are, of course, authorized to invalidate laws that have been enacted by Congress or by a state legislature but that those courts find to violate some provision of the Constitution. Nevertheless, those who have pondered the matter have always recognized that the ideal of judicial review has basically antidemocratic and antimajoritarian facets that require some justification in this Nation, which prides itself on being a self-governing representative democracy.

All who have studied law, and many who have not, are familiar with John Marshall's classic defense of judicial review in his opinion for the Court in *Marbury v. Madison*.[6] I will summarize very briefly the thrust of that answer, with which I fully agree, because while it supports the Holmes version of the phrase "living Constitution," it also suggests some outer limits for the brief writer's version.

The ultimate source of authority in this Nation, Marshall said, is not Congress, not the states, not for that matter the Supreme Court of the United States. The people are the ultimate source of authority; they have parceled out the authority that originally resided entirely with them by adopting the original Constitution and by later amending it. They have granted some authority to the federal government and have reserved authority not granted it to the states or to the people individually. As between the branches of the federal government, the people have given certain authority to the President, certain authority to Congress, and certain authority to the federal judiciary. In the Bill of Rights they have erected protections for specified individual rights against the actions of the federal government. From today's perspective we might add that they have placed restrictions on the authority of the state governments in the Thirteenth, Fourteenth, and Fifteenth amendments.

In addition, Marshall said that if the popular branches of government—state legislatures, the Congress, and the Presidency—are operating within the authority granted to them by the Constitution, their judgment and not that of the Court must obviously prevail. When these branches overstep the authority given them by the Constitution, in the case of the President and the Congress, or invade protected individual rights, and a constitutional challenge to their action is raised in a lawsuit brought in federal court, the Court must prefer the Constitution to the government acts.

John Marshall's justification for judicial review makes the provision for an independent federal judiciary not only understandable but also thoroughly desirable. Since the judges will be merely interpreting an instrument framed by the people, they should be detached and objective. A mere change in public opinion since the adoption of the Constitution, unaccompanied by a constitutional amendment, should not change the meaning of the Constitution. A merely temporary majoritarian groundswell should not abrogate some individual liberty truly protected by the Constitution.

Clearly Marshall's explanation contains certain elements of either ingenuousness or ingeniousness, which tend to grow larger as our constitutional history extends over a longer period of time. The Constitution is in many of its parts obviously not a specifically worded document but one couched in general phraseology. There is obviously wide room for honest difference of opinion over the meaning of general phrases in the Constitution; any particular Justice's decision when a question arises under one of these general phrases will depend to some extent on his own philosophy of constitutional law. One may nevertheless concede all of these problems that inhere in Marshall's justification of judicial review, yet feel that his justification for nonelected judges exercising the power of judicial review is the only one consistent with democratic philosophy of representative government.

Marshall was writing at a time when the governing generation remembered well not only the deliberations of the framers of the Constitution at Philadelphia in the summer of 1787 but also the debates over the ratification of the Constitution in the 13 colonies. The often heated discussions that took place from 1787, when Delaware became the first state to ratify the Constitution,[7] until 1790, when recalcitrant Rhode Island finally joined the Union,[8] were themselves far more representative of the give-and-take of public decision making by a constituent assembly than is the ordinary enactment of a law by Congress or by a state legislature. Patrick Henry had done all he could to block ratification in Virginia,[9] and the opposition of the Clinton faction in New York had provoked Jay, Hamilton, and Madison to their brilliant effort in defense of the Constitution, the *Federalist Papers*.[10] For Marshall, writing the *Marbury v. Madison* opinion in 1803, the memory of the debates in which the people of the 13 colonies had participated only a few years before could well have fortified his conviction that the Constitution was, not merely in theory but in fact as well, a fundamental charter that had emanated from the people.

One senses no similar connection with a popularly adopted constituent act in what I have referred to as the brief writer's version of the living Constitution. The brief writer's version seems instead to be based upon the proposition that federal judges, perhaps judges as a whole, have a role of their own, quite independent of popular will, to play in solving society's problems. Once we have abandoned the idea that the authority of the courts to declare laws unconstitutional is somehow tied to the language of the Constitution that the people adopted, a judiciary exercising the power of judicial review appears in a quite different light. Judges then are no longer the keepers of the covenant; instead they are a small group of fortunately situated people with a roving commission to second-guess Congress, state legislatures, and state and federal administrative officers concerning what is best for the country. Surely there is no justification for a third legislative branch in the federal government, and there is even less justification for a federal legislative branch's reviewing on a policy basis the laws enacted by the legislatures of the 50 states. Even if one were to disagree with me on this point, the members of a third branch of the federal legislature at least ought to be elected by and responsible to constituencies, just as in the case of the other two branches of Congress. If there is going to be a council of revision, it ought to have at least some connection with popular feeling. Its members either ought to stand for reelection on occasion, or their terms should expire and they should be allowed to continue serving only if reappointed by a popularly elected Chief Executive and confirmed by a popularly elected Senate.

The brief writer's version of the living Constitution is seldom presented in its most naked form, but is instead usually dressed in more attractive garb. The argument in favor of this approach generally begins with a sophisticated wink—why pretend that there is any ascertainable content to the general phrases of the Constitution as they are written since, after all, judges constantly disagree about their meaning? We are all familiar with Chief Justice Hughes's famous aphorism that "We are under a Constitution, but the Constitution is what the judges say it is."[11] We all know the basis of Marshall's justification for judicial review, the argument runs, but it is necessary only to keep the window dressing in place. Any sophisticated student of the subject knows that judges need not limit themselves to the intent of the framers, which is very difficult to determine in any event. Because of the general language used in the Constitution, judges should not hesitate to use their authority to make the Constitution relevant and useful in solving the problems of modern society. The brief writer's version of the living Constitution envisions all of the above conclusions.

At least three serious difficulties flaw the brief writer's version of the living Constitution. First, it misconceives the nature of the Constitution, which was designed to enable the popularly elected branches of government, not the judicial branch, to keep the country abreast of the times. Second, the brief writer's version ignores the Supreme Court's disastrous experiences when in the past it embraced contemporary, fashionable notions of what a living Constitution should contain. Third, however socially desirable the goals sought to be advanced by the brief writer's version, advancing them through a freewheeling, nonelected judiciary is quite unacceptable in a democratic society.

It seems to me that it is almost impossible, after reading the record of the Founding Fathers' debates in Philadelphia, to conclude that they intended the Constitution itself to suggest answers to the manifold problems that they knew would confront succeeding generations. The Constitution that they drafted was indeed intended to endure indefinitely, but the reason for this very well-founded hope was the general language by which national authority was granted to Congress and the Presidency. These two branches were to furnish the motive power within the federal system, which was in turn to coexist with the state governments; the elements of government having a popular constituency were looked to for the solution of the numerous and varied problems that the future would bring. Limitations were indeed placed upon both federal and state governments in the form of both a division of powers and express protection for individual rights. These limitations, however, were not themselves designed to solve the problems of the future, but were instead designed to make certain that the constituent branches, when *they* attempted to solve those problems, should not transgress these fundamental limitations.

Although the Civil War Amendments were designed more as broad limitations on the authority of state governments, they too were enacted in response to practices that the lately seceded states engaged in to discriminate against and mistreat the newly emancipated freed men. To the extent that the language of these amendments is general, the courts are of course warranted in giving them an application coextensive with their language. Nevertheless, I greatly doubt that even men like Thad Stevens and John Bingham, leaders of the radical Republicans in Congress, would have thought any portion of the Civil War Amendments, except section five of the Fourteenth Amendment,[12] was designed to solve problems that society might confront a century later. I think they would have said that those amendments were designed to prevent abuses from ever recurring in which the states had engaged prior to that time.

The second difficulty with the brief writer's version of the living Constitution lies in its inattention to or rejection of the Supreme Court's historical experience gleaned from similar forays into problem solving.

Although the phrase "living Constitution" may not have been used during the nineteenth century and the first half of this century, the idea represented by the brief writer's version was very much in evidence during both periods. The apogee of the living Constitution doctrine during the nineteenth century was the Supreme Court's decision in *Dred Scott v. Sandford.*[13] In that case the question at issue was the status of a Negro who had been carried by his master from a slave state into a territory made free by the Missouri Compromise. Although thereafter taken back to a slave state, Dred Scott claimed that upon previously reaching free soil he had been forever emancipated. The Court, speaking through Chief Justice Taney, held that Congress was without power to legislate upon the issue of slavery even in a territory governed by it, and that therefore Dred Scott had never become free. Congress, the Court held, was virtually powerless to check or limit the spread of the institution of slavery.

The history of this country for some 30 years before the *Dred Scott* decision demonstrates the bitter frustration which that decision brought to large elements of the population who opposed any expansion of slavery. In 1820 when Maine was seeking admission as a free state and Missouri as a slave state, a fight over the expansion of slavery engulfed the national legislative halls and resulted in the Missouri Compromise,[14] which forever banned slavery from those territories lying north of a line drawn through the southern boundary of Missouri.[15] This was a victory for the antislavery forces in the North, but the Southerners were prepared to live with it. At the time of the Mexican War in 1846, Representative David Wilmot of Pennsylvania introduced a bill, later known as the Wilmot Proviso,[16] that would have precluded the opening to slavery of any territory acquired as a result of the Mexican War.[17] This proposed amendment to the Missouri Compromise was hotly debated for years both in and out of Congress.[18] Finally in 1854 Senator Stephen A. Douglas shepherded through Congress the Kansas-Nebraska Act,[19] which in effect repealed the Missouri Compromise and enacted into law the principle of "squatter sovereignty": the people in each of the new territories would decide whether or not to permit slavery.[20] The enactment of this bill was, of course, a victory for the proslavery forces in Congress and a defeat for those opposed to the expansion of slavery. The great majority of the antislavery groups, as strongly as they felt about the matter, were still willing to live with the decision of Congress.[21] They were not willing, however, to live with the *Dred Scott* decision.

The Court in *Dred Scott* decided that all of the agitation and debate in Congress over the Missouri Compromise in 1820, over the Wilmot Proviso a generation later, and over the Kansas-Nebraska Act in 1854 had amounted to absolutely nothing. It was, in the words of Macbeth, "A tale told by an idiot, full of sound and fury, signifying nothing."[22] According to the Court, the decision had never been one that Congress was entitled to make; it was one that the Court alone, in construing the Constitution, was empowered to make.

The frustration of the citizenry, who had thought themselves charged with the responsibility for making such decisions, is well expressed in Abraham Lincoln's First Inaugural Address:

> [T]he candid citizen must confess that if the policy of the government, upon vital questions affecting the whole people, is to be irrevocably fixed by decisions

> of the Supreme Court, the instant they are made, in ordinary litigation between parties in personal actions, the people will have ceased to be their own rulers, having to that extent practically resigned their government into the hands of that eminent tribunal.[23]

The *Dred Scott* decision, of course, was repealed in fact as a result of the Civil War and in law by the Civil War Amendments. The injury to the reputation of the Supreme Court that resulted from the *Dred Scott* decision, however, took more than a generation to heal. Indeed, newspaper accounts long after the *Dred Scott* decision bristled with attacks on the Court, and particularly on Chief Justice Taney, unequalled in their bitterness even to this day.

The brief writer's version of the living Constitution made its next appearance, almost as dramatically as its first, shortly after the turn of the century in *Lochner v. New York*.[24] The name of the case is a household word to those who have studied constitutional law, and it is one of the handful of cases in which a dissenting opinion has been overwhelmingly vindicated by the passage of time. In *Lochner* a New York law that limited to ten the maximum number of hours per day that could be worked by bakery employees was assailed on the ground that it deprived the bakery employer of liberty without due process of law. A majority of the Court held the New York maximum hour law unconstitutional, saying, "Statutes of the nature of that under review, limiting the hours in which grown and intelligent men may labor to earn their living, are mere meddlesome interferences with the rights of the individual. . . ."[25]

The Fourteenth Amendment, of course, said nothing about any freedom to make contracts upon terms that one thought best, but there was a very substantial body of opinion outside the Constitution at the time of *Lochner* that subscribed to the general philosophy of social Darwinism as embodied in the writing of Herbert Spencer in England and William Graham Sumner in this country. It may have occurred to some of the Justices who made up a majority in *Lochner*, hopefully subconsciously rather than consciously, that since this philosophy appeared eminently sound and since the language in the due process clause was sufficiently general not to rule out its inclusion, why not strike a blow for the cause? The answer, which has been vindicated by time, came in the dissent of Mr. Justice Holmes:

> [A] constitution is not intended to embody a particular economic theory, whether of paternalism and the organic relation of the citizen to the state or of *laissez faire*. It is made for people of fundamentally differing views, and the accident of our finding certain opinions natural and familiar or novel and even shocking ought not to conclude our judgment upon the question whether statutes embodying them conflict with the Constitution of the United States.[26]

One reads the history of these episodes in the Supreme Court to little purpose if he does not conclude that prior experimentation with the brief writer's expansive notion of a living Constitution has done the Court little credit. There remain today those, such as wrote the brief from which I quoted, who appear to cleave nevertheless to the view that the experiments of the Taney Court before the Civil War, and of the Fuller and Taft Courts in the first part of this century, ended in failure not because they sought to bring into the Constitution a principle that the great majority of objective scholars would have to conclude was not there but because they sought to bring into the Constitution the *wrong* extraconstitutional principle. This school of thought appears to feel that while added protection for slave owners was clearly unacceptable and safeguards for businessmen threatened with ever-expanding state regulation were not desirable, expansion of the protection accorded to individual liberties against the state or to the interest of "discrete and insular" minorities,[27] such as prisoners, must stand on a quite different, more favored footing. To the extent, of course, that such a distinction may legitimately be derived from the Constitution itself, these latter principles do indeed stand on an entirely different footing. To the extent that one must, however, go beyond even a generously fair reading of the language and intent of that document in order to subsume these principles, it seems to me that they are not really distinguishable from those espoused in *Dred Scott* and *Lochner*.

The third difficulty with the brief writer's notion of the living Constitution is that it seems to ignore totally the nature of political value judgments in a democratic society. If such a society adopts a constitution and incorporates in that constitution safeguards for individual liberty, these safeguards indeed do take on a generalized moral rightness or goodness. They assume a general social acceptance neither because of any intrinsic worth nor because of any unique origins in someone's idea of natural justice but instead simply because they have been incorporated in a constitution by the people. Within the limits of our Constitution, the representatives of the people in the executive branches of the state and national governments enact laws. The laws that emerge after a typical political struggle in which various individual value judgments are debated likewise take on a form of moral goodness because they have been enacted into positive law. It is the fact of their enactment that gives them whatever moral claim they have upon us as a society, however, and not any independent virtue they may have in any particular citizen's own scale of values.

Beyond the Constitution and the laws in our society, there simply is no basis other than the individual conscience of the citizen that may serve as a platform for the launching of moral judgments. There is no conceivable way in which I can logically demonstrate to you that the judgments of my conscience are superior to the judgments of your conscience, and vice versa. Many of us necessarily feel strongly and deeply about our own moral judgments, but they remain only personal moral judgments until in some way given the sanction of law.

As Mr. Justice Holmes said in his famous essay on natural law:

> Certitude is not the test of certainty. We have been cocksure of many things that were not so.... One cannot be wrenched from the rocky crevices into which one is thrown for many years without feeling that one is attacked in one's life. What we most love and revere generally is determined by early associations. I love granite rocks and barberry bushes, no doubt because with them were my earliest joys that reach back through the past eternity of my life. But while one's experience thus makes certain preferences dogmatic for oneself, recognition of how they came to be so leaves one able to see that others, poor souls, may be equally dogmatic about something else. And this again means skepticism.[28]

This is not to say that individual moral judgments ought not to afford a springboard for action in society, for indeed they are without doubt the most common and most powerful wellsprings for action when one believes that questions of right and wrong are involved. Representative government is predicated upon the idea that one who feels deeply upon a question as a matter of conscience will seek out others of like view or will attempt to persuade others who do not initially share that view. When adherents to the belief become sufficiently numerous, he will have the necessary armaments required in a democratic society to press his views upon the elected representatives of the people, and to have them embodied into positive law.

Should a person fail to persuade the legislature, or should he feel that a legislative victory would be insufficient because of its potential for future reversal, he may seek to run the more difficult gauntlet of amending the Constitution to embody the view that he espouses. Success in amending the Constitution would, of course, preclude succeeding transient majorities in the legislature from tampering with the principle formerly added to the Constitution.

The brief writer's version of the living Constitution, in the last analysis, is a formula for an end run around popular government. To the extent that it makes possible an individual's persuading one or more appointed federal judges to impose on other individuals a rule of conduct that the popularly elected branches of government would not have enacted and the voters have not and would not have embodied in the Constitution, the brief writer's version of the living Constitution is genuinely corrosive of the fundamental values of our democratic society.

Notes

1. See *Hearings on Nominations of William H. Rehnquist and Lewis F. Powell Jr., Before the Senate Committee on the Judiciary,* 92d Cong., 1st Sess., 87 (1971).
2. 252 U.S. 416 (1920).
3. Ibid., at 433.
4. U.S. Constitution, Amendments XIII, XIV, and XV.
5. *Fay v. New York,* 332 U.S. 261, 282 (1947) (Jackson, J.).
6. 5 U.S. (1 Cranch) 137 (1803).
7. F. Thorpe, *A Constitutional History of the American People,* Vol. 2, 18 (New York: Harper & Bros., 1898).
8. Ibid., at 191.
9. Ibid., at 81, 91–95.
10. Ibid., at 134–139.
11. C. Hughes, *Addresses and Papers of Charles Evans Hughes* 139 (New York: Putnam's, 1908).
12. "The Congress shall have power to enforce, by appropriate legislation, the provisions of this article." U.S. Constitution, Amendment XIV, 5.
13. 60 U.S. (19 How.) 393 (1857).
14. Act of 6 March 1820, ch. 22, 3 Stat. 545.
15. See Thorpe, supra note 7, at 366–377 and 433.
16. Act of 19 June 1862, ch. 111, 12 Stat. 432.
17. Thorpe, supra note 7, at 430.
18. Ibid., at 430–432.
19. Act of 30 May 1854, ch. 59, 10 Stat. 277.
20. See Thorpe, supra note 7, at 518–521.
21. Ibid., at 536–542.
22. Shakespeare, *Macbeth,* V.v. 19.
23. First Inaugural Address by Abraham Lincoln, 4 March 1861, in A. Lincoln, *Complete Works of Abraham Lincoln* 171–172, ed. by J. Nicolay (1894).
24. 198 U.S. 45 (1905).
25. Ibid., at 61.
26. Ibid., at 75–76 (Holmes, J., dis. op.).
27. *United States v. Carolene Products Co.,* 304 U.S. 144, 152 n. 4 (1938).
28. O.W. Holmes, "Natural Law," in *Collected Legal Papers* 310, 311 (New York: Peter Smith, 1920).

CHAPTER 17

A Relativistic Constitution

William Wayne Justice
Judge, U.S. District Court, Eastern District of Texas (1968–1998)

AFTER A DEBATE of nearly 200 years, a debate which has never lacked for participants, it may well be that all that can be said about judicial review and its legitimacy has already been said.

But it would be a mistake to assume that modern debate on the subject, however intense, has brought us any closer to a resolution of the problems that a federal judiciary and the institution of judicial review have posed for our contemporary society.

A relatively recent contribution to this debate concerning judicial review was an address by Mr. Justice Rehnquist, entitled "The Notion of a Living Constitution."[1] Justice Rehnquist focused upon a passage from a brief filed in a federal district court on behalf of state prisoners which complained of the conditions of their confinement. The brief writer urged relief from the district court, as "the voice and conscience of contemporary society,"[2] on the ground that the other branches of government had failed to act. Justice Rehnquist criticized this formulation by pointing out that the American form of government is a democratic one, founded on the principle of government by the consent of the governed. Within this framework, the only legitimate justification for judicial review is the one so eloquently propounded by Chief Justice Marshall in *Marbury v. Madison*[3]: that courts, when they strike down an act of a legislative body, do so by the command of the people as embodied in the Constitution. It is therefore not within the constitutional power of a federal judge to remedy every condition which he views as a social evil. Rather, values in a democratic society are best identified through the democratic branches of government.

Acknowledgment to Chief Judge William Wayne Justice for excerpts from his article in 52 University of Colorado Law Review *19 (1980).*

At first glance, there seems little to disagree with in this formulation. On closer reading, however, I discerned three areas which may warrant a response: first, Justice Rehnquist's view of the place of judicial review in a democracy; second, his emphasis on, indeed, his exaltation of, relativism as a constitutional principle; and last, his quick derision of the brief writer's position.

Justice Rehnquist looked first to Marshall's defense of judicial review in *Marbury v. Madison,* according to which the Constitution, as the authoritative voice of the people, must prevail over any legislative acts which conflict with it. This explanation, in Justice Rehnquist's opinion, is "the only one consistent with [a] democratic philosophy of representative government."[4] My problem with it is twofold: First, as Alexander Bickel has convincingly pointed out,[5] the opinion in *Marbury v. Madison* not only begs the question, it begs the wrong question. Obviously, the Constitution is the supreme authority to which all governmental acts must conform; the difficult question is, why should the courts rather than the other two branches be the arbiters of the Constitution? In other words, the necessity for review goes without saying; the real question is, why *judicial* review?

My second objection goes to Justice Rehnquist's expressed desire to find a theory of review that is consistent with a democratic philosophy of government. This is the first instance in the speech of what develops into a recurring tendency, that is, to criticize judicial review, not according to the Constitution, but rather according to some extraconstitutional notion of democracy. The Constitution unquestionably contains some distinctly nonmajoritarian elements. The whole notion of binding future majorities to values they may, from time to time, desire to reject hardly represents adherence to pure majoritarianism. And most noteworthy, Article III withdraws one of the three key governmental functions from popular control. I do not mean that our Constitution is inconsistent with the principles of a self-governing, representative democracy, but I do insist that, rather than judging our Constitution by some abstract, personal, and perhaps arbitrary theory of "democracy," we should judge such a theory by the light of our venerated, and justly venerated, Constitution.

These two objections are intimately related. The answer to the question, why the judiciary should be the guardian of the Constitution, tells us something also about the kind of democracy that our Constitution guarantees. *Marbury v. Madison* takes the easy way out and avoids these questions. Chief Justice Marshall chose to cast the first judicial establishment of judicial review in terms that would least offend the People: he credited the People with superiority over their representatives, rather than according judges, in enforcing the commands of the Constitution, the power to override the representatives of the People.

A far more probing and contemporary justification of judicial review than Justice Marshall's intentional sleight of hand is to be found in Alexander Hamilton's *Federalist* No. 78,[6] published in 1788. The main point of *Federalist* No. 78

is to explain the importance of an independent judiciary. Independent means independent of the *People*; precisely, that judges are not elected. Hamilton did not apologize for this feature; he celebrated it and extolled its virtues. And in meeting head-on the difficult and politically sensitive question why judicial review rather than Congressional or executive review, Hamilton answered, because *judges are independent*.

> The complete independence of the courts of justice is peculiarly essential in a limited [C]onstitution,... one which contains specified exceptions to the legislative authority.... Limitations of this kind can be preserved in practice no other way than through the medium of courts of justice, whose duty it must be to declare all acts contrary to the manifest tenor of the [C]onstitution void. Without this, all the reservations of particular rights or privileges would amount to nothing.[7]

This is the justification of judicial review, in Hamilton's words the "bulwark," the "excellent barrier to the encroachments and oppressions of the representative body."[8]

I have come to believe that Hamilton's argument for what might seem to be the most undemocratic aspect of judicial review turns on the distinction between what the People adopt as a "solemn and authoritative act," as he characterized it; and what they might be tempted to decide, equally authoritatively—but less solemnly—later on. A great many of the individual rights set out in the Constitution were a restatement of English principles: the principles of Magna Carta, the Petition of Rights, the Commonwealth Parliament, and the Revolution of 1688. Others came as the result of our own experience. Nearly all, whether of English or American derivation, were the aftermath of wars, revolutions, insurrections, and civil disturbances. At such times, it appears that those involved are invested with a sense of urgency to memorialize the rights they have so painfully obtained in the form of a "solemn and authoritative act," as though they realize that they may later desire to modify the principles and be tempted to retract them in practice.

A very early and eloquent formulation of this view was suggested by a man of no mean democratic credentials, Thomas Jefferson. Writing in 1781 in his "Notes on the State of Virginia," Jefferson defended the importance of a bill of rights:

> Even in a government which fully reflects the "spirit of the People" ... is the spirit of the times an infallible, a permanent reliance? ... The spirit of the times may alter, will alter. Our rulers will become corrupt, our people careless.... It can never be too often represented, that the time for fixing every essential right on a legal basis is while our rulers are honest, and ourselves united. From the conclusion of this war, we shall be going downhill.[9]

The often-made comparison between the Bill of Rights and contemporary public opinion polls reflecting adverse views as to certain of the enumerated rights seems to support Jefferson's point; perhaps we have indeed gone "downhill." But I would suggest that Jefferson's statement applies even more strongly to those constitutional amendments adopted in the afterglow of the Civil War. In the wake of decades of debate and years of blood, the nation solemnly and authoritatively adopted certain essential principles. Slavery was forbidden, and also outlawed were whatever modified forms of oppression that were substituted for it. The nation committed itself to "equal protection of the laws." The theretofore important principle of relative autonomy for the individual states in their internal affairs was sacrificed to the ideal of the equal application of laws to all citizens.

The generosity of the language chosen reflects the largeness of spirit that prevailed at the time. I feel that the decision to preserve that breadth of spirit represented a hedge against what those who adopted the amendments were afraid they might feel in a less exalted moment. There can certainly be no doubt that the history of Reconstruction and of the first half of the twentieth century show a significant backsliding from the authoritative principles solemnly adopted as a result of our most severe national crisis.

To return to Justice Rehnquist, I wholeheartedly agree with him that judicial review must be confined to the application of the Constitution which the people have adopted. A "generously fair reading of the language and intent of that document,"[10] as he put it, is the only basis for a justifiable judicial decision. But the Justice argued for what amounts to a very minimal judicial review. He derived his views at least in part from what I regard as his rather extreme view of democracy, rather than the more complicated and differentiated governmental structure which the Constitution creates. In several instances, he made deprecatory comments concerning the nonelective status of federal judges. It is, of course, easy to understand that a member of the judiciary who feels compelled to apologize for his nonelected position might feel more uncomfortable in marshaling the Constitution against the will of the majority than would a judge not similarly disposed.

However, the address revealed a second, related, source of his argument for judicial impotence, one that I feel is alien to the Constitution—Justice Rehnquist's attachment to moral relativism. He argued that, since no value can be demonstrated to be intrinsically better or worse than any others, a particular value is *authoritative* only when it can claim majority support. I will seek to show that this sort of uncritical deference to the will of the majority goes far beyond judicial restraint and the intention of the Framers, toward judicial abdication. The key to this understanding I perceive in the decisions of Justice Oliver Wendell Holmes.

Justice Rehnquist began his discussion by identifying two "quite different" meanings to which the phrase "a living Constitution" is susceptible. One he attributed to an anonymous brief writer and the other to Justice Holmes. The Holmes version comes from his famous decision in *Missouri v. Holland*,[11] and reads as follows:

> [W]hen we are dealing with words that also are a constituent act, like the Constitution of the United States, we must realize that they have called into life a being the development of which could not have been foreseen completely by the most gifted of its begetters. It was enough for them to realize or to hope that they had created an organism; it has taken a century and has cost their successors much sweat and blood to prove that they created a nation.

A closer look at the context of this passage casts a rather curious light on what Justice Rehnquist called the Holmesian view of a "living Constitution," and with which, he stated, one could hardly disagree.

Missouri v. Holland involved a suit by the state of Missouri seeking to enjoin federal game wardens from enforcing the Migratory Bird Treaty Act of 1918, as an unconstitutional interference with the rights reserved to the states by the Tenth Amendment. The federal government, concerned with the imminent extinction of several species of migratory birds, had entered into a treaty with Great Britain which prohibited the killing, capturing, or selling of these birds except under regulations to be issued by the Secretary of Agriculture. Injunctive relief was denied by the Supreme Court. The language quoted by Justice Rehnquist, though vague in the extreme, acquires a very specific meaning in this context. First of all, the "being," the "organism" referred to in the passage, is not the Constitution at all; it is, rather, the nation that the Constitution created and, specifically, the federal legislative power. This power is what is living, and hence growing and developing. The Constitution is alive, in this sense, only insofar as it expands to give scope to governmental powers. Far from acting as any kind of limit on government action, the Constitution permits virtually anything Congress decides to do.

As a model of a living Constitution, this view has one distinctive limitation: it provides only for living governmental powers; it says nothing about whether the constitutional *limits* on governmental powers are alive as well. In terms of judicial review, this version of the living Constitution recommends restraint to the point of abdication.

Indeed, Holmes's entire body of work on the Court documents this tendency toward abdication. As Professor Walter Berns has pointed out,[12] we tend to view Holmes's decisions uncritically, even admiringly, because his theory of judicial review happened to correspond to the political views of New Deal reformers, much of whose handiwork has since been vindicated. What we tend to forget, although it is necessarily the other side of the relativist coin, is the number of Holmes's decisions which subsequent history has condemned. In *Bailey v. Alabama*,[13] a Negro plaintiff challenged a statutory system which maintained poor Negroes in a forced condition of peonage. Led by the conservative Justice Hughes, the Court held the system to violate the Thirteenth Amendment's prohibition of involuntary servitude. Holmes preferred to accept the legislature's characterization of the system as a voluntary contractual one and dissented. In *Patsone v. Pennsylvania*,[14] Holmes led the Court to uphold a statute making it unlawful for aliens to kill wild birds or animals or to possess guns. Once again, accepting the legislature's unsupported assumption that the "aliens were the peculiar source of evil,"[15] Holmes resorted to a degree of judicial review which was no review at all, and the law stood.

Finally, and most distressingly, Holmes wrote the infamous majority opinion in *Buck v. Bell*,[16] holding constitutionally valid a state's system of compulsory sterilization of the feebleminded. Although this program clearly intruded into the sacrosanct zone courts now know and respect as personal privacy, Holmes employed his habitually relaxed deference to legislative choice. Asking no questions about the effectiveness of the program, its even handedness, or necessity, he upheld the law. "The principle that sustains compulsory vaccination," he reasoned, "is broad enough to cover cutting the Fallopian tubes."[17] Realizing the worst fears of all antirelativists, Holmes thus equated the elimination of smallpox with the elimination of children.

Holmes's relativism, which Justice Rehnquist professed to swallow whole, when revealed in this naked form, may shock us; but it is more relevant to us today in a different sense—in its relation to the Constitution, which I see as one of repugnancy. The main deficiency of philosophical relativism as a constitutional principle is that it is clearly a latter-day excrescence. The Framers gave no indication that they joined Justice Holmes in seeing "no reason for attributing to man a significance different in kind from that which belongs to a baboon or to a grain of sand."[18] They devoted their best efforts toward providing an environment in which men could achieve a happier existence, through the fullest exercise of their faculties.

This intense concern with the nature and quality of human existence is expressed in the Declaration of Independence, the Preamble to the Constitution, and throughout the *Federalist Papers*. And, although not spelled out in the body of the Constitution in so many words, its presence there is unmistakable, not only in its "majestic generalities,"[19] but in the very fact of the Constitution itself, whose Framers sought to bind future generations. My point is simply that if the relativism of Holmes and Justice Rehnquist had been conceived to be true by the Framers, there would have been no reason for any rights to have been written into a constitution. After all, those rights are only the preferences or "value judgments" of one set of men, and there would have been no reason for them to put on a "legal basis" which would make them difficult for later men, with differing opinions, to change. Following this reasoning, if the men of 1787 wanted religious freedom, they would have merely enacted a statute; why saddle us with their values? If the men of 1867 disliked slavery, a statute would have been sufficient, and would have left later majorities more free to change their minds.

This theory of relativism *implies* that any law more permanent than what a given majority favors is unwarranted. That view is attributable in part to our modern historical circumstance. As an historical observation, I cannot fault the notion that it is a lack of any common religious or moral order that leaves us with a system of law that receives its legitimacy largely from incarnating the focused energies of the body politic. But it is one thing to observe that popular will has become a substitute for any coherent moral vision, and quite another to celebrate this transition from principle to will. I cannot agree with Justice Rehnquist that, as a normative proposition, it is "the fact of their enactment that gives the law whatever moral claim they have upon us as a society."[20] This is a suggestion that consensus is, in itself, a sufficient principle of order. That proposition, under a constitutional system such as ours, cannot be true.

I have understood the source of our enduring and venerable ideals to be more than the *vox populi.* To vest the law with a purely systemic morality is to find in majority sentiment a degree of legitimacy that is simply undeserved. Walter Lippmann urged, many years ago, that we dare not pretend that the principle of majority rule is anything more than a rule of practicality.[21] It is simply a mechanism for decision making, so that we may govern ourselves. The plain fact of the matter is that the majority is sometimes wrong. Lippmann warned that the rule of the majority

> may easily become an absurd tyranny if we regard it worshipfully, as though it were more than a political device. We have lost all sense of its true meaning when we imagine that the opinion of fifty-one percent is in some high fashion the true opinions of the whole hundred percent, or indulge in the sophistry that the rule of the majority is based upon the ultimate equality of man.[22]

Certainly the will of a transient majority should not lightly be permitted to overturn hard-won constitutional rights.

As I have sought to make clear, the inclination of the People to make certain laws more permanent than others must come from a belief that certain values are more important than others. In adopting a constitution, men voluntarily impose limitations on themselves and on future generations, because at that juncture they perceive that their best selves have triumphed. Justice Rehnquist and his mentor, Holmes, apparently do not share this understanding of the implicit reason for a constitution. Because their relativism can offer no real justification for the Constitution's power to bind, they tend to minimize that power, by discouraging its exercise.

But in so doing, they take great liberties with the Constitution. The "democratic theory" on which our Constitution is based is not indifferent to the substance of the People's rule. A complicated government with branches all derived from the People, some more and some less, was instituted in order to secure certain rights. Those rights are just as fundamental to our system as are the democratic principles that were also adopted. Judicial review may seem anomalous in the light of a "democratic theory" which dogmatically insists on popular choice but is dogmatically skeptical about what the people choose; it is not anomalous in a constitution which attempts to reconcile the principle of popular choice with inherent rights.

So far, I have tried to demonstrate that Justice Rehnquist began by adopting Marshall's appealing, popular justification for judicial review rather than the more intellectually candid one expressed by Hamilton in *Federalist* No. 78, and proceeded from this false beginning to a falsely restrictive sense of how judicial review should be exercised.

As my final point, I would like to offer a partial defense of the so-called brief writer's position, and in so doing complete the picture of how the Justice's version of judicial restraint, as set out in his speech, was derived not from a conservative or interpretivist view of the Constitution, with which I might differ only as a question of degree, but rather from the substitution of his own relativist majoritarian ideals for those embodied in the Constitution, a substitution which I cannot accept at all.

Justice Rehnquist criticized two main points in the brief writer's position: first, that "the federal judiciary may address themselves to a social problem simply because other branches of government have failed or refused to do so"; and second, that "[t]hese same judges, responsible to no constituency whatever," are expected to speak as "the voice and conscience of contemporary society" and as "the measure of the modern conception of human dignity."[23] Certainly the language here is a bit inflated; after all, the writer was seeking to persuade. But are the points made so contemptible as Justice Rehnquist made them out to be? My "generously fair" reading of the words convinces me that, on the contrary, they represent quite traditional constitutional thought.

The first point was made as part of the brief writer's argument that, as a discrete and insular minority, prisoners are entitled to heightened judicial solicitude. The language of "discrete and insular" minority is, of course, Justice Stone's from the famous footnote 4 of the *Carolene Products* case.[24] Justice Stone, in urging general judicial restraint when reviewing legislative acts, excepted those laws disadvantaging classes whose access to the representative processes was practically nonexistent. This seems to me perfectly consistent with Hamilton's description of the judiciary as a bulwark against majoritarian excesses, and with the language of the equal protection clause. It must have seemed so to others as well, since footnote 4 has become the source and mainstay of the Supreme Court's equal protection doctrine. While it would be premature to form an opinion about whether prisoners in fact constitute a discrete and insular minority, it would have been odd had their counsel neglected to urge it, and certainly not contemptible that he did.

The brief writer's second point is equally arguable. Like all other suits of this nature, the prisoner's complaint must necessarily have included a claim under the Eighth Amendment, which prohibits "cruel and unusual punishments." Justice Rehnquist never quoted, or even referred to, the constitutional provisions invoked. Yet any mode of judicial review must at least begin with the language of the Constitution. "Cruel and unusual" are subjective words; they are not susceptible of fixed, qualitative meanings. "Cruel" is a word of emotional charge; "unusual" requires comparison. Both take on meaning in the context of the facts. It is virtually uncontroverted that the Framers of the Constitution and their constituents contemplated judicial review to enforce the Bill of Rights. Knowing this, they refrained from prohibiting only dismemberment and other punishments frowned on at the time in favor of the more general language, just as after the Civil War the framers of the Fourteenth Amendment chose not to limit its protection only to freed slaves. Once again, I reserve judgment on the merits of the brief writer's argument that certain prison conditions conflict with the Eighth Amendment. Certainly, I interpret nothing in the Constitution as a "roving commission" inviting me to enforce my own personal values; but, directly confronting the Eighth Amendment, which Justice Rehnquist refrained from doing in his speech, I do not feel that the Constitution allows me to dismiss the argument out of hand. After all, it was in an Eighth Amendment case, *Trop v. Dulles,*[25] that the Supreme Court said "the words of the Amendment are not precise, and ... their scope is not static. The Amendment must draw its meaning from the evolving standards of decency that mark the progress of a maturing society."[26]

By paraphrasing these arguments and by ignoring the constitutional provisions behind them, the Justice appears to have distorted and obscured what is meritorious in them, and once again in the Holmesian mode, seems to have replaced judicial review with virtual abdication, calling it restraint. The brief writer suggested "that if the states' legislatures and governors, or Congress and the President, have not solved a particular social problem, then the federal court may act." Justice Rehnquist's answer was: "I do not believe that this argument will withstand rational analysis. Even in the face of a conceded social evil, a reasonably representative legislature may decide to do nothing."[27]

With this last statement I cannot disagree. But neither do I find it terribly useful to a judge trying to interpret the Constitution. Identifying something as a social evil does not advance a judge's task. There are all varieties of social evils. Some, like police policies of coercing confessions or making unreasonable searches, are unconstitutional. Others, like inadequate flood control and 7 percent unemployment, are not. Still others, concerning a state's administration of its welfare system or its prisons, may pose a close question. Justice Rehnquist's use of the phrase "social evil" perhaps emblematizes my main point of departure with the Justice. The phrase starts out with a political conclusion where a textual inquiry should begin. It blurs and obscures where there should be clarification and analysis. And it ends before any questions are asked, not with informed restraint, but with abdication.

In closing, I call your attention to the words of Professor Thayer: "The tendency of a common and easy resort to [judicial review], now lamentably too common, is to dwarf the political capacity of the people, and to deaden its sense of moral responsibility. It is not a light thing to do that."[28] I wholly agree with that sentiment. Let it be emphasized that I would prefer a regime in which the popular branches were sensitive to and respectful of constitutional restraints, so that judicial review would be unnecessary. I infinitely would favor legislative and administrative reform of prisons to attempts at reform by the judiciary. Similarly I would have preference for voluntary compliance with the Fourth Amendment to the exclusionary rule. I likewise would prefer that legislative encroachments and oppressions, against which the Framers intended Article III to be the bulwark, be few and far between, and that government by the People and respect for individual rights coexist.

But I also agree with the view of Justice Cardozo, who spoke to precisely this threat—the possibility that courts may come to oppress legislative initiative. This danger, according to Cardozo,

> must be balanced against those of independence from all restraint, independence on the part of public officers elected for brief terms, without the guiding force of a continuous tradition. On the whole, I believe the latter dangers to be the more formidable of the two. Great maxims, if they may be violated with impunity, are honored often with lip service, which passes easily into irreverence. The restraining power of the judiciary does not manifest its chief worth in the few cases in which the legislature has gone beyond the lines that mark the limits of discretion. Rather shall we find its chief worth in making vocal and audible the ideals that might otherwise be silenced, in giving them continuity of life and of expression, in guiding and directing choice within the limits where choice ranges. This function should preserve to the courts the power that now belongs to them, if only the power is exercised with insight into social values, and with suppleness of adaptation to changing social needs.[29]

Notes

1. W. Rehnquist, "The Notion of a Living Constitution," 54 *Texas Law Review* 693 (1976).
2. Ibid., at 695.
3. 5 U.S. (1 Cranch) 137 (1803).
4. Rehnquist, supra note 1, at 697.
5. A. Bickel, *The Least Dangerous Branch* 2 (Indianapolis: Bobbs-Merrill, 1962).
6. *The Federalist,* No. 78, ed. by J. C. Hamilton (Philadelphia: Lippincott, 1873).
7. Ibid., at 576–577.
8. Ibid., at 575.
9. T. Jefferson, *The Life and Selected Writings of Jefferson* 277, ed. by A. Koch and W. Peden (New York: Random House, 1944).
10. Rehnquist, supra note 1, at 704.
11. 252 U.S. 416, 433 (1920).
12. W. Berns, *The First Amendment and the Future of American Democracy* 163 (New York: Basic Books, 1976).
13. 219 U.S. 219 (1911).
14. 232 U.S. 138 (1914).
15. Ibid., at 144.
16. 274 U.S. 200 (1927).
17. Ibid., at 207.
18. O.W. Holmes, *The Holmes-Pollock Letters*, Vol. 2, 252, ed. by M. DeWolfe Howe (Cambridge: Belknap Press, 1961).
19. *Fay v. New York,* 332 U.S. 261, 282 (1947) (Jackson, J.).
20. Rehnquist, supra note 1, at 704.
21. C. Rossiter and J. Lare, eds., *The Essential Lippmann* (New York: Random House, 1963).
22. Ibid., at 13.
23. Rehnquist, supra note 1, at 695
24. *United States v. Carolene Products Co.,* 304 U.S. 144 (1938).
25. 356 U.S. 96 (1958).
26. Ibid., at 100.
27. Rehnquist, supra note 1, at 700.
28. J. Thayer, *John Marshall* 106–107 (Boston: Houghton, Mifflin, 1901).
29. B. Cardozo, *The Nature of the Judicial Process* 93–94 (New Haven: Yale University Press, 1921).

CHAPTER 18

The Jurisprudence of Judicial Restraint

A Return to the Moorings

J. Clifford Wallace

Judge, U.S. Court of Appeals, Ninth Circuit (1972–1996) and Judge, U.S. District Court, Southern District of California (1970–1972)

My purpose here is to sketch the theory and practice of, and argue for, a philosophy of judicial restraint. The opposite of judicial activism, judicial restraint has sometimes been referred to as "strict constructionism" or "interpretivism."[1] "Strict constructionism" or "interpretivism," in the natural meaning of those terms, is, as will emerge later, part, but only part, of judicial restraint.

Judicial restraint, as I will use the phrase, is not tied to any narrow sectarian politics, but rather is based upon concerns of legal predictability, uniformity, and judicial economy, and most importantly, upon values of liberty and democracy that are widely shared by our American citizens. Indeed, judicial restraint is dictated by the Constitution. My argument is that our Republic would be best served if the judiciary returned to those moorings.

The Constitution and the Theory of Judicial Restraint

Although the language of the Constitution is not as reminiscent of John Locke as is that of the Declaration of Independence, the substance of the Constitution shows the influence of Locke's theory that the central purpose of government is the

Acknowledgment to Judge J. Clifford Wallace for his lecture delivered at the National Law Center, George Washington University (September 25, 1981), appearing in 50 George Washington Law Review *1 (1981).*

protection of individual rights such as life, liberty, and private property. This purpose establishes one element of any judicial philosophy. The courts must protect constitutional rights against infringement, even infringement by the legally elected representatives of the majority. This, then, is one respect in which the Constitution is not entirely democratic. There are limits on what the majority may do.

For example, the representatives of the majority may not, without going through the amendment process, pass a bill of attainder, establish cruel and unusual punishment, or make race a condition of suffrage. In practice,[2] amendment requires a supermajority. Thus, although the Constitution imposes no absolute limits[3] on popular decision making, constitutional protections and structures do represent significant practical restraints on the scope of majoritarian democracy.

The Constitution includes a number of devices designed, at least in part, to protect the citizenry. The division of authority between the states and the federal government, for example, insures both that certain basic rights will be respected throughout the territory of the United States and that a wide range of decisions affecting rights will be made by a government less distant from the individual than is the federal government. Moreover, the danger that government will infringe rights is diminished whenever there is more than one center of power. The oppressive potential of a unified government is total. In a federal system, such total oppression is less likely because it requires the close cooperation of many different centers of power. Thus, our federal system wisely reserves all powers to the states except those delegated to the central government.

The Framers also designed the division of authority among three branches of the federal government to protect individual rights. The very separateness of the branches curtails the risk of oppression in the same fashion as does the division of power between federal and state governments. The more their separateness and relative equality are maintained, the less is the likelihood that the governmental branches will be united in undermining constitutional protections.

Beyond this, however, the Framers intended the judicial branch to have a special role in the protection of rights. One of the motivations for creating this unique role for the judicial branch may have been a distrust of the other branches. The Framers probably feared most the executive branch of government because they had fresh in their minds the oppressive potential of a king. Legislatures were, however, not free of suspicion. During the Confederation period the state legislatures had inspired widespread distrust. Many thought that democracy was getting out of hand by violating rights of citizens in an excessive zeal for equality. Oppression by the judicial branch was not feared as much by the Framers, presumably because in their experience the colonial and state courts had been relatively benign. As is well known, Hamilton considered the judiciary the "least dangerous" and "weakest" branch.[4] This perhaps explains why the Constitution neither expressly directs nor restrains the judiciary very much.

The partisans of both judicial activism and judicial restraint agree that government cannot act beyond the outer limits established by constitutional boundaries without becoming subject to judicial intervention. The controversial question is just where those limits are and thus how extensive the territory is within which government can function free of judicial intervention.

To answer this question we must look to a second aspect of our Constitution—its democratic side. The Constitution establishes the framework for a federal representative democracy and guarantees to the states a "republican form of government."[5]

The Founders structured the democracy of the federal government to ameliorate what some of them perceived as egalitarian excesses of democracy. The federal democracy, then, is a limited democracy. The Constitution imposes external limits, such as the Bill of Rights, and internal devices of indirect voting and representation. Most of the internal checks on the federal democracy remain. Similarly, the Founders intended the "republican form of government" clause to embrace a wide range of political forms of state governments. Regardless, however, of the built-in checks on the federal democracy and latitude afforded state governments, the Framers intended the basic form of both the federal government and state governments to be democratic in the broad sense. Citizens would make decisions, directly or indirectly. I wish now to focus upon this democratic aspect of our governmental enterprise.

Difficult cases concerning whether a decision by Congress, a state legislature, or elected officials falls within the permissible range of discretion afforded those bodies or officials often test one's belief in judicial restraint. An examination of the value of democracy can assist one in arriving at an answer in these controversial cases. If democracy is an intrinsic, fundamental value, then the area of legislative discretion is presumably larger than it would be if democracy were a minor or derivative value.

Democracy is, I believe, intrinsically and fundamentally valuable. Therefore, judges, mindful of the Constitution, must be extremely cautious in taking decisions away from elected representatives and elected officials.

The opposing theory is that democracy is simply an instrumental value. Under the instrumental theory, democracy is valuable only to the extent that it produces substantively "better" decisions than would any other available decision-making procedure. This view has the corollary that democracy should be replaced by a benevolent dictator or a computer if one can be found that will make better decisions.

If one believes that the value of democracy is only instrumental and if one runs across a congressional enactment that is clearly unwise, then one has a duty to correct the mistake, if possible. A democratic decision procedure that is corrected in an undemocratic fashion when clearly wrong is better, instrumentally speaking, than the same procedure without the correction.

We may fairly assume that no judge believes that he or she can correct any enactment that comes before the court solely because it is perceived to be unwise. At the least there must be some colorable argument for unconstitutionality or a rationale for interpreting the statute in a way that overrides legislative intent. If one believes in the instrumental theory of democracy, however, one is likely to find the required constitutional argument or statutory construction when faced with what one perceives to be a bad statute.

A noninstrumental theory of democracy, by contrast, places value in the democratic process even when decisions fall short of the best possible—indeed even when the majority makes a decision that is stupid, irrational, or completely wrong-headed. As a private citizen one may vote directly or indirectly against bad legislation while still believing that the majority, because it is the majority, has a right to be mistaken. The majority does not have a right to make just any sort of mistake, of course, because constitutional limits remain. The noninstrumentalist, however, believes that, aside from the constitutional restraints, it is better that the majority make a wrong decision than that a judge make the decision, even if the judge would make a socially more beneficial decision. As a judge, he or she will be careful to allow only the legislature to develop social policy. Such a judge believes that, aside from what is proscribed by the Constitution, the legislature has a right to be wrong. A judge who believes in the intrinsic value of democracy will, then, shrink from abrogating legislative decisions and will look for ways to uphold legislation rather than to strike it down.

A corollary of the noninstrumental theory of democracy is that it is better for the majority to make a mistaken policy decision, within broad limits, than for a judge to make a correct one. That is, the process by which the decision is made may have greater value than the decision itself.

I hope that, on reflection, you will agree that democracy is intrinsically valuable. If you are not yet persuaded, let me give an argument for the proposition.

The starting assumption of my argument is that *liberty* is intrinsically valuable. This assumption is very nearly an article of faith of our American political philosophy. It is better to be free and hungry than to be a well-fed slave. We do think that, as a general rule, people make better decisions for themselves than others would make for them, but this instrumental advantage of liberty is secondary. Freedom is necessary for a realization of what makes human beings human. To take away a person's power to make decisions—his or her autonomy—is an extreme measure only slightly less severe than taking away the power to think.

My argument for the intrinsic value of democracy is that democracy is an extension of liberty into the realm of social decision making. One cannot consistently be an instrumentalist about democracy and believe that liberty is intrinsically valuable. This rather abstract-sounding philosophical claim can be illustrated by a homely example. Suppose that five co-owners of a building are in disagreement whether it should be painted white or blue. If there were only one owner, he would be free to paint the building as he chose. His choice would not be frustrated. With five persons of differing opinions, however, some choices will inevitably be frustrated. A majority decision minimizes the number of persons whose choices are frustrated. In this way, democracy most nearly approximates the liberty of a single free decision maker. In general, majoritarian democracy is more respectful of individual autonomy than is any other social decision-making procedure that guarantees a decision. Therefore, the same respect for human autonomy that underlies liberty underlies democracy as well and establishes its intrinsic value.

Liberty and democracy can, of course, come into conflict. The majority may vote to restrict liberty. To resolve this conflict between the two intrinsic values, one must answer this question: Which decisions are to be made individually and which collectively through the democratic process? The Constitution provides part of the answer to this question by establishing limits on the powers of Congress and the states. A great many issues, however, are not committed by the Constitution either to the democratic process or to individual decision.

Consider a decision that really should, as a matter of sound political philosophy or moral theory, be left to the individual, but that is not reserved to the individual by the Constitution. Suppose that Congress or a state legislature passes an act deciding the issue and thus takes it out of the hands of the individual. There are, I believe, federal and state statutes of this description. Possible examples include state laws requiring drivers to wear seat belts and federal laws removing cyclamates from the market. Alternatively, consider taxation. From a theoretical perspective, every tax dollar limits the individual taxpayer's effective freedom by restricting his or her capacity to make purchases or investments. Some of this loss of freedom through taxation is, of course, well-justified by the federal or state programs supported by the revenues. Not every spending program, however, is sufficiently worthwhile to provide an adequate justification for taxation. I will leave you free to nominate your own candidates for the least worthwhile state and federal spending programs.

Certainly we can all agree that there are some laws that restrict individual liberty in ways that are unwise, though constitutionally permissible. Activists would argue that in at least some such cases, the judiciary should step in to vindicate liberty on the theory that the intrinsic value of liberty outweighs the intrinsic value of democracy.

The problem is in identifying an unwise, though constitutional, limitation on liberty. I may be confident that a particular statute is unwise. The legislature, however, may have been just as confident that the statute represented good social policy. Are judges, as a group, better at making judgments of social policy than are legislatures? Certainly legislatures, with their committees, staffs, and deliberative processes, are institutionally better-equipped to investigate the consequences of policy decisions than are the courts. I do not believe that one gains added wisdom or a keener perception of social value merely by becoming a judge. Indeed, because a judge is removed from the political process while a legislator is constantly immersed in it, the legislator is more closely exposed to the basic needs of society.

There undoubtedly remain cases in which an omniscient Being could verify that the judge's instincts are better than those of the legislature. But the judge does not have that perception, and his or her subjective confidence is a wholly inadequate substitute for objective omniscience. There is, in this instance, a process deficiency.

A judge cannot act on the belief that he or she knows better than the legislature on a question of policy, because the judge can never be justifiably certain that he or she is right even when the judge happens to be right. In this way, appropriate judicial humility weighs against judicial activism. Thus, even when the intrinsic value of liberty or other values outweigh the intrinsic value of democracy, there is no justification for judicial activism.

The intrinsic value of democracy thus provides a general theoretical underpinning for judicial restraint—an underpinning not undermined by the possibility that in a given case other values may be more important than democracy.

But the important value of democracy underlies only one aspect of judicial restraint. Other aspects I will describe only briefly, not because they are unimportant, but because they are easy to identify and analyze. Concern for legal predictability and for the coherence of the legal system as a whole also fosters judicial restraint. These values suggest following the natural interpretation of statutory language and case law. They also suggest a general caution towards legal innovation.

Legal economy further justifies judicial restraint. Many disputes are better resolved in a nonjudicial setting. Courts are cost-effective, for the most part, in settling disputes. They become cost-ineffective when asked to re-engineer social structures and reorganize social priorities.

Litigation does not produce wealth. On its civil side, it is primarily a means of redistributing wealth, and a very expensive means at that. One party wins; the other pays. Both incur litigation expenses. Society pays directly, in supporting the courts, and indirectly, through losses in productivity. No other nation devotes as much of its resources to litigation as ours does. In this era of international economic competition, we should hardly wish to excel in the category of litigation expense. Judicial restraint addresses this problem by being cautious about jurisdiction and the extension of causes of action.

Finally, judicial restraint is consistent with and complementary to the balance of power among the three independent branches. It accomplishes this in two ways. First, judicial restraint not only recognizes the equality of the other two branches with the judiciary, but also fosters that equality by minimizing interbranch interference by the judiciary. In this analysis, judicial restraint might better be called judicial respect; that is, respect by the judiciary for the other coequal branches. In contrast, judicial activism's unpredictable results make the judiciary a moving target and thus decrease the ability to maintain equality with the co-branches. Restraint stabilizes the judiciary so it may better function in a system of interbranch equality.

Second, judicial restraint tends to protect the independence of the judiciary. When courts become engaged in social legislation, almost inevitably voters, legislators, and other elected officials will conclude that the activities of judges should be closely monitored. If judges act like legislators, it follows that judges should be elected like legislators. This is counterproductive. The touchstone of an independent federal judiciary has been its removal from the political process. Even if this removal has sometimes been less than complete, it is an ideal worthy of support and one that has had valuable effects.

The constitutional trade-off for independence is that judges must restrain themselves from the areas reserved to the other, separate branches. Thus, judicial restraint complements the twin, overarching values of the independence of the judiciary and the separation of powers.

The Practical Application of Judicial Restraint

So much for the theory of judicial restraint. I would now like to say something about its practice. By way of summary, the overall and abstract conception of judicial restraint, as I understand it, is that to avoid usurping the policy-making role of democratically elected bodies and officials, a judge should always hesitate to declare statutes or governmental actions unconstitutional and cautious to supplement or modify statutes when construing them. Courts should make as little social policy as possible consistent with deciding properly presented controversies. As a corollary, judges should remain keenly aware of the possibility that a controversy is not, in fact, properly before them and should resist the temptation to decide an issue broader than the one actually before the court.

Constitutional law is perhaps the realm in which questions of judicial activism and judicial restraint are of most interest. Because constitutional law concerns the interpretation of a legal document in the light of prior case law, it combines the considerations involved in the statutory and common-law contexts. If there were no common-law legacy, judicial restraint would apply to constitutional interpretation just as it does to the interpretation of statutes. Drawing on the discussion of statutory interpretation, and temporarily assuming away the existence of case law, I would tentatively suggest the following principles:

1. Stand by the clear language of the Constitution unless doing so is manifestly counter to the Framers' intent.
2. Clarify unclear constitutional language in line with the Framers' intent if that intent is ascertainable with reasonable certainty.
3. If neither of the prior principles applies, clarify unclear constitutional language by selecting the alternative that least restricts the discretion of elected lawmakers and officials.
4. If none of the prior principles applies, clarify unclear constitutional language in line with the best estimate of the Framers' intent or in the manner most congruent with prior expectations.

This approach is at odds with the popular "living Constitution" or "growing Constitution" theory of interpretation, with its touchstone—current social attitudes. Conceivably, current social attitudes might be relevant to constitutional interpretation. I find no constitutional language, however, that explicitly builds current social attitudes into the Constitution. Still, the Framers possibly intended certain specific clauses of the Constitution or its amendments to be read as if they contained variables ranging over social attitudes. For example, one might argue that the Framers used the term "cruel and unusual punishment" in the Eighth Amendment to provide for a varying societal approach.

Although it is possible that the Framers intended to write this sort of flexibility into the Constitution, constitutional language to that effect is absent. The burden of historical proof should therefore be on those who assert that the Framers intended a so-called living Constitution.

Some have argued that a constitution is by its very nature a growing document. The Framers could not have intended otherwise, the argument runs, because they could not have intended to put the future into a straitjacket.[6] This is an extremely tenuous historical hypothesis upon which to base an all-inclusive constitutional theory. More importantly, it is unlikely that the Framers, who made the Constitution so difficult to change by amendment, would have made it so easy to change by reference to sociological surveys.

In addition, squaring the belief held by the Framers' generation in self-evident truth and inalienable rights with the normative relativity of the "growing Constitution" theory is difficult. The relativity of truth and rights would have made no more sense to the Framers than it would have to John Locke, that is, no sense at all. In short, I strongly suspect that the "living" or "growing" Constitution is a twentieth-century theory anachronistically projected back onto the eighteenth and nineteenth centuries.

The living Constitution theory also displays a naive faith in consistent moral and social progress. The idea that the Constitution changes with shifting public opinion seems relatively benign if one expects public opinion to become more enlightened with the passage of time. If, however, one expects public opinion to become more enlightened with the passage of time, one may not want a constitution at all. Why not simply have a democratic body without any restrictions on its decisions—like the British Parliament? Why should a less enlightened past put *any* restrictions on a more enlightened future?

Constitution making apparently assumes a less than complete optimism about the consistency of future political progress. In this light, consider the possibility that due to various tragic circumstances our country is shaken by a wave of bigotry and racism. Are we to assume that drafters of the Fourteenth Amendment intended the meaning of the equal protection clause to change under these circumstances, losing its bite? Far more likely, they intended the Fourteenth Amendment not only to remedy the precise problem facing them, but to protect against possible future changes in the composition and racial views of the enfranchised electorate.

At this point, I may appear to be inconsistent. Earlier I argued in favor of judicial restraint by citing the intrinsic value of democracy. Now I argue against the "living Constitution" theory by citing the Framers' fears of future electorates. There is, however, no inconsistency. The Constitution, the Framers' intent, and our proper attitude towards the Constitution all have democratic as well as nondemocratic aspects. There can be no doubt that the Constitution establishes outer bounds on legislation and official conduct. What I have been arguing just now is that there is no good reason to believe that the Framers intended those bounds to change with time and public opinion, short of amendment. To conclude that the bounds are stationary, however, is not yet to establish their location. The democratic component of judicial restraint encourages placing those outer bounds as widely as the language of the Constitution permits in order to maximize the area of legislative discretion in solving social problems.

In fact, there is much less reason to think that the constitutional limits must change with time if they do not cover too broad a range of subjects to begin with. A constitution is properly a short document; like the Ten Commandments, it needs to say very little to be of great importance. It guards the most vital political structures and most fundamental human rights in an unyielding and changeless way. Exactly because it intrudes on future democratic decisions only in the most important respects, it deserves serious attention when it does speak. It should not be trivialized. A constitution interpreted so broadly that it plays the same role as social legislation must change as social conditions change. There is, however, no need for such a constitution. We have Congress and the state legislatures to write laws in the light of changing conditions. By accepting the Constitution as a brief set of fixed guiding principles, it may be applied to new situations, but not modified by ever-changing public opinion. Thus, the democratic aspect of judicial restraint is complementary to the view that the Framers intended the Constitution to "grow" only through amendment.

The "living Constitution" school and others that see the major role of the judiciary as a social instrument to effectuate change may be suspected of a certain historical one-sidedness. They favor a growing Constitution only when it grows their way. More generally, activism loses much of its appeal if one considers the possibility of a court composed of judges whose activism favored social positions diametrically opposed to one's own philosophy. I will discuss this problem in general in its historical setting in a few moments.

So far, in discussing constitutional interpretation, I have operated under the enormously simplifying assumption that there is no case law. For better and for worse, there is a great deal of case law. Much of it is sound in terms of the canons of judicial restraint. Some of it is not.

For a judge, and especially a judge below the Supreme Court, the case law of a higher court, and usually that of the judge's own court, is given, even when it is wrong. Judicial restraint that did not follow binding precedent would not be worthy of its name. There is a difference, however, between following precedent and extending it. Predictability and uniformity increase when a judge applies a precedent to an analogous set of facts. The closer the analogy, the more judicial restraint will tend to favor the application. This is only a tendency, however.

If the extension runs counter to the principles of judicial restraint regarding constitutional interpretation, this conflict will provide a reason for refusing to extend the precedent. Whether extending the precedent to new areas is the judicially restrained course of action, all things considered, depends upon the closeness of the precedent to the new area and its degree of perceived wrongness. In making the determination, the judge must take into account the rationale of the precedent because the rationale is relevant to considerations of predictability and uniformity.

Judicial Restraint's Response to Judicial Activism

The abstract theory of judicial restraint that I discussed earlier may in certain respects sound a little radical—although I would say it is radical only in the sense of returning to the origin, the fundamental moorings of the Constitution and our judicial heritage. The underlying values of judicial restraint are not those of any particular political party or ideology, but rather are the values of liberty, democracy, predictability, uniformity, and judicial economy. By the very nature of judicial restraint, there can be nothing radical, in the popular sense, about its practice. It requires that one play the game with strict attention to the rules. Its model of the judge is more that of neutral expounder of justice under law than that of a moral reformer. It recognizes that the judge is not the complete problem-solver, but one part of a team. It requires him or her to give proper deference to the other independent branches, even when he or she believes that they have made an incorrect choice of policy.

Judicial restraint only rarely permits one to overturn the law made by activist judges. This obviously gives such judges a certain advantage, because judges who deplore their innovations will nonetheless often retain, though rarely extend, them.

If left entirely unchecked, periodic activist inroads over the years could emasculate fundamental doctrines and undermine the separation of powers. Judges may therefore overturn judicial decisions in certain special circumstances: if the decisions are clearly wrong, have important effects, and would otherwise be difficult to negate.

A constitutional case will more often meet the third of these conditions than will a case concerning statutory construction. An incorrect interpretation of a statute can be set aside by Congress through a more explicit enactment. A constitutional misinterpretation, however, may do continuing damage because of the difficulty of the amendment process. Similarly, because of the institutional centrality of the Constitution and because of its unique role of protecting the citizenry, a constitutional case will very often meet the second condition—importance. Constitutional cases may also provide the best examples of the first condition—clear error. They will tend to be clearly wrong, for example, when judges, influenced by "living Constitution" jurisprudence, spin twentieth-century sociology out of the eighteenth- or nineteenth-century language.

The activist judge must not therefore assume, particularly in constitutional cases, that judicially restrained successors will let stand every activist misconstruction of the Constitution. Undoing an activist mistake does not offend the democratic values underlying restraint. Indeed, undoing antidemocratic forays supports those values. But such a course may offend predictability and perhaps uniformity. For these reasons, judges must approach the overturning process with the greatest care. These considerations, however, do not totally militate against the necessary overruling of precedent. Predictability and uniformity are important instrumental values, but they are outweighed when the great values of our Constitution are at stake.

Thus, even when, in overruling precedent, judicial restraint most nearly resembles activism, it maintains a general consistency with its underlying principles. Those principles demand the neutralization of activist judicial decisions that fundamentally distort the Constitution.

Judicial restraint is also consistent in its application to different historical periods. Its practice does not vary with changing political currents among legislators and judges. It adheres to a consistency of principle.

Judicial activism, by contrast, has no such consistency. Many who deplored the activism of the economic substantive due process era earlier in this century praised the activism of the Warren Court. Although one may try to draw subtle jurisprudential distinctions, I must be excused for suspecting that the only real difference was pure politics unattached to constitutional principles. Virtue seemed to be dictated by the result. In one era, these theorists found the legislatures more congenial to their political preferences than was the bench. In the later era, this relationship was reversed. A judicial doctrine that waxes and wanes with the political tides is unworthy of the name "philosophy." It is nothing more than a rationalization of a willingness to use whatever means are expedient to reach one's preferred results. Regardless of one's political or social view, one should reject such a judicial approach.

Notes

1. E.g., J. Ely, *Democracy and Distrust* (Cambridge: Harvard University Press, 1980).
2. Even if the state legislatures accurately reflect their constituents, a majority can, in theory, amend the Constitution. This is because only a bare majority in each of three-fourths of the states need approve the amendment. The citizens of the remaining one-quarter of the states, which might be the most populous states, might unanimously disapprove.
3. There is one exception. Article V prohibits depriving a state of equal suffrage in the Senate without consent of the state. Presumably this clause of Article V and the relevant parts of Article I, Sec. 3, are unamendable.
4. *The Federalist,* No. 78, at 504, ed. by S. Miltell (Washington, D.C.: National Home Library Foundation, 1938).
5. U.S. Constitution, Art. IV, Sec. 4, cl. 1.
6. E.g., M. Perry, "Abortion, Public Morals, and the Police Power," 23 *U.C.L.A. Law Review* 689, 713 (1977).

CHAPTER 19

Tradition and Morality in Constitutional Law

Robert H. Bork

Judge, U.S. Court of Appeals, District of Columbia Circuit (1981–1988)

WHEN A JUDGE undertakes to speak in public about any subject that might be of more interest than the law of incorporeal hereditaments he embarks upon a perilous enterprise. There is always, as I have learned with some pain, someone who will write a story finding it sensational that a judge should say anything. There is some sort of notion that judges have no general ideas about law or, if they do, that, like pornography, ideas are shameful and ought not to be displayed in public to shock the squeamish. For that reason, I come before you, metaphorically at least, clad in a plain brown wrapper.

One common style of speech on occasions such as this is that which paints a bleak picture, identifies even bleaker trends, and then ends on a note of strong and, from the evidence presented, wholly unwarranted optimism. I hope to avoid both extremes while talking about sharply divergent ideas that are struggling for dominance within the legal culture. While I think it serious and potentially of crisis proportions, I speak less to thrill you with the prospect of doom—which is always good fun—than to suggest to you that law is an arena of ideas that is too often ignored by intellectuals interested in public policy. Though it was not always so, legal thought has become something of an intellectual enclave. Too few people are aware of the trends there and the importance of those trends for public policy.

Acknowledgment to Judge Robert H. Bork for the Francis Boyer Lectures on Public Policy given at the American Enterprise Institute. Copyright 1984 by the American Enterprise Institute for Public Policy Research, Washington, D.C.

It is said that, at a dinner given in his honor, the English jurist Baron Parke was asked what gave him the greatest pleasure in the law. He answered that his greatest joy was to write a "strong opinion." Asked what that might be, the baron said, "It is an opinion in which, by reasoning with strictly legal concepts, I arrive at a result no layman could conceivably have anticipated."

That was an age of formalism in the law. We have come a long way since then. The law and its acolytes have since become steadily more ideological and more explicit about that fact. That is not necessarily a bad thing: there are ideologies suitable, indeed indispensable, for judges, just as there are ideologies that are subversive of the very idea of the rule of law. It is the sharp recent growth in the latter that is worrisome for the future.

We are entering, I believe, a period in which our legal culture and constitutional law may be transformed, with even more power accruing to judges than is presently the case. There are two reasons for that. One is that constitutional law has very little theory of its own and hence is almost pathologically lacking in immune defenses against the intellectual fevers of the larger society as well as against the disorders that were generated by its own internal organs.

The second is that the institutions of the law, in particular the schools, are becoming increasingly converted to an ideology of the Constitution that demands just such an infusion of extraconstitutional moral and political notions. A not untypical example of the first is the entry into the law of the First Amendment of the old, and incorrect, view that the only kinds of harm that a community is entitled to suppress are physical and economic injuries. Moral harms are not to be counted because to do so would interfere with the autonomy of the individual. That is an indefensible definition of what people are entitled to regard as harms.

The result of discounting moral harm is the privatization of morality, which requires the law of the community to practice moral relativism. It is thought that individuals are entitled to their moral beliefs but may not gather as a community to express those moral beliefs in law. Once an idea of that sort takes hold in the intellectual world, it is very likely to find lodgment in constitutional theory and then in constitutional law. The walls of the law have proved excessively permeable to intellectual osmosis. Out of prudence, I will give but one example of the many that might be cited.

A state attempted to apply its obscenity statute to a public display of an obscene word. The Supreme Court majority struck down the conviction on the grounds that regulation is a slippery slope and that moral relativism is a constitutional command. The opinion said, "The principle contended for by the State seems inherently boundless. How is one to distinguish this from any other offensive word?" One might as well say that the negligence standard of tort law is inherently boundless, for how is one to distinguish the reckless driver from the safe one? The answer in both cases is, by the common sense of the community. Almost all judgments in the law are ones of degree, and the law does not flinch from such judgments except when, as in the case of morals, it seriously doubts the community's right to define harms. Moral relativism was even more explicit in the majority opinion, however, for the Court observed, apparently thinking the observation decisive: "One man's vulgarity is another's lyric." On that ground, it is difficult to see how law on any subject can be permitted to exist.

But the Court immediately went further, reducing the whole question to one of private preference, saying: "We think it is largely because governmental officials cannot make principled distinctions in this area that the Constitution leaves matters of taste and style so largely to the individual." Thus, the community's moral and aesthetic judgments are reduced to questions of style and those are then said to be privatized by the Constitution. It testifies all the more clearly to the power of ideas floating in the general culture to alter the Constitution that this opinion was written by a justice generally regarded as moderate to conservative in his constitutional views.

George Orwell reminded us long ago about the power of language to corrupt thought and the consequent baleful effects upon politics. The same deterioration is certainly possible in morality. But I am not concerned about the constitutional protection cast about an obscene word. Of more concern is the constitutionalizing of the notion that moral harm is not harm legislators are entitled to consider. As Lord Devlin said, "What makes a society is a community of ideas, not political ideas alone but also ideas about the way its members should behave and govern their lives." A society that ceases to be a community increases the danger that weariness with turmoil and relativism may bring about an order in which many more, and more valuable, freedoms are lost than those we thought we were protecting.

I do not know the origin of the notion that moral harms are not properly, legally cognizable harms, but it has certainly been given powerful impetus in our culture by John Stuart Mill's book *On Liberty*. Mill, however, was a man of two minds and, as Gertrude Himmelfarb has demonstrated, Mill himself usually knew better than this. Miss Himmelfarb traces the intellectual themes of *On Liberty* to Mill's wife. It would be ironic, to put it no higher, if we owed major features of modern American constitutional doctrine to Harriet Taylor Mill, who was not, as best I can remember, one of the framers at Philadelphia.

It is unlikely, of course, that a general constitutional doctrine of the impermissibility of legislating moral standards will ever be framed. So the development I have cited, though troubling, is really only an instance of a yet more worrisome phenomenon, and that is the capacity of ideas that originate outside the Constitution to influence judges, usually without their being aware of it, so that those ideas are elevated to constitutional doctrine. We have seen that repeatedly in our history. If one may complain today that the Constitution did not adopt John Stuart Mill's *On Liberty*, it was only a few judicial generations ago, when economic laissez-faire somehow got into the Constitution, that Justice Holmes wrote in dissent that the Constitution "does not enact Mr. Herbert Spencer's *Social Statics*."

Why should this be so? Why should constitutional law constantly be catching colds from the intellectual fevers of the general society?

The fact is that the law has little intellectual or structural resistance to outside influences, influences that should properly remain outside. The striking, and peculiar, fact about a field of study so old and so intensively cultivated by men and women of first-rate intelligence is that the law possesses very little theory about itself. I once heard George Stigler remark with some astonishment: "You lawyers have nothing of your own. You borrow from the social sciences, but you have no discipline, no core, of your own." And, a few scattered insights here and there aside, he was right. This theoretical emptiness at its center makes law, particularly constitutional law, unstable, a ship with a great deal of sail but a very shallow keel, vulnerable to the winds of intellectual or moral fashion, which it then validates as the commands of our most basic compact.

This weakness in the law's intellectual structure may be exploited by new theories of moral relativism and egalitarianism now the dominant mode of constitutional thinking in a number of leading law schools. The attack of these theories upon older assumptions has been described by one Harvard law professor as a "battle of cultures," and so it is. It is fair to think, then, that the outcome of this confused battle may strongly affect the constitutional law of the future and hence the way in which we are governed.

The constitutional ideologies growing in the law schools display three worrisome characteristics. They are increasingly abstract and philosophical; they are sometimes nihilistic; they always lack what law requires, democratic legitimacy. These tendencies are new, much stronger now than they were even ten years ago, and certainly nothing like them appeared in our past.

Up to a few years ago most professors of constitutional law would probably have agreed with Joseph Story's dictum in 1833: "Upon subjects of government, it has always appeared to me, that metaphysical refinements are out of place. A constitution of government is addressed to the common-sense of the people, and never was designed for trials of logical skill or visionary speculation." But listen to how Nathan Glazer today perceives the lawyer's task, no doubt because of the professors he knows: "As a political philosopher or a lawyer, I would try to find basic principles of justice that can be defended and argued against all other principles. As a sociologist, I look at the concrete consequences, for concrete societies."

Glazer's perception of what more and more lawyers are doing is entirely accurate. That reality is disturbing. Academic lawyers are not going to solve the age-old problems of political and moral philosophy any time soon, but the articulated premise of their abstract enterprise is that judges may properly reason to constitutional decisions in that way. But judges have no mandate to govern in the name of contractarian or utilitarian or what-have-you philosophy rather than according to the historical Constitution. Judges of this generation, and much more, of the next generation, are being educated to engage in really heroic adventures in policy making.

The abstract, universalistic style of legal thought has a number of dangers. For one thing, it teaches disrespect for the actual institutions of the American polity. These institutions are designed to achieve compromise, to slow change, to dilute absolutisms. They embody wholesome inconsistencies. They are designed, in short, to do things that abstract generalizations about the just society tend to bring into contempt.

More than this, the attempt to define individual liberties by abstract reasoning, though intended to broaden liberties, is actually likely to make them more vulnerable. Our constitutional liberties arose out of historical experience and out of political, moral, and religious sentiment. They do not rest upon any general theory. Attempts to frame a theory that removes from democratic control areas of life the framers intended to leave there can only succeed if abstractions are regarded as overriding the constitutional text and structure, judicial precedent, and the history that gives our rights life, rootedness, and meaning. It is no small matter to discredit the foundations upon which our constitutional freedoms have always been sustained and substitute as a bulwark only abstractions of moral philosophy. The difference in approach parallels the difference between the American and French revolutions, and the outcome for liberty was much less happy under the regime of "the rights of man."

It is perhaps not surprising that abstract, philosophical approaches to law often produce constitutional nihilism. Some of the legal philosophers have begun to see that there is no overarching theory that can satisfy the criteria that are required. It may be, as Friedrich Hayek suggested, that nihilism naturally results from sudden disillusion when high expectations about the powers of abstract reasoning collapse. The theorists, unable to settle for practical wisdom, must have a single theoretical construct or nothing. In any event, one of the leading scholars has announced, in a widely admired article, that all normative constitutional theories, including the theory that judges must only interpret the law, are necessarily incoherent. The apparently necessary conclusion—that judicial review is, in that case, illegitimate—is never drawn. Instead, it is proposed that judges simply enforce good values, or rather the values that seem to the professor good. The desire for results appears to be stronger than the respect for legitimacy, and, when theory fails, the desire to use judicial power remains.

This brings into the open the fundamental antipathy to democracy to be seen in much of the new legal scholarship. The original Constitution was devoted primarily to the mechanisms of democratic choice. Constitutional scholarship today is dominated by the creation of arguments that will encourage judges to thwart democratic choice. Though the arguments are, as you might suspect, cast in terms of expanding individual freedom, that is not their result. One of the freedoms, the major freedom, of our kind of society is the freedom to choose to have a public morality. As Chesterton put it, "What is the good of telling a community that it has every liberty except the liberty to make laws? The liberty to make laws is what constitutes a free people." The makers of our Constitution thought so too, for they provided wide powers to representative assemblies and ruled only a few subjects off limits by the Constitution.

The new legal view disagrees both with the historical Constitution and with the majority of living Americans about where the balance between individual freedom and social order lies.

Leading legal academics are increasingly absorbed with what they call "legal theory." That would be welcome, if it were real, but what is generally meant is not theory about the sources of law, or its capacities and limits, or the prerequisites for its vitality, but rather the endless exploration of abstract philosophical principles. One would suppose that we can decide nothing unless we first settle the ultimate questions of the basis of political obligation, the merits of contractarianism, rule or act utilitarianism, the nature of the just society, and the like. Nor surprisingly, the politics of the professors becomes the command of the Constitution. As Richard John Neuhaus puts it, "the theorists' quest for universality becomes simply the parochialism of a few intellectuals," and he notes "the limitations of theories of justice that cannot sustain a democratic consensus regarding the legitimacy of law."

Sometimes I am reminded of developments in another, perhaps parallel, field. I recall one evening listening to a rather traditional theologian bemoan the intellectual fads that were sweeping his field. Since I had a very unsophisticated view of theology, I remarked with some surprise that his church seemed to have remarkably little doctrine capable of resisting these trends. He was offended and said there had always been tradition. Both of our fields purport to rest upon sacred texts, and it seemed odd that in both the main bulwark against heresy should be only tradition. Law is certainly like that. We never elaborated much of a theory—as distinguished from mere attitudes—about the behavior proper to constitutional judges. As Alexander Bickel observed, all we ever had was a tradition, and in the last 30 years that has been shattered.

Now we need theory, theory that relates the framers' values to today's world. That is not an impossible task by any means, but it is a good deal more complex than slogans such as "strict construction" or "judicial restraint" might lead you to think. It is necessary to establish the proposition that the framers' intentions with respect to freedoms are the sole legitimate premise from which constitutional analysis may proceed. It is true that a willful judge can often clothe his legislation in sophistical argument and the misuse of history. But hypocrisy has its value. General acceptance of correct theory can force the judge to hypocrisy and, to that extent, curb his freedom. The theorists of moral abstraction are devoted precisely to removing the judge's guilt at legislating and so removing the necessity for hypocrisy. Worse still, they would free the intellectually honest judge from constraints he would otherwise recognize and honor.

It is well to be clear about the role moral discourse should play in law. Neuhaus is entirely correct in saying

> whatever else law may be, it is a human enterprise in response to human behavior, and human behavior is stubbornly entangled with beliefs about right and wrong. Law that is recognized as legitimate is therefore related to—even organically related to, if you will—the larger universe of moral discourse that helps shape human behavior. In short, if law is not also a moral enterprise, it is without legitimacy or binding force.

To that excellent statement I would add only that it is crucial to bear in mind what kind of law, and what legal institutions, we are talking about. In a constitutional democracy the moral content of law must be given by the morality of the framer or the legislator, never by the morality of the judge. The sole task of the latter—and it is a task quite large enough for anyone's wisdom, skill, and virtue—is to translate the framer's or the legislator's morality into a rule to govern unforeseen circumstances. That abstinence from giving his own desires free play, that continuing and self-conscious renunciation of power, that is the morality of the jurist.

CHAPTER 20

What Am I, a Potted Plant?

The Case Against Strict Constructionism

Richard A. Posner

Judge, U.S. Court of Appeals, Seventh Circuit (1981–)

MANY PEOPLE, not all of conservative bent, believe that modern American courts are too aggressive, too "activist," too prone to substitute their own policy preferences for those of the elected branches of government. This may well be true. But some who complain of judicial activism espouse a view of law that is too narrow. And a good cause will not hallow a bad argument.

This point of view often is called "strict constructionism." A more precise term would be "legal formalism." [On this view, issues] of the "public good" can "be decided legitimately only with the consent of the governed." Judges have no legitimate say about these issues. Their business is to address issues of private rights, that is, "to decide whether the right exists—in the Constitution or in a statute—and, if so, what it is; but at that point inquiry ceases." The judge may not use "discretion and the weighing of consequences" to arrive at his decisions and he may not create new rights. The Constitution is a source of rights, but only to the extent that it embodies "fundamental and clearly articulated principles of government." There must be no judicial creativity or "policy-making."

In short, there is a political sphere, where the people rule, and there is a domain of fixed rights, administered but not created or altered by judges. The first is the sphere of discretion, the second of application. Legislators make the law; judges find and apply it.

Acknowledgment to Judge Richard A. Posner for remarks excerpted in 197 The New Republic *23 (1987). Reprinted by permission of* The New Republic, *© 1987, The New Republic, Inc.*

There has never been a time when the courts of the United States, state or federal, behaved consistently in accordance with this idea. Nor could they, for reasons rooted in the nature of law and legal institutions, in the limitations of human knowledge, and in the character of a political system.

"Questions about the public good" and "questions about private rights" are inseparable. The private right is conferred in order to promote the public good. So in deciding how broadly the right shall be interpreted, the court must consider the implications of its interpretation for the public good. For example, should an heir who murders his benefactor have a right to inherit from his victim? The answer depends, in part anyway, on the public good that results from discouraging murders. Almost the whole of so-called private law, such as property, contract, and tort law, is instrumental to the public end of obtaining the social advantages of free markets. Furthermore, most private law is common law—that is, law made by judges rather than by legislators or by constitution-framers. Judges have been entrusted with making policy from the start.

Often when deciding difficult questions of private rights courts have to weigh policy considerations. If a locomotive spews sparks that set a farmer's crops afire, has the railroad invaded the farmer's property right or does the railroad's ownership of its right of way implicitly include the right to emit sparks? If the railroad has such a right, shall it be conditioned on the railroad's taking reasonable precautions to minimize the danger of fire? If, instead, the farmer has the right, shall it be conditioned on his taking reasonable precautions? Such questions cannot be answered sensibly without considering the social consequences of alternative answers.

A second problem is that when a constitutional convention, a legislature, or a court promulgates a rule of law, it necessarily does so without full knowledge of the circumstances in which the rule might be invoked in the future. When the unforeseen circumstance arises—it might be the advent of the motor vehicle or of electronic surveillance, or a change in attitudes toward religion, race, and sexual propriety—a court asked to apply the rule must decide, in light of information not available to the promulgators of the rule, what the rule should mean in its new setting. That is a creative decision, involving discretion, the weighing of consequences, and, in short, a kind of legislative judgment—though, properly, one more confined than if the decision were being made by a real legislature. A court that decides, say, that copyright protection extends to the coloring of old black-and-white movies is making a creative decision, because the copyright laws do not mention colorization. It is not being lawless or usurpative merely because it is weighing consequences and exercising discretion.

Or if a court decides (as the Supreme Court has done in one of its less controversial modern rulings) that the Fourth Amendment's prohibition against unreasonable searches and seizures shall apply to wiretapping, even though no trespass is committed by wiretapping and hence no property right is invaded, the court is creating a new right and making policy. But in a situation not foreseen and expressly provided for by the Framers of the Constitution, a simple reading out of a policy judgment made by the Framers is impossible.

Even the most carefully drafted legislation has gaps. The Constitution, for example, does not say that the federal government has sovereign immunity—the right, traditionally enjoyed by all sovereign governments, not to be sued without its consent. Nevertheless, the Supreme Court held that the federal government has sovereign immunity. Is this interpolation usurpative? The Federal Tort Claims Act, a law waiving sovereign immunity so citizens can sue the government, makes no exception for suits by members of the armed services who are injured through the negligence of their superiors. Nevertheless the Supreme Court has held that the act was not intended to provide soldiers with a remedy. The decision may be right or wrong, but it is not wrong just because it is creative. The Eleventh Amendment to the Constitution forbids a citizen of one state to sue "another" state in federal court without the consent of the defendant state. Does this mean that you can sue your own state in federal court without the state's consent? That's what the words seem to imply, but the Supreme Court has held that the Eleventh Amendment was intended to preserve the sovereign immunity of the states more broadly. The Court thought this was implied by the federalist system that the Constitution created. Again the Court may have been right or wrong, but it was not wrong just because it was creative.

Opposite the unrealistic picture of judges who apply law but never make it hangs an unrealistic picture of a populist legislature that acts only "with the consent of the governed." Speaking for myself, I find that many of the political candidates whom I have voted for have failed to be elected and that those who have been elected have then proceeded to enact much legislation that did not have my consent. Given the effectiveness of interest groups in the political process, much of this legislation probably didn't have the consent of a majority of citizens. Politically, I feel more governed than self-governing. In considering whether to reduce constitutional safeguards to slight dimensions, we should be sure to have a realistic, not an idealized, picture of the legislative and executive branches of government, which would thereby be made more powerful than they are today.

To banish all discretion from the judicial process would indeed reduce the scope of constitutional rights. The framers of a constitution who want to make it a charter of liberties and not just a set of constitutive rules face a difficult choice. They can write specific provisions, and thereby doom their work to rapid obsolescence or irrelevance; or they can write general provisions, thereby delegating substantial discretion to the authoritative interpreters, who in our system are the judges. The U.S. Constitution is a mixture of specific and general provisions. Many of the specific provisions have stood the test of time amazingly well or have been amended without any great fuss. This is especially true of the rules establishing the structure and procedures of Congress. Most of the specific provisions creating rights, however, have fared poorly. Some have proved irksomely anachronistic—for example, the right to a jury trial in federal court in all cases at law if the stakes exceed $20. Others have become dangerously anachronistic, such as the right to bear arms. Some have even turned topsy-turvy, such as the provision for indictment by grand jury. The grand jury has become an instrument of prosecutorial investigation rather than a protection for the criminal suspect. If the Bill of Rights had consisted entirely of specific provisions, it would have aged very rapidly and would no longer be a significant constraint on the behavior of government officials.

Many provisions of the Constitution, however, are drafted in general terms. This creates flexibility in the face of unforeseen changes, but it also creates the possibility of multiple interpretations, and this possibility is an embarrassment for a theory of judicial legitimacy that denies that judges have any right to exercise discretion. A choice among semantically plausible interpretations of a text, in circumstances remote from those contemplated by its drafters, requires the exercise of discretion and the weighing of consequences. Reading is not a form of deduction; understanding requires a consideration of consequences. If I say, "I'll eat my hat," one reason that my listeners will "decode" this in non-literal fashion is that I couldn't eat a hat if I tried. The broader principle, which applies to the Constitution as much as to a spoken utterance, is that if one possible interpretation of an ambiguous statement would entail absurd or terrible results, that is a good reason to adopt an alternative interpretation.

Even the decision to read the Constitution narrowly, and thereby "restrain" judicial interpretation, is not a decision that can be read directly from the text. The Constitution does not say, "Read me broadly," or, "Read me narrowly." That decision must be made as a matter of political theory, and will depend on such things as one's view of the springs of judicial legitimacy and of the relative competence of courts and legislatures in dealing with particular types of issues.

Consider the provision in the Sixth Amendment that "in all criminal prosecutions, the accused shall enjoy the right … to have the Assistance of Counsel for his defense." Read narrowly, this just means that the defendant can't be forbidden to retain counsel; if he can't afford counsel, or competent counsel, he is out of luck. Read broadly, it guarantees even the indigent the effective assistance of counsel; it becomes not just a negative right to be allowed to hire a lawyer but a positive right to demand the help of the government in financing one's defense. Either reading is compatible with the semantics of the provision, but the first better captures the specific intent of the Framers. At the time the Sixth Amendment was written, English law forbade a criminal defendant to have the assistance of counsel unless abstruse questions of law arose in his case. The Framers wanted to do away with this prohibition. But, more broadly, they wanted to give criminal defendants protection against being railroaded. When they wrote, government could not afford, or at least did not think it could afford, to hire lawyers for indigent criminal defendants. Moreover, criminal trials were short and simple, so it was not ridiculous to expect a person to defend himself without a lawyer if he couldn't afford to hire one. Today the situation is different. Not only can the society easily afford to supply lawyers to poor people charged with crimes, but modern criminal law and procedure are so complicated that an unrepresented defendant will usually be at a great disadvantage....

Everyone professionally connected with law knows that, in Oliver Wendell Holmes's famous expression, judges legislate "interstitially," which is to say they make law, only more cautiously, more slowly, and in more principled, less partisan, fashion than legislators. The attempt to deny this truism entangles "strict constructionists" in contradictions....

The liberal judicial activists may be imprudent and misguided in their efforts to enact the liberal political agenda into constitutional law, but it is no use pretending that what they are doing is not interpretation but "deconstruction," not law but politics, because it involves the exercise of discretion and a concern with consequences and because it reaches results not foreseen 200 years ago. It may be bad law because it lacks firm moorings in constitutional text, or structure, or history, or consensus, or other legitimate sources of constitutional law, or because it is reckless of consequences, or because it oversimplifies difficult moral and political questions. But it is not bad law, or no law, just because it violates the tenets of strict construction.

CHAPTER 21

Originalism

The Lesser Evil

Antonin Scalia

*Justice, Supreme Court of the United States (1986–)
and Judge, U.S. Court of Appeals, District of Columbia Circuit
(1982–1986)*

It may surprise the layman, but it will surely not surprise the lawyers here, to learn that originalism is not, and had perhaps never been, the sole method of constitutional exegesis. It would be hard to count on the fingers of both hands and the toes of both feet, yea, even on the hairs of one's youthful head, the opinions that have in fact been rendered not on the basis of what the Constitution originally meant, but on the basis of what the judges currently thought it desirable for it to mean. That is, I suppose, the sort of behavior Chief Justice Hughes was referring to when he said the Constitution is what the judges say it is. But in the past, nonoriginalist opinions have almost always had the decency to lie, or at least to dissemble, about what they were doing—either ignoring strong evidence of original intent that contradicted the minimal recited evidence of an original intent congenial to the court's desires, or else not discussing original intent at all, speaking in terms of broad constitutional generalities with no pretense of historical support.... It is only in relatively recent years, however, that nonoriginalist exegesis has, so to speak, come out of the closet, and put itself forward overtly as an intellectually legitimate device. To be sure, in support of its venerability as a legitimate interpretive theory there is often trotted out John Marshall's statement in *McCulloch v. Maryland* that "we

Acknowledgment to Justice Antonin Scalia for excerpts from the William Howard Taft Constitutional Law Lecture given at the University of Cincinnati (September 16, 1988), which appears in 57 University of Cincinnati Law Review *849 (1989).*

must never forget it is a constitution we are expounding"[1]—as though the implication of that statement was that our interpretation must change from age to age. But that is a canard. The real implication was quite the opposite: Marshall was saying that the Constitution had to be interpreted generously because the powers conferred upon Congress under it had to be broad enough to serve not only the needs of the federal government originally discerned but also the needs that might arise in the future. If constitutional interpretation could be adjusted as changing circumstances required, a broad initial interpretation would have been unnecessary.

Those who have not delved into the scholarly writing on constitutional law for several years may be unaware of the explicitness with which many prominent and respected commentators reject the original meaning of the Constitution as an authoritative guide. Harvard Professor Laurence H. Tribe, for example, while generally conducting his constitutional analysis under the rubric of the open-ended textual provisions such as the Ninth Amendment, does not believe that the originally understood content of those provisions has much to do with how they are to be applied today. The Constitution, he has written, "invites us, and our judges, to expand on the ... freedoms that are uniquely our heritage,"[2] and "invites a collaborative inquiry, involving both the Court and the country, into the contemporary content of freedom, fairness, and fraternity."[3] Stanford Dean Paul Brest, having (in his own words) "abandoned both consent and fidelity to the text and original understanding as the touchstones of constitutional decisionmaking,"[4] concludes that "the practice of constitutional decisionmaking should enforce those, but only those, values that are fundamental to our society."[5] While Brest believes that the "text," "original understanding," "custom," "social practices," "conventional morality," and "precedent" all strongly inform the determination of those values, the conclusions drawn from all these sources are "defeasible in the light of changing public values."[6] Yale Professor Owen Fiss asserts that, whatever the Constitution might originally have meant, the courts should give "concrete meaning and application" to those values that "give our society an identity and inner coherence [and] its distinctive public morality."[7] Oxford Professor (and expatriate American) Ronald Dworkin calls for "a fusion of constitutional law and moral theory."[8] Harvard Professor Richard Parker urges, somewhat more specifically, that constitutional law "take seriously and work from (while no doubt revising) the classical conception of a republic, including its elements of relative equality, mobilization of citizenry, and civic virtue."[9] More specifically still, New York University Professor David Richards suggests that it would be desirable for the courts' constitutional decisions to follow the contractarian moral theory set forth in Professor John Rawls' treatise, *A Theory of Justice*.[10] And I could go on.

The principal theoretical defect of nonoriginalism, in my view, is its incompatibility with the very principle that legitimizes judicial review of constitutionality. Nothing in the text of the Constitution confers upon the courts the power to inquire into, rather than passively assume, the constitutionality of federal statutes. That power is, however, reasonably implicit because, as Marshall said in *Marbury v. Madison,* (1) "[i]t is emphatically the province and duty of the judicial department to say what the law is," (2) "[i]f two laws conflict with each other, the courts must decide on the operation of each," and (3) "the constitution is to be considered, in court, as a paramount law."[11] Central to that analysis, it seems to me, is the perception that the Constitution, though it has an effect superior to other laws, is in its nature the sort of "law" that is the business of the courts—an enactment that has a fixed meaning ascertainable through the usual devices familiar to those learned in the law. If the Constitution were not that sort of a "law," but a novel invitation to apply current societal values, what reason would there be to believe that the invitation was addressed to the courts rather than to the legislature? One simply cannot say, regarding that sort of novel enactment, that "[i]t is emphatically the province and duty of the judicial department" to determine its content. Quite to the contrary, the legislature would seem a much more appropriate expositor of social values, and its determination that a statute is compatible with the Constitution should, as in England, prevail.

Apart from the frailty of its theoretical underpinning, nonoriginalism confronts a practical difficulty reminiscent of the truism of elective politics that "You can't beat somebody with nobody." It is not enough to demonstrate that the other fellow's candidate (originalism) is no good; one must also agree upon another candidate to replace him. Just as it is not very meaningful for a voter to vote "non-Reagan," it is not very helpful to tell a judge to be a "nonoriginalist." If the law is to make any attempt at consistency and predictability, surely there must be general agreement not only that judges reject one exegetical approach (originalism), but that they adopt another. And it is hard to discern any emerging consensus among the nonoriginalists as to what this might be. Are the "fundamental values" that replace original meaning to be derived from the philosophy of Plato, or of Locke, or Mills, or Rawls, or perhaps from the latest Gallup poll? This is not to say that originalists are in entire agreement as to what the nature of their methodology is; as I shall mention shortly, there are some significant differences. But as its name suggests, it by and large represents a coherent approach, or at least an agreed-upon point of departure. As the name "nonoriginalism" suggests (and I know no other, more precise term by which this school of exegesis can be described), it represents agreement on nothing except what is the wrong approach.

Finally, I want to mention what is not a defect of nonoriginalism, but one of its supposed benefits that seems to me illusory. A bit earlier I quoted one of the most prominent nonoriginalists, Professor Tribe, to the effect that the Constitution "invites us, and our judges, to expand on the ... freedoms that are uniquely our heritage."[12] I think it fair to say that that is a common theme of nonoriginalists in general. But why, one may reasonably ask—once the original import of the Constitution is cast aside to be replaced by the "fundamental values" of the current society—why are we invited only to "expand on" freedoms, and not to contract them as well? Last Term we decided a case, *Coy v. Iowa,*[13] in which, at the trial of a man accused of taking indecent liberties with two young girls, the girls were permitted to testify separated from the defendant by a screen which prevented them from seeing him. We held that, at least absent a specific finding that these particular witnesses needed such protection, this procedure violated that provision of the Sixth Amendment that assures a criminal defendant the right "to be confronted with the witnesses against him."[14] Let us hypothesize, however (a hypothesis that may well be true), that modern American society is much more conscious of, and averse to, the effects of "emotional trauma" than was the society of 1791, and that it is, in addition, much more concerned about the emotional frailty of children and the sensitivity of young women regarding sexual abuse. If that is so, and if the nonoriginalists are right, would it not have been possible for the Court to hold that, even though in 1791 the confrontation clause clearly would not have permitted a blanket exception for such testimony, it does so today? Such a holding, of course, could hardly be characterized as an "expansion upon" preexisting freedoms. Or let me give another example that is already history: I think it highly probable that over the past two hundred years the Supreme Court, though not avowedly under the banner of "nonoriginalist" interpretation, has in fact narrowed the contract clause of the Constitution[15] well short of its original meaning.[16] Perhaps we are all content with that development—but can it possibly be asserted that it represented an expansion, rather than a contraction, of individual liberties? Our modern society is undoubtedly not as enthusiastic about economic liberties as were the men and women of 1789; but we should not fool ourselves into believing that because we like the result the result does not represent a contraction of liberty. Nonoriginalism, in other words, is a two-way street that handles traffic both to and from individual rights.

Let me turn next to originalism, which is also not without its warts. Its greatest defect, in my view, is the difficulty of applying it correctly. Not that I agree with, or even take very seriously, the intricately elaborated scholarly criticisms to the effect that (believe it or not) words have no meaning. They have meaning enough, as the scholarly critics themselves must surely believe when they choose to express their views in text rather than music. But what is true is that it is often exceedingly difficult to plumb the original understanding of an ancient text. Properly done, the task requires the consideration of an enormous mass of material—in the case of the Constitution and its Amendments, for example, to mention only one element, the records of the ratifying debates in all the states. Even beyond that, it requires an evaluation of the reliability of that material—many of the reports of the ratifying debates, for example, are thought to be quite unreliable. And further still, it requires immersing oneself in the political and intellectual atmosphere of the time—somehow placing out of mind knowledge that we have which an earlier age did not, and putting on beliefs, attitudes, philosophies, prejudices and loyalties that are not those of our day. It is, in short, a task sometimes better suited to the historian than the lawyer....

I can be much more brief in describing what seems to me the second most serious objection to originalism: In its undiluted form, at least, it is medicine that seems too strong to swallow. Thus, almost every originalist would adulterate it with the doctrine of *stare decisis*—so that *Marbury v. Madison* would stand even if Professor Raoul Berger should demonstrate unassailably that it got the meaning of the Constitution wrong. (Of course recognizing *stare decisis* is seemingly even more incompatible with nonoriginalist theory: If the most solemnly and democratically adopted text of the Constitution and its Amendments can be ignored on the basis of current values, what possible basis could there be for enforced adherence to a legal decision of the Supreme Court?) But *stare decisis* alone is not enough to prevent originalism from being what many would consider too bitter a pill. What if some state should enact a new law providing public lashing, or branding of the right hand, as punishment for certain criminal offenses? Even if it could be demonstrated unequivocally that these were not cruel and unusual measures in 1791, and even though no prior Supreme Court decision has specifically disapproved them, I doubt whether any federal judge—even among the many who consider themselves originalists—would sustain them against an Eighth Amendment challenge. It may well be, as Professor Henry Monaghan persuasively argues, that this cannot legitimately be reconciled with originalist philosophy—that it represents the unrealistic view of the Constitution as a document intended to create a perfect society for all ages to come, whereas in fact it was a political compromise that did not pretend to create a perfect society even for its own age (as its toleration of slavery, which a majority of the founding generation recognized as an evil, well enough demonstrates).[17] Even so, I am confident that public flogging and handbranding would not be sustained by our courts, and any espousal of originalism as a practical theory of exegesis must somehow come to terms with that reality.

One way of doing so, of course, would be to say that it was originally intended that the cruel and unusual punishment clause would have an evolving content—that "cruel and unusual" originally meant "cruel and unusual for the age in question" and not "cruel and unusual in 1791." But to be faithful to originalist philosophy, one must not only say this but demonstrate it to be so on the basis of some textual or historical evidence. Perhaps the mere words "cruel and unusual" suggest an evolutionary intent more than other provisions of the Constitution, but that is far from clear; and I know of no historical evidence for that meaning. And if the faint-hearted originalist is willing simply to posit such an intent for the "cruel and unusual punishment" clause, why not for the due process clause, the equal protection clause, the privileges and immunity clause, etc.? When one goes down that road, there is really no difference between the faint-hearted originalist and the moderate nonoriginalist, except that the former finds it comforting to make up (out of whole cloth) an original evolutionary intent, and the latter thinks that superfluous. It is, I think, the fact that most originalists are faint-hearted and most nonoriginalists are moderate (that is, would not ascribe evolving content to such clear provisions as the requirement that the President be no less than thirty-five years of age) which accounts for the fact that the sharp divergence between the two philosophies does not produce an equivalently sharp divergence in judicial opinions.

Having described what I consider the principal difficulties with the originalist and nonoriginalist approaches, I suppose I owe it to the listener to say which of the two evils I prefer. It is originalism. I take the need for theoretical legitimacy seriously, and even if one assumes (as many nonoriginalists do not even bother to do) that the Constitution was originally meant to expound evolving rather than permanent values, as I discussed earlier I see no basis for believing that supervision of the evolution would have been committed to the courts. At an even more general theoretical level, originalism seems to me more compatible with the nature and purpose of a Constitution in a democratic system. A democratic society does not, by and large, need constitutional guarantees to insure that its laws will reflect "current values." Elections take care of that quite well. The purpose of constitutional guarantees—and in particular those constitutional guarantees of individual rights that are at the center of this controversy—is precisely to prevent the law from reflecting certain changes in original values that the society adopting the Constitution thinks fundamentally undesirable. Or, more precisely, to require the society to devote to the subject the long and hard consideration required for a constitutional amendment before those particular values can be cast aside.

I also think that the central practical defect of nonoriginalism is fundamental and irreparable: the impossibility of achieving any consensus on what, precisely, is to replace original meaning, once that is abandoned. The practical defects of originalism, on the other hand, while genuine enough, seem to me less severe. While it may indeed be unrealistic to have substantial confidence that judges and lawyers will find the correct historical answer to such refined questions of original intent as the precise content of "the executive Power," for the vast majority of questions the answer is clear. The death penalty, for example, was not cruel and unusual punishment because it is referred to in the Constitution itself; and the right of confrontation by its plain language meant, at least, being face-to-face with the person testifying against one at trial. For the nonoriginalist, even these are open questions. As for the fact that originalism is strong medicine, and that one cannot realistically expect judges (probably myself included) to apply it without a trace of constitutional perfectionism, I suppose I must respond that this is a world in which nothing is flawless, and fall back upon G. K. Chesterton's observation that a thing worth doing is worth doing badly.

It seems to me, moreover, that the practical defects of originalism are defects more appropriate for the task at hand—that is, less likely to aggravate the most significant weakness of the system of judicial review and more likely to produce results acceptable to all. If one is hiring a reference-room librarian and has two applicants, between whom the only substantial difference is that the one's normal conversational tone tends to be too loud and the other's too soft, it is pretty clear which of the imperfections should be preferred. Now the main danger in judicial interpretation of the Constitution—or, for that matter, in judicial interpretation of any law—is that the judges will mistake their own predilections for the law. Avoiding this error is the hardest part of being a conscientious judge; perhaps no conscientious judge ever succeeds entirely. Nonoriginalism, which under one or another formulation invokes "fundamental values" as the touchstone of constitutionality, plays precisely to this weakness. It is very difficult for a person to discern a difference between those political values that he personally thinks most important, and those political values that are "fundamental to our society." Thus, by the adoption of such a criterion judicial personalization of the law is enormously facilitated. (One might reduce this danger by insisting that the new "fundamental values" invoked to replace original meaning be clearly and objectively manifested in the laws of the society. But among all the varying tests suggested by nonoriginalist theoreticians, I am unaware that that one ever appears. Most if not all nonoriginalists, for example, would strike down the death penalty, though it continues to be widely adopted in both state and federal legislation.)

Originalism does not aggravate the principal weakness of the system, for it establishes a historical criterion that is conceptually quite separate from the preferences of the judge himself. And the principal defect of that approach—that historical research is always difficult and sometimes inconclusive—will, unlike nonoriginalism, lead to a more moderate rather than a more extreme result. The inevitable tendency of judges to think that the law is what they would like it to be will, I have no doubt, cause most errors in judicial historiography to be made in the direction of projecting upon the age of 1789 current, modern values—so that as applied, even as applied in the best of faith, originalism will (as the historical record shows) end up as something of a compromise. Perhaps not a bad characteristic for a constitutional theory. Thus, nonoriginalists can say, concerning the principal defect of originalism, "Oh happy fault." Originalism is, it seems to me, the librarian who talks too softly. Having made that endorsement, I hasten to confess that in a crunch I may prove a faint-hearted originalist. I cannot imagine myself, any more than any other federal judge, upholding a statute that imposes the punishment of flogging. But then I cannot imagine such a case's arising either. In any event, in deciding the cases before me I expect I will rarely be confronted with making the stark choice between giving evolutionary content (not yet required by *stare decisis*) and not giving evolutionary content to particular constitutional provisions. The vast majority of my dissents from nonoriginalist thinking (and I hope at least some of those dissents will be majorities) will, I am sure, be able to be framed in the terms that, even if the provision in question has an evolutionary content, there is inadequate indication that any evolution in social attitudes has occurred.[18] That—to conclude this largely theoretical talk on a note of reality—is the real dispute that appears in the case: not between nonoriginalists on the one hand and pure originalists on the other, concerning the validity of looking at all to current values; but rather between, on the one hand, nonoriginalists, faint-hearted originalists and pure-originalists-accepting-for-the-sake-of-argument-evolutionary-content, and, on the other hand, other adherents of the same three approaches, concerning the nature and degree of evidence necessary to demonstrate that constitutional evolution has occurred.

I am left with a sense of dissatisfaction, as I am sure you are, that a discourse concerning what one would suppose to be a rather fundamental—indeed, the most fundamental—aspect of constitutional theory and practice should end so inconclusively. But it should come as no surprise. We do not yet have an agreed-upon theory for interpreting statutes, either. I find it perhaps too laudatory to say that this is the genius of the common law system; but it is at least its nature.

Notes

1. *McCulloch v. Maryland*, 17 U.S. (4 Wheat.) 316, 407 (1819).
2. L. Tribe, *God Save This Honorable Court* 45 (New York: Random House, 1985).
3. L. Tribe, *American Constitutional Law* 771 (Westbury, N.Y.: The Foundation Press, 2d ed. 1988).
4. P. Brest, "The Misconceived Quest for the Original University," 60 *Boston University Law Review* 204, 226 (1980).
5. Ibid., at 227.
6. Ibid., at 229.
7. O. Fiss, "The Supreme Court 1978 Term—Foreword: The Forms of Justice," 93 *Harvard Law Review* 1, 9, 11 (1979).
8. R. Dworkin, *Taking Rights Seriously* 149 (Cambridge: Harvard University Press, 1977).

9. R. Parker, "The Past of Constitutional Theory—And Its Future," 42 *Ohio State Law Journal* 223, 258 n. 146 (1981).
10. D. Richards, "Constitutional Privacy, The Right to Die and the Meaning of Life: A Moral Analysis," 22 *William & Mary Law Review* 327, 344–347 (1981).
11. *Marbury v. Madison,* 5 U.S. (1 Cranch.) 137, 177 (1803).
12. L. Tribe, supra note 2, at 45.
13. *Coy v. Iowa*, 108 S.Ct. 2798 (1988).
14. Ibid. at 2800.
15. U.S. Const. Art. I, Sec. 10, Cl. 2.
16. See, e.g., *Home Building and Loan Association v. Blaisdell*, 290 U.S. 398 (1934).
17. See H. Monaghan, "Our Perfect Constitution," 56 *New York University Law Review* 353 (1981).
18. See, e.g., *Thompson v. Oklahoma*, 108 S.Ct. 2687, 2711 (1988) (Scalia, J., dissenting).

CHAPTER 22

The Constitution
A Living Document

Thurgood Marshall
Justice, Supreme Court of the United States (1967–1991) and Judge, U.S. Court of Appeals, Second Circuit (1962–1965)

THE YEAR 1987 marks the 200th anniversary of the United States Constitution. A Commission has been established to coordinate the celebration. The official meetings, essay contests, and festivities have begun. The planned commemoration will span three years, and I am told 1987 is "dedicated to the memory of the Founders and the document they drafted in Philadelphia."[1] We are to "recall the achievements of our Founders and the knowledge and experience that inspired them, the nature of the government they established, its origins, its character, and its ends, and the rights and privileges of citizenship, as well as its attendant responsibilities."[2]

Like many anniversary celebrations, the plan for 1987 takes particular events and holds them up as the source of all the very best that has followed. Patriotic feelings will surely swell, prompting proud proclamations of the wisdom, foresight, and sense of justice shared by the framers and reflected in a written document now yellowed with age. This is unfortunate—not the patriotism itself, but the tendency for the celebration to oversimplify, and overlook the many other events that have been instrumental to our achievements as a nation. The focus of this celebration invites a complacent belief that the vision of those who debated and compromised in Philadelphia yielded the "more perfect Union" it is said we now enjoy.

I cannot accept this invitation, for I do not believe that the meaning of the Constitution was forever "fixed" at the Philadelphia Convention. Nor do I find the wis-

Acknowledgment to Justice Thurgood Marshall for his remarks at the annual seminar of the San Francisco Patent and Trademark Law Association (May 16, 1987).

dom, foresight, and sense of justice exhibited by the framers particularly profound. To the contrary, the government they devised was defective from the start, requiring several amendments, a civil war, and momentous social transformation to attain the system of constitutional government, and its respect for the individual freedoms and human rights, that we hold as fundamental today. When contemporary Americans cite "The Constitution," they invoke a concept that is vastly different from what the framers barely began to construct two centuries ago.

For a sense of the evolving nature of the Constitution we need look no further than the first three words of the document's preamble: "We the People." When the Founding Fathers used this phrase in 1787, they did not have in mind the majority of America's citizens. "We the People" included, in the words of the framers, "the whole Number of free Persons." [3] On a matter so basic as the right to vote, for example, Negro slaves were excluded, although they were counted for representational purposes—at three-fifths each. Women did not gain the right to vote for over a hundred and thirty years.[4]

These omissions were intentional. The record of the framers' debates on the slave question is especially clear:the Southern states acceded to the demands of the New England states for giving Congress broad power to regulate commerce, in exchange for the right to continue the slave trade. The economic interests of the regions coalesced: New Englanders engaged in the "carrying trade" would profit from transporting slaves from Africa as well as goods produced in America by slave labor. The perpetuation of slavery ensured the primary source of wealth in the Southern states.

Despite this clear understanding of the role slavery would play in the new republic, use of the words "slaves" and "slavery" was carefully avoided in the original document. Political representation in the lower House of Congress was to be based on the population of "free Persons" in each state, plus three-fifths of all "other Persons." [5] Moral principles against slavery, for those who had them, were compromised, with no explanation of the conflicting principles for which the American Revolutionary War had ostensibly been fought: the self-evident truths "that all men are created equal, that they are endowed by their Creator with certain unalienable Rights, that among these are Life, Liberty and the pursuit of Happiness." [6]

It was not the first such compromise. Even these ringing phrases from the Declaration of Independence are filled with irony, for an early draft of what became that declaration assailed the King of England for suppressing legislative attempts to end the slave trade and for encouraging slave rebellions.[7] The final draft adopted in 1776 did not contain this criticism. And so again at the Constitutional Convention eloquent objections to the institution of slavery went unheeded, and its opponents eventually consented to a document which laid a foundation for the tragic events that were to follow.

Pennsylvania's Gouverneur Morris provides an example. He opposed slavery and the counting of slaves in determining the basis for representation in Congress. At the Convention he objected that

> the inhabitant of Georgia [or] South Carolina who goes to the coast of Africa, and in defiance of the most sacred laws of humanity tears away his fellow creatures from their dearest connections and damns them to the most cruel bondages, shall have more votes in a Government instituted for protection of the rights of mankind, than the Citizen of Pennsylvania or New Jersey who views with a laudable horror, so nefarious a practice.[8]

And yet Gouverneur Morris eventually accepted the three-fifths accommodation. In fact, he wrote the final draft of the Constitution, the very document the bicentennial will commemorate.

As a result of compromise, the right of the Southern states to continue importing slaves was extended, officially, at least until 1808. We know that it actually lasted a good deal longer, as the framers possessed no monopoly on the ability to trade moral principles for self-interest. But they nevertheless set an unfortunate example. Slaves could be imported, if the commercial interests of the North were protected. To make the compromise even more palatable, customs duties would be imposed at up to ten dollars per slave as a means of raising public revenues.[9]

No doubt it will be said, when the unpleasant truth of the history of slavery in America is mentioned during this bicentennial year, that the Constitution was a product of its times, and embodied a compromise which, under other circumstances, would not have been made. But the effects of the framers' compromise have remained for generations. They arose from the contradiction between guaranteeing liberty and justice to all, and denying both to Negroes.

The original intent of the phrase "We the People" was far too clear for any ameliorating construction. Writing for the Supreme Court in 1857, Chief Justice Taney penned the following passage in the *Dred Scott* case,[10] on the issue of whether, in the eyes of the framers, slaves were "constituent members of the sovereignty," and were to be included among "We the People":

> We think they are not, and that they are not included, and were not intended to be included.... They had for more than a century before been regarded as beings of an inferior order, and altogether unfit to associate with the white race ...; and so far inferior, that they had no rights which the white man was bound to respect; and that the negro might justly and lawfully be reduced to slavery for his benefit.... [A]ccordingly, a negro of the African race was regarded ... as an article of property, and held, and bought and sold as such.... [N]o one seems to have doubted the correctness of the prevailing opinion of the time.[11]

And so, nearly seven decades after the Constitutional Convention, the Supreme Court reaffirmed the prevailing opinion of the framers regarding the rights of Negroes in America. It took a bloody civil war before the thirteenth amendment could be adopted to abolish slavery, though not the consequences slavery would have for future Americans.

While the Union survived the civil war, the Constitution did not. In its place arose a new, more promising basis for justice and equality, the fourteenth amendment, ensuring protection of the life, liberty, and property of all persons against deprivations without due process, and guaranteeing equal protection of the laws. And yet almost another century would pass before any significant recognition was obtained of the rights of black Americans to share equally even in such basic opportunities as education, housing, and employment, and to have their votes counted, and counted equally. In the meantime, blacks joined America's military to fight its wars and invested untold hours working in its factories and on its farms, contributing to the development of this country's magnificent wealth and waiting to share in its prosperity.

What is striking is the role legal principles have played throughout America's history in determining the condition of Negroes. They were enslaved by law, emancipated by law, disenfranchised and segregated by law; and, finally, they have begun to win equality by law. Along the way, new constitutional principles have emerged to meet the challenges of a changing society. The progress has been dramatic, and it will continue.

The men who gathered in Philadelphia in 1787 could not have envisioned these changes. They could not have imagined, nor would they have accepted, that the document they were drafting would one day be construed by a Supreme Court to which had been appointed a woman and the descendent of an African slave. "We the People" no longer enslave, but the credit does not belong to the framers. It belongs to those who refused to acquiesce in outdated notions of "liberty," "justice," and "equality," and who strived to better them.

And so we must be careful, when focusing on the events which took place in Philadelphia two centuries ago, that we not overlook the momentous events which followed, and thereby lose our proper sense of perspective. Otherwise, the odds are that for many Americans the bicentennial celebration will be little more than a blind pilgrimage to the shrine of the original document now stored in a vault in the National Archives. If we seek, instead, a sensitive understanding of the Constitution's inherent defects, and its promising evolution through 200 years of history, the celebration of the "Miracle at Philadelphia"[12] will, in my view, be a far more meaningful and humbling experience. We will see that the true miracle was not the birth of the Constitution, but its life, a life nurtured through two turbulent centuries of our own making, and a life embodying much good fortune that was not.

Thus, in this bicentennial year, we may not all participate in the festivities with flag-waving fervor. Some may more quietly commemorate the suffering, struggle, and sacrifice that has triumphed over much of what was wrong with the original document, and observe the anniversary with hopes not realized and promises not fulfilled. I plan to celebrate the bicentennial of the Constitution as a living document, including the Bill of Rights and the other amendments protecting individual freedoms and human rights.

Notes

1. Commission on the Bicentennial of the United States Constitution, *First Report* (September 1985), at 7.
2. Ibid., at 6.
3. U.S. Constitution, Art. I, Sec. 2.
4. U.S. Constitution, Amend. XIX.
5. U.S. Constitution, Art. I, Sec. 2.
6. The Declaration of Independence, paragraph 2 (U.S. 1776).
7. See C. Becker, *The Declaration of Independence:A Study in the History of Political Ideas* 147 (New York:Vintage Books, 1970).
8. M. Farrand, ed., *The Records of the Federal Convention of 1787,* Vol. 2, 222 (New Haven:Yale University Press, 1911).
9. U.S. Constitution, Art. I, Sec. 9.
10. *Dred Scott v. Sandford*, 60 U.S. 393, 404, 407–408 (1857).
11. Ibid., at 405, 407–408.
12. C.D. Bowen, *Miracle at Philadelphia:The Story of the Constitutional Convention, May to September 1787* (Boston:Little, Brown, 1966).

CHAPTER 23

The Constitution of the United States

Contemporary Ratification

William J. Brennan Jr.
Justice, Supreme Court of the United States (1956–1990) and Justice, Supreme Court of New Jersey (1952–1956)

IT WILL PERHAPS not surprise you that the text I have chosen for exploration is the amended Constitution of the United States, which, of course, entrenches the Bill of Rights and the Civil War Amendments, and draws sustenance from the bedrock principles of another great text, the Magna Carta. So fashioned, the Constitution embodies the aspirations to social justice, brotherhood, and human dignity that brought this nation into being. The Declaration of Independence, the Constitution, and the Bill of Rights solemnly committed the United States to be a country where the dignity and rights of all persons were equal before all authority. In all candor we must concede that part of this egalitarianism in America has been more pretension than realized fact. But we are an aspiring people with faith in progress. Our amended Constitution is the lodestar for our aspirations. Like every text worth reading, it is not crystalline. The phrasing is broad and the limitations of its provisions are not clearly marked. Its majestic generalities and ennobling pronouncements are both luminous and obscure. This ambiguity of course calls forth interpretation, the interaction of reader and text. The encounter with the Constitutional text has been, in many senses, my life's work....

Acknowledgment to Justice William J. Brennan Jr. for his address on constitutional interpretation at the Text and Teaching Symposium, Georgetown University (October 12, 1985).

The Constitution is fundamentally a public text—the monumental charter of a government and a people—and a Justice of the Supreme Court must apply it to resolve public controversies. For, from our beginnings, a most important consequence of the constitutionally created separation of powers has been the American habit, extraordinary to other democracies, of casting social, economic, philosophical, and political questions in the form of law suits, in an attempt to secure ultimate resolution by the Supreme Court. In this way, important aspects of the most fundamental issues confronting our democracy may finally arrive in the Supreme Court for judicial determination. Not infrequently, these are the issues upon which contemporary society is most deeply divided. They arouse our deepest emotions. The main burden of my 29 Terms on the Supreme Court has thus been to wrestle with the Constitution in this heightened public context, to draw meaning from the text in order to resolve public controversies.

Two other aspects of my relation to this text warrant mention. First, constitutional interpretation for a federal judge is, for the most part, obligatory. When litigants approach the bar of the court to adjudicate a constitutional dispute, they may justifiably demand an answer. Judges cannot avoid a definitive interpretation because they feel unable to, or would prefer not to, penetrate to the full meaning of the Constitution's provisions. Unlike literary critics, judges cannot merely savor the tensions or revel in the ambiguities inhering in the text—judges must resolve them.

Second, consequences flow from a Justice's interpretation in a direct and immediate way. A judicial decision respecting the incompatibility of Jim Crow with a constitutional guarantee of equality is not simply a contemplative exercise in defining the shape of a just society. It is an order—supported by the full coercive power of the State—that the present society change in a fundamental aspect. Under such circumstances the process of deciding can be a lonely, troubling experience for fallible human beings conscious that their best may not be adequate to the challenge. We Justices are certainly aware that we are not final because we are infallible; we know that we are infallible only because we are final. One does not forget how much may depend on the decision. More than the litigants may be affected. The course of vital social, economic, and political currents may be directed.

These three defining characteristics of my relation to the constitutional text—its public nature, obligatory character, and consequentialist aspect—cannot help but influence the way I read that text. When Justices interpret the Constitution they speak for their community, not for themselves alone. The act of interpretation must be undertaken with full consciousness that it is, in a very real sense, the community's interpretation that is sought. Justices are not platonic guardians appointed to wield authority according to their personal moral predilections.

Precisely because coercive force must attend any judicial decision to countermand the will of a contemporary majority, the Justices must render constitutional interpretations that are received as legitimate. The source of legitimacy is, of course, a wellspring of controversy in legal and political circles. At the core of the debate is what the late Yale Law School professor Alexander Bickel labeled "the counter-majoritarian difficulty." Our commitment to self-governance in a representative democracy must be reconciled with vesting in electorally unaccountable Justices the power to invalidate the expressed desires of representative bodies on the ground of inconsistency with higher law. Because judicial power resides in the authority to give meaning to the Constitution, the debate is really a debate about how to read the text, about constraints on what is legitimate interpretation.

There are those who find legitimacy in fidelity to what they call "the intentions of the Framers." In its most doctrinaire incarnation, this view demands that Justices discern exactly what the Framers thought about the question under consideration and simply follow that intention in resolving the case before them. It is a view that feigns self-effacing deference to the specific judgments of those who forged our original social compact. But in truth it is little more than arrogance cloaked as humility. It is arrogant to pretend that from our vantage we can gauge accurately the intent of the Framers on application of principle to specific, contemporary questions. All too often, sources of potential enlightenment such as records of the ratification debates provide sparse or ambiguous evidence of the original intention. Typically, all that can be gleaned is that the Framers themselves did not agree about the application or meaning of particular constitutional provisions, and hid their differences in cloaks of generality. Indeed, it is far from clear whose intention is relevant—that of the drafters, the congressional disputants, or the ratifiers in the states?—or even whether the idea of an original intention is a coherent way of thinking about a jointly drafted document drawing its authority from a general assent of the states. And apart from the problematic nature of the sources, our distance of two centuries cannot but work as a prism refracting all we perceive. One cannot help but speculate that the chorus of lamentations calling for interpretation faithful to "original intention"—and proposing nullification of interpretations that fail this quick litmus test—must inevitably come from persons who have no familiarity with the historical record.

Perhaps most importantly, while proponents of this facile historicism justify it as a depoliticization of the judiciary, the political underpinnings of such a choice should not escape notice. A position that upholds constitutional claims only if they were within the specific contemplation of the Framers in effect establishes a presumption of resolving textual ambiguities against the claim of constitutional right. It is far from clear what justifies such a presumption against claims of right. Nothing intrinsic in the nature of interpretation—if there is such a thing as the "nature" of interpretation—commands such a passive approach to ambiguity. This is a choice no less political than any other; it expresses antipathy to claims of the minority to rights against the majority. Those who would restrict claims of right to the values of 1789 specifically articulated in the Constitution turn a blind eye to social progress and eschew adaptation of overarching principles to changes of social circumstance.

Another, perhaps more sophisticated, response to the potential power of judicial interpretation stresses democratic theory: because ours is a government of the people's elected representatives, substantive value choices should by and large be left to them. This view emphasizes not the transcendent historical authority of the Framers but the predominant contemporary authority of the elected branches of government. Yet it has similar consequences for the nature of proper judicial interpretation. Faith in the majoritarian process counsels restraint. Even under more expansive formulations of this approach, judicial review is appropriate only to the extent of ensuring that our democratic process functions smoothly. Thus, for example, we would protect the freedom of speech merely to ensure that the people are heard by their representatives, rather than as a separate, substantive value. When, by contrast, society tosses up to the Supreme Court a dispute that would require invalidation of a legislature's substantive policy choice, the Court generally would stay its hand because the Constitution was meant as a plan of government and not as an embodiment of fundamental substantive values.

The view that all matters of substantive policy should be resolved through the majoritarian process has appeal under some circumstances, but I think it ultimately will not do. Unabashed enshrinement of majority will would permit the imposition of a social caste system or wholesale confiscation of property so long as a majority of the authorized legislative body, fairly elected, approved. Our Constitution could not abide such a situation. It is the very purpose of a Constitution—and particularly of the Bill of Rights—to declare certain values transcendent, beyond the reach of temporary political majorities. The majoritarian process cannot be expected to rectify claims of minority right that arise as a response to the outcomes of that very majoritarian process. As James Madison put it:

> The prescription in favor of liberty ought to be levelled against that quarter where the greatest danger lies, namely, that which possesses the highest prerogative of power. But this is not found in either the Executive or Legislative departments of Government, but in the body of the people, operating by the majority against the minority.[1]

Faith in democracy is one thing, blind faith quite another. Those who drafted our Constitution understood the difference. One cannot read the text without admitting that it embodies substantive value choices; it places certain values beyond the power of any legislature. Obvious are the separation of powers; the privilege of the Writ of Habeas Corpus; prohibition of Bills of Attainder and ex post facto laws; prohibition of cruel and unusual punishments; the requirement of just compensation for official taking of property; the prohibition of laws tending to establish religion or enjoining the free exercise of religion; and, since the Civil War, the banishment of slavery and official race discrimination. With respect to at least such principles, we simply have not constituted ourselves as strict utilitarians. While the Constitution may be amended, such amendments require an immense effort by the people as a whole.

To remain faithful to the content of the Constitution, therefore, an approach to interpreting the text must account for the existence of these substantive value choices and must accept the ambiguity inherent in the effort to apply them to modern circumstances. The Framers discerned fundamental principles through struggles against particular malefactions of the Crown; the struggle shapes the particular contours of the articulated principles. But our acceptance of the fundamental principles has not and should not bind us to those precise, at times anachronistic, contours. Successive generations of Americans have continued to respect these fundamental choices and adopt them as their own guide to evaluating quite different historical practices. Each generation has the choice to overrule or add to the fundamental principles enunciated by the Framers; the Constitution can be amended or it can be ignored. Yet with respect to its fundamental principles, the text has suffered neither fate. Thus, if I may borrow the words of an esteemed predecessor, Justice Robert Jackson, the burden of judicial interpretation is to translate "the majestic generalities of the Bill of Rights, conceived as part of the pattern of liberal government in the eighteenth century, into concrete restraints on officials dealing with the problems of the twentieth century."[2]

We current Justices read the Constitution in the only way that we can:as twentieth-century Americans. We look to the history of the time of framing and to the intervening history of interpretation. But the ultimate question must be:what do the words of the text mean in our time? For the genius of the Constitution rests not in any static meaning it might have had in a world that is dead and gone, but in the adaptability of its great principles to cope with current problems and current needs. What the constitutional fundamentals meant to the wisdom of other times cannot be their measure to the vision of our time. Similarly, what those fundamentals mean for us, our descendants will learn, cannot be the measure to the vision of their time. This realization is not, I assure you, a novel one of my own creation. Permit me to quote from one of the opinions of our Court, *Weems v. United States*, written nearly a century ago:

> Time works changes, brings into existence new conditions and purposes. Therefore, a principle to be vital must be capable of wider application than the mischief

> which gave it birth. This is peculiarly true of constitutions. They are not ephemeral enactments, designed to meet passing occasions. They are, to use the words of Chief Justice John Marshall, "designed to approach immortality as nearly as human institutions can approach it." The future is their care and provision for events of good and bad tendencies of which no prophesy can be made. In the application of a constitution, therefore, our contemplation cannot be only of what has been, but of what may be.[3]

Interpretation must account for the transformative purposes of the text. Our Constitution was not intended to preserve a preexisting society but to make a new one, to put in place new principles that the prior community had not sufficiently recognized. Thus, for example, when we interpret the Civil War Amendments to the charter—abolishing slavery, guaranteeing blacks equality under law, and guaranteeing blacks the right to vote—we must remember that those who put them in place had no desire to enshrine the status quo. Their goal was to make over their world, to eliminate all vestige of slave caste. Having discussed at some length how I, as a Supreme Court Justice, interact with this text, I think it is time to turn to the fruits of this discourse. For the Constitution is a sublime oration on the dignity of man, a bold commitment by a people to the ideal of libertarian dignity protected through law. Some reflection is perhaps required before this can be seen.

The Constitution on its face is, in large measure, a structuring text, a blueprint for government. And when the text is not prescribing the form of government, it is limiting the powers of that government. The original document, before addition of any of the amendments, does not speak primarily of the rights of man but of the abilities and disabilities of government. When one reflects on the text's preoccupation with the scope of government as well as its shape, however, one comes to understand that what this text is about is the relationship of the individual and the state. The text marks the metes and bounds of official authority and individual autonomy. When one studies the boundary that the text marks out, one gets a sense of the vision of the individual embodied in the Constitution.

As augmented by the Bill of Rights and the Civil War Amendments, this text is a sparkling vision of the supremacy of the human dignity of every individual. This vision is reflected in the very choice of democratic self-governance:the supreme value of a democracy is the presumed worth of each individual. And this vision manifests itself most dramatically in the specific prohibitions of the Bill of Rights, a term which I henceforth will apply to describe not only the original first eight amendments, but the Civil War Amendments as well. It is a vision that has guided us as a people throughout our history, although the precise rules by which we have protected fundamental human dignity have been transformed over time in response to both transformations of social condition and evolution of our concepts of human dignity.

Until the end of the nineteenth century, freedom and dignity in our country found meaningful protection in the institution of real property. In a society still largely agricultural, a piece of land provided men not just with sustenance but with the means of economic independence, a necessary precondition of political independence and expression. Not surprisingly, property relationships formed the heart of litigation and of legal practice, and lawyers and judges tended to think stable property relationships the highest aim of the law.

But the days when common-law property relationships dominated litigation and legal practice are past. To a growing extent economic existence now depends on less certain relationships with government—licenses, employment, contracts, subsidies, unemployment benefits, tax exemptions, welfare, and the like. Government participation in the economic existence of individuals is pervasive and deep. Administrative matters and other dealings with government are at the epicenter of the exploding law. We turn to government and to the law for controls which would never have been expected or tolerated before this century, when a man's answer to economic oppression or difficulty was to move two hundred miles west. Now hundreds of thousands of Americans live entire lives without any real prospect of the dignity and autonomy that ownership of real property could confer. Protection of the human dignity of such citizens requires a much modified view of the proper relationship of individual and state.

In general, problems of the relationship of the citizen with government have multiplied and thus have engendered some of the most important constitutional issues of the day. As government acts ever more deeply upon those areas of our lives once marked "private," there is an even greater need to see that individual rights are not curtailed or cheapened in the interest of what may temporarily appear to be the "public good." And as government continues in its role of provider for so many of our disadvantaged citizens, there is an even greater need to ensure that government act with integrity and consistency in its dealings with these citizens. To put this another way, the possibilities for collision between government activity and individual rights will increase as the power and authority of government itself expands, and this growth, in turn, heightens the need for constant vigilance at the collision points. If our free society is to endure, those who govern must recognize human dignity and accept the enforcement of constitutional limitations on their power conceived by the Framers to be necessary to preserve that dignity and the air of freedom which is our proudest heritage. Such recognition will not come from a technical understanding of the organs of government, or the new forms of wealth they administer. It requires something different, something deeper—a personal confrontation with the wellsprings of our society. Solutions of constitutional questions from that perspective have become the great challenge of the modern era. All the talk in the last half-decade about shrinking the government does not alter this reality or the challenge it imposes. The modern activist state is a concomitant of the complexity of modern society; it is inevitably with us. We must meet the challenge rather than wish it were not before us.

The challenge is essentially, of course, one to the capacity of our constitutional structure to foster and protect the freedom, the dignity, and the rights of all persons within our borders, which it is the great design of the Constitution to secure. During the time of my public service, this challenge has largely taken shape within the confines of the interpretive question whether the specific guarantees of the Bill of Rights operate as restraints on the power of state government. We recognize the Bill of Rights as the primary source of express information as to what is meant by constitutional liberty. The safeguards enshrined in it are deeply etched in the foundation of America's freedoms. Each is a protection with centuries of history behind it, often dearly bought with the blood and lives of people determined to prevent oppression by their rulers. The first eight amendments, however, were added to the Constitution to operate solely against federal power. It was not until the Thirteenth and Fourteenth Amendments were added, in 1865 and 1868, in response to a demand for national protection against abuses of state power, that the Constitution could be interpreted to require application of the first eight amendments to the states.

It was in particular the Fourteenth Amendment's guarantee that no person be deprived of life, liberty, or property without process of law that led us to apply many of the specific guarantees of the Bill of Rights to the states. In my judgment, Justice Cardozo best captured the reasoning that brought us to such decisions when he described what the Court has done as a process by which the guarantees "have been taken over from the earlier articles of the federal bill of rights and brought within the Fourteenth Amendment by a process of absorption ... [that] has had its source in the belief that neither liberty nor justice would exist if [those guarantees] ... were sacrificed."[4] But this process of absorption was neither swift nor steady. As late as 1922 only the Fifth Amendment guarantee of just compensation for official taking of property had been given force against the states. Between then and 1956 only the First Amendment guarantees of speech and conscience and the Fourth Amendment ban of unreasonable searches and seizures had been incorporated—the latter, however, without the exclusionary rule to give it force. As late as 1961, I could stand before a distinguished assemblage of the bar at New York University's James Madison Lecture and list the following as guarantees that had not been thought to be sufficiently fundamental to the protection of human dignity so as to be enforced against the state:the prohibition of cruel and unusual punishments, the right against self-incrimination, the right to assistance of counsel in a criminal trial, the right to confront witnesses, the right to compulsory process, the right not to be placed in jeopardy of life or limb more than once upon accusation of a crime, the right not to have illegally obtained evidence introduced at a criminal trial, and the right to a jury of one's peers.

The history of the quarter century following that James Madison Lecture need not be told in great detail. Suffice it to say that each of the guarantees listed above has been recognized as a fundamental aspect of ordered liberty. Of course, the above catalogue encompasses only the rights of the criminally accused, those caught, rightly or wrongly, in the maw of the criminal justice system. But it has been well said that there is no better test of a society than how it treats those accused of transgressing against it. Indeed, it is because we recognize that incarceration strips a man of his dignity that we demand strict adherence to fair procedure and proof of guilt beyond a reasonable doubt before taking such a drastic step. These requirements are, as Justice Harlan once said, "bottomed on a fundamental value determination of our society that it is far worse to convict an innocent man than to let a guilty man go free."[5] There is no worse injustice than wrongly to strip a man of his dignity. And our adherence to the constitutional vision of human dignity is so strict that even after convicting a person according to these stringent standards, we demand that his dignity be infringed only to the extent appropriate to the crime and never by means of wanton infliction of pain or deprivation. I interpret the Constitution plainly to embody these fundamental values.

Of course the constitutional vision of human dignity has, in this past quarter century, infused far more than our decisions about the criminal process. Recognition of the principle of "one person, one vote" as a constitutional one redeems the promise of self-governance by affirming the essential dignity of every citizen in the right to equal participation in the democratic process. Recognition of so-called "new property" rights in those receiving government entitlements affirms the essential dignity of the least fortunate among us by demanding that government treat with decency, integrity, and consistency those dependent on its benefits for their very survival. After all, a legislative majority initially decides to create governmental entitlements; the Constitution's Due Process Clause merely provides protection for entitlements thought necessary by society as a whole. Such due process rights prohibit government from imposing the devil's bargain of bartering away human dignity in exchange for human sustenance. Likewise, recognition of full equality for women—equal protection of the laws—ensures that gender has no bearing on claims to human dignity.

Recognition of broad and deep rights of expression and of conscience reaffirm the vision of human dignity in many ways. They too redeem the promise of self-governance by facilitating—indeed demanding—robust, uninhibited, and wide-open debate on issues of public importance. Such public debate is, of course, vital to the development and dissemination of political ideas. As importantly, robust public discussion is the crucible in which personal political convictions are forged. In our democracy, such discussion is a political duty; it is the essence of self-government. The constitutional vision of human dignity rejects the possibility of political orthodoxy imposed from above; it respects the right of each individual to form and to express political judgments, however far they may deviate from the mainstream and however unsettling they might be to the powerful or the elite. Recognition of these rights of expression and conscience also frees up the private space for both intellectual and spiritual development free of government dominance, either blatant or subtle. Justice Brandeis put it so well sixty years ago when he wrote: "Those who won our independence believed that the final end of the State was to make men free to develop their faculties; and that in its government the deliberative forces should prevail over the arbitrary. They valued liberty both as an end and as a means."[6]

I do not mean to suggest that we have in the last quarter century achieved a comprehensive definition of the constitutional ideal of human dignity. We are still striving toward that goal, and doubtless it will be an eternal quest. For if the interaction of this Justice and the constitutional text over the years confirms any single proposition, it is that the demands of human dignity will never cease to evolve.

Indeed, I cannot in good conscience refrain from mention of one grave and crucial respect in which we continue, in my judgment, to fall short of the constitutional vision of human dignity. It is in our continued tolerance of state-administered execution as a form of punishment. I make it a practice not to comment on the constitutional issues that come before the Court, but my position on this issue, of course, has been for some time fixed and immutable. I think I can venture some thoughts on this particular subject without transgressing my usual guideline too severely.

As I interpret the Constitution, capital punishment is under all circumstances cruel and unusual punishment prohibited by the Eighth and Fourteenth Amendments. This is a position of which I imagine you are not unaware. Much discussion of the merits of capital punishment has in recent years focused on the potential arbitrariness that attends its administration, and I have no doubt that such arbitrariness is a grave wrong. But for me, the wrong of capital punishment transcends such procedural issues. As I have said in my opinions, I view the Eighth Amendment's prohibition of cruel and unusual punishments as embodying to a unique degree moral principles that substantively restrain the punishments our civilized society may impose on those persons who transgress its laws. Foremost among the moral principles recognized in our cases and inherent in the prohibition is the primary principle that the state, even as it punishes, must treat its citizens in a manner consistent with their intrinsic worth as human beings. A punishment must not be so severe as to be utterly and irreversibly degrading to the very essence of human dignity. Death for whatever crime and under all circumstances is a truly awesome punishment. The calculated killing of a human being by the state involves, by its very nature, an absolute denial of the executed person's humanity. The most vile murder does not, in my view, release the state from constitutional restraints on the destruction of human dignity. Yet an executed person has lost the very right to have rights, now or ever. For me, then, the fatal constitutional infirmity of capital punishment is that it treats members of the human race as nonhumans, as objects to be toyed with and discarded. It is, indeed, "cruel and unusual." It is thus inconsistent with the fundamental premise of the Clause that even the most base criminal remains a human being possessed of some potential, at least, for common human dignity.

This is an interpretation to which a majority of my fellow Justices—not to mention, it would seem, a majority of my fellow countrymen—does not subscribe. Perhaps you find my adherence to it, and my recurrent publication of it, simply contrary, tiresome, or quixotic. Or perhaps you see in it a refusal to abide by the judicial principle of *stare decisis*, obedience to precedent. In my judgment, however, the unique interpretive role of the Supreme Court with respect to the Constitution demands some flexibility with respect to the call of *stare decisis*. Because we are the last word on the meaning of the Constitution, our views must be subject to revision over time, or the Constitution falls captive, again, to the anachronistic views of long-gone generations. I mentioned earlier the judge's role in seeking out the community's interpretation of the Constitutional text. Yet, again in my judgment, when a Justice perceives an interpretation of the text to have departed so far from its essential meaning, that Justice is bound, by a larger constitutional duty to the community, to expose the departure and point toward a different path. On this issue, the death penalty, I hope to embody a community striving for human dignity for all, although perhaps not yet arrived.

You have doubtless observed that this description of my personal encounter with the constitutional text has in large portion been a discussion of public developments in constitutional doctrine over the last quarter century. That, as I suggested at the outset, is inevitable because my interpretive career has demanded a public reading of the text. This public encounter with the text, however, has been a profound source of personal inspiration. The vision of human dignity embodied there is deeply moving. It is timeless. It has inspired Americans for two centuries, and it will continue to inspire as it continues to evolve. That evolutionary process is inevitable and, indeed, it is the true interpretive genius of the text.

If we are to be as a shining city upon a hill, it will be because of our ceaseless pursuit of the constitutional ideal of human dignity. For the political and legal ideals that form the foundation of much that is best in American institutions—ideals jealously reserved and guarded throughout our history—still form the vital force in creative political thought and activity within the nation today. As we adapt our institutions to the ever-changing conditions of national and international life, those ideals of human dignity—liberty and justice for all individuals—will continue to inspire and guide us because they are entrenched in our Constitution. The Constitution with its Bill of Rights thus has a bright future, as well as a glorious past, for its spirit is inherent in the aspirations of our people.

Notes

1. *Annals of Congress: The Debates and Proceedings in the Congress of the United States* 437 (Washington, D.C.: Gales and Seaton, 1834).
2. *West Virginia State Board of Education v. Barnette,* 319, 624, 639 (1943).
3. *Weems v. United States* 317, 349 (1910).
4. *Palko v. Connecticut,* 302 U.S. 319, 326 (1937).
5. *In re Winship*, 397 U.S. 358, 372 (1970).
6. *Whitney v. California,* 274 U.S. 357 (1927).

CHAPTER 24

Speaking in a Judicial Voice

Reflections on *Roe v. Wade*

Ruth Bader Ginsburg

Justice, Supreme Court of the United States (1993–)
and Judge, U.S. Court of Appeals, District of Columbia Circuit (1980–1993)

IN *The Federalist* No. 78, Alexander Hamilton said that federal judges, in order to preserve the people's rights and privileges, must have authority to check legislation and acts of the executive for constitutionality. But he qualified his recognition of that awesome authority. The judiciary, Hamilton wrote, from the very nature of its functions, will always be "the least dangerous" branch of government, for judges hold neither the sword nor the purse of the community; ultimately, they must depend upon the political branches to effectuate their judgments. Mindful of that reality, the effective judge, I believe and will explain why in these remarks, strives to persuade, and not to pontificate. She speaks in "a moderate and restrained" voice, engaging in a dialogue with, not a diatribe against, co-equal departments of government, state authorities, and even her own colleagues. . . .

Moving from the style to the substance of third branch decisionmaking, I will stress in the remainder of these remarks that judges play an interdependent part in our democracy. They do not alone shape legal doctrine but, as I suggested at the outset, they participate in a dialogue with other organs of government, and with the people as well. "Judges do and must legislate," Justice Holmes "recognized without hesitation," but "they can do so," he cautioned, "only interstitially; they are confined from molar to molecular motions." Measured motions seem to me

---

Acknowledgment to Justice Ruth Bader Ginsburg for excerpts from her essay "Speaking in a Judicial Voice," which appears in 67 New York University Law Review *1185 (1992).*

right, in the main, for constitutional as well as common law adjudication. Doctrinal limbs too swiftly shaped, experience teaches, may prove unstable. The most prominent example in recent decades is *Roe v. Wade*.[1] To illustrate my point, I have contrasted that breathtaking 1973 decision with the Court's more cautious dispositions, contemporaneous with *Roe*, in cases involving explicitly sex-based classifications, and will further develop that comparison here.

The seven to two judgment in *Roe v. Wade* declared "violative of the Due Process Clause of the Fourteenth Amendment" a Texas criminal abortion statute that intolerably shackled a woman's autonomy; the Texas law "excepted from criminality only a life-saving procedure on behalf of the pregnant woman." Suppose the Court had stopped there, rightly declaring unconstitutional the most extreme brand of law in the nation, and had not gone on, as the Court did in *Roe*, to fashion a regime blanketing the subject, a set of rules that displaced virtually every state law then in force. Would there have been the twenty-year controversy we have witnessed, reflected most recently in the Supreme Court's splintered decision in *Planned Parenthood v. Casey*?[2] A less encompassing *Roe*, one that merely struck down the extreme Texas law and went no further on that day, I believe and will summarize why, might have served to reduce rather than to fuel controversy.

In the 1992 *Planned Parenthood* decision, the three controlling Justices accepted as constitutional several restrictions on access to abortion that could not have survived strict adherence to *Roe*. While those Justices did not closely consider the plight of women without means to overcome the restrictions, they added an important strand to the Court's opinions on abortion—they acknowledged the intimate connection between a woman's "ability to control her reproductive life" and her "ability ... to participate equally in the economic and social life of the Nation." The idea of the woman in control of her destiny and her place in society was less prominent in the *Roe* decision itself, which coupled with the rights of the pregnant woman the free exercise of her physician's medical judgment. The *Roe* decision might have been less of a storm center had it both homed in more precisely on the women's equality dimension of the issue and, correspondingly, attempted nothing more bold at that time than the mode of decisionmaking the Court employed in the 1970s gender classification cases.

In fact, the very Term *Roe* was decided, the Supreme Court had on its calendar a case that could have served as a bridge, linking reproductive choice to disadvantageous treatment of women on the basis of their sex. The case was *Struck v. Secretary of Defense*;[3] it involved a Captain the Air Force sought to discharge in Vietnam War days. Perhaps it is indulgence in wishful thinking, but the *Struck* case, I believe, would have proved extraordinarily educational for the Court and had large potential for advancing public understanding. Captain Susan Struck was a career officer. According to her commanding officer, her performance as a manager and nurse was exemplary. Captain Struck had avoided the drugs and the alcohol that hooked many service members in the late 1960s and early 1970s, but she did become pregnant while stationed in Vietnam. She undertook to use, and in fact used, only her accumulated leave time for childbirth. She declared her intention to place, and in fact placed, her child for adoption immediately after birth. Her religious faith precluded recourse to abortion.

Two features of Captain Struck's case are particularly noteworthy. First, the rule she challenged was unequivocal and typical of the time. It provided: "A woman officer will be discharged from the service with the least practicable delay when a determination is made by a medical officer that she is pregnant." To cover any oversight, the Air Force had a back-up rule: "The commission of any woman officer will be terminated with the least practicable delay when it is established that she ... has given birth to a living child while in a commissioned officer status."

A second striking element of Captain Struck's case was the escape route available to her, which she chose not to take. Air Force regulations current at the start of the 1970s provided: "The Air Force Medical Service is not subject to State laws in the performance of its functions. When medically indicated or for reasons involving medical health, pregnancies may be terminated in Air Force hospitals ... ideally before 20 weeks gestation."

Captain Struck argued that the unwanted discharge she faced unjustifiably restricted her personal autonomy and dignity; principally, however, she maintained that the regulation mandating her discharge violated the equal protection of the laws guarantee implicit in the fifth amendment's due process clause. She urged that the Air Force regime differentiated invidiously by allowing males who became fathers, but not females who became mothers, to remain in service and by allowing women who had undergone abortions, but not women who delivered infants, to continue their military careers. Her pleas were unsuccessful in the lower courts, but on October 24, 1972, less than three months before the *Roe* decision, the Supreme Court granted her petition for *certiorari*.

At that point the Air Force decided it would rather switch than fight. At the end of November 1972, it granted Captain Struck a waiver of the once unwaivable regulation and permitted her to continue her service as an Air Force officer. The Solicitor General promptly and successfully suggested that the case had become moot.

Given the parade of cases on the Court's full calendar, it is doubtful that the Justices trained further attention on the *Struck* scenario. With more time and space for reflection, however, and perhaps a female presence on the Court, might the Justices have gained at least these two insights? First, if even the military, an institution not known for avant-garde policy, had taken to providing facilities for abortion, then was not a decision of *Roe*'s muscularity unnecessary? Second, confronted with Captain Struck's unwanted discharge, might the Court have comprehended an argument, or at least glimpsed a reality, it later resisted—that disadvantageous treatment of a woman because of her pregnancy and reproductive choice is a paradigm case of discrimination on the basis of sex? What was the assumption underlying the differential treatment to which Captain Struck was exposed? The regulations that mandated her discharge were not even thinly disguised. They declared, effectively, that responsibility for children disabled female parents, but not male parents, for other work—not for biological reasons, but because society had ordered things that way.

Captain Struck had asked the Court first to apply the highest level of scrutiny to her case, to hold that the sex-based classification she encountered was a "suspect" category for legislative or administrative action. As a fallback, she suggested to the Court an intermediate standard of review, one under which prescriptions that worked to women's disadvantage would gain review of at least heightened, if not the very highest, intensity. In the course of the 1970s, the Supreme Court explicitly acknowledged that it was indeed applying an elevated, labeled "intermediate," level of review to classifications it recognized as sex-based....

Until 1971, women did not prevail before the Supreme Court in any case charging unconstitutional sex discrimination. In the years from 1971 to 1982, however, the Court held unconstitutional, as violative of due process or equal protection constraints, a series of state and federal laws that differentiated explicitly on the basis of sex.

The Court ruled in 1973, for example, that married women in the military were entitled to the housing allowance and family medical care benefits that Congress had provided solely for married men in the military.[4] Two years later, the Court held it unconstitutional for a state to allow a parent to stop supporting a daughter once she reached the age of 18, while requiring parental support for a son until he turned 21.[5] In 1975, and again in 1979, the Court declared that state jury-selection systems could not exclude or exempt women as a class.[6] In decisions running from 1975 to 1980, the Court deleted the principal explicitly sex-based classifications in social insurance[7] and workers' compensation schemes.[8] In 1981, the Court said nevermore to a state law designating the husband "head and master" of the household.[9] And in 1982, in an opinion by Justice O'Connor, the Court held that a state could not limit admission to a state nursing college to women only.[10]

The backdrop for these rulings was a phenomenal expansion, in the years from 1961 to 1971, of women's employment outside the home, the civil rights movement of the 1960s and the precedents set in that struggle, and a revived feminist movement, fueled abroad and in the United States by Simone de Beauvoir's remarkable 1949 publication, *The Second Sex*. In the main, the Court invalidated laws that had become obsolete, retained into the 1970s by only a few of the states. In a core set of cases, however, those dealing with social insurance benefits for a worker's spouse or family, the decisions did not utterly condemn the legislature's product. Instead, the Court, in effect, opened a dialogue with the political branches of government. In essence, the Court instructed Congress and state legislatures:rethink ancient positions on these questions. Should you determine that special treatment for women is warranted, i.e., compensatory legislation because of the sunken-in social and economic bias or disadvantage women encounter, we have left you a corridor in which to move. But your classifications must be refined, adopted for remedial reasons, and not rooted in prejudice about "the way women (or men) are." In the meantime, the Court's decrees removed no benefits; instead, they extended to a woman worker's husband, widower, or family benefits Congress had authorized only for members of a male worker's family.

The ball, one might say, was tossed by the Justices back into the legislators' court, where the political forces of the day could operate. The Supreme Court wrote modestly, it put forward no grand philosophy; but by requiring legislative reexamination of once customary sex-based classifications, the Court helped to ensure that laws and regulations would "catch up with a changed world."

Roe v. Wade, in contrast, invited no dialogue with legislators. Instead, it seemed entirely to remove the ball from the legislators' court. In 1973, when *Roe* was issued, abortion law was in a state of change across the nation. As the Supreme Court itself noted, there was a marked trend in state legislatures "toward liberalization of abortion statutes." That movement for legislative change ran parallel to another law revision effort then underway—the change from fault to no-fault divorce regimes, a reform that swept through the state legislatures and captured all of them by the mid–1980s.

No measured motion, the *Roe* decision left virtually no state with laws fully conforming to the Court's delineation of abortion regulation still permissible. Around that extraordinary decision, a well-organized and vocal right-to-life movement rallied and succeeded, for a considerable time, in turning the legislative tide in the opposite direction.

Constitutional review by courts is an institution that has been for some two centuries our nation's hallmark and pride. Two extreme modes of court intervention in social change processes, however, have placed stress on the institution. At one extreme, the Supreme Court steps boldly in front of the political process, as some believe it did in *Roe*. At the opposite extreme, the Court in the early part of the twentieth century found—or thrust—itself into the rearguard opposing change, striking down, as unconstitutional, laws embodying a new philosophy of economic regulation at odds with the nineteenth century's laissez-faire approach. Decisions at both of these poles yielded outcries against the judiciary in certain quarters. The Supreme Court, particularly, was labeled "activist" or "imperial," and its precarious position as final arbiter of constitutional questions was exposed.

I do not suggest that the Court should never step ahead of the political branches in pursuit of a constitutional precept. *Brown v. Board of Education*,[11] the 1954 decision declaring racial segregation in public schools offensive to the equal protection principle, is the case that best fits the bill. Past the midpoint of the twentieth century, apartheid remained the law-enforced system in several states, shielded by a constitutional interpretation the Court itself advanced at the turn of the century—the "separate but equal" doctrine.

In contrast to the legislative reform movement in the states, contemporaneous with *Roe*, widening access to abortion, prospects in 1954 for state legislation dismantling racially segregated schools were bleak. That was so, I believe, for a reason that distances race discrimination from discrimination based on sex. Most women are life partners of men; women bear and raise both sons and daughters. Once women's own consciousness was awakened to the unfairness of allocating opportunity and responsibility on the basis of sex, education of others—of fathers, husbands, sons as well as daughters—could begin, or be reinforced, at home. When blacks were confined by law to a separate sector, there was no similar prospect for educating the white majority.

It bears emphasis, however, that *Brown* was not an altogether bold decision. First, Thurgood Marshall and those who worked with him in the campaign against racial injustice, carefully set the stepping stones leading up to the landmark ruling. Pathmarkers of the same kind had not been installed prior to the Court's decision in *Roe*. Second, *Brown* launched no broadside attack on the Jim Crow system in all its institutional manifestations. Instead, the Court concentrated on segregated schools; it left the follow-up for other days and future cases. A burgeoning civil rights movement—which *Brown* helped to propel—culminating in the Civil Rights Act of 1964, set the stage for the Court's ultimate total rejection of Jim Crow legislation.

Significantly, in relation to the point I just made about women and men living together, the end of the Jim Crow era came in 1967, thirteen years after *Brown*:the case was *Loving v. Virginia*,[12] the law under attack, a state prohibition on interracial marriage. In holding that law unconstitutional, the Court effectively ruled that, with regard to racial classifications, the doctrine of "separate but equal" was dead—everywhere and anywhere within the governance of the United States.

The framers of the Constitution allowed to rest in the Court's hands large authority to rule on the Constitution's meaning; but the framers, as I noted at the outset, armed the Court with no swords to carry out its pronouncements. President Andrew Jackson in 1832, according to an often-told legend, said of a Supreme Court decision he did not like: "The Chief Justice has made his decision, now let him enforce it." With prestige to persuade, but not physical power to enforce, with a will for self-preservation and the knowledge that they are not "a bevy of Platonic Guardians," the Justices generally follow, they do not lead, changes taking place elsewhere in society. But without taking giant strides and thereby risking a backlash too forceful to contain, the Court, through constitutional adjudication, can reinforce or signal a green light for a social change. In most of the post–1970 gender-classification cases, unlike *Roe*, the Court functioned in just that way. It approved the direction of change through a temperate brand of decisionmaking, one that was not extravagant or divisive. *Roe*, on the other hand, halted a political process that was moving in a reform direction and thereby, I believe, prolonged divisiveness and deferred stable settlement of the issue. The most recent *Planned Parenthood* decision notably retreats from *Roe* and further excludes from the High Court's protection women lacking the means or the sophistication to surmount burdensome legislation. The latest decision may have had the sanguine effect, however, of contributing to the ongoing revitalization in the 1980s and 1990s of the political movement in progress in the early 1970s, a movement that addressed not simply or dominantly the courts but primarily the people's representatives and the people themselves. That renewed force, one may hope, will—within a relatively short span—yield an enduring resolution of this vital matter in a way that affirms the dignity and equality of women.

Notes

1. *Roe v. Wade*, 410 U.S. 113 (1973).
2. *Planned Parenthood of Southeastern Pennsylvania v. Casey*, 505 U.S. 833 (1992).
3. *Struck v. Secretary of Defense*, 409 U.S. 1071 (1972).
4. *Frontiero v. Richardson*, 411 U.S. 677 (1975).
5. *Stanton v. Stanton*, 421 U.S. 7 (1975).
6. *Taylor v. Louisiana*, 419 U.S. 522 (1975); and *Duren v. Missouri*, 439 U.S. 76 (1979).
7. *Weinberger v. Wiesenfeld*, 420 U.S. 636 (1975); *Califano v. Goldfarb*, 430 U.S. 199 (1977); *Califano v. Westcott*, 443 U.S. 76 (1979).
8. *Wengler v. Druggists Mut. Ins. Co.*, 446 U.S. 142 (1980).
9. *Kirchberg v. Feenstra*, 450 U.S. 455 (1981).
10. *Mississippi Univ. for Women v. Hogan*, 458 U.S. 718 (1982).
11. *Brown v. Board of Education*, 347 U.S. 483 (1954).
12. *Loving v. Virginia*, 388 U.S. 1 (1967).

CHAPTER 25

Our Democratic Constitution

Stephen G. Breyer
Justice, Supreme Court of the United States (1994–) and Judge, U.S. Court of Appeals, First Circuit (1980–1994)

THE UNITED STATES is a nation built on principles of human liberty—a liberty that embraces concepts of democracy. The French political philosopher Benjamin Constant understood the connection. He distinguished between liberty as practiced by the ancient Greeks and Romans and the "liberty" of the eighteenth- and nineteenth-century "moderns."[1] Writing thirty years after the French Revolution and not long after the adoption of our American Constitution, Constant said that the "liberty of the ancients" consisted of an "active and constant participation in collective power." The ancient world, he added, believed that liberty consisted of "submitting to all the citizens, without exception, the care and assessment of their most sacred interests."... Constant distinguished that "liberty of the ancients" from the more "modern liberty" consisting of "individual independence" from governmental restriction....

I shall argue that, when judges interpret the Constitution, they should place greater emphasis upon the "ancient liberty," that is, the people's right to "an active and constant participation in collective power." I believe that increased emphasis upon this active liberty will lead to better constitutional law—law that will promote governmental solutions consistent with individual dignity and community need.

At the same time, my discussion will illustrate an approach to constitutional interpretation that places considerable weight upon consequences—consequences

Acknowledgment to Justice Stephen G. Breyer for permission to reprint excerpts from the James Madison Lecture, "Our Democratic Constitution," appearing in 77 New York University Law Review *245 (2002).*

valued in terms of basic constitutional purposes. It disavows a contrary constitutional approach, a more "legalistic" approach that places too much weight upon language, history, tradition, and precedent alone while understating the importance of consequences. If the discussion helps to convince you that the more "consequential" approach has virtue, so much the better.

Three basic views underlie my discussion. First, the Constitution, considered as a whole, creates a framework for a certain kind of government. Its general objectives can be described abstractly as including: (1) democratic self-government; (2) dispersion of power (avoiding concentration of too much power in too few hands); (3) individual dignity (through protection of individual liberties); (4) equality before the law (through equal protection of the law); and (5) the rule of law itself....

Second, the Court, while always respecting language, tradition, and precedent, nonetheless has emphasized different general constitutional objectives at different periods in its history. Thus one can characterize the early nineteenth century as a period during which the Court helped to establish the authority of the federal government, including the federal judiciary. During the late nineteenth and early twentieth centuries, the Court underemphasized the Constitution's efforts to secure participation by black citizens in representative government—efforts related to the participatory "active liberty" of the ancients. At the same time, it overemphasized protection of property rights, such as an individual's freedom to contract without government interference, to the point where President Franklin [Delano] Roosevelt commented that the Court's *Lochner*-era decisions had created a legal "no-man's land" that neither state nor federal regulatory authority had the power to enter.[2]

The New Deal Court and the Warren Court reemphasized "active liberty." The former did so by dismantling various *Lochner*-era distinctions, thereby expanding the scope of democratic self-government. The latter did so by interpreting the Civil War Amendments in light of their purposes to mean what they say, thereby helping African Americans become members of the nation's community of self-governing citizens—a community that the Court expanded further in its "one person, one vote" decisions.[3]

More recently, in my view, the Court has again underemphasized the importance of the citizen's active liberty. I will argue for a contemporary reemphasis that better combines "the liberty of the ancients" with that "freedom of governmental restraint" that Constant called "modern."

Third, the real-world consequences of a particular interpretive decision, valued in terms of basic constitutional purposes, play an important role in constitutional decision making. To that extent, my approach differs from that of judges who would place nearly exclusive interpretive weight upon language, history, tradition, and precedent. In truth, the difference is one of degree. Virtually all judges, when interpreting a constitution or a statute, refer at one time or another to language, to history, to tradition, to precedent, to purpose, and to consequences. Even those who take a more literal approach to constitutional interpretation sometimes find consequences and general purposes relevant. But the more "literalist" judge tends to ask those who cannot find an interpretive answer in language, history, tradition, and precedent alone to rethink the problem several times before making consequences determinative. The more literal judges may hope to find, in language, history, tradition, and precedent, objective interpretive standards; they may seek to avoid an interpretive subjectivity that could confuse a judge's personal idea of what is good for that which the Constitution demands; and they may believe that these "original" sources more readily will yield rules that can guide other institutions, including lower courts. These objectives are desirable, but I do not think the literal approach will achieve them, and, in any event, the constitutional price is too high....

To focus upon that active liberty, to understand it as one of the Constitution's handful of general objectives, will lead judges to consider the constitutionality of statutes with a certain modesty. That modesty embodies an understanding of the judges' own expertise compared, for example, with that of a legislature. It reflects the concern that a judiciary too ready to "correct" legislative error may deprive "the people" of "the political experience, and the moral education and stimulus that come from ... correcting their own errors." It encompasses that doubt, caution, prudence, and concern—that state of not being "too sure" of oneself—that Learned Hand described as the "spirit of liberty."[4] In a word, it argues for traditional "judicial restraint."...

I begin with free speech and campaign finance reform. The campaign finance problem arises out of the recent explosion in campaign costs along with a vast disparity among potential givers.... A very small number of individuals underwrite a very large share of these enormous costs.... The basic constitutional question, as you all know, is not the desirability of reform legislation but whether, how, or to what extent the First Amendment permits the legislature to impose limitations or ceilings on the amounts individuals, organizations, or parties can contribute to a campaign or on the kinds of contributions they can make. The Court has considered this kind of question several times; I have written opinions in several of those cases; and here I shall rephrase (not go beyond) what I already have written.

One cannot (or, at least, I cannot) find an easy answer to the constitutional questions in language, history, or tradition. The First Amendment's language says that Congress shall not abridge "the freedom of speech." But it does not define "the freedom of speech" in any detail. The nation's founders did not speak directly about campaign contributions....

Neither can I find answers in purely conceptual arguments. Some argue, for example, that "money is speech"; others say "money is not speech." But neither contention helps much. Money is not speech, it is money. But the expenditure of money enables speech; and that expenditure is often necessary to communicate a message, particularly in a political context. A law that forbids the expenditure of money to convey a message could effectively suppress that communication.

Nor does it resolve the matter simply to point out that campaign contribution limits inhibit the political "speech opportunities" of those who wish to contribute more. Indeed, that is so. But the question is whether, in context, such a limitation abridges "the freedom of speech." And to announce that this kind of harm could never prove justified in a political context is simply to state an ultimate constitutional conclusion; it is not to explain the underlying reasons.

To refer to the Constitution's general participatory self-government objective, its protection of "active liberty" is far more helpful. That is because that constitutional goal indicates that the First Amendment's constitutional role is not simply one of protecting the individual's "negative" freedom from governmental restraint. The amendment in context also forms a necessary part of a constitutional system designed to sustain that democratic self-government. The amendment helps to sustain the democratic process both by encouraging the exchange of ideas needed to make sound electoral decisions and by encouraging an exchange of views among ordinary citizens necessary to their informed participation in the electoral process. It thereby helps to maintain a form of government open to participation (in Constant's words, by "all the citizens, without exception").

The relevance of this conceptual view lies in the fact that the campaign finance laws also seek to further the latter objective. They hope to democratize the influence that money can bring to bear upon the electoral process, thereby building public confidence in that process, broadening the base of a candidate's meaningful financial support, and encouraging greater public participation. They consequently seek to maintain the integrity of the political process—a process that itself translates political speech into governmental action. Seen in this way, campaign finance laws, despite the limits they impose, help to further the kind of open public political discussion that the First Amendment also seeks to encourage, not simply as an end, but also as a means to achieve a workable democracy.

For this reason, I have argued that a court should approach most campaign finance questions with the understanding that important First Amendment-related interests lie on both sides of the constitutional equation, and that a First Amendment presumption hostile to government regulation, such as "strict scrutiny," is consequently out of place. Rather, the court considering the matter without the benefit of presumptions must look realistically at the legislation's impact, both its negative impact on the ability of some to engage in as much communication as they wish and the positive impact upon the public's confidence and consequent ability to communicate through (and participate in) the electoral process....

I am not saying that focus upon active liberty will automatically answer the constitutional question in particular campaign finance cases. I argue only that such focus will help courts find a proper route for arriving at an answer. The positive constitutional goal implies a systemic role for the First Amendment; and that role, in turn, suggests a legal framework, that is, a more particular set of questions for the Court to ask. Modesty suggests where, and how, courts should defer to legislatures in doing so. The suggested inquiry is complex. But courts both here and abroad have engaged in similarly complex inquiries where the constitutionality of electoral laws is at issue. That complexity is demanded by a Constitution that provides for judicial review of the constitutionality of electoral rules while granting Congress the effective power to secure a fair electoral system....

I turn next to federalism. My example suggests a need to examine consequences valued in terms of active liberty.

The Court's recent federalism cases fall into three categories. First, the Court has held that Congress may not write laws that "commandeer" a state's legislative or executive officials, say by requiring a state legislature to write a particular kind of law (for example, a nuclear waste storage law)[5] or by requiring a local official to spend time enforcing a federal policy (for example, requiring a local sheriff to see whether a potential gun buyer has a criminal record).[6] Second, the Court has limited Congress's power (under the Commerce Clause or the Fourteenth Amendment) to force a state to waive its Eleventh Amendment immunity from suit by private citizens.[7] Third, the Court has limited the scope of Congress's Commerce Clause powers, finding that gun possession near local schools and violence against women in local communities did not sufficiently "affect" interstate commerce.[8]

Although I dissented in each recent case, I recognize that each holding protects liberty in its negative form—to some degree. Each of them, in one respect or another, makes it more difficult for the federal government to tell state and local governments what they must do. To that extent they free citizens from certain restraints that a more distant central government might otherwise impose. But constitutional principles of federalism involve active as well as negative freedom. They impose limitations upon the distant central government's decision making not simply as an antirestrictive end but also as a democracy-facilitating means.

My colleague Justice [Sandra Day] O'Connor has set forth many of the basic connections. By guaranteeing state and local governments broad decision making authority, federalist principles facilitate "novel social and economic experiments," secure decisions that rest on knowledge of local circumstances, and help to develop a sense of shared purposes among local citizens. Through increased transparency, they make it easier for citizens to hold government officials accountable. And by bringing government closer to home, they help maintain a sense of local community. In all these ways they facilitate and encourage citizen participation in governmental decision making—Constant's classical ideal. We must evaluate the Court's federalism decisions in terms of both forms of liberty—their necessary combination. When we do so, we shall find that a cooperative federalism, allocating specific problem-related roles among national and state governments, will protect both forms of liberty today, including the active liberty that the Court's decisions overlook.

A concrete example drawn from toxic chemical regulation exemplifies the kind of technologically based problem modern governments are asked to solve. Important parts of toxic substance regulation must take place at the national level. Chemical substances ignore state boundaries as they travel through air, water, or soil, and consequently they may affect the environment in more than one state. Their regulation demands a high level of scientific and technical expertise to which the federal government might have ready access, at least initially. A federal regulator might be better able than state regulators to create, for example, a uniform risk discourse designed to help ordinary citizens better understand the nature of risk. And only a federal regulator could set minimum substantive standards designed to avoid a race to the bottom among states hoping to attract industry.

At the same time, certain aspects of the problem seem better suited for decentralized regulation by state or local governments. The same amounts of the same chemical may produce different toxic effects depending upon local air, water, or soil conditions. The same standard will have different economic effects in different communities. And affected citizens in different communities may value the same level of toxic substance cleanup quite differently. To what point should we clean up the local waste dump and at what cost?

Modern efforts to create more efficient regulation recognize the importance of that local involvement. They seek a kind of cooperative federalism that would, for example, have federal officials make expertise available to state and local officials while seeking to separate expert and fact-related matters from more locally based questions of value. They would also diminish reliance upon classical command-and-control regulation, supplementing that regulation with incentive-based, less restrictive regulatory methods, such as taxes and marketable rights. Such efforts, by placing greater power to participate and to decide in the hands of individuals and localities, can further both the negative and active liberty interests that underlie federalist principles. But will the Court's recent federalism decisions encourage or discourage those cooperative, or incentive-based, regulatory methods?

In my view, the "commandeering" decisions, such as *United States v. Printz*, might well hinder a cooperative program, for they could prevent Congress from enlisting local officials to check compliance with federal minimum standards.

Rather, Congress would have to create a federal enforcement bureaucracy (or, perhaps, create unnecessary federal spending programs). Given ordinary bureaucratic tendencies, that fact, other things being equal, will make it harder, not easier, to shift regulatory power to state and local governments. It will make it more difficult, not easier, to experiment with incentive-based regulatory methods. And while some argue that Congress can bypass the "commandeering" decisions through selective and aggressive exercise of its spending power (at least as that doctrine currently exists), there is little evidence that Congress has taken this path.

I can make this same point with another example underlined by the tragic events of September 11. In a dissenting opinion, Justice [John Paul] Stevens wrote that the "threat of an international terrorist, may require a national response before federal personnel can be made available to respond.... Is there anything [in the Constitution] ... that forbids the enlistment of state officers to make that response effective?" That enlistment, by facilitating the participation of local and state officials, would help both the cause of effective security coordination and the cause of federalism.

The Eleventh Amendment decisions could hinder the adoption of certain kinds of "less restrictive" regulatory methods. Suppose, for example, that Congress, reluctant to expand the federal regulatory bureaucracy, wished to encourage citizen suits as a device for ensuring state-owned (as well as privately owned) toxic waste dump compliance. Or suppose that Congress, in order to encourage state or local governments to impose environmental taxes, provided for suits by citizens seeking to protest a particular tax assessment or to obtain a tax refund.

Decisions in the third category—the Court's recent Commerce Clause power decisions—would neither prohibit nor facilitate citizen participation in "cooperative" or "incentive-based" regulatory programs. Still, the Court's determination to reweigh congressional evidence of "interstate effects" creates uncertainty about how much evidence is needed to find the constitutionally requisite effect. And certain portions of the Court's reasoning, such as its refusal to aggregate "noneconomic" causes of interstate effects, create considerable doctrinal complexity.[9] Both may leave Congress uncertain about its ability to legislate the details of a cooperative federal, state, local, and regulatory framework. This uncertainty, other things being equal, makes it less likely that Congress will enact those complex laws—laws necessarily of national scope. To that extent, one can see these decisions as unhelpful to the cause of active liberty.

I do not claim that these consequences alone can prove the majority's holding wrong. I suggest only that courts ask certain consequence-related questions and not rely entirely upon logical deduction from text or precedent. I ask why the Court should not at least consider the practical effects on local democratic self-government when it elaborates the Constitution's principles of federalism—principles that seek to further that kind of government....

I next turn to a different kind of example. It focuses upon current threats to the protection of privacy, defined as the power to "control information about oneself." It seeks to illustrate what active liberty is like in modern America when we seek to arrive democratically at solutions to important technologically based problems. And it suggests a need for judicial caution and humility when certain privacy matters, such as the balance between free speech and privacy, are at issue.

First, I must describe the "privacy" problem. That problem is unusually complex. It clearly has become even more so since the terrorist attacks. For one thing, those who agree that privacy is important disagree about why. Some emphasize the need to be left alone, not bothered by others, or that privacy is important because it prevents people from being judged out of context. Some emphasize the way in which relationships of love and friendship depend upon trust, which implies a sharing of information not available to all. Others find connections between privacy and individualism, in that privacy encourages nonconformity. Still others find connections between privacy and equality, in that limitations upon the availability of individualized information leads private businesses to treat all customers alike. For some, or all, of these reasons, legal rules protecting privacy help to ensure an individual's dignity.

For another thing, the law protects privacy only because of the way in which technology interacts with different laws. Some laws, such as trespass, wiretapping, eavesdropping, and search-and-seizure laws, protect particular places or sites, such as homes or telephones, from searches and monitoring. Other laws protect not places, but kinds of information, for example, laws that forbid the publication of certain personal information even by a person who obtained that information legally. Taken together these laws protect privacy to different degrees depending upon place, individual status, kind of intrusion, and type of information.

Further, technological advances have changed the extent to which present laws can protect privacy. Video cameras now monitor shopping malls, schools, parks, office buildings, city streets, and other places that present law leaves unprotected. Scanners and interceptors can overhear virtually any electronic conversation. Thermal imaging devices detect activities taking place within the home. Computers record and collate information obtained in any of these ways and others. This technology means an ability to observe, collate, and permanently record a vast amount of information about individuals that the law previously may have made available for collection but which, in practice, could not easily have been recorded and collected. The nature of the current or future privacy threat depends upon how this technological/legal fact will affect differently situated individuals.

These circumstances mean that efforts to revise privacy law to take account of the new technology will involve, in different areas of human activity, the balancing of values in light of predictions about the technological future....

The complex nature of these problems calls for resolution through a form of participatory democracy. Ideally, that participatory process does not involve legislators, administrators, or judges imposing law from above. Rather, it involves law revision that bubbles up from below. Serious complex changes in law are often made in the context of a national conversation involving, among others, scientists, engineers, businessmen and women, and the media, along with legislators, judges, and many ordinary citizens whose lives the new technology will affect. That conversation takes place through many meetings, symposia, and discussions, through journal articles and media reports, through legislative hearings and court cases. Lawyers participate fully in this discussion, translating specialized knowledge into ordinary English, defining issues, creating consensus. Typically, administrators and legislators then make decisions, with courts later resolving any constitutional issues that those decisions raise. This "conversation" is the participatory democratic process itself.

The presence of this kind of problem and this kind of democratic process helps to explain, because it suggests a need for, judicial caution or modesty. That is why, for example, the Court's decisions so far have hesitated to preempt that process. In one recent case the Court considered a cell phone conversation that an unknown private individual had intercepted with a scanner and delivered to a radio station.[10] A statute forbade the broadcast of that conversation, even though the radio station itself had not planned or participated in the intercept. The Court had to determine the scope of the station's First Amendment right to broadcast given the privacy interests that the statute sought to protect. The Court held that the First Amendment trumped the statute, permitting the radio station to broadcast the information. But the holding was narrow. It focused upon the particular circumstances present, explicitly leaving open broadcaster liability in other, less innocent, circumstances.

The narrowness of the holding itself serves a constitutional purpose. The privacy "conversation" is ongoing. Congress could well rewrite the statute, tailoring it more finely to current technological facts, such as the widespread availability of scanners and the possibility of protecting conversations through encryption. A broader constitutional rule might itself limit legislative options in ways now unforeseeable. And doing so is particularly dangerous where statutory protection of an important personal liberty is at issue.

By way of contrast, the Court held unconstitutional police efforts to use, without a warrant, a thermal imaging device placed on a public sidewalk.[11] The device permitted police to identify activities taking place within a private house. The case required the Court simply to ask whether the residents had a reasonable expectation that their activities within the house would not be disclosed to the public in this way—a well-established Fourth Amendment principle. Hence the case asked the Court to pour new technological wine into old bottles; it did not suggest that doing so would significantly interfere with an ongoing democratic policy conversation.

The privacy example suggests more by way of caution. It warns against adopting an overly rigid method of interpreting the Constitution—placing weight upon eighteenth-century details to the point where it becomes difficult for a twenty-first-century court to apply the document's underlying values. At a minimum it suggests that courts, in determining the breadth of a constitutional holding, should look to the effect of a holding on the ongoing policy process, distinguishing, as I have suggested, between the "eavesdropping" and the "thermal heat" types of cases. And it makes clear that judicial caution in such matters does not reflect the fact that judges are mitigating their legal concerns with practical considerations. Rather, the Constitution itself is a practical document—a document that authorizes the Court to proceed practically when it examines new laws in light of the Constitution's enduring, underlying values.

My fourth example concerns equal protection and voting rights, an area that has led to considerable constitutional controversy. Some believe that the Constitution prohibits virtually any legislative effort to use race as a basis for drawing electoral-district boundaries—unless, for example, the effort seeks to undo earlier invidious race-based discrimination.[12] Others believe that the Constitution does not so severely limit the instances in which a legislature can use race to create majority-minority districts. Without describing in detail the basic argument between the two positions, I wish to point out the relevance to that argument of the Constitution's democratic objective.

That objective suggests a simple, but potentially important, constitutional difference in the electoral area between invidious discrimination, penalizing members of a racial minority, and positive discrimination, assisting members of racial minorities. The Constitution's Fifteenth Amendment prohibits the former, not simply because it violates a basic Fourteenth Amendment principle, namely that the government must treat all citizens with equal respect, but also because it denies minority citizens the opportunity to participate in the self-governing democracy that the Constitution creates. By way of contrast, affirmative discrimination ordinarily seeks to enlarge minority participation in that self-governing democracy. To that extent it is consistent with, and indeed furthers, the Constitution's basic democratic objective. That consistency, along with its more benign purposes, helps to mitigate whatever lack of equal respect any such discrimination might show to any disadvantaged member of a majority group.

I am not saying that the mitigation will automatically render any particular discriminatory scheme constitutional. But the presence of this mitigating difference supports the view that courts should not apply the strong presumptions of unconstitutionality that are appropriate where invidious discrimination is at issue. My basic purpose, again, is to suggest that reference to the Constitution's "democratic" objective can help us apply a different basic objective, here that of equal protection. And in the electoral context, the reference suggests increased legislative authority to deal with multiracial issues.

My last example focuses upon statutory interpretation and a potential relationship between active liberty and statutory drafting. Students of modern government complain that contemporary political circumstances too often lead Congress to ignore its own committees and to draft legislation, through amendments, on the House or Senate floor. This tendency may reflect a membership that is closely divided between the parties, single-interest pressure groups that (along with overly simplified media reporting) discourage compromise, or an election system in which voters tend to hold individuals rather than parties responsible. The consequence is legislation that is often silent, ambiguous, or even contradictory in respect to key interpretive questions. In such cases the true answer as to what Congress intended about such issues as the creation of a private right of action, the time limits governing an action, the judicial deference due an agency's interpretation of the statute, or other technical questions of application may well be that no one in Congress thought about the matter.

How are courts, which must find answers, to interpret these silences? Of course, courts first will look to a statute's language, structure, and history to help determine the statute's purpose, and then use that purpose, along with its determining factors, to help find the answer. But suppose that these factors, while limiting the universe of possible answers, do not themselves prove determinative. What then?

At this point courts are typically pulled in one of two directions. The first is linguistic. The judge may try to tease further meaning from language and structure, followed by application of language-based canons of interpretation designed to limit subjective judicial decision making.[13] The second is purposive. Instead of deriving an artificial meaning through the use of general canons, the judge will ask instead how a (hypothetical) reasonable member of Congress, given the statutory language, structure, history, and purpose, would have answered the question, had it been presented. The second approach has a theoretical advantage. It reminds the judge of the law's democratic source, that is, that it is in Congress, not the courts, where the Constitution places the authority to enact a statute. And it has certain practical advantages sufficient in my view to overcome any risk of subjectivity.

The Court recently considered the matter in an administrative law case. The question was whether a court should defer to a customs inspector's on-the-spot ad hoc interpretation of a customs statute. A well-known administrative law case, *Chevron v. Natural Resources Defense Council*,[14] sets forth an interpretive canon stating that, when an agency-administered statute is ambiguous, courts should defer to a reasonable agency interpretation. But how absolute is *Chevron*'s canon? Does it mean that courts should normally defer or always defer? The Court held that *Chevron* was not absolute. It required deference only where Congress would have wanted deference. And the Court suggested criteria for deciding what Congress would have wanted where Congress provided no indication and perhaps did not think about the matter.

Why refer to a hypothetical congressional desire? Why produce the complex and fictional statement, "it seems unlikely Congress would have wanted courts to defer here"? The reason is that the fiction provides guidance of a kind roughly similar to that offered by Professor [Arthur Linton] Corbin's "reasonable contracting party" in contract cases.[15] It focuses the judge's attention on the fact that democratically elected individuals wrote the statute in order to satisfy certain human purposes. And it consequently increases the likelihood that courts will ask what those individuals would have wanted in light of those purposes. In this instance, I believe the approach favored reading exceptions into *Chevron*'s canon where necessary to further those statutory purposes.

That flexibility is important. Dozens of different agencies apply thousands of different statutes containing untold numbers of lacunae in untold numbers of different circumstances. In many circumstances, as *Chevron* suggests, deference makes sense; but in some circumstances deference does not make sense. The metaphor—by focusing on what a reasonable person likely would have wanted—helps bring courts to that conclusion. To treat *Chevron*'s rule purely as a judicial canon is less likely to do so....

The instances I have discussed encompass different areas of law—speech, federalism, privacy, equal protection, and statutory interpretation. In each instance, the discussion has focused upon a contemporary social problem—campaign finance, workplace regulation, environmental regulation, information-based technological change, race-based electoral districting, and legislative politics. In each instance, the discussion illustrates how increased focus upon the Constitution's basic democratic objective might make a difference—in refining doctrinal rules, in evaluating consequences, in applying practical cautionary principles, in interacting with other constitutional objectives, and in explicating statutory silences. In each instance, the discussion suggests how that increased focus might mean better law. And "better" in this context means both (1) better able to satisfy the Constitution's purposes, and (2) better able to cope with contemporary problems. The discussion, while not proving its point purely through logic or empirical demonstration, uses examples to create a pattern. The pattern suggests a need for increased judicial emphasis upon the Constitution's democratic objective.

My discussion emphasizes values underlying specific constitutional phrases, sees the Constitution itself as a single document with certain basic related objectives, and assumes that the latter can inform a judge's understanding of the former. Might that discussion persuade those who prefer to believe that the keys to constitutional interpretation instead lie in specific language, history, tradition, and precedent and who fear that a contrary approach would permit judges too often to act too subjectively?

Perhaps so, for several reasons. First, the area of interpretive disagreement is more limited than many believe. Judges can, and should, decide most cases, including constitutional cases, through the use of language, history, tradition, and precedent. Judges will often agree as to how these factors determine a provision's basic purpose and the result in a particular case. And where they differ, their differences are often differences of modest degree. Only a handful of constitutional issues—though an important handful—are as open in respect to language, history, and basic purpose as those that I have described. And even in respect to those issues, judges must find answers within the limits set by the Constitution's language. Moreover, history, tradition, and precedent remain helpful, even if not determinative.

Second, those more literalist judges who emphasize language, history, tradition, and precedent cannot justify their practices by claiming that is what the Framers wanted, for the Framers did not say specifically what factors judges should emphasize when seeking to interpret the Constitution's open language. Nor is it plausible to believe that those who argued about the Bill of Rights, and made clear that it did not contain an exclusive detailed list, had agreed about what school of interpretive thought should prove dominant in the centuries to come. Indeed, the Constitution itself says that the "enumeration" in the Constitution of some rights "shall not be construed to deny or disparage others retained by the people."...

Third, judges who reject a literalist approach deny that their decisions are subjective and point to important safeguards of objectivity. A decision that emphasizes values, no less than any other, is open to criticism based upon (1) the decision's relation to the other legal principles (precedents, rules, standards, practices, institutional understandings) that it modifies; and (2) the decision's consequences, that is, the way in which the entire bloc of decision-affected legal principles subsequently affects the world. The relevant values, by limiting interpretive possibilities and guiding interpretation, themselves constrain subjectivity; indeed, the democratic values that I have emphasized themselves suggest the importance of judicial restraint. An individual constitutional judge's need for consistency over time also constrains subjectivity.

Fourth, the literalist does not escape subjectivity, for his tools, language, history, and tradition can provide little objective guidance in the comparatively small set of cases about which I have spoken. In such cases, the Constitution's language is almost always nonspecific. History and tradition are open to competing claims and rival interpretations. Nor does an emphasis upon rules embodied in precedent necessarily produce clarity, particularly in borderline areas or where rules are stated abstractly. Indeed, an emphasis upon language, history, tradition, or prior rules in such cases may simply channel subjectivity into a choice about: Which history? Which tradition? Which rules? The literalist approach will then produce a decision that is no less subjective but which is far less transparent than a decision that directly addresses consequences in constitutional terms.

Finally, my examples point to offsetting consequences—at least if "literalism" tends to produce the legal doctrines (related to the First Amendment, to federalism, to statutory interpretation, to equal protection) that I have criticized. Those doctrines lead to consequences at least as harmful, from a constitutional perspective, as any increased risk of subjectivity. In the ways that I have set out, they undermine the Constitution's efforts to create a framework for democratic government—a government that, while protecting basic individual liberties, permits individual citizens to govern themselves....

[T]he Constitution provides a framework for the creation of democratically determined solutions, which protect each individual's basic liberties and assure that individual equal respect by government, while securing a democratic form of government. We judges cannot insist that Americans participate in that government, but we can make clear that our Constitution depends upon their participation....

Notes

1. B. Constant, "The Liberty of the Ancients Compared with That of the Moderns," (1819) in *Political Writings* 309, 309–328 (Biancamaria Fontana trans. & ed., 1988).
2. See, e.g., *Lochner v. New York*, 198 U.S. 45 (1905) striking down workplace health regulations on substantive due process grounds. W. E. Leuchtenburg, *The Supreme Court Reborn* 133 (New York: Oxford University Press, 1995).
3. See, e.g., *Reynolds v. Sims*, 377 U.S. 533 (1964) requiring application of the "one person, one vote" principle to state legislatures; *Baker v. Carr*, 369 U.S. 186 (1962) finding that the Equal Protection Clause justified federal court intervention to review voter apportionment; *Gomillion v. Lightfoot*, 364 U.S. 339 (1960) striking down racial gerrymandering on Fifteenth Amendment grounds.
4. L. Hand, *The Spirit of Liberty* 190 (New York:Knopf, 2d ed. 1952); cf. at 109 "If [a judge] is in doubt, he must stop, for he cannot tell that the conflicting interests in the society for which he speaks would have come to a just result...."
5. *New York v. United States*, 505 U.S. 144 (1992).
6. *Printz v. United States*, 521 U.S. 898, 921 (1997).
7. E.g., *Board of Trustees of the University of Alabama v. Garrett*, 531 U.S. 356 (2001) holding that suits under the Americans with Disabilities Act for money damages against states are barred by the Eleventh Amendment; *Seminole Tribe v. Florida*, 517 U.S. 44 (1996) holding that Congress cannot abrogate the state's sovereign immunity under Article I.
8. *United States v. Morrison*, 529 U.S. 598 (2000) Violence Against Women Act; *United States v. Lopez*, 514 U.S. 549 (1995) (Gun-Free School Zones Act).

9. See *United States v. Lopez*, 514 U.S. 549, 625–631 (1995) (Breyer, J., dissenting) detailing shortcomings of the Court's approach.
10. *Bartnicki v. Vopper*, 532 U.S. 514, 518–519 (2001).
11. *Kyllo v. United States*, 536 U.S. 27, 40 (2001).
12. See, e.g., *Hunt v. Cromartie*, 526 U.S. 541 (1999) overturning a district court's grant of summary judgment in a racial gerrymandering case because the state legislature's motivation was in dispute.
13. See, e.g., A. Scalia, "Common-Law Courts in a Civil-Law System: The Role of United States Federal Courts in Interpreting the Constitution and Laws," in A. Gutmann ed., *A Matter of Interpretation: Federal Courts and the Law* 26-27 (Princeton: Princeton University Press, 1997).
14. *Chevron U.S.A. Inc. v. Natural Resources Defense Council, Inc.*, 467 U.S. 837 (1984).
15. See J.D. Calamari and J.M. Perillo, *The Law of Contracts* 3.10 2d ed. (1977).

CHAPTER 26

Against Constitutional Theory

Richard A. Posner

Judge, U.S. Court of Appeals, Seventh Circuit (1981–)

CONSTITUTIONAL THEORY, as I shall use the term, is the effort to develop a generally accepted theory to guide the interpretation of the Constitution of the United States. It is distinct on the one hand from inquiries of a social scientific character into the nature, provenance, and consequences of constitutionalism—the sort of thing one associates mainly with historians and political scientists, such as Charles Beard, Jon Elster, and Stephen Holmes—and on the other hand from commentary on specific cases and doctrines, the sort of thing one associates with legal doctrinalists, such as Kathleen Sullivan, Laurence Tribe, and William Van Alstyne. A number of scholars straddle this divide, such as Ronald Dworkin and Lawrence Lessig, and although I mean to keep to one side of it in this lecture, the straddle is no accident. Constitutional theorists are normativists; their theories are meant to influence the way judges decide difficult constitutional cases; when the theorists are law-trained, as most of them are, they cannot resist telling their readers which cases they think were decided consistently with or contrary to their theory. Most constitutional theorists, indeed, believe in social reform through judicial action. Constitutional theory that is strongly influenced by moral theory has additional problems, as I have discussed recently and will not repeat here.

I must stress at the outset the limited domain of constitutional theory. Nothing pretentious enough to warrant the name of theory is required to decide cases in which the text or history of the Constitution provides sure guidance. No theory is required to determine how many Senators each state may have. Somewhat more difficult interpretive issues, such as whether the self-incrimination clause should be

---

Acknowledgment to Judge Richard A. Posner for excerpts from his lecture "Against Constitutional Theory," which appears in 73 New York University Law Review *1 (1998).*

interpreted as forbidding the prosecutor to comment on the defendant's failure to take the stand, can be resolved pretty straightforwardly by considering the consequences of rival interpretations....

Constitutional theory in the sense in which I am using the term is at least as old as the *Federalist* papers. And yet after more than two centuries no signs of closure or even, it seems to me, of progress, are visible. The reason is that constitutional theory has no power to command agreement from people not already predisposed to accept the theorist's policy prescriptions. It has no power partly because it is normative, partly because interpretation, the subject of constitutional theory, is not susceptible of theoretical resolution, and partly because normativists in general and lawyers (and as I said most constitutional theorists are lawyers, albeit professors of law rather than practicing lawyers) do not like to be backed into a corner by committing themselves to a theory that might be falsified by data, just as no practicing lawyer wants to take a position that might force him to concede that his client has no case. Neither type of lawyer wants the validity of his theory to be a hostage to what a factual inquiry might bring to light. But as a result, constitutional theory, while often rhetorically powerful, lacks the agreement-coercing power of the best natural and social science.

An even more serious problem is that constitutional theory is not responsive to, and indeed tends to occlude, the greatest need of constitutional adjudicators, which is the need for empirical knowledge.... I know that just getting the facts right can't decide a case. There has to be an analytic framework to fit the facts into; without it they can have no normative significance. Only I don't think that constitutional theory can supply that framework. Nor that the design of the framework, as distinct from fitting the facts into it, is the big problem in constitutional law today. The big problem is not lack of theory, but lack of knowledge—lack of the very knowledge that academic research, rather than the litigation process, is best designed to produce. But it is a different kind of research from what constitutional theorists conduct.

The leading theorists are intelligent people, and it is possible that their lively debates have a diffuse but cumulatively significant impact on the tone and texture and occasionally even on the outcomes of constitutional cases. (Whether it is a good impact is a different question, and one that cannot be answered on the basis of existing knowledge.) If the theorists do not have a large audience among judges, and I do not think they do, they have a large audience among their own students and hence among the judges' law clerks, whose influence on constitutional law, though small, is not completely negligible. Yet the real significance of constitutional theory is, I believe, as a sign of the increased academification of law school professors, who are much more inclined than they used to be to write for other professors rather than for judges and practitioners.... Constitutional theory today circulates in a medium that is largely opaque to the judge and the practicing lawyer.

The problem in political theory to which constitutional theory is offered as a solution is that our judicially enforceable Constitution gives the judges an unusual amount of power. This was seen as problematic long before the democratic principle became as central to our concept of government as it is now. Hamilton's solution to the problem, drawing on what was already an age-old formalist tradition stretching back to Cicero and shortly to be echoed by John Marshall, was to assert that it was the law that was supreme, not the judges, since judges are (in Blackstone's phrase, but it is also Hamilton's sense) just the oracles, the mouthpieces, of the law.

After a century of judicial willfulness, this position was difficult to maintain with a straight face. The Constitution had obviously made the judges a competing power center. James Bradley Thayer argued in the 1890s that this was bad because it sapped the other branches of government of initiative and responsibility. He urged courts to enforce a constitutional right only when the existence of the right, as a matter of constitutional interpretation, was clear beyond a reasonable doubt....

Thayer is the father of the "outrage" school of constitutional interpretation, whose most notable practitioner was Holmes. Holmes's position was not identical to Thayer's; nor were Cardozo's and Frankfurter's positions identical to Holmes's, though there are broad affinities among all four. This school teaches that to be justified in trying to stymie the elected branches of government it shouldn't be enough that the litigant claiming a constitutional right has the better of the argument; it has to be a lot better; the alleged violation of the Constitution has to be certain (Thayer's position), or stomach-turning (Holmes's "puke" test), or shocking to the conscience (Frankfurter's test), or, a synthesis of the positions (one supported by Holmes's dissent in *Lochner* [*v. New York*][1], the sort of thing no reasonable person could defend. The school of outrage is almost interchangeable with the doctrine of judicial self-restraint when that doctrine is understood as seeking to minimize the occasions on which the courts annul the actions of other branches of government. The judge who is self-restrained in this sense wishes to take a back seat to the other branches of government, but is stirred to action if his sense of justice is sufficiently outraged.

I own to considerable sympathy with this way of approaching constitutional issues. And when the outrage approach is tied, as I have just suggested it can be, to the doctrine of judicial self-restraint—a doctrine that is founded on reasons—the approach is no longer so purely visceral as my initial description may have suggested. But I cannot pretend that outrage or even self-restraint furnishes much in the way of guidance to courts grappling with difficult issues. And I could defend the approach convincingly only by showing, what may be impossible as a practical matter to do, that decisions invalidating statutes or other official actions as unconstitutional, when the decision could not have been justified under Thayer's or Holmes's or Cardozo's or Frankfurter's approach, have done more harm than good.

Hamilton-style formalism now has a defender in Justice Scalia. But he lacks the courage of his convictions. For he takes extreme libertarian positions with respect to such matters as affirmative action and freedom of speech on the ground that these positions are dictated not by the Constitution but by the cases interpreting the Constitution. Take away the adventitious operation of *stare decisis* and Scalia is left with a body of constitutional law of remarkable meagerness—which is not an objection but which requires a greater effort at justification than he has been able to offer. Indeed he has offered little by way of justification other than bromides about democracy. Complaining that the Supreme Court is undemocratic begs the question. The Court is part of the Constitution, which in its inception was rich in undemocratic features, such as the indirect election of the President and of the Senate, and a highly restricted franchise. The Constitution still has major undemocratic features. They include the method of apportionment of the Senate, which results in weighting the votes of people in sparsely populated states much more heavily than the votes of people in densely populated states; the election of the President on the basis of electoral rather than popular votes, which could result in the election of a candidate who had lost the popular vote; the expansion of constitutional rights brought about by the Bill of Rights and the Fourteenth Amendment, which curtails the powers of the elected branches of government; and, of course, lifetime appointment of federal judges who exercise considerable political power by virtue of the expansion of rights to which I just referred. The Supreme Court is certainly undemocratic in a sense, but not in a sense that makes it anomalous in the political system created by the Constitution, given the other "undemocratic" features that I have mentioned. A further drawback to Scalia's approach is that it requires judges to be political theorists, so that they know what "democracy" is, and also to be historians, because it takes a historian to reconstruct the original meaning of centuries-old documents.

Most constitutional theorizing in this century has taken a nonformalistic direction, unlike that of a Hamilton or a Scalia. We may begin with Learned Hand's argument that the Bill of Rights provides so little guidance to judges that it ought to be deemed (largely) nonjusticiable, and move on to Herbert Wechsler's prompt riposte that constitutional law can be stabilized by judicial evenhandedness, what he called "neutral principles," soon recognized as merely principles and since principles can be bad as well as good, Wechsler's riposte failed. Focus then shifted to an effort to identify good principles to guide constitutional decisionmaking. Leading candidates include John Hart Ely's principle of "representation reinforcement" and Ronald Dworkin's principle of egalitarian natural justice. These are substantive political principles, and they founder on the authors' lack of steady interest in and firm grasp of the details of public policy. I have complained elsewhere about the egregious underspecialization of constitutional lawyers and theorists, and I don't want to repeat myself. People who devote most of their lives to the study of political theory and constitutional doctrine do not thereby equip themselves to formulate substantive principles designed to guide decisionmaking across the vast range of difficult issues that spans affirmative action and exclusionary zoning, legislative apportionment and prison administration, telecommunications and euthanasia, the education of alien children and the administration of capital punishment, to name just a few current and recent issues in constitutional law.

The constitutional theories propounded by the formalists, by Thayer and his followers, and by Wechsler, were procedural in the sense of offering a method of analysis rather than a master substantive principle in the style of Ely or Dworkin. The formulation of procedural theories has continued. . . .

Constitutional theorists want to influence constitutional practice. One cannot read Ely and Dworkin and the others without sensing a strong desire to influence judicial decisions or even (in Dworkin's case) the composition of the Supreme Court—for one remembers his polemic against the appointment of Bork. And Scalia is on the Supreme Court. But to get the richest rewards available within the modern legal academic community a professor has to do "theory," and this tends to alienate the professors from the judges. . . .

I would like to see an entirely different kind of constitutional theorizing. It would set itself the difficult—although, from the perspective of today's theorists, the intellectually modest—task of exploring the operation and consequences of constitutionalism. It would ask such questions as, what difference has it made for press freedom and police practices in the United States compared to England that we have a judicially enforceable Bill of Rights and England does not? How influenced are judges in constitutional cases by public opinion? How influenced is public opinion by constitutional decisions? Are constitutional issues becoming more complex, and if so, what are the courts doing to keep abreast of the complexities? Does intrusive judicial review breed constitutionally dubious statutes by enabling legislators to shift political hot potatoes to the courts? What is the effect of judicial activism on judicial workloads and is there a feedback loop here, activism producing heavy workloads that in turn cause the judges to become restrained in order to reduce the number of cases and thus alleviate the workload pressures? Does the Court try to prevent the formation of interest groups that might obtain constitutional amendments that would curtail the Court's power or abrogate some of its doctrines, or to encourage the formation of interest groups that will defend the Court's prerogatives? And what role do interest groups play in constitution-making and -amending? In the appointment of Supreme Court Justices? In the reception of Supreme Court decisions by the media and through the media the public? Above all, what are the actual and likely effects of particular decisions and doctrines? Did *Brown v. Board of Education*[2] improve the education of blacks? Did *Roe v. Wade*[3] retard abortion law reform at the state level? What effect have the apportionment cases had on public policy? Did the Warren Court's decisions expanding the constitutional rights of criminal defendants contribute to the increase in the crime rate in the 1960s and 1970s and provoke a legislative backlash, increasing the severity of sentences? These questions have not been entirely ignored, but the literature on them is meager, and law professors have contributed very little to it. Exploring these questions would be a more fruitful use of academic time and brains than continuing the 200-hundred-year-old game of political rhetoricizing that we call constitutional theory. Some of these questions might actually be answerable, and the answers would alter constitutional practice more than theorizing has done or can do. Thus I am in radical disagreement with Dworkin, who insists that cases in which facts or consequences matter to sound constitutional decisionmaking are "rare."...

I am not advocating the transformation of litigation into a setting for generating or marshaling social scientific data and for testing social scientific hypotheses. The capability of the courts to conduct scientific or social scientific research is extremely limited, and perhaps nil. But their assimilative powers are greater. I would like to see the legal professoriat redirect its research and teaching efforts toward fuller participation in the enterprise of social science, and by doing this make social science a better aid to judges' understanding of the social problems that get thrust at them in the form of constitutional issues. What the judges should do until the professoriat accepts this challenge and makes real progress in the study of race relations, sexual activity, euthanasia, education theory, and the other areas of social life that are generating constitutional issues these days is an issue that I shall defer until I have explained what seem to me to be the unfortunate consequences of judicial ignorance of the social realities behind the issues with which they grapple....

Brown v. Board of Education is increasingly considered a flop when regarded as a case about education, which is how the Court pretended (presumably for political reasons) to regard it. For there is no solid evidence that it led to an improvement in the education of blacks or even to substantial public-school integration. It is better viewed as a case about racial subordination, whereas the exclusion of women by the Virginia Military Institute [in *United States v. Virginia*][4] cannot be regarded with a straight face as the warp or woof of a tapestry of sex subordination, given the political and economic power of American women.

I shall end with a few remarks about the *Romer* [*v. Evans*][5] case. This is the second scrape that the Supreme Court has had with homosexuality, the first being of course *Bowers v. Hardwick*,[6] and the most remarkable thing about both judicial performances is the Court's unwillingness or inability to talk realistically about the phenomenon. The majority opinion in *Bowers* and Chief Justice Burger's concurrence treat it as an uncontroversially reprobated horror, like pedophilia, while the dissents in *Bowers* and the majority opinion in *Romer* treat it as a socially irrelevant innate condition like being left-handed, and Justice Scalia's dissent in *Romer* treats homosexual rights as a sentimental charitable project of the intelligentsia, like the protection of harp seals. The majority opinion in *Romer* finds, sensibly enough, that the constitutional amendment under challenge, which barred local governments from forbidding discrimination against homosexuals, was motivated by hostility toward homosexuality. The Court then holds that hostility is not an adequate justification for treating one class of people differently from another. And that is just about all there is in the opinion. Ignored are the questions that an ordinary person, his mind not fogged by legal casuistry, would think central: why there is hostility to homosexuality and whether the challenged amendment was a rational expression of that hostility.

Many religious people, Christian and Jewish, believe that homosexual activity is morally wrong. There is no way to assess the validity of this belief, and what weight if any such a belief should be given in a constitutional case seems to me an equally indeterminate question. The belief in equality that informs the *VMI* opinion is as much an article of faith as the Judeo-Christian antipathy to homosexuality, and to suppose that securing equality for homosexuals is part of the meaning of the Equal Protection Clause is equally a leap of faith. In any event, most Americans, whether religious or not, dislike homosexuality and in particular do not want their children to become homosexuals. They are not sure whether homosexuality is acquired or innate, but, unconvinced that it is purely the latter, they worry about their children becoming homosexual through imitation or seduction. They also worry about AIDS spreading from the homosexual to the heterosexual population (although this fear has abated with the peaking of the epidemic). For these and other reasons, most people dislike the flaunting of homosexual relationships and activities. They particularly do not want government to endorse homosexuality as a way of life entitled to the same respect that we accord to heterosexual relationships particularly within marriage. An ordinance forbidding discrimination in housing, employment, or public accommodations on the basis of sexual orientation is naturally viewed as a form of public endorsement of homosexuality.

My own view is that there is compelling scientific evidence that homosexual preference is genetic or at least congenital, and not acquired, so that the fear of homosexual "contagion" from flaunting or public endorsement of the homosexual way of life is groundless. And it is as likely that increasing the rights of homosexuals would reduce AIDS-producing sex among homosexuals as decreasing them would. No allusion to the scientific and social scientific evidence bearing on the phenomenon of homosexuality was made in the *Romer* opinion, however, so that as it stands the Court seems prepared to forbid discrimination against homosexuals even if the Colorado ban on protective legislation for homosexuals is entirely rational discrimination—the equivalent of "discriminating" against air line pilots who have the misfortune to be old or infirm and as a result are grounded against their will.

There are analogies, which may have been in the minds of some of the Justices, between hostility to homosexuals and other, now discredited hostilities, such as anti-Semitism, just as there is an analogy between racial and sexual segregation of public facilities. But analogies, to repeat an earlier point less contentiously, invite inquiry into difference and similarity; they should not be permitted to elide inquiry. Hostility to homosexuals is plainly a different phenomenon from anti-Semitism and has to be analyzed on its own terms, which the Court has refused to do. Some manifestations of that hostility may be so egregious, hurtful, mean-spirited, even barbarous that the courts should invalidate them without waiting to find out a lot about the phenomenon. But merely barring local governments from making efforts to prevent peaceable private discrimination and by doing so to be seen as endorsing the homosexual way of life falls far short of savagery.

My point is not so much that *Romer* and the *VMI* case were decided incorrectly as that the decisions are so barren of any engagement with reality that the issue of their *correctness* scarcely arises. It is the lack of an empirical footing that is and always has been the Achilles heel of constitutional law, not the lack of a good constitutional theory. But this raises the question of what the courts are to do in difficult constitutional cases when their ignorance is irremediable, though one hopes only temporarily so. Judges don't yet know enough about the role of women in the military, or about the causes of homosexual orientation, to base decisions in cases such as *Romer* and *VMI* on the answers to these empirical questions. Inevitably, the judge's vote in such a case will turn on his values and temperament. Those judges who believe (a belief likely to reflect a judge's values and temperament rather than a theory of judicial review) in judicial self-restraint, in the sense of wanting to minimize the occasions on which the courts annul the actions of other branches of government, will consider ignorance of the consequences of a challenged governmental policy that is not completely outrageous a compelling reason for staying the judicial hand in the absence of sure guidance from constitutional text, history, or precedent. (An important qualification: many constitutional issues can be resolved on the basis of these conventional legal materials.) Activists will plow ahead. These poles will not meet until much more is known about the consequences of judicial activism and judicial self-restraint. So one thing that we may hope for through the application of the methods of scientific theory and empirical inquiry to constitutional law is the eventual accumulation of enough knowledge to enable judges at least to deal sensibly with their uncertainty about the consequences of their decisions. Ultimately many of the uncertainties may be dispelled. Until that happy day arrives, the most we can realistically ask of the judges is that they be mindful of the limitations of their knowledge. And I do not mean knowledge of constitutional theory.

Notes

1. *Lochner v. New York*, 198 U.S. 45 (1905).
2. *Brown v. Board of Education*, 347 U.S. 483 (1954).
3. *Roe v. Wade*, 410 U.S. 113 (1973).
4. *United States v. Virginia*, 518 U.S. 515 (1996).
5. *Romer v. Evans*, 517 U.S. 620 (1996).
6. *Bowers v. Hardwick*, 478 U.S. 186 (1986).

CHAPTER 27

The Importance of Comparative Law

Aharon Barak
Chief Justice, Supreme Court of Israel (1995–2006)

I HAVE FOUND COMPARATIVE LAW to be of great assistance in realizing my role as a judge. The case law of the courts of the United States, Australia, Canada, the United Kingdom, and Germany have helped me significantly in finding the right path to follow. Indeed, comparing oneself to others allows for greater self-knowledge. With comparative law, the judge expands the horizon and the interpretative field of vision. Comparative law enriches the options available to us. In different legal systems, similar legal institutions often fulfill corresponding roles, and similar legal problems (such as hate speech, privacy, and now the fight against terrorism) arise. To the extent that these similarities exist, comparative law becomes an important tool with which judges fulfill their role in a democracy ("microcomparison"). Moreover, because many of the basic principles of democracy are common to democratic countries, there is good reason to compare them ("macrocomparison"). Indeed, different democratic legal systems often encounter similar problems. Examining a foreign solution may help a judge choose the best local solution. This usefulness applies both to the development of the common law and to the interpretation of legal texts.

Naturally, one must approach comparative law cautiously, remaining cognizant of its limitations. Comparative law is not merely the comparison of laws. A useful comparison can exist only if the legal systems have a common ideological basis. The judge must be sensitive to the uniqueness of each legal system. Nonetheless, when the judge is convinced that the relative social, historical, and religious circumstances create a common ideological basis, it is possible to refer to a foreign legal system for a source of comparison and inspiration. Indeed, the importance of

---

Acknowledgment to Princeton University Press for excerpts from The Judge in a Democracy *by Aharon Barak, © Princeton, N.J.: Princeton University Press 2006.*

comparative law lies in extending the judge's horizons.... Of course, there is no obligation to refer to comparative law. Additionally, even when comparative law is consulted, the final decision must always be local. The benefit of comparative law is in expanding judicial thinking about the possible arguments, legal trends, and decision-making structures available.

Comparative law is a tool that aids in constitutional and statutory interpretation. This assistance may work on three levels. The first concerns interpretive theory. Comparative law helps the judge better understand the place of interpretation and the role of the judge [as] an interpreter.... Before judges decide their own position on the issue, they would do well to consider how other legal systems treat the question. The second level at which judges rely on comparative law is connected with democracy's fundamental values. Democracies share common fundamental values. Democracy must infringe on certain fundamental values in order to maintain others. It is important for judges to know how foreign law treats this question and what techniques it uses. Does it employ a technique of balancing or of categorization? Why is one technique preferred over another? Every legal system grapples with the issue of constitutional limitations on human rights. What are these limitations, and what technique was used to reach them? What are the remedies for violating an unlawful order, and how can they be determined? The third level of aid provided by comparative law concerns the solutions it offers to specific situations. For example, how protected is racist speech? Is affirmative action recognized? How does the foreign system deal with terrorism? Of course, the resolution of these issues is intrinsically local. However, in different legal systems, they have a common core, in that they reflect the problems of democracy and the complexity of human relations. Again, I do not advocate adopting the foreign arrangement. It is never binding. I just advocate an open approach, one that recognizes that for all our singularity, we are not alone. That recognition will enrich our own legal systems if we take the trouble to understand how others respond in situations similar to those we encounter....

Comparative Law and Interpretation of the Constitution

Comparative law can help judges determine the objective purpose of a constitution. Democratic countries have several fundamental principles in common. As such, legal institutions often fulfill similar functions across countries. From the purpose that one gives democratic legal system attributes to a constitutional arrangement, one can learn about the purpose of that constitutional arrangement in another legal system. Indeed, comparative constitutional law is a good source of expanded horizons and cross-fertilization of ideas across legal systems. This is clearly the case when the constitutional text of one country has been influenced by the constitutional text of another. But even in the absence of any (direct or indirect) influence of one constitutional text on another, there is still a basis for interpretive inspiration. For example, a constitution may refer expressly to democratic values or democratic societies. But even without such a reference, the interpretive influence of comparative law is proper. This is the case with regard to determining the scope of human rights, resolving particularly difficult issues such as abortion and the death penalty, and determining constitutional remedies.

Nonetheless, as we have seen, interpretive inspiration is only proper if there is an ideological basis common to the two legal systems and a common allegiance to the basic democratic principles. A common basis of democracy, however, is a necessary but insufficient condition for comparative analysis. As judges, we must also examine whether there is anything in the historical development and social conditions that makes the local and the foreign system different enough to render interpretive inspiration impracticable.

But when there is an adequate similarity, interpretive inspiration is proper. This is the case with regard to inspiration from the law of another democratic country. It is also the case with regard to interpretive inspiration from international law, as various international conventions enshrine constitutional values. These conventions influence the formation of the objective purpose of different constitutional texts. The case law of international and national courts that interpret these conventions ought to serve as a basis for the interpretation of the constitutions of various nations.

Use of Comparative Law in Practice

The use of comparative law for the development of the common law and the interpretation of legal texts is determined by the tradition of the legal system. Israeli law, for example, makes extensive use of comparative law. When Israeli courts encounter an important legal problem, they frequently examine foreign law. United Kingdom law, Canadian law, and Australian law is commonplace. Those with the linguistic ability also refer to Continental law, and sometimes we use English translations of Continental (mainly German, French, and Italian) legal literature.

In countries of the British Commonwealth, there is much cross-fertilization. Each such nation refers to United Kingdom case law. United Kingdom judges refer to Commonwealth case law, and Commonwealth judges in turn refer to each other's case law. The Supreme Court of Canada is particularly noteworthy for its frequent and fruitful use of comparative law. As such, Canadian law serves as a source of inspiration for many countries around the world. The generous use of comparative law can be found in the opinions of the South African Constitutional Court. In South Africa's Constitution, it is explicitly determined that:

> When interpreting the Bill of Rights, a court, tribunal, or forum—
>
> a. must promote the values that underline an open and democratic society based on human dignity, equality, and freedom;
>
> b. must consider international law; and
>
> c. may consider foreign law.

Regrettably, until very recently the United States Supreme Court has made little use of comparative law. Many democratic countries draw inspiration from the United States Supreme Court, particularly in its interpretation of the United States Constitution. By contrast, some Justices of the United States Supreme Court do not cite foreign case law in the judgments. They fail to make use of an important source of inspiration, one that enriches legal thinking, makes the law more creative, and strengthens the democratic ties and foundations of different legal systems.... Of course, American law in general, and its constitutional law in particular, is rich and developed. American law is comprised of not one but fifty-one legal systems. Nonetheless, I think that it is always possible to learn new things even from other democratic legal systems that, in their turn, have learned from American law. As Judge Guido Calabresi rightly said, "Wise parents do not hesitate to learn from their children." There appears to be the beginning of a change in the United States Supreme Court's attitude toward comparative law. In some recent cases, Supreme Court justices have cited case law from other jurisdictions. Is the Court moving toward wider use of comparative law?

CHAPTER 28

The Two Faces of Judicial Activism

William Wayne Justice
Judge, U.S. District Court, Eastern District of Texas (1968–1998)

For the past twenty years, every United States Supreme Court nominee has come with a presidential warranty that he or she will be a jurist who interprets the law rather than makes it. It has become commonplace for political officeseekers and officeholders of all ideological stripes to make "judicial activism" the target of much demagogic bluster. Several of my own decisions have been made into campaign issues in Texas gubernatorial races and numerous local political contests. Indeed,... East Texans are casting their ballots in a primary election in which one of the candidates for State Representative has expended considerable rhetoric condemning the consent decrees and orders I approved and issued in the prison reform case of *Ruiz v. Estelle*.[1]

What has been missing from much of this verbal attack is the clear identification of its subject. "Judicial activism" is, more often than not, a code word used to induce public disapproval of a court action that a politician opposes, but is powerless to overturn. In most cases, the mindless incantation of this phrase amounts to a political ritual, which touches the congregation of voters on an emotional level without provoking any reasoned discourse among them. Even within the legal profession, defenders and decriers of "judicial activism" sometimes fail to see the need to explain just what it is they are debating.

Because my name has appeared on the "ten most wanted list" of judicial activists for much of my nearly quarter-century on the bench, I have found it

Acknowledgment to Chief Judge William Wayne Justice for his article "The Two Faces of Judicial Activism," in 61 George Washington Law Review *1 (1992).*

worthwhile to devote some thought to the essential elements of this offense. The charge of judicial activism conflates and confuses two quite distinct juridical activities. On the one hand, this label has been applied to decisions whereby judicial precedents or statutory schemes are overturned based upon the constitutional values determined by the judges considering the case.[2] On the other hand, the term "judicial activism" is used to describe the expansive remedies imposed and monitored by federal district courts pursuant to evidentiary showings of constitutional injury.[3]

The institutional and philosophical implications of these two different forms of "judicial activism" are quite separate. To employ the same terminology for both is misleading. I shall refer to the two forms as "jurisprudential activism" and "remedial activism," respectively. This distinction is not made in an effort to brand one as illegitimate and tout the other as valid. Rather, I hope this demarcation will show that what is condemned as "judicial activism," in reality, comprises two traditional and unexceptionable juridical enterprises. The consistency of each form of activism with democratic theory depends entirely upon the circumstances of a particular case.

Jurisprudential activism in American law dates to the earliest years of the Republic. The first and one of the most successful practitioners of this technique was Chief Justice John Marshall. Condemnation of Chief Justice Marshall's decisions as subversion of the popular will by unelected members of the third branch of the government was a tenet of faith in both Jeffersonian and Jacksonian democracy.[4] In contrast to the opponents of judicial activism in recent years, Jeffersonian and Jacksonian populists did not face a well-established tradition of court invalidation of legislative acts, nor was there much extant American legal precedent. The legitimacy of judicial review was seriously contestable at that time, and, therefore, the terms of the debate over jurisprudential activism were genuine.

As is well known, *Marbury v. Madison* first articulated the principle that the Supreme Court was the ultimate arbiter of the Constitution.[5] Chief Justice Marshall expounded upon this role in *Marbury* and *McCulloch v. Maryland,*[6] without citing any precedent and relying almost exclusively on his own constitutional wisdom. These decisions surely represented jurisprudential activism of the first order, as well as incidentally carrying out the Federalist political program that had gone down to defeat at the ballot box.[7]

The notion that the judiciary must invalidate unconstitutional government actions has since become an established part of our constitutional system, and has been recognized as such for at least the past century and a half.[8] The sound and fury of politicians and pundits aside, because "[i]t is emphatically the province and duty of the judicial department to say what the law is,"[9] jurisprudential activism is constitutionally mandated and, in and of itself, quite proper.

The random launching of barbs against the judiciary obscures what should be the subject of discussion: How does a judge determine what the Constitution means? The debate over this inquiry is often portrayed as a disagreement over process and the role of the Judicial Branch. I believe that is an inapt depiction. Justice William Brennan and Chief Justice William Rehnquist did not disagree that the Court should strike down unconstitutional laws, rather, they had vastly different concepts of which laws were unconstitutional.[10] Their disputes, like most since ratification of the Constitution, were over what our constitutional values should be.

One of the longest running dramas in American political life may be entitled appropriately "The Quest for Constitutional Meaning." Even though this "production" has entered its third century, some are reluctant to recognize that its plot is inevitably political and strongly value-laden. From Chief Justice John Marshall to Justice Thurgood Marshall, whenever the Court determined whether an act was constitutional, the Court—by definition—created constitutional meaning. When the Court's constitutional vision either has varied too far from precedent or majoritarian preference, or was not ratified by subsequent societal and doctrinal developments, it has been labelled jurisprudential "activism." Some examples from history are instructive.

Dred Scott[11] is one of the most thoroughly condemned forays into this type of activism. When Chief Justice Roger Taney declared the Missouri Compromise to be an invalid legislative enactment in that case, he made a legal determination about the meaning of the Constitution regarding African-Americans, human rights, and property.[12] When the failings of Chief Justice Taney's judicial reasoning are elaborated, his constitutional values are what disturb us. Although *Dred Scott* was only the second time the Supreme Court invalidated congressional legislation, we do not reject the notion that it was the Court's role to decide whether the statutory enactment comported with our fundamental law.

In *Bradwell v. Illinois,*[13] the Supreme Court discerned no constitutional injury in a statute that prohibited women from practicing law. The systematic enforcement of white superiority was given constitutional blessing in *Plessy v. Ferguson.*[14] In *Lochner v. New York,*[15] the Court employed a particular economic philosophy to find a Fourteenth Amendment right to make a contract to toil until one died from exhaustion. What is so very wrong about each of these decisions is the actual judicial reasoning employed to create substantive constitutional meaning. It is my hope that we share a different overriding view of the human condition one hundred years later than when these cases were decided. But, whether we call it natural law or basic notions of humanity, the necessary consultation of an extratextual source for constitutional interpretation is jurisprudential activism.

Though it is infrequently a thing of beauty, jurisprudential activism is definitely in the eye of the beholder. Some decried the actions of the Supreme Court in striking down major portions of the New Deal—for the benefit of the propertied few—as an unwarranted exercise of raw judicial power.[16] Others perceived the wholesale rejection in the mid–1930s of legal precedents, only to uphold almost identical legislation just a few years later, to be the offending conduct.[17] In truth, both were examples of jurisprudential activism. Certainly, the words of the Constitution did not change in 1937; the members of the Court did. But there is more to it than that. Professor Bruce Ackerman has persuasively contended that a constitutional revolution occurred in 1937, for only the second time since ratification—the other being Reconstruction.[18]

As Professor John Ely has argued, *Carolene Products,*[19] with its famous footnote four in which the Court committed itself to protecting the powerless from the excesses of the political process, embodied the Justices' new constitutional philosophy.[20] When the Court makes such a sea-change in constitutional interpretation, it is certainly engaging in jurisprudential activism. Whether such action will be accepted depends upon (1) the particular direction abandoned; (2) the new course plotted; and (3) the reasons articulated to justify the shift. Posterity, for the most part, has endorsed the constitutional revolution of 1937 and its legitimacy has not been disputed widely over the past fifty years.

The Warren Court articulated a constitutional philosophy that supported individual rights against state power,[21] human rights over property rights,[22] and equality in place of hierarchy.[23] Because it rejected certain outmoded precedents and angered many, the Warren Court was condemned as a paradigm of jurisprudential activism.[24] Instead, however, legal commentators should have argued about the values the Justices identified as being constitutionally paramount, the ideas rejected, and the Court's rationale for imposing change. Platitudes about the need for judicial restraint do not advance the dialogue about what our constitutional system should be.

At this very moment, we may well be on the verge of a restoration of the ancien régime. Last term, in *Payne v. Tennessee,*[25] the Rehnquist Court decreed that it was not necessarily bound by recent precedents, i.e., those of the Warren and Burger Courts, that were "badly reasoned" or "decided by the narrowest of margins, over spirited dissents challenging the basic underpinnings of those decisions," other than in property or contract cases.[26] Confronting the reality that the Court creates constitutional meaning, Justices Marshall and Blackmun retorted:

> The text of the Constitution is rarely so plain as to be self-executing; invariably, this Court must develop mediating principles and doctrines in order to bring the text of constitutional provisions to bear on particular facts. Thus, to rebut the

> charge of personal lawmaking, Justices who would discard the mediating principles embodied in precedent must do more than state that they are following the "text" of the Constitution; they must explain why they are entitled to substitute their mediating principles for those that are already settled in the law.[27]

As the Rehnquist Court hands down its decisions..., it appears beyond a doubt that the Court will engage in considerable jurisprudential activism. It also seems readily apparent that the Court will abdicate its critical role as protector of the powerless. To put it plainly, we are returning to an age where the courts once again support the state and its most propertied inhabitants. I, for one, despair this regression. But those who oppose this constitutional counterrevolution have their work cut out for them. The Rehnquist Court has explained its decisions, and will justify them, as being part of its assigned role to say what the law is and what the Constitution means.[28]

The first type of activism that I have described, jurisprudential activism, is not one of which I can be justly accused. I have made very little law in my judicial career, for the simple reason that I am in a poor position to do so. As a district court judge, every legal ruling I make is reviewable *de novo* by the United States Court of Appeals for the Fifth Circuit and, ultimately, by the Supreme Court. The members of the Federalist Society can rest assured that the present composition of these courts all but guarantees that I shall not be making any law in the near future. Where I am most accused of activism is with respect to the broad and comprehensive remedies that I have ordered in institutional reform cases. Some say that I have usurped the power of the state legislature, meddled in areas beyond the expertise of the court, and imposed my own philosophy and sociological conclusions.[29]

I disagree wholeheartedly with these allegations, and I would move to quash the indictment. When properly practiced, remedial activism is completely consistent with the obligation of a district court judge to determine the existence of constitutional injuries and impose appropriate remedies based upon the evidence adduced in the case. When such a remedy is called for, the adversarial nature of the judicial process—particularly the consideration of the testimony of expert witnesses—enables the court to order remedies that are neither arbitrary, tyrannical, nor the products of its own imagination, but rather remedies that flow logically from the court's findings in the case.

Given reasonable and cooperative parties, a court needs to take few remedial steps of its own initiation. But it should be emphasized that when confronted with an obstinate, obdurate and unregenerate defendant, a more detailed remedy is needed. If a decree is only in general terms, such a defendant will find it easy to disobey and defy the decree without fear of contempt, by making the contention that the order is too vague to guide future conduct. In such instances, a court must "ratchet-down" on the defendant, by successive, more detailed supplemental decrees, until compliance is eventually achieved.

Therefore, I firmly believe that when a defendant exhibits a stubborn and perverse resistance to change, extensive court-ordered relief is both necessary and proper. I have spoken only of what creates the necessity. The propriety of a detailed remedy comes from the judicial office itself. The Supreme Court has said, time and again, that once a constitutional violation is found, a federal court is required to tailor the scope of the remedy to fit the nature and extent of the injury.[30]

Similar to its duty to say what the law is, a court's obligation to ensure full compliance with the law is nothing new. Liberal federal judges did not recently invent the notion that an intrusive remedy is necessary in some circumstances to ensure adherence to the dictates of law. In family court, for example, a judge restructures the most basic human relationships, with or without the consent of the parties, pursuant to fairly general standards of equity. For several hundred years, courts of equity—acting through various agents such as receivers and bankruptcy trustees—have made decisions about how businesses will be run and actually have operated them. Thus, I contend that when a state institution is constitutionally bankrupt, intrusive court action is needed as much as in the case of the financial bankruptcy of a megacorporation.

I would like to use two of my cases as examples of what I have termed remedial activism. They are *Morales v. Turman,*[31] and *Ruiz v. Estelle,*[32] both of which involved the rights of incarcerated individuals. *Morales v. Turman* was a challenge to the treatment of juveniles in reform schools run by the Texas Youth Council. A five-week trial in 1973 revealed truly shocking conditions in many of these state institutions. These conditions included widespread brutality that was tolerated and often encouraged by the top officials in the institutions; arbitrary disciplinary procedures coupled with often harsh and degrading punishments; and woefully inadequate rehabilitation procedures.[33]

After almost a year of exhaustively reviewing the trial testimony and the proposed findings of fact submitted by all parties, I ordered comprehensive relief coextensive with the wholesale constitutional violations. The order placed limits on permissible punishments, such as solitary confinement, detailed the disciplinary procedures that the Constitution insisted must be followed, and mandated the closing of the two worst schools.[34] I also ordered the parties to submit plans for improving the treatment and rehabilitation of juveniles, and appointed an ombudsman to monitor the court's order.[35]

I created none of this out of whole cloth. Rather, the facts of the case and the testimony of eminent experts supported the necessity of each and every step to remedy the clearly established constitutional violations. Although most in the media greeted the findings of legal injury with favor, the remedial portion of the order was labelled by the *Dallas Morning News* as a "Judicial Coup d'Etat."[36] Changes in the law and evidence of improvement in the reform schools while the case was on appeal caused the Fifth Circuit to order a new trial three years later.[37] Following further wrangling, the parties eventually reached a settlement. Pursuant to the terms of the settlement, the Texas Legislature and Board of Directors of the Texas Youth Council embarked firmly upon the path of reform.

Morales illustrates an old adage: If you are confronted with a refractory mule, in order to get its attention, you need to hit it—hard—right between the eyes. In *Morales*, the recalcitrant state institution was stimulated to action by the attention-getting, detailed, remedial order. The former chairperson of the National Institute of Corrections has labelled *Morales* a "sterling example of successful court-induced [, as opposed to court-mandated,] change."[38] Because the defendants eventually adopted the spirit and general thrust of the court's order, it can be said fairly that the *Morales* decision induced dramatic and beneficial change in the Texas juvenile justice system.

My experience with *Ruiz*, the Texas prison case, was similar but received considerably more media attention than *Morales*. There, the trial lasted 159 days and involved over 350 witnesses. After a year and a half of analysis, I made detailed findings of severe overcrowding, inadequate security, widespread brutality stemming from the use of inmates to keep discipline, lack of health care, arbitrary and harsh discipline, and obstruction of access to the courts.[39] I ordered relief which has been justly described as "more comprehensive and specific than any other prison order ever issued by a federal court."[40] The relief included details as specific as the amount of exercise to be permitted to inmates, the number of guards assigned to a unit, and the space allowance for prisoners housed in dormitories. The specificity of the order resulted from the truly active and fanatical opposition of the defendants in the pre-trial, trial, and post-trial phases of the case. Much of the remedial order was affirmed on appeal, though some portions were subsequently modified in some respects and strengthened in others by stipulations of the parties.

The *Ruiz* case established little, if any, new law, and I discovered no new rights lurking in the penumbras of enumerated constitutional rights. Although it is true that the Eighth Amendment prohibitions are based on "concepts of dignity, civilized standards, humanity, and decency,"[41] the determination that a prison is not in compliance with the Constitution does not imply the imposition of personal ideology. Instead, the determination results from the application of judicial precedents and factual reality, which the adversarial process is designed to foster. Simply ordering the Texas prisons to hire more prison guards based purely on my personal opinion would have been both an arbitrary and an arrogant use of power. Every aspect of the relief that I ordered was based on the evidence presented in my court.

I make no apologies for the comprehensive relief I ordered in this and other cases. Having found a constitutional violation by a state institution, I acted upon the belief that simply declaring a practice unconstitutional was not the limit of my duty as a judge. Judges are more than social critics. The power of the law and justice lies in actions, not pronouncements. Given my sworn oath to uphold the Constitution, I feel compelled to obliterate any practices contrary to it by any means necessary. I believe my remedies were "activist" only in the literal sense that they were not passive. As Judge Richard Posner has remarked, we on the bench are not potted plants.[42] To this day, I sincerely maintain that I simply was following the law.

I would like now to address directly the criticisms of my extensive remedies. At the most simplistic level, it is argued that federal courts simply have no business telling a state how to operate its prison system, its schools, or any other public institution. This, of course, is pure nonsense. Sadly, this is some of the favorite rhetoric of demagogic politicians of both parties and some individuals who sit on the bench. Critics of *Brown v. Board of Education* made the same argument ... and they have been left on the dung heap of history. Just as the judges charged with implementing *Brown* encountered the stubbornness of Jim Crow, state bureaucratic institutions often develop an entrenched culture and a set of habits that will not be changed merely by pounding a magic gavel and solemnly intoning that its practices are unconstitutional. Southern states ignored the Supreme Court segregation decisions;[43] in like manner, state institutions often will be fiercely resistant to court-imposed changes to business as usual. As experience has shown, a legal decision without effective sanction amounts to no law.

A slightly more sophisticated criticism is that courts should defer to the experienced judgment of the state institution. Just because state officials have made a decision, however, does not make it either correct or constitutional. First, high officials often are unaware of conditions in their own agencies. The practices uncovered at the *Morales* trial, for example, were as much a revelation for the Director of the Texas Youth Council as they were for me. Second, agency heads often take any criticism of the agency personally, and, consequently, they are unable to evaluate objectively the agency's performance. Finally, bureaucratic inertia often results in supervisors who are both unaware of and unconcerned with the latest developments in their fields. When in doubt, they simply do things the way that they have always been done.

This brings me to the most serious criticism of my activism. That criticism is the argument of institutional incompetence, that a single judge is simply not equipped to make important decisions about how a state institution should be run. As a general matter, I completely agree. As a judge, I am no more an expert in prison administration or school reform than I am in business arrangements or automobile accidents. Yet I am often called upon to make legal and factual conclusions with respect to these and other topics. I have to deal with all of these cases in the same general way, by ruling on the basis of the law and the record, and by using my common sense and making credibility determinations when the testimony and evidence conflict. I wholeheartedly concur that the institutions themselves should be left to correct their own unconstitutional practices, if they attempt to do so in good faith. But such an attempt seldom is made in the real world, where not every politician and bureaucrat has a respect for constitutional requirements. The desirability of court-ordered and court-monitored institutional reform is about equal to the desirability of having a democracy. It is the worst system, except for all the others.

Although I agree with commentators, such as Professor Abram Chayes, who note that institutional reform cases challenge the traditional and limited bipolar model of the lawsuit typical of contract and tort cases,[44] it is also important to me to stress that my remedial orders in institutional litigation are simply part of the traditional duties of a judge. In both private law and public law disputes, the issue of what remedy must be imposed presents unique analytic problems and is distinct from the finding of liability. In contract cases, the measure of damages may depend on factual determinations regarding mitigation, and whether there were consequential damages. In some tort cases, damages and injunctive relief issues sometimes occupy more of the court's time than liability.

Furthermore, even in a so-called public law institutional reform case, the judge is still constrained by certain hallmarks of judicial decisionmaking:(1) the judge must make a decision on every grievance presented; (2) the judge must listen to the witnesses and arguments of both sides; and (3) the judge must justify his decision. These safeguards—which, I emphasize, are not imposed on state legislators and executive officers, who also make decisions profoundly affecting the welfare of the community—make it more likely that a judge's decision regarding the remedy to be imposed will be reliable and well-considered.

That being said, I fully acknowledge that protracted and intrusive intervention of the courts in public institutions presents its own set of problems. As a judge, my job is to decide cases, not administer prisons. Furthermore, as Professor Judith Resnick has pointed out, a judge who becomes too personally involved in the management of any litigation can lose objectivity in the same way that the institution itself does.[45]

There are ample ways to avoid these problems, however. For example, I would much rather have the parties agree to relief than to order it myself. Thus, in *Ruiz*, I gave the parties a general outline of what had to be accomplished and ordered the parties to meet and to attempt to reach agreement. After the affirmance of the case on appeal, the parties reached agreement on many issues, making it unnecessary to impose more detailed remedies. I also appointed a special master in *Ruiz*, and a monitor in *Morales*, to oversee compliance with consent decrees and court-ordered remedies. In *Ruiz*, the special master also has attended the settlement negotiations. As a result, my involvement in these cases was episodic and only consisted of participation in court proceedings.

It does not take a rocket scientist to discover that litigation is a poor alternative to capable and caring performance by the state officials in the first instance. But if the state institutions fail to measure up to what the Constitution or other law demands, and the executive and legislative branches of state government take no remedial steps, litigation may be the only way to bring justice to the continuously expanding number of victims of the state's malfeasance. Remedial activism, the ordering of detailed remedies in institutional reform cases, is nothing more than an application of the traditional role of the judge:to resolve disputes and remedy wrongs. That the disputes involve arguments over how our public institutions should be run, rather than private law disputes between two individuals or businesses, is a difference of degree rather than of kind. What most distinguishes institutional reform litigation from other forms is its massive size. The remedies ordered by courts in institutional reform litigation will, of necessity, usually be more detailed and more complicated than in other cases.

Unless we are to do away with the Constitution, federal courts will continue to be called upon to order state institutions to remedy constitutional violations, and such remedies ordinarily will be more specific than a mere prohibition of illegal activity. Unless one is prepared to reduce constitutional guarantees to a form of words—a practice that is currently in vogue—one cannot question the proposition that if a constitutional violation is found, it must be remedied. If the law makes empty promises of justice and courts stand by—impotently watching constitutional violations persist without taking action to correct them—then we do not fulfill the promises of equal protection and due process. The question is not whether relief will be ordered for constitutional injuries, but what the relief will be.

In conclusion, I believe that attaching the label of "judicial activism" to the two kinds of juridical conduct I have discussed today is simply a rhetorical device to avoid making a more convincing attack on the results that the judge has reached. Those who oppose the Supreme Court's recent reactionary jurisprudential activism, as well as its unwarranted truncation of the lower courts' ability to ensure compliance with the Constitution, must do more than invoke the charge of "judicial activism." They must confront—and somehow refute and surmount—the mean-spirited and callous values that are being identified as constitutionally preeminent, the inadequacy of the reasons given for the selection of them, and the inconsistencies between the judiciary's words and deeds....

Notes

1. *Ruiz v. Estelle,* 503 F. Supp. 1265 (S.D. Tex. 1980), *aff'd* in part, vacated in part, and modified in part, 679 F.2d 1115 (5th Cir.), amended in part and vacated in part, 688 F.2d 266 (5th Cir. 1982), *cert.* denied, 460 U.S. 1042 (1983).
2. See, e.g., R. Berger, "New Theories of 'Interpretation':The Activist Flight from the

Constitution," 47 *Ohio State Law Journal* 7, 8 (1986); Judge F.M. Johnson Jr., "The Role of the Judiciary with Respect to the Other Branches of Government," 11 *Georgia Law Review* 455, 468–469 (1977); Mark V. Tushnet, "Comment: The Role of the Supreme Court: Judicial Activism or Self-Restraint," 47 *Maryland Law Review* 147, 149–150 (1987).

3. See, e.g., D.E. Edwards, "Judicial Misconduct and Politics in the Federal System: A Proposal for Revising the Judicial Councils Act," 75 *California Law Review* 1071, 1080 & n. 65 (1987); J.O. Newman, "Between Legal Reasoning and Neutral Principles: The Legitimacy of Institutional Values," 72 *California Law Review* 200, 209 (1984).
4. See, e.g., C.M. Wiltze, *The Jefferson Tradition in American Democracy* 173 (1935); W.H. Ridgway, "Introduction: The Role of the Supreme Court: Judicial Activism or Self-Restraint," 47 *Maryland Law Review* 115 (1987).
5. *Marbury v. Madison,* 5 U.S. (1 Cranch) 137, 177 (1803).
6. *McCulloch v. Maryland,* 17 U.S. (4 Wheat.) 316, 326 (1819).
7. See, e.g., R.H. Bork, *The Tempting of America:The Political Seduction of the Law* 21 (New York:Free Press, 1990) stating that Chief Justice Marshall's appointment on the heels of Jefferson's election was meant "to preserve the national judiciary as a Federalist Party stronghold"; G.A. Spann, "Pure Politics," 88 *Michigan Law Review* 1971, 1978 n.18 (1990) stating that political considerations guided Chief Justice Marshall in *Marbury,* and that his true objective in denying Marbury's commission "was to establish a power of judicial review that would enable the recently defeated Federalist party to retain political power through its hold over the life-tenured judiciary."
8. See, e.g., *United States v. Munoz-Florez,* 495 U.S. 385, 396–397 (1990), "[T]he principle that the courts will strike down a law when Congress has passed it in violation of such a command has been well settled for almost two centuries."
9. *Marbury v. Madison,* 5 U.S. (1 Cranch), at 177.
10. For example, Justice Brennan held that a Texas flag burning statute was unconstitutional because it infringed on conduct "sufficiently imbued with elements of communication" without being adequately justified by a government interest. *Texas v. Johnson,* 491 U.S. 397, 406–407 (1989). Chief Justice Rehnquist, on the other hand, believed that the American flag is the symbol embodying our Nation and does not represent the views or expression of any individual—thus, not implicating freedom of speech—and would have upheld the flag burning statute. Ibid., at 429 (Rehnquist, C.J., dissenting).
11. *Dred Scott v. Sandford,* 60 U.S. (19 How.) 393 (1857).
12. Ibid. The Court held that an African-American could not be a United States citizen and could not sue in a federal court, and proclaimed that under the Constitution, Congress was powerless to prohibit slavery in the territories. Ibid., at 406, 452.
13. *Bradwell v. Illinois,* 83 U.S. (16 Wall.) 130 (1873).
14. *Plessy v. Ferguson,* 163 U.S. 537 (1896), overruled by *Brown v. Board of Education,* 347 U.S. 483 (1954).
15. *Lochner v. New York,* 198 U.S. 45 (1905), overruled by *Day-Brite Lighting, Inc. v. Missouri,* 342 U.S. 421 (1952).
16. See, e.g., S.L. Winter, "Indeterminancy and Incommensurability in Constitutional Law," 78 *California Law Review* 1441, 1463 (1990).

17. See, e.g., T.W. Merril, "The Economics of Public Use," 72 *Cornell Law Review* 61, 68 (1986).
18. B. Ackerman, "Constitutional Politics/Constitutional Law," 99 *Yale Law Journal* 453, 487–490 (1989).
19. *United States v. Carolene Products Co.,* 304 U.S. 144 (1938).
20. J.H. Ely, *Democracy and Distrust: A Theory of Judicial Review* 75–77 (Cambridge: Harvard University Press, 1980). The Court refused to depart from its standard of review in interstate commerce cases, stating that "legislation affecting ordinary commercial transactions is not to be pronounced unconstitutional unless ... it is of such a character as to preclude the assumption that it rests upon some rational basis within the knowledge and experience of the legislators." *Carolene Products,* 304 U.S. at 152. Footnote four, however, expressed the Court's willingness to depart from its deferential standard of review of statutes "directed at particular religions, national, or racial minorities" where prejudice "tends to curtail the operation of those political processes ordinarily to be relied upon to protect minorities, and which may call for a correspondingly more searching judicial inquiry." Ibid., at 153 n. 4 (citations omitted).
21. See, e.g., *Griswold v. Connecticut,* 381 U.S. 479 (1965) holding that a state may not prohibit the use of contraception by married persons; *Yates v. United States,* 354 U.S. 298 (1957) holding that the federal government may not prohibit the mere advocacy of forcible overthrow of the United States, overruled by *Burks v. United States,* 437 U.S. 1 (1978).
22. See, e.g., *Sniadach v. Family Finance Corp.,* 395 U.S. 337 (1969) holding that prejudgment garnishment of wages without prior hearing violates due process; *Sherbert v. Verner,* 374 U.S. 398 (1963) holding that a state may not terminate a citizen's unemployment compensation for refusing to work on the Sabbath.
23. See, e.g., *Reynolds v. Sims,* 377 U.S. 533 (1964) holding that the Equal Protection Clause requires equal state legislative representation for all citizens; *Brown v. Board of Education,* 347 U.S. 483 (1954) holding that a state may not deny its citizens the opportunity for education on equal terms.
24. See, e.g., A.M. Bickel, *Politics and the Warren Court* xi (New York: Harper & Row, 1965) "[In reapportionment decisions,] the Court has intervened unwisely beyond the limits of effective legal action, into the necessary work of politics"; P.B. Kurland, *Politics, the Constitution and the Warren Court* 90–91 (Chicago:University of Chicago Press, 1970) "The list of opinions destroyed by the Warren Court reads like a table of contents from an old constitutional law casebook"; R.H. Bork, "Neutral Principles and Some First Amendment Problems," 47 *Indiana Law Journal* 1, 6 (1971) "[N]o argument that is both coherent and respectable can be made supporting a Supreme Court that chooses fundamental values because a Court that makes rather than implements value choices cannot be squared with the presuppositions of a democratic society."
25. *Payne v. Tennessee,* 111 S.Ct. 2597 (1991).
26. Ibid. at 2609–2611.
27. Ibid. at 2624 n. 3 (Marshall, J., dissenting).
28. See, e.g., *Texas v. Johnson,* 491 U.S. 397, 421, 434 (1989), "The Court's role as final expositor of the Constitution is well established" (Rehnquist, C.J., dissenting); *Patter-*

son v. McLean Credit Union, 491 U.S. 164, 188 (1989) stating that the Supreme Court's "role is limited to interpreting what Congress may do and has done"; *Federal Election Comm'n v. Massachusetts Citizens for Life, Inc.,* 479 U.S. 238, 263 (1986) stating that the Supreme Court's duty is to "enforce the demands of the Constitution."

29. See, e.g., Rep. J. Culberson, "Give Texans Back State Control of Their Prisons," *Houston Chronicle* 1 (12 April 1992); W. Rawls Jr., "Judges' Authority in Prison Reform Attacked," *New York Times,* A1 (18 May 1982).
30. See, e.g., *Maine v. Moulton,* 474 U.S. 159, 191 (1985) stating that remedies should be tailored to the injury; *United States v. Gouveia,* 467 U.S. 180, 201 (1984) (same); *Rushen v. Spain,* 464 U.S. 114, 117 (1983) (same); *United States v. Morrison,* 449 U.S. 361, 364 (1981) (same).
31. *Morales v. Turman,* 383 F. Supp. 53 (E.D. Tex. 1974), *rev'd,* 535 F.D. 864 (5th Cir. 1976).
32. *Ruiz v. Estelle,* 503 F. Supp. 1265 (S.D. Tex. 1980), *aff'd* in part, vacated in part, and modified in part, 679 F.2d 1115 (5th Cir.), amended in part and vacated in part, 688 F.2d 266 (5th Cir.), *cert.* denied, 460 U.S. 1042 (1983).
33. *Morales,* 383 F. Supp. at 72–77 (brutality); ibid. at 78–83 (arbitrary disciplinary procedures); ibid. at 92–100 (inadequate rehabilitative procedures).
34. Ibid., at 77–78 (limits on punishment); ibid. at 83–85 (detailed disciplinary procedures); ibid. at 121–126 (closing of two schools).
35. Ibid. at 120–121.
36. D. West, "Judicial Coup d'Etat," *Dallas Morning News,* 2D (23 July 1976).
37. *Morales v. Turman,* 562 F.2d 993 (5th Cir. 1977).
38. F. R. Kemerer, *William Wayne Justice:A Judicial Biography* 179–180 (1991).
39. *Ruiz v. Estelle,* 503 F. Supp. 1265, 1277–1285 (S.D. Tex. 1980) (overcrowding), *aff'd* in part, vacated in part, and modified in part, 679 F.2d 1115 (5th Cir.), amended in part and vacated in part, 688 F.2d 266 (5th Cir. 1982), *cert.* denied, 460 U.S. 1042 (1983); ibid. at 1288–1294 (inadequate security); ibid. at 1299–1303 (brutality); ibid. at 1307–1328 (lack of health care); ibid. at 1346–1350 (arbitrary and harsh discipline); ibid. at 1367–1370 (obstruction of access to courts).
40. Kemerer, supra note 38, at 377.
41. *Estelle v. Gamble,* 429 U.S. 97, 102 (1976) quoting *Jackson v. Nishop,* 404 F.2d 571, 579 (8th Cir. 1968).
42. *Tagatz v. Marquette University,* 861 F.2d 1040, 1045 (7th Cir. 1988).
43. See, e.g., J. Bass, *Unlikely Heroes* 17, 64, 128–131, 177–218 (New York: Simon & Schuster, 1981) describing how the state governments of Alabama, Louisiana, Mississippi, and Texas refused to comply with *Brown.*
44. See A. Chayes, "The Role of the Judge in Public Law Litigation," 89 *Harvard Law Review* 1281, 1282–1290 (1976).
45. J. Resnick, "Managerial Judges," 96 *Harvard Law Review* 374, 424–431 (1982).

Part IV

The Judiciary and Federal Regulation

Line Drawing and Statutory Interpretation

"It is in the courts and not the legislature that our citizens primarily feel the keen, cutting edge of the law."[1] Reiterating that view of New Jersey State Supreme Court chief justice Arthur T. Vanderbilt, Justice Tom Clark once observed: "In a democracy the national welfare should be the primary objective of the legislature whose statutes may quickly pattern effective measures to that end. The courts, on the other hand, have the duty of interpreting and enforcing such legislation. Theirs is the machinery through which law finds its teeth."[2]

Judicial participation in regulatory politics at the federal level greatly increased after the New Deal, particularly during the 1960s and 1970s, because of congressional creation of new administrative agencies and legislation aimed at ensuring civil rights and liberties as well as promoting health, safety, and consumer and environmental protection. Appeals of administrative decisions, for instance, rose more than fivefold.

The growing importance of statutory interpretation, along with constitutional interpretation, is evident as well in the changing character of the business of the Supreme Court. In historical perspective, the Court gradually became a tribunal of constitutional and statutory interpretation. During roughly the first decade of the Court's history, over 40 percent of its business consisted in admiralty prize cases. Approximately 50 percent of the docketed cases raised questions of law—largely diversity actions (suits by citizens of different states) and other matters of common law—with the remaining 10 percent matters such as equity, including one probate case.[3] Litigation before the Court was not immune from socioeconomic changes after the Civil War brought by Reconstruction and the Industrial Revolution. In 1882, for instance, the number of admiralty suits dropped to less than 4 percent.

Almost 40 percent of the decisions handed down still dealt with either disputes about common law or questions of jurisdiction, practice, and procedure. Over 43 percent of the Court's business, however, resolved issues of statutory interpretation; less than 4 percent were matters of constitutional law. The decline in admiralty and common-law adjudication, and the concomitant rise in cases concerning statutory and constitutional interpretation, reflect the impact in the late nineteenth century of changing socioeconomic conditions and increasing congressional legislation. In 1890, Justice Stephen Field observed:

> Thus by the new agencies of steam and electricity in the movement of machinery and transmission of intelligence, creating railways and steamboats, telegraphs and telephones, and adding almost without number to establishments for the manufacture of factories, transactions are carried on to an infinitely greater extent than before between different states, leading to innumerable controversies between their citizens, which have found their way to [the Supreme Court] for decision.[4]

In the twentieth century, particularly after the Judiciary Act of 1925 enlarged the Court's discretionary jurisdiction, the trend continued toward a Supreme Court that principally decides issues of constitutional and statutory interpretation. Over 40 percent of the cases disposed of by full or *per curiam* opinion now involve matters of constitutional law, while almost 40 percent deal with statutory interpretation. The remaining cases resolve matters of practice and procedure, administrative law, taxation, and other claims against the government.[5]

The contemporary Supreme Court is therefore not primarily concerned, as it once was, with resolving disputes per se; but instead with providing uniformity, stability, and predictability to the law—principally by means of constitutional and statutory interpretation. "The legislature does not speak with finality as to the meaning of its own powers," Justice Benjamin Cardozo noted. "The final word is for the courts."[6] Invalidation of congressional legislation steadily increased throughout the twentieth century as the Supreme Court assumed a special role in safeguarding individual freedoms against encroachments by Congress. The Court, for example, developed doctrines such as "void for vagueness" and "statutory overbreadth" when striking down legislation that it viewed as impinging on First Amendment freedoms. With the expansion of congressional legislation and the emergence of the so-called administrative state, the Court also assumed an important role in providing guidance to lower federal courts and administrative agencies by clarifying and supervising the implementation of congressional mandates. An appellate court, in Judge Jerome Frank's words, "is, vis-à-vis the Supreme Court, 'merely a reflector, serving as a judicial moon.' Judges on such a court usually must, as best they can, cautiously follow new 'doctrinal trends' ... [a]s their duty is usually to learn, 'not the congressional intent, but the Supreme Court's intent.'"[7]

Statutory interpretation is no less vexatious than constitutional interpretation, and perhaps often more difficult due to the doctrine of *stare decisis.* "The Court has felt far freer," Justice Lewis Powell explained, "to reverse constitutional decisions than it has to reverse the interpretation of statutes"[8] because of the need for stability in the law and respect for the principle of separation of powers.

The starting point and first rule of statutory interpretation is strict adherence to the text, to the plain meaning of statutory language. As Justice Oliver Wendell Holmes put it: "We do not inquire what the legislature meant; we ask only what the statute means."[9] Statutory language, however, is often ambiguous, especially in the areas of antitrust and health, safety, and environmental legislation. "Such is the character of human language," Chief Justice John Marshall recognized, "that no word conveys to the mind in all situations, one single definite idea."[10] The task of the judge, according to Justice Holmes, remains "to work out, from what is expressly said and done, what would have been said with regard to events not definitely before the minds of the parties, if those events had been considered."[11]

Interpretation of statutes thus frequently moves beyond the text to the context of legislation—to congressional testimony, hearings, floor debate, and history—in a quest for "the intent" of Congress. Congressional history has become more important because legislation typically does not express a clear intent; instead it is a mandate for federal agencies to regulate and implement policy. This is in part because Congress rarely agrees on the precise details of an enactment or anticipates all possible applications of a statute. Justice Cardozo put the problem this way:

> The difficulties of so-called interpretation arise when the legislature has had no meaning at all; when the question which is raised on the statute never occurred to it; when what the judges have to do is, not to determine what the legislature did mean on a point which was present to its mind, but to guess what it would have intended on a point not present to its mind, if the point had been present.[12]

Senators and members of the House of Representatives, moreover, are susceptible to special-interest groups, given to "logrolling" on matters of little immediate concern to their particular constituents, and dependent on their staffs for drafting and negotiating statutory language. Issues that should be settled during the legislative process are left for courts to resolve; and judges confront deliberate ambiguities in statutory language or instances of congressional silence and no certain, unambiguous congressional history.

The ambiguities of language and congressional silence or conflicting records render the task of statutory interpretation truly challenging, inviting considerable judicial creativity. Justice Felix Frankfurter, in Chapter 29, further examines the problems of text, context, and congressional intent. He also contrasts the interpretative styles and approaches of Justices Holmes, Cardozo, and Louis Brandeis. A former congressman and federal court of appeals judge, Abner Mikva, provides another perspective:

> When I was in Congress I used to get irritated at the way I felt courts were misinterpreting what I considered the clear meaning of a piece of legislation. I am convinced now that, almost without exception, judges really are trying to do what Congress says but that the meanings just aren't as clear when you're looking at them in the isolation of a court case.[13]

Despite the problems of ambiguity and congressional silence, Justice Brandeis was wont to say, "to supply omissions transcends the judicial function."[14] Nonetheless, justices at times do supply omissions and rewrite statutory language. Justice William Brennan, for example, in *United Steelworkers of America v. Weber,* argued—over the forceful dissents of Chief Justice Warren Burger and Justice William Rehnquist—that "a thing may be within the letter of the statute and yet not within the statute, because not within its spirit nor within the intention of its makers."[15]

When Congress delegates authority to an agency but the enabling legislation and congressional history are challenged, the alternatives to judicial rewriting of a statute are either to uphold the agency's view of the legislation or to invoke the nondelegation doctrine—striking down the legislation as impermissibly broad, without clear standards for guiding agency action.

Historically, the Court has permitted agencies to "fill in the details"[16] of legislation in recognition of the fact that Congress cannot foresee all possible applications of a statute and that implementation of legislation often requires the expertise of administrative agencies. On that basis the Court upholds broad delegations of power to federal agencies and independent regulatory commissions. The Interstate Commerce Commission, for example, was authorized to fix "just and reasonable" rates; the Federal Trade Commission is empowered to eliminate "unfair methods of competition"; the Securities and Exchange Commission is charged with maintaining "a fair and orderly market" on "just and equitable principles of trade"; and the Federal Communications Commission is authorized to regulate radio and television licenses on a standard of "public convenience, interest, or necessity."

The nondelegation doctrine, though invoked during the heyday of the New Deal,[17] has been infrequently employed by the Supreme Court, although state courts continue to enforce the doctrine against state legislation. In the view of Justice Thurgood Marshall and others, the nondelegation doctrine is "moribund"[18] and ought to be laid to rest. By contrast, Chief Justice Rehnquist urged its utility in preserving the separation of powers between Congress and the executive branch.[19]

During the late 1960s and 1970s Congress and the Supreme Court in fact encouraged lower court supervision of regulatory policies, especially with regard to health, safety, and environmental regulation. Judicial oversight of the administrative process grew in part because of the fear that new agencies—such as the Environmental Protection Agency (EPA), the Occupational Safety and Health Administration (OSHA), and the Consumer Product Safety Commission (CPSC)—would be "captured" by special interest groups and in part because of a distrust of agency expertise and a demand for more public participation in the formulation of regulatory policies. Supervision of the regulatory process by generalist federal judges was encouraged by Congress and the judiciary in three ways: by "liberalizing" the law of standing and thus permitting more citizen lawsuits challenging agency actions and inactions; by "judicializing" the process of administrative decision making and rule making in order to ensure public participation and open, adjudicative-type examination of all competing views of regulatory action; and by heightening the standards for judicial review of final agency decisions. By the early 1980s there thus emerged, in Judge Harold Leventhal's words, "a new era in administrative law."[20]

The form and extent of judicial intervention in regulatory policies bears emphasizing, for it reflects basic differences in judicial self-perception. Federal judges differ in their perceptions of their role and capacity as "generalists" to scrutinize complex, science-policy regulations, for example.

The U.S. Court of Appeals for the District of Columbia Circuit remains the primary lower federal appellate court for challenging legislation authorizing administrative regulations, given that Congress gave it virtually complete jurisdiction over challenges to new statutes. For decades it was sharply divided over the kind of review that should be given to the procedural and scientific basis for regulatory action. The complexity of the issues was not the problem, Judge David Bazelon maintained, since courts review no less vexing economic issues when reviewing Federal Communications Commission (FCC) and Security and Exchange Commission (SEC) decisions. Rather, environmental and other science-policy disputes confront judges who have no "knowledge and training to assess the merits of competing scientific arguments," with vexatious issues over which there frequently exists no scientific consensus. Even if there were agreement within the scientific community, basic moral-political choices remain—choices that in a constitutional democracy should be ventilated in a public forum. For Judge Bazelon, lack of judicial competence implies judicial self-restraint. Courts should not substitute their judgments for those of scientific and administrative experts: "Courts are not the agency either to resolve the factual disputes, or to make the painful value choices."[21] Judges, however, are presumably experts on process, and adherence to judicial self-restraint on substantive matters need not preclude judicial activism on procedural grounds. According to Judge Bazelon:

> [I]n cases of great technological complexity, the best way for courts to guard against unreasonable or erroneous administrative decisions is not for judges themselves to scrutinize the technical merits of each decision. Rather, it is to establish a decision that can be held up to the scrutiny of the scientific community and the public.[22]

The federal judiciary thus should supervise the process of administrative decision making and, when necessary, impose procedural requirements in order to ensure public participation, open discussion, and the reasoned elaboration of the scientific basis for an agency's regulations.

By contrast, Judge Harold Leventhal championed the view that although deference should be shown to administrative and scientific expertise, judges should engage in "enough steeping" in technical matters to permit informed, substantive review of administrative decisions. With searching review, a judge "becomes aware, especially from a combination of danger signals, that the agency has not really taken a 'hard look' at the salient problems, and has not genuinely engaged in reasoned decision making."[23] The "hard look" approach required judges to do more than, as Judge Henry Friendly said, simply look for "good faith efforts of agencies."[24] A court, according to Judge Leventhal, should "penetrate to the underlying decisions of an agency decision to satisfy itself that the agency has exercised a reasoned discretion with reasons that do not deviate from or ignore the ascertainable legislative intent."[25] Although courts should not innovate procedurally or substitute more rigorous processes for those adopted by agencies, judges are capable of informing themselves about scientific and technical matters and thus may scrutinize, criticize, and overturn the basis for administrative decisions.

The hard-look approach was endorsed by the Supreme Court in *Vermont Yankee Nuclear Power Corporation v. Natural Resources Defense Council, Inc.*[26] Yet it demanded a great deal of judges and provided little guidance and a pretext for judicial intervention in the regulatory process when reviewing agencies' final decisions. Not all federal judges share the ability or personal dedication of Judge Leventhal to master all the technical details of complex science-policy disputes. They typically find such litigation perplexing, taxing, and time-consuming. As one federal judge remarked with regard to the adjudication of science-policy disputes: "In environmental litigation we are constantly placed in a position of choosing between the lies told by the fisherman's experts and the lies told by [the] utility company's experts. The overwhelming temptation for an appellate court is to accept the original fact finder's conclusion as to which expert was telling the smallest lie."[27]

As the composition of the Supreme Court and the federal bench has changed, due to appointments made by Republican Presidents Ronald Reagan, George H. W. Bush, and George W. Bush, so did the doctrines bearing on judicial deference to federal agencies' construction of their legislative mandates and authorizations. In *Chevron v. Natural Resources Defense Council* (1984),[28] the Court held that when statutory language is "silent or ambiguous with respect to the specific issue, the question for the court is whether the agency's answer is based on a permissible construction of the statute." Furthermore, the Court subsequently reaffirmed *Chevron*'s guidelines for judicial deference to administrative interpretations and reinterpretations of statutes in *Rust v. Sullivan,*[29] among other decisions.

Although the Supreme Court has signaled greater judicial deference to Executive Branch rule making and interpretation of statutes, the matter of statutory construction and the use of congressional history continue to be vigorously debated; even members of the Court are bitterly divided. While a strong advocate of relying on "original intent" in constitutional interpretation, Justice Antonin Scalia, for example, has championed a "plain meaning" approach to statutory interpretation and emphatically rejects a probing use of congressional histories. By contrast, Justice Stephen Breyer has defended the use of congressional history in construing federal statutes.[30] In Chapter 30, Court of Appeals for the Seventh Circuit Judge Frank H. Easterbrook discusses some aspects of the contemporary debate over the use, abuse, and misuse of legislative history in statutory construction.

Notes

1. Arthur T. Vanderbilt, *The Challenge of Law Reform* 4 (Princeton: Princeton University Press, 1955).
2. Thomas C. Clark, "Random Thoughts on the Court's Interpretation of Individual Rights," 1 *Houston Law Review* 75 (1963).
3. Based on data in J. Goebel Jr., "Appendix: The Business of the Supreme Court, 1789–1801," in *History of the Supreme Court of the United States: Antecedents and Beginnings to 1801*, at 796–798 (New York: Macmillan, 1971).
4. Stephen J. Field, "The Centenary of the Supreme Court of the United States," 24 *American Law Review* 23 (1890).
5. Based on analysis by the author. For further discussion, see David M. O'Brien, *Storm Center: The Supreme Court in American Politics* 8th ed. (New York: Norton, 2008).
6. Benjamin N. Cardozo, *The Paradoxes of Legal Science* 99 (New Haven: Yale University Press, 1929).
7. Jerome Frank, *Courts on Trial* 307 (Princeton: Princeton University Press, 1959).
8. Lewis J. Powell, "Constitutional Interpretation: An Interview with Justice Lewis Powell," *Kenyon College Alumni Bulletin* 14, 15 (Summer 1979).

9. Oliver W. Holmes, "The Theory of Legal Interpretation," in *Collected Legal Papers* 207 (New York: Harcourt, Brace, 1920).
10. *McCulloch v. Maryland,* 17 U.S. (4 Wheat.) 316, 414 (1819).
11. Oliver W. Holmes, *The Common Law* 303 (Boston: Little, Brown, 1881).
12. Benjamin N. Cardozo, *The Nature of the Judicial Process* 15 (New Haven: Yale University Press, 1921).
13. "Q. and A.: Abner J. Mikva: On Leaving Capitol Hill for the Bench," *Washington Post,* B8, col. 3 (May 12, 1983).
14. *Iselin v. United States,* 270 U.S. 245, 251 (1926).
15. *United Steelworkers of America v. Weber,* 443 U.S. 193, 201 (1979), quoting *Holy Trinity Church v. United States,* 143 U.S. 457, 459 (1892).
16. *Wayman v. Southard,* 23 U.S. (10 Wheat.) 1 (1825).
17. See, e.g., *Schechter Poultry Co. v. United States,* 295 U.S. 495, 529 (1935).
18. *FPC v. New England Power Co.,* 415 U.S. 345, 353 (1974).
19. See *Industrial Union Department, AFL-CIO v. American Petroleum Institute,* 448 U.S. 607, 671–688 (1980) (Rehnquist, J., con. op.).
20. Harold Leventhal, "Environmental Decisionmaking and the Role of the Courts," 122 *University of Pennsylvania Law Review* 509 (1974).
21. David L. Bazelon, "Coping with Technology Through the Legal Process," 62 *Cornell Law Review* 817, 822 (1977).
22. *International Harvester Co. v. Ruckelshaus,* 478 F.2d 615, 653 (D.C. Cir. 1973) (Bazelon, J., con. op.).
23. *Ethyl Corp. v. EPA,* 541 F.2d 1, 20 (D.C. Cir. 1976).
24. *New York City v. United States,* 344 F. Supp. 929 (E.D.N.Y. 1972). See also Henry J. Friendly, "Some Kind of Hearing," 123 *University of Pennsylvania Law Review* 1267 (1975).
25. *Greater Boston Television Corp. v. FCC,* 444 F.2d 841, 850 (D.C. Cir. 1970).
26. *Vermont Yankee Nuclear Power Corp. v. Natural Resources Defense Council, Inc.,* 435 U.S. 519 (1978).
27. Quoted by Maurice Rosenberg, "Contemporary Litigation in the United States," in Harry W. Jones, ed., *Legal Institutions Today: English and American Approaches Compared* 152, 158 (New York: American Bar Association, 1977).
28. *Chevron v. Natural Resources Defense Council,* 467 U.S. 837 (1984).
29. *Rust v. Sullivan,* 500 U.S. 173 (1991).
30. See, e.g., *United States v. Lopez,* 514 U.S. 549 (1995) (Breyer, J., dis. op.).

CHAPTER 29

Some Reflections on the Reading of Statutes

Felix Frankfurter
Justice, Supreme Court of the United States (1939–1965)

THOUGH IT HAS its own preoccupations and its own mysteries, and above all its own jargon, judicial construction ought not to be torn from its wider, non-legal context. Anything that is written may present a problem of meaning, and that is the essence of the business of judges in construing legislation. The problem derives from the very nature of words. They are symbols of meaning. But unlike mathematical symbols, the phrasing of a document, especially a complicated enactment, seldom attains more than approximate precision. If individual words are inexact symbols, with shifting variables, their configuration can hardly achieve invariant meaning or assured definiteness. Apart from the ambiguity inherent in its symbols, a statute suffers from dubieties. It is not an equation or a formula representing a clearly marked process, nor is it an expression of individual thought to which is imparted the definiteness a single authorship can give. A statute is an instrument of government partaking of its practical purposes but also of its infirmities and limitations, of its awkward and groping efforts. With one of his flashes of insight, Mr. Justice Johnson called the science of government "the science of experiment."[1] The phrase, uttered 125 years ago, has a very modern ring, for time has only served to emphasize its accuracy. To be sure, laws can measurably be improved with improvement in the mechanics of legislation, and the need for interpretation is usually in inverse ratio to the care and imagination of draftsmen. The area for judicial construction may be contracted. A large area is bound to remain.

Acknowledgment to the Association of the Bar of the City of New York City for permission to reprint portions of Justice Felix Frankfurter's essay from 2 Record of the Association of the Bar of the City of New York *213 (1947), copyright Association of the Bar of the City of New York.*

The difficulties are inherent not only in the nature of words, of composition, and of legislation generally. They are often intensified by the subject matter of an enactment. Moreover, government sometimes solves problems by shelving them temporarily. The legislative process reflects that attitude. Statutes as well as constitutional provisions at times embody purposeful ambiguity or are expressed with a generality for future unfolding. "The prohibition contained in the Fifth Amendment refers to infamous crimes—a term obviously inviting interpretation in harmony with conditions and opinions prevailing from time to time."[2] And Mr. Justice Cardozo once remarked, "a great principle of constitutional law is not susceptible of comprehensive statement in an adjective."[3]

The intrinsic difficulties of language and the emergence after enactment of situations not anticipated by the most gifted legislative imagination, reveal doubts and ambiguities in statutes that compel judicial construction. The process of construction, therefore, is not an exercise in logic or dialectic: The aids of formal reasoning are not irrelevant; they may simply be inadequate. The purpose of construction being the ascertainment of meaning, every consideration brought to bear for the solution of that problem must be devoted to that end alone. To speak of it as a practical problem is not to indulge a fashion in words. It must be that, not something else. Not, for instance, an opportunity for a judge to use words as "empty vessels into which he can pour anything he will"—his caprices, fixed notions, even statesmanlike beliefs in a particular policy. Nor, on the other hand, is the process a ritual to be observed by unimaginative adherence to well-worn professional phrases. To be sure, it is inescapably a problem in the keeping of the legal profession and subject to all the limitations of our adversary system of adjudication. When the judge, selected by society to give meaning to what the legislature has done, examines the statute, he does so not in a laboratory or in a classroom. Damage has been done or exactions made, interests are divided, passions have been aroused, sides have been taken. But the judge, if he is worth his salt, must be above the battle. We must assume in him not only personal impartiality but intellectual disinterestedness. In matters of statutory construction also it makes a great deal of difference whether you start with an answer or with a problem.

The Judge's Task

Everyone has his own way of phrasing the task confronting judges when the meaning of a statute is in controversy. Judge Learned Hand speaks of the art of interpretation as "the proliferation of purpose." Who am I not to be satisfied with Learned Hand's felicities? And yet that phrase might mislead judges intellectually less disciplined than Judge Hand. It might justify interpretations by judicial libertines, not merely judicial libertarians. My own rephrasing of what we are driving at is probably no more helpful, and is much longer than Judge Hand's epigram. I should say that the troublesome phase of construction is the determination of the extent to which extraneous documentation and external circumstances may be allowed to infiltrate the text on the theory that they were part of it, written in ink discernible to the judicial eye.

Chief Justice White was happily endowed with the gift of finding the answer to problems by merely stating them. Often have I envied him this faculty but never more than in recent years. No matter how one states the problem of statutory construction, for me, at least, it does not carry its own answer. Though my business throughout most of my professional life has been with statutes, I come to you empty-handed. I bring no answers. I suspect the answers to the problems of an art are in its exercise. Not that one does not inherit, if one is capable of receiving it, the wisdom of the wise. But I confess unashamedly that I do not get much nourishment from books on statutory construction, and I say this after freshly reexamining them all, scores of them.

When one wants to understand or at least get the feeling of great painting, one does not go to books on the art of painting. One goes to the great masters. And so I have gone to great masters to get a sense of their practice of the art of interpretation. However, the art of painting and the art of interpretation are very different arts. Law, Holmes told us, becomes civilized to the extent that it is self-conscious of what it is doing. And so the avowals of great judges regarding their process of interpretation and the considerations that enter into it are of vital importance, though that ultimate something called the judgment upon the avowed factors escapes formulation and often, I suspect, even awareness. Nevertheless, an examination of some 2,000 cases, the bulk of which directly or indirectly involve matters of construction, ought to shed light on the encounter between the judicial and the legislative processes, whether that light be conveyed by hints, by explicit elucidation, or, to mix the metaphor, through the ancient test, by their fruits.

And so I have examined the opinions of Holmes, Brandeis, and Cardozo and sought to derive from their treatment of legislation what conclusions I could fairly draw, freed as much as I could be from impressions I had formed in the course of the years.

Holmes came to the Supreme Court before the great flood of recent legislation, while the other two, especially Cardozo, appeared at its full tide. The shift in the nature of the Court's business led to changes in its jurisdiction, resulting in a concentration of cases involving the legislative process. Proportionately to their length of service and the number of opinions, Brandeis and Cardozo had many more statutes to construe. And the statutes presented for their interpretation became increasingly complex, bringing in their train a quantitatively new role for administrative regulations. Nevertheless, the earliest opinions of Holmes on statutory construction, insofar as he reveals himself, cannot be distinguished from Cardozo's last opinion, though the latter's process is more explicit.

A judge of marked individuality stamps his individuality on what he writes, no matter what the subject. What is however striking about the opinions of the three Justices in this field is the essential similarity of their attitude and of their appraisal of the relevant. Their opinions do not disclose a private attitude for or against extension of governmental authority by legislation, or towards the policy of particular legislation, which consciously or imperceptibly affected their judicial function in construing laws. It would thus be a shallow judgment that found in Mr. Justice Holmes's dissent in the *Northern Securities* case[4] an expression of his disapproval of the policy behind the Sherman Law. His habit of mind—to be as accurate as one can—had a natural tendency to confine what seemed to him familiar language in a statute to its familiar scope. But the proof of the pudding is that his private feelings did not lead him to invoke the rule of indefiniteness to invalidate legislation of which he strongly disapproved[5] or to confine language in a constitution within the restrictions which he gave to the same language in a statute.[6]

The reservations I have just made indicate that such differences as emerge in the opinions of the three Justices on statutory construction are differences that characterize all of their opinions, whether they are concerned with interpretation or constitutionality, with admiralty or patent law. They are differences of style. In the case of each, the style is the man.

If it be suggested that Mr. Justice Holmes is often swift, if not cavalier, in his treatment of statutes, there are those who level the same criticism against his opinions generally. It is merited in the sense that he wrote, as he said, for those learned in the art. I need hardly add that for him "learned" was not a formal term comprehending the whole legal fraternity. When dealing with problems of statutory construction also he illumined whole areas of doubt and darkness with insights enduringly expressed, however briefly. To say, "We agree to all the generalities about not supplying criminal laws with what they omit, but there is no canon against using common sense in construing laws as saying what they obviously mean," *Roschen v. Ward*[7] is worth more than most of the dreary writing on how to construe penal legislation. Again when he said that "the meaning of a sentence is to be felt rather than to be proved,"[8] he expressed the wholesome truth that the final rendering of the meaning of a statute is an act of judgment. He would shudder at the thought that by such a statement he was giving comfort to the school of visceral jurisprudence. Judgment is not drawn out of the void but is based on the correlation of imponderables all of which need not, because they cannot, be made explicit. He was expressing the humility of the intellectual that he was, whose standards of exactitude distrusted pretensions of certainty, believing that legal controversies that are not frivolous almost always involve matters of degree, and often degree of the nicest sort. Statutory construction implied the exercise of choice, but precluded the notion of capricious choice as much as choice based on private notions of policy. One gets the impression that in interpreting statutes Mr. Justice Holmes reached meaning easily, as was true of most of his results, with emphasis on the language in the totality of the enactment and the felt reasonableness of the chosen construction. He had a lively awareness that a statute was expressive of purpose and policy, but in his reading of it he tended to hug the shores of the statute itself, without much re-enforcement from without.

Mr. Justice Brandeis, on the other hand, in dealing with these problems as with others, would elucidate the judgment he was exercising by proof or detailed argument. In such instances, especially when in dissent, his opinions would draw on the whole arsenal of aids to construction. More often than either Holmes or Cardozo, Brandeis would invoke the additional weight of some "rule" of construction. But he never lost sight of the limited scope and function of such "rules." Occasionally, however, perhaps because of the nature of a particular statute, the minor importance of its incidence, the pressure of judicial business or even the temperament of his law clerk, whom he always treated as a co-worker, Brandeis disposed of a statute even more dogmatically, with less explicit elucidation, than did Holmes.

For Cardozo, statutory construction was an acquired taste. He preferred common law subtleties, having great skill in bending them to modern uses. But he came to realize that problems of statutory construction had their own exciting subtleties and gave ample employment to philosophic and literary talents. Cardozo's elucidation of how meaning is drawn out of a statute gives proof of the wisdom and balance which, combined with his learning, made him a great judge. While the austere style of Brandeis seldom mitigated the dry aspect of so many problems of statutory construction, Cardozo managed to endow even these with the glow and softness of his writing. The differences in the tone and color of their style as well as in the moral intensity of Brandeis and Cardozo made itself felt when they wrote full-dress opinions on problems of statutory construction. Brandeis almost compels by demonstration; Cardozo woos by persuasion.

Scope of the Judicial Function

From the hundreds of cases in which our three Justices construed statutes one thing clearly emerges. The area of free judicial movement is considerable. These three remembered that laws are not abstract propositions. They are expressions of policy arising out of specific situations and addressed to the attainment of particular ends. The difficulty is that the legislative ideas which laws embody are both explicit and immanent. And so the bottom problem is: What is below the surface of the words and yet fairly a part of them? Words in statutes are not unlike words in a foreign language in that they too have "associations, echoes, and overtones." Judges must retain the associations, hear the echoes, and capture the overtones. In one of his very last opinions, dealing with legislation taxing the husband on the basis of the combined income of husband and wife, Holmes wrote: "The statutes are the outcome of a thousand years of history.... They form a system with echoes of different moments, none of which is entitled to prevail over the other."[9]

Even within their area of choice the courts are not at large. They are confined by the nature and scope of the judicial function in its particular exercise in the field of interpretation. They are under the constraints imposed by the judicial function in our democratic society. As a matter of verbal recognition certainly, no one will gainsay that the function in construing a statute is to ascertain the meaning of words used by the legislature. To go beyond it is to usurp a power which our democracy has lodged in its elected legislature. The great judges have constantly admonished their brethren of the need for discipline in observing the limitations. A judge must not rewrite a statute, neither to enlarge nor contract it. Whatever temptations the statesmanship of policy making might wisely suggest, construction must eschew interpolation and evisceration. He must not read in by way of creation. He must not read out except to avoid patent nonsense of internal contradiction. "If there is no meaning in it," said Alice's King, "that saves a world of trouble, you know, as we needn't try to find any." Legislative words presumably have meaning and so we must try to find it.

This duty of restraint, this humility of function as merely the translator of another's command, is a constant theme of our Justices. It is on the lips of all judges, but seldom, I venture to believe, has the restraint which it expresses, or the duty which it enjoins, been observed with so consistent a realization that its observance depends on the self-conscious discipline. Cardozo put it this way: "We do not pause to consider whether a statute differently conceived and framed would yield results more consonant with fairness and reason. We take this statute as we find it."[10] It was expressed more fully by Mr. Justice Brandeis when the temptation to give what might be called a more liberal interpretation could not have been wanting. "The particularization and detail with which the scope of each provision, the amount of the tax thereby imposed, and the incidence of the tax, were specified, preclude an extension of any provision by implication to any other subject.... What the Government asks is not a construction of a statute, but, in effect, an enlargement of it by the court, so that what was omitted, presumably by inadvertence, may be included within its scope."[11] An omission, at the time of enactment, whether careless or calculated, cannot be judicially supplied however much later wisdom may recommend the inclusion.

The vital difference between initiating policy, often involving a decided break with the past, and merely carrying out a formulated policy, indicates the relatively narrow limits within which choice is fairly open to courts and the extent to which interpreting the law is inescapably making law. To say that, because of this restricted field of interpretive declaration, courts make law just as do legislatures is to deny essential features in the history of our democracy. It denies that legislation and adjudication have had different lines of growth, serve vitally different purposes, function under different conditions, and bear different responsibilities. The judicial process of dealing with words is not at all Alice in Wonderland's way of dealing with them. Even in matters legal some words and phrases, though very few, approach mathematical symbols and mean substantially the same to all who have occasion to use them. Other law terms like "police power" are not symbols at all but labels for the results of the whole process of adjudication. In between lies a gamut of words with different denotations as well as connotations. There are varying shades of compulsion for judges behind different words, differences that are due to the words themselves, their setting in a text, their setting in history. In short, judges are not unfettered glossators. They are under a special duty not to overemphasize the episodic aspects of life and not to undervalue its organic processes—its continuities and relationships. For judges at least it is important to remember that continuity with the past is not only a necessity but even a duty.

The Process of Construction

Let me descend to some particulars.

The text. Though we may not end with the words in construing a disputed statute, one certainly begins there. You have a right to think that a hoary platitude, but it is a platitude too often not observed at the bar. In any event, it may not take you to the end of the road. The Court no doubt must listen to the voice of Congress. But often Congress cannot be heard clearly because its speech is muffled. Even when it has spoken, it is as true of Congress as of others that what is said is what the listener hears. Like others, judges too listen with what psychologists used to call the apperception mass, which I take it means in plain English that one listens with what is already in one's head. One more caution is relevant when one is admonished to listen attentively to what a statute says. One must also listen attentively to what it does not say.

We must, no doubt, accord the words the sense in which Congress used them. That is only another way of stating the central problem of decoding the symbols. It will help to determine for whom they were meant. Statutes are not archaeological documents to be studied in a library. They are written to guide the actions of men. As Mr. Justice Holmes remarked upon some Indian legislation, "The word was addressed to the Indian mind." [12] If a statute is written for ordinary folk, it would be arbitrary not to assume that Congress intended its words to be read with the minds of ordinary men. If they are addressed to specialists, they must be read by judges with the minds of the specialists.

The context. Legislation is a form of literary composition. But construction is not an abstract process equally valid for every composition, not even for every composition whose meaning must be judicially ascertained. The nature of the composition demands awareness of certain pre-suppositions. For instance, the words in a constitution may carry different meanings from the same words in a statute precisely because "it is a constitution we are expounding." The reach of this consideration was indicated by Mr. Justice Holmes in language that remains fresh no matter how often repeated:

> When we are dealing with words that also are a constituent act, like the Constitution of the United States, we must realize that they have called into life a being the development of which could not have been foreseen completely by the most gifted of its begetters. It was enough for them to realize or to hope that they had created an organism; it has taken a century and has cost their successors much sweat and blood to prove that they created a nation. The case before us must be considered in the light of our whole experience and not merely in that of what was said a hundred years ago.[13]

And so, the significance of an enactment, its antecedents as well as its later history, its relation to other enactments, all may be relevant to the construction of words for one purpose and in one setting but not for another. Some words are confined to their history; some are starting points for history. Words are intellectual and moral currency. They come from the legislative mint with some intrinsic meaning. Sometimes it remains unchanged. Like currency, words sometimes appreciate or depreciate in value.

"Proliferation of Purpose"

You may have observed that I have not yet used the word "intention." All these years I have avoided speaking of the "legislative intent," and I shall continue to be on my guard against using it. The objection to "intention" was indicated in a letter by Mr. Justice Holmes which the recipient kindly put at my disposal:

> Only a day or two ago—when counsel talked of the intention of a legislature, I was indiscreet enough to say I don't care what their intention was. I only want to know what the words mean. Of course the phrase often is used to express a conviction not exactly thought out—that you construe a particular clause or expression by considering the whole instrument and any dominant purposes that it may express. In fact intention is a residuary clause intended to gather up whatever other aids there may be to interpretation beside the particular words and the dictionary.

If that is what the term means, it is better to use a less beclouding characterization. Legislation has an aim; it seeks to obviate some mischief, to supply an inadequacy, to effect a change of policy, to formulate a plan of government. That aim, that policy is not drawn, like nitrogen, out of the air; it is evinced in the language of the statute, as read in the light of other external manifestations of purpose. That is what the judge must seek and effectuate, and he ought not be led off the trail by tests that have overtones of subjective design. We are not concerned with anything subjective. We do not delve into the mind of legislators or their draftsmen, or committee members.

Unhappily, there is no table of logarithms for statutory construction. No item of evidence has a fixed or even average weight. One or another may be decisive in one set of circumstances, while of little value elsewhere. A painstaking, detailed report by a Senate Committee bearing directly on the immediate question may settle the matter. A loose statement even by a chairman of a committee, made impromptu in the heat of debate, less informing in cold type than when heard on the floor, will hardly be accorded the weight of an encyclical.

Spurious use of legislative history must not swallow the legislation so as to give point to the quip that only when legislative history is doubtful do you go to the statute. While courts are no longer confined to the language, they are still confined by it. Violence must not be done to the words chosen by the legislature. Unless indeed no doubt can be left that the legislature has in fact used a private code, so that what appears to be violence to language is merely respect to special usage. In the end, language and external aids, each accorded the authority deserved in the circumstances, must be weighed in the balance of judicial judgment. Only if its premises are emptied of their human variables, can the process of statutory construction have the precision of a syllogism. We cannot avoid what Mr. Justice Cardozo deemed inherent in the problem of construction, making "a choice between uncertainties. We must be content to choose the lesser."[14]

Notes

1. *Anderson v. Dunn,* 6 Wheat. 204, 226 (1821).
2. Mr. Justice Brandeis in *United States v. Moreland,* 258 U.S. 433, 451 (1922).
3. *Carter v. Carter Coal Co.,* 298 U.S. 238, 327 (1936).
4. *Northern Securities Co. v. United States,* 193 U.S. 197, 400 (1904).
5. Compare *Nash v. United States,* 229 U.S. 373 (1913) and *International Harvester Co. v. Kentucky,* 234 U.S. 216 (1914).
6. Compare *Towne v. Eisner,* 245 U.S. 418 (1918) and *Eisner v. Macomber,* 252 U.S. 189 (1920).
7. *Roschen v. Ward,* 279 U.S. 337, 339 (1929).
8. *United States v. Johnson,* 221 U.S. 488, 496 (1911).

9. *Hoeper v. Tax Commission,* 284 U.S. 206, 219 (1931).
10. *Anderson v. Wilson,* 289 U.S. 20, 27 (1933).
11. *Iselin v. United States,* 270 U.S. 245, 250, 251 (1926).
12. *Fleming v. McCurtain,* 215 U.S. 56, 60 (1909).
13. *Missouri v. Holland,* 252 U.S. 416, 433 (1920).
14. *Burnet v. Guggenheim,* 288 U.S. 280, 288 (1933).

CHAPTER 30

What Does Legislative History Tell Us?

Frank H. Easterbrook

Judge, U.S. Court of Appeals, Seventh Circuit (1985–)

LEGISLATIVE HISTORY IS out of the doldrums. For decades judges pawed through legislative history without much theory about what they were doing or why. Judges were atheoretic, the rest of the bar largely apathetic. How times have changed! Discussions of the role of legislative history, of statutory interpretation in general, have erupted both on the bench and in the academy. For the first time in 50 years there is a sustained, interesting debate about how to understand statutes, the meat of the business in federal courts. Debate ranges over questions of political philosophy, political economy, and epistemology—as it must when the question is, What counts as law in our constitutional republic, and how do we identify that law?...

People of good will disagree about where the common weal lies. An assumption that legislation points toward it is not so much a rule of interpretation as it is wishful thinking coupled with a hope that judges can pick up the torch. Realistic understanding of statutes treats them as compromises. Still, it may be possible to nudge the outcome a little in the direction of goodness. Can a gaggle of lawyers with no training in social science and insulation (by tenure) from the pulse of America do this? Are they authorized to do it, if they can?...

Justice Scalia insisted in *Green v. Bock Laundry Machine Co.*[1] that the legislative history of Rule 609 was neither illuminating nor relevant.... Justice Scalia insists that "law" lies in the enacted texts rather than in the legislators' intents. Yet this does not always lead him to disregard the history of an enactment. Well it

Acknowledgment to Judge Frank H. Easterbrook for excerpts from "What Does Legislative History Tell Us?" which appears in 66 ITT Chicago-Kent Law Review *441 (1990).*

should not, as *Green* shows. Rule 609(a)(1) says that a witness's criminal record may be admitted when "the court determines that the probative value of admitting this evidence outweighs its prejudicial value to the defendant." Why only the effect on "the defendant"? One possibility is that the text is a garble, and that it really means "the litigant" or "the criminal defendant." Another is that the phrase demonstrates a limited domain for Rule 609—that the rule applies only to criminal cases (the only kind in which the Rules of Evidence generally give special consideration to "defendants") and is inapplicable to civil cases, making "the defendant" sensible as it stands but precluding universal application.

Which is it? All of the Justices assumed that Rule 609 has universal application, producing a considerable problem in interpretation and need for triage. The majority of the Justices trudged through the legislative history and concluded that Congress wanted convictions to be automatically admissible to impeach any witness in a civil case; the dissenting Justices used the same methods yet reached a different destination; Justice Scalia got off the bus....

Suppose we start in a different place, with the question: "What makes us think that Rule 609 applies to civil cases?" One answer might be that the Rules of Evidence are supposed to apply to all litigation, as Rule 1101(b) says. But the jarring reference to "the defendant" in Rule 609(a)(1) suggests a more restricted domain. Legislative history may be useful in showing the scope of an enactment. If we turn to the debates (as eight Justices did) we find a pitched battle ending in a compromise. Combatants wrangled about the treatment of criminal defendants. The compromise was about their rights, nothing more.

Words do not have natural meanings; language is a social enterprise. Textualists, like other users of language, want to know its context, including assumptions shared by the speakers and the intended audience. Words in legislation may be terms of legal art. Debates and remarks may tell us whether the words in a statute appeal to a lay understanding or to a technical one. Because laws themselves do not have purposes or spirits—only the authors are sentient—it may be essential to mine the context of the utterance out of the debates, just as we learn the limits of a holding from reading the entire opinion. When litigants appeal to a precedent, the judge's first inquiry is whether the old decision contains a rule of decision for today's case. Many an opinion concerns the same subject without resolving it. On learning this, the judge takes what is to be learned from the reasoning but seeks "authority" elsewhere. Just as cases have limited domains of authority, so with statutes, and again context matters. What we learn from consulting the debates behind Rule 609 is that the statute is limited to criminal cases. Any particular meaning in civil cases is fanciful—invention, not construction. Why invent a meaning for Rule 609? Every statute has limits; once we discover the limit of Rule 609, we may put it down and seek the answer to our problem elsewhere.

As it turns out, "elsewhere" is close at hand. Rule 403 says that evidence, although relevant, may be excluded "if its probative value is substantially outweighed by the danger of unfair prejudice." If Rule 609 concerns only criminal cases, then Rule 403 supplies the rule for civil cases. Courts should take the "danger of unfair prejudice" into account, but without either torturing the language or employing the judges' own systems of values. The majority concluded that the structure of the rules was against this outcome, and Justice Scalia agreed. Yet their argument shows that the wrong question begets an irrelevant answer. The majority asked whether "Rule 403 overrides Rule 609" and answered that it does not because Rule 609 contains its own balancing test:the specific controls the general. Indisputable, if Rule 609 applies to civil cases. Asking whether Rule 403 "overrides" Rule 609 begs the answer to that question.

No degree of skepticism concerning the value of legislative history allows us to escape its use. Especially not when we know that laws have no "spirit," that they are complex compromises with limits and often with conflicting provisions, the proponents of which have discordant understandings. Legislative history shows the extent of agreement....

What else ought courts do with legislative history? Doubts about the value of legislative history arise not because the context of a law is unimportant, but because snippets from the debates so often have been used in lieu of the text, or as an excuse to nudge the law closer to the view of the losers in the legislative battle (a class that may include the judge). The text of the statute—and not the intent of those who voted for or signed it—is the law. To discard an intentionalist view of statutory meaning is to limit dramatically the use of legislative history.

We may no longer plumb the history to discover where the sponsors wanted to go; compromises place limits on how far they were able to proceed in that direction. We may no longer assume that anticipated effects dictate the meaning of rules. Statutes commonly contain means, rules of conduct, while legislative history describes what the drafters intended these rules to achieve. But only the rules are enacted, not all predictions come true, and some unexpected things are bound to happen. Laws therefore have effects not recognized in the committee reports. In the main, shared meaning in the legislative process is limited to the rules to be established; expectations about what these rules will do diverge much more widely. (Sometimes Congress enacts objectives, as in the antitrust laws when instructing the courts to prevent "monopoly"; these laws properly receive interpretation quite distinct from those that prescribe means rather than ends.)

Because the text is the law, we may not properly use colloquy to engage in "imaginative reconstruction." What distinguishes laws from the results of opinion polls conducted among legislators is that the laws survived a difficult set of procedural hurdles and either passed by a two-thirds vote or obtained the

President's signature. Even the most astute inductions about what Congress "would have done" if faced with a problem are just paths not taken.

Consider the difference between interpreting a statute and interpreting a contract. Contracts, like laws, may have omissions and ambiguities. It is standard practice to fill in the blanks of a contract, or interpret its ambiguities, by supplying terms that we believe the parties would have reached themselves if costs of bargaining were low. This is imaginative reconstruction in practice. It works because contracting parties generally have a single objective (making money), implying a standard by which to write or disambiguate terms. The institution of contract becomes more useful when courts relieve parties of the need to dicker over everything in advance (or receive unexpected jolts if they do not). Everyone gains, at least *ex ante*, when the legal rules allow parties to conserve on bargaining costs. Legislators do not have common objectives, so the basis for imputing agreement to them is weaker than the foundation for this technique in private law. More important, the constitutional rules are designed to increase, not minimize, the "costs" of enacting statutes. The complex of hurdles, in the context of the limited time each legislature has to act, is an essential part of the plan. So a method of interpretation appropriate to contracts is inappropriate to legislation, and with it goes one use of history. Legislative history has become less important because there is less to use it for....

Judge Posner urges us to treat an unclear (or mistaken) law as a garbled command to a secretary ("cancel today's lunch date with X," when the calendar shows that the date is with Y), or to a platoon leader ("Go [static]").[2] Everyone can tell that action is essential, but what action? The secretary or platoon leader had best make a quick choice, and in neither case is literal compliance appropriate....

I agree with ... Posner that a good secretary, nanny, or sergeant avoids empty-headed literalism. We hire agents for their expertise and judgment as well as for their ability to follow orders; good agents know when to deviate from a command in order to achieve more of the principal's objective. Still, it does not follow that courts ought to treat legislation the way nannies treat recipes for soup. Examples concerning secretaries, soldiers, and the like have several things in common:they posit a single living principal, a single agent, and a single maxim. None of these holds true when the time comes to interpret statutes.

Statutes are drafted by multiple persons, often with conflicting objectives. There will not be a single objective, and discretionary interpretation favors some members of the winning coalition over others. (Maybe it favors the losers!) An agent's hands are more closely tied when the principal names a means without having a clear objective. Moreover, the parallel to a private agent such as the nanny supposes an ongoing relationship, one in which discretion by the agent best serves the principal's current objectives. With legislation, the "principal" is not the sitting Congress but the enacting one (or perhaps the polity as a whole). This brings into play the many rules that tie the hands of those principals—and perforce of their agents, as it is difficult to give a constitutional theory that endows the judiciary with greater legislative discretion than Congress possesses. Legislators cannot create laws without satisfying constitutional requirements (bicameral approval and the like), plus internal requirements (consideration by committees, and so on). The drafters go out of office and lose the ability to update their decisions; the current legislature may update or be passive (and passivity may stem from still more procedural obstacles rather than agreement with the rules in place).

Still more differences separate the legislature-judge relationship from the common principal-agent one. Laws are designed to control the conduct of strangers to the transactions, not just of the judges. Rules must be publicized to be effective (to be "rules of law" at all). Addressees need predictability so they may plan for compliance, for the rearrangement of the rest of their lives. Usually the addressees (the platoon commanders or nannies) are not judges. They are businesses or the executive branch of government. They may be hostile to the constraints; their purposes diverge from the legislators' objectives. If they do not obey, they are not fired (as private agents may be); instead they are brought to court. If addressees must be able to vary the commands in order to fulfill their objectives, then undermining is likely too. What role is left for judges? To descend from the hills and shoot the wounded? Judges too may be hostile to the commands, or may believe that the supporters did not do "enough." Private agents acting on these views would be discharged; judges have tenure.

My point is simple: an understanding of agency appropriate to one-on-one transactions is not appropriate to the business of writing and implementing statutes. To the extent it is a useful analogy, it shows why the laws' addressees—private persons or the executive branch—should have discretion in interpretation. It may show, for example, why courts defer to administrative agencies' interpretation of the law, and why public officials have immunity from liability in damages. So used, however, this analogy diminishes the role of the courts in governance, and of legislative history in judging.

So far I have identified only one proper use of legislative history: establishing the domain of the statute. Putting a law in context is not the exclusive use of legislative history. The model of the United Kingdom and many European nations, which disdain legislative history, is not open to courts of the United States because of differences in the way laws are drafted. In England the Office of Parliamentary Counsel drafts the government's bills; in France the Conseil d'Etat reviews the government's *projet d'loi.* Most other nations have similar institutions, which embody legal society's wisdom about good drafting. They do more than dot i's and cross [check] references. They catch and remove ambiguities; they revise laws so that they will achieve anticipated results after the application of the canons of construction;

they comb the books for inconsistent rules to be amended or removed; they add statutes of limitation and specify the extent of private rights of action. Parliamentary systems give the government control over the content of law, the leisure to get things right before introducing bills, and confidence that the proposed text will be enacted as is. Legislative history may be disregarded in these nations because (a) these other mechanisms take care of most of the problems for which we use legislative history, and (b) the parliaments do not draft laws at all, but knuckle under to the cabinet's wishes (or bring down the government). It would overstate the role of a parliament to put much weight on speeches for or about the government's legislation.

Congress, unlike a parliament, really "makes" the law—usually from scratch. Thoughts of the authors matter (and sometimes the legislative history really does speak for the authors). Bills are drafted by junior staffs of legislators, abused by amendments from multiple and conflicting sources, and often hammered into shape at the very end of the session, with little time for review. This process puts great pressure on the ability of words to carry meaning—often a meaning all participants shared, but which a drafter could not make idiotproof. Intelligent, modest use of the background of American laws can do much to bring the execution into line with the plan.

Provided we avoid romanticism about what we read, avoid a belief that all participants were striving for the same goals, avoid a belief that the results must be consistent and in line with "sound" policy (meaning the judge's views of policy). We may not use legislative history to wrench a statute from its moorings, to shift the level of generality. Laws may be precise but expectations (values) about effects nebulous and conflicting. Emphasizing these "values" enables the reader to shift levels of generality, a tactic that lets the interpreter move pretty much at will. A case from last term shows how this works.[3] Maryland allowed children to testify in criminal trials by closed circuit television. That way the child would never need to look the accused child-abuser in the eye. Five Justices concluded that this satisfied the confrontation clause of the sixth amendment. The Court asked: "Why do we have confrontation?" to which it answered, roughly, "So that defendants may receive fair trials." Then it asked: "Did this defendant get a fair trial?" to which it answered, "Yes." That was that.

Confrontation vanished in the shuffle. The real Constitution does not say "All trials must be fair." It contains a series of rules, which the drafters anticipated would produce fair trials. Shifting the level of generality—emphasizing the anticipated effects of a rule while slighting the rule itself—is a method of liberating judges from rules. When rules vanish, so does the claim of judges to have the final word. Yet often the point of employing legislative history is to find something on a plane of generality different from the statute, to facilitate this maneuver. It is a use that must be resisted not only if we wish to carry out the enacted rule, but also if we wish to have laws that produce replicable decisions. A corps of judges allowed to play with the level of generality will move every which way, defeating the objective of justice (equal treatment) under law.

Enough. This is a comment, not a screed. A few notes bring this to a close:

1. The objective of statutory interpretation is to give the text a meaning appropriate to our particular constitutional republic. It is a republic with institutions (federalism, bicameralism, a president with veto power) that distinguish it from the democracies of Europe. A method of interpretation based on hermeneutics slights the differences between law and literature, and between a parliamentary system and our federal republic. Literary interpretation liberates the reader; novelty is rewarding and rewarded. Laws do not liberate their addressees, and novelty is penalized. Creative scholars get tenure; creative subjects of legal regulation get fined. No one supposes that the same method of interpretation is right for Shakespeare and laws in the United States, China, Iraq, and Germany.
2. Many scholars disagree with the analysis I have ventured here and elsewhere. Controversy goes with the territory. Justices of the Supreme Court regularly disagree with each other's methods as well as their conclusions.... Hotly disputed statements may be correct. At all events, the proponent of a method of interpretation that depends on Hans-Georg Gadamer's hermeneutics ought not equate controversy with error....
3. Textualism and distrust of legislative history may be confused with conservative politics. Overlap ought to be coincidental, however. If the textualist is interpreting laws written in a more conservative era, the results will appear "conservative" to modern eyes. Sometimes, however, the change goes the other way. The "conservatives" in the confrontation clause case used the Warren Court's usual kit of tools to get 'round an inconvenient text, and the textualist (Justice Scalia) stumped for the result favorable to the criminal defendant. When the text is to the left of today's consensus, textualism produces results that are politically "liberal."

When Congress is to the left of the president, yielding a bench that is "conservative" from Congress' perspective, everyone should support textualism. It allows the legislature to achieve its objectives. In years past a resort to legislative history, and a boost in the level of generality, has been used by a bench to move the law and the Constitution to the left. Conservatives cried out in dismay, objecting to method as well as result. Textualism as a method is politically neutral, preserving the compromises of the enacting legislature. Neutrality is an objective any bench ought to strive for—and the more power the interpreter possesses, the more assiduously the interpreter should seek neutrality.

Notes

1. *Green v. Bock Laundry Machine Co.,* 490 U.S. 504 (1989).
2. R.A. Posner, *The Problems of Jurisprudence* 267–278 (Cambridge: Harvard University Press, 1990).
3. *Maryland v. Craig*, 497 U.S. 836 (1990).

Part V

Our Dual Constitutional System

The Bill of Rights and the States

The very purpose of a bill of rights, Justice Robert Jackson observed, "was to withdraw certain subjects from the vicissitudes of political controversy, to place them beyond the reach of majorities and officials and to establish them as legal principles to be applied by the Courts. One's right to life, liberty, and freedom of worship and assembly, and other fundamental rights may not be submitted to vote; they depend on the outcome of no election."[1] By contrast, Justice Antonin Scalia has staked out the position that under the guarantees of the Bill of Rights there should be no exceptions made for religious minorities from generally applicable laws, observing that:

> Values that are protected against government interference through enshrinement in the Bill of Rights are not thereby banished from the political process.... It may fairly be said that leaving accommodation to the political process will place at a relative disadvantage those religious practices that are not widely engaged in; but that unavoidable consequence of democratic government must be preferred to a system in which each conscience is a law unto itself or in which judges weigh the social importance of all laws against the centrality of religious beliefs.[2]

The Bill of Rights, like the Constitution, emerged from considerable debate, numerous compromises, and remains a matter of controversy. A bill of rights, Alexander Hamilton argued in *The Federalist* No. 84, was "not only unnecessary ... but would even be dangerous." Any enumeration of rights was unnecessary because "the Constitution itself, in every rational sense, and to every useful purpose, is a bill of rights."[3] Parchment guarantees might also prove dangerous, he thought, by prohibiting the exercise of powers for which no express authority was granted to the national government. In our dual constitutional system, Hamilton reasoned, the national government possesses only limited, expressly delegated powers, and thus civil liberties are secure and subject to state constitutions enforced by state courts. By contrast, James Madison and Thomas Jefferson advanced libertarian arguments for adopting a federal bill of rights, but even they differed in their understanding of the rights to be secured. Madison, like Hamilton, worried about the potential problems arising from a declaration of rights. In a letter to Jefferson, Madison explained:

> My own opinion has always been in favor of a bill of rights; provided it be so framed not to imply powers not meant to be included in the enumeration.... I have not viewed it in an important light ... [however, because] there is a great reason to fear that a positive declaration of some of the most essential rights could not be obtained in the requisite latitude.[4]

Jefferson agreed that any declaration of rights inevitably poses problems of inclusion and exclusion, yet contended that "half a loaf is better than no bread. If we cannot secure all our rights, let's secure what we can."[5] Responding to Madison's fears, he added:

> In the arguments in favor of a declaration of rights, you omit one which has great weight to me, the legal check which it puts into the hands of the judiciary. This is a body, which if rendered independent, and kept strictly to their own department, merits great confidence for their learning and integrity.[6]

Both Madison and Jefferson came to view a bill of rights as providing, through the judiciary, a check on a coercive national government and a way to ensure "the requisite latitude" of civil rights and liberties. Madison, nonetheless, was more libertarian than Jefferson, proposing that neither the states nor the national government "shall violate the equal rights of conscience" of any citizen.[7] Ratified on December 15, 1791, the Bill of Rights applied only to the national government and therefore was to Hamilton superfluous, and possibly dangerous. To Madison it was an insufficient safeguard for individual freedom, particularly with regard to the states. To Jefferson it was a reaffirmation both of the limits of the national government and of the reserved powers of the states.

"Bills of rights give assurance to the individual of the preservation of his liberty," Justice Benjamin Cardozo noted. "They do not define the liberty they promise."[8] The courts, as Madison and Jefferson foresaw, assumed a guardianship role in defining and protecting civil rights and liberties. As a guardian of the Bill of Rights, the Supreme Court forged a constitutional revolution with profound consequences for individual freedom and federalism. On the one hand, as Justice Hugo Black explains in Chapter 31, the Court assumed the vexatious task of defining the nature and scope of the enumerated guarantees, thereby limiting the coercive powers of the national government. On the other hand, as Justice William Brennan details in Chapter 32, the Court also extended guarantees of the Bill of Rights to the states under the Fourteenth Amendment's due process clause, which prohibits any state from "depriving a person of life, liberty, or property without due process of law."

With notably few exceptions, the guarantees of the Bill of Rights have been enlarged and nationalized. On a selective, incremental, case-by-case basis in the early and middle twentieth century the Court applied them to the states via incorporation into the due process clause of the Fourteenth Amendment. In addition, in *Griswold v. Connecticut* the Court interpreted various amendments—the First, Third, Fourth, Fifth, and Ninth Amendments—to secure an unenumerated but enforceable constitutional right of privacy, which also applies to the states. Table V.1 lists the guarantees enforceable against both the national government and the states.

Although the Supreme Court nationalized the Bill of Rights, a majority of the justices failed to agree on a justification for incorporating those provisions into the Fourteenth Amendment. This was due to shifting alliances among the justices, differing judicial philosophies, and the Court's changing composition. At one extreme, some justices—including Chief Justice John Marshall in *Barron v. Baltimore,* one of his last major decisions—maintained that the Bill of Rights as ratified applies only to the national government. After the adoption of the Fourteenth Amendment in 1868, however, some justices contended that congressional leaders intended the amendment to incorporate and apply the guarantees of the Bill of Rights to the states. The first Justice John Marshall Harlan, for one, thus urged the "total incorporation" of the Bill of Rights.[9] Drawing inspiration from Madison's libertarian precepts, as he explains in Chapter 31, Justice Black similarly advocates total incorporation and an "absolutist" interpretation of enumerated guarantees. In recognition of the history of the Bill of Rights and our dual constitutional system, most justices nonetheless tend to view incorporation as a matter of balancing particular liberties against state police powers and interests in law enforcement. Justice Cardozo contended that some but not all of the provisions of the Bill of Rights have a "preferred position" because they are "implicit in the concept of ordered liberty." He therefore urged the "selective incorporation" and extension of the First Amendment, for example, but not the Fourth Amendment's guarantee against "unreasonable searches and seizures."[10] In particular cases, Justice Felix Frankfurter argued that only those rights required by "fundamental fairness," or whose violation "shocks the conscience," are enforceable against the states.[11] At the other extreme, Justices Frank Murphy, Wiley Rutledge, and William Douglas advanced a position of "total incorporation-plus" other unenumerated yet allegedly "fundamental rights."[12]

Table V.1 The Nationalization of the Bill of Rights: A Process of Selective Incorporation-Plus

Amendment	*Year*	*Case*
V. "Fair use" and "just compensation"	1896	*Missouri Pacific Railway Co. v. Nebraska*
	1897	*Chicago B. & O. R.R. v. Chicago*
I. Freedom of speech	1927	*Fiske v. Kansas; Gitlow v. New York* (dictum, 1925)
I. Freedom of the press	1931	*Near v. Minnesota*
VI. Fair trial and right to counsel in capital cases	1932	*Powell v. Alabama*
I. Freedom of religion	1934	*Hamilton v. Regents of the U. of California* (dictum)
I. Freedom of assembly (and right to petition)	1937	*DeJonge v. Oregon*
I. Free exercise of religious belief	1940	*Cantwell v. Connecticut*
I. Separation of church and state	1947	*Everson v. Board of Education of Ewing Tp.*
VI. Right to public trial	1948	*In re Oliver*
IV. Right against unreasonable search and seizures	1949	*Wolf v. Colorado*
I. Freedom of association	1958	*NAACP v. Alabama*
IV. Exclusionary rule	1961	*Mapp v. Ohio*
VIII. Right against cruel and unusual punishment	1962	*Robinson v. California*
VI. Right to counsel in all felony cases	1963	*Gideon v. Wainwright*
V. Right against self-incrimination	1964	*Mallory v. Hogan*
VI. Right to confront witnesses	1965	*Pointer v. Texas*
I, III, IV, V, and IX. Right of privacy	1965	*Griswold v. Connecticut*
VI. Right to impartial jury	1966	*Parker v. Gladden*
VI. Right to speedy trial	1967	*Klopfer v. North Carolina*
VI. Right to compulsory process for obtaining witnesses	1967	*Washington v. Texas*
VI. Right to jury trial in serious crime	1968	*Duncan v. Louisiana*
V. Right against double jeopardy	1969	*Benton v. Maryland*
VI. Right to counsel in all criminal cases entailing a jail term	1972	*Argersinger v. Hamlin*

Note: The only provisions of the Bill of Rights that have not been extended to the states are the Second, Third, and Seventh amendments, as well as the Fifth Amendment's guarantee for indictment by a grand jury, and the Eighth Amendment's rights against excessive fines and bail.

The Supreme Court's nationalization of the Bill of Rights profoundly altered our dual constitutional system and the relationship between federal and state courts. With the increasing prominence of the federal judiciary, the role of state courts tends to be overshadowed. Yet the work of the Supreme Court and the federal judiciary, Justice Brennan appropriately cautioned, "must not divert attention from the vital importance of the work of the state courts in the administration of justice. Actually the composite work of the courts of the 50 states probably has greater significance in measuring how well America attains the ideal of equal justice for all." [13]

State courts continue to handle the overwhelming volume of all litigation—well over 90 percent of all filings. In 2007–2008, for instance, there were over 257,000 cases filed in federal district courts, and about 58,000 filed in federal appellate courts. By comparison, state courts faced more than an estimated 40 million cases. The type of litigation in state courts also tends to diverge from that in federal courts. Apart from criminal cases, the largest portion of state supreme court litigation, for instance, involves economic issues—whether relating to state regulation of public utilities, zoning, and small businesses, or labor relations and workers' compensation, natural resources, energy, and the environment. Litigation varies from state to state as well, depending on factors such as population size, urbanization, and socioeconomic conditions.

The important role of state courts in the administration of justice is underscored, as Justice Brennan emphasized, when we remind ourselves that the Supreme Court intrudes in state court policymaking in only a very narrow class of litigation—the class of cases in which the state courts deal with federal questions. Federal questions rarely emerge from the grist of the state courts. In Justice Brennan's words: "If cases were grains of sand, federal question cases would be hard to find on the beach. The final and vital decisions of most controversies upon which depend life, liberty, and property are made by the state courts." [14] If a case does not raise a substantial federal question or was decided on "adequate and independent state grounds" [15]—for example, a state constitution or bill of rights—then the Court declines review, respecting the principle of comity between federal and state judiciaries.

State courts thus continue to play a crucial role in the administration of justice, particularly as "guardians of our liberties" when interpreting and applying state constitutions and bills of rights. State bills of rights tend to be neglected due to the nationalization of the federal Bill of Rights. Yet Justices Brennan and Hans Linde of the Oregon State Supreme Court, in Chapters 32 and 33, respectively, argue that state courts should look first to their own bills of rights. This is so both because those guarantees historically precede the nationalization of the Bill of Rights, and because it is more appropriate to apply them first, given the logic of federalism and our dual constitutional system. Moreover, Justices Brennan and

Linde indicate that state courts need not always follow the leadership of federal courts, and that by interpreting their own state constitutions and bills of rights, state courts may chart their own boundaries for protecting civil rights and liberties, such as the Massachusetts state supreme court's ruling that its state constitution forbids discriminating against same-sex marriages, among other rulings. Finally, in Chapter 34 New York Court of Appeals chief judge Judith S. Kaye offers an assessment of the role of state courts in constitutional and statutory interpretation at "the dawn of a new century."

Notes

1. *West Virginia State Board of Education v. Barnette,* 319 U.S. 624, 638 (1943).
2. *Employment Division, Dept. of Human Resources of Oregon v. Smith,* 494 U.S. 872 (1990).
3. Alexander Hamilton, *The Federalist,* No. 84, at 513–514, ed. C. Rossiter, (New York: Mentor Books, 1961).
4. Thomas Jefferson, Letter from James Madison to Thomas Jefferson (October 17, 1788), *The Papers of Thomas Jefferson,* Vol. 14, at 16 and 18, ed. J. Boyd (Princeton: Princeton University Press, 1955).
5. Ibid., at 659.
6. Ibid.
7. *Annals of Congress,* Vol. 1, at 766 (Washington, D.C.: Gates and Seaton, 1834).
8. Benjamin N. Cardozo, "Paradoxes of Legal Science," in *Selected Writings of Benjamin Nathan Cardozo,* at 311, ed. M. Hall (New York: Fallon, 1947).
9. See *Hurtado v. California,* 110 U.S. 516 (1884).
10. See *Palko v. Connecticut,* 302 U.S. 319 (1937).
11. See *Adamson v. California,* 332 U.S. 46 (1947); and *Rochin v. California,* 342 U.S. 165 (1952).
12. See *Adamson v. California,* 332 U.S. 46 (1947) (Murphy, J., and Rutledge, J.); and *Griswold v. Connecticut,* 381 U.S. 479 (1965) (Douglas, J.).
13. William J. Brennan Jr., Address, Pennsylvania Bar Association (February 3, 1960), appearing in 31 *Pennsylvania Bar Association Quarterly* 393, 394 (1960).
14. Ibid., at 398.
15. See *Michigan v. Long,* 463 U.S. 1036 (1983).

CHAPTER 31

The Bill of Rights

Hugo L. Black
Justice, Supreme Court of the United States (1937–1971)

WHAT IS A BILL OF RIGHTS? In the popular sense it is any document setting forth the liberties of the people. I prefer to think of our Bill of Rights as including all provisions of the original Constitution and Amendments that protect individual liberty by barring government from acting in a particular area or from acting except under certain prescribed procedures. I have in mind such clauses in the body of the Constitution itself as those which safeguard the right of habeas corpus, forbid bills of attainder and ex post facto laws, guarantee trial by jury, and strictly define treason and limit the way it can be tried and punished. I would certainly add to this list the last constitutional prohibition in Article Six that "no religious Test shall ever be required as a Qualification to any Office or public Trust under the United States."

I shall speak to you about the Bill of Rights only as it bears on powers of the Federal Government. Originally, the first ten amendments were not intended to apply to the states but, as the Supreme Court held in 1883 in *Barron v. Baltimore,*[1] were adopted to quiet fears extensively entertained that the powers of the big new national government "might be exercised in a manner dangerous to liberty." I believe that by virtue of the Fourteenth Amendment, the first ten amendments are now applicable to the states, a view I stated in *Adamson v. California.*[2] I adhere to that view. In this talk, however, I want to discuss only the extent to which the Bill of Rights limits the Federal Government.

In applying the Bill of Rights to the Federal Government there is today a sharp difference of views as to how far its provisions should be held to limit the lawmaking

---

Acknowledgment to New York University Law Review *for permission to reprint excerpts from Justice Hugo L. Black's article "The Bill of Rights," from 35* New York University Law Review *865 (1960).*

power of Congress. How this difference is finally resolved will, in my judgment, have far-reaching consequences upon our liberties. I shall first summarize what those different views are.

Some people regard the prohibitions of the Constitution, even its most unequivocal commands, as mere admonitions which Congress need not always observe. This viewpoint finds many different verbal expressions. For example, it is sometimes said that Congress may abridge a constitutional right if there is a clear and present danger that the free exercise of the right will bring about a substantive evil that Congress has authority to prevent. Or it is said that a right may be abridged where its exercise would cause so much injury to the public that this injury would outweigh the injury to the individual who is deprived of the right. Again, it is sometimes said that the Bill of Rights' guarantees must "compete" for survival against general powers expressly granted to Congress and that the individual's right must, if outweighed by the public interest, be subordinated to the Government's competing interest in denying the right. All of these formulations, and more with which you are doubtless familiar, rest, at least in part, on the premise that there are no "absolute" prohibitions in the Constitution, and that all constitutional problems are questions of reasonableness, proximity, and degree. This view comes close to the English doctrine of legislative omnipotence, qualified only by the possibility of a judicial veto if the Supreme Court finds that a congressional choice between "competing" policies has no reasonable basis.

I cannot accept this approach to the Bill of Rights. It is my belief that there *are* "absolutes" in our Bill of Rights, and that they were put there on purpose by men who knew what words meant, and meant their prohibitions to be "absolutes." The whole history and background of the Constitution and Bill of Rights, as I understand it, belies the assumption or conclusion that our ultimate constitutional freedoms are no more than our English ancestors had when they came to this new land to get new freedoms. The historical and practical purposes of a Bill of Rights, the very use of a written constitution, indigenous to America, the language the Framers used, the kind of three-department government they took pains to set up, all point to the creation of a government which was denied all power to do some things under any and all circumstances, and all power to do other things except precisely in the manner prescribed.

The form of government which was ordained and established in 1789 contains certain unique features which reflected the Framers' fear of arbitrary government and which clearly indicate an intention absolutely to limit what Congress could do. The first of these features is that our Constitution is written in a single document. Such constitutions are familiar today and it is not always remembered that our country was the first to have one. Certainly one purpose of a written constitution is to define and therefore more specifically limit government powers. An all-powerful government that can act as it pleases wants no such constitution—unless to fool the people. England had no written constitution and this once proved a source of tyranny, as our ancestors well knew. Jefferson said about this departure from the English type of government: "Our peculiar security is in possession of a written Constitution. Let us not make it a blank paper by construction."[3]

A second unique feature of our Government is a Constitution supreme over the legislature. In England, statutes, Magna Charta, and later declarations of rights had for centuries limited the power of the King, but they did not limit the power of Parliament. Although commonly referred to as a constitution, they were never the "supreme law of the land" in the way in which our Constitution is, much to the regret of statesmen like Pitt the elder. Parliament could change this English "Constitution"; Congress cannot change ours. Ours can only be changed by amendments ratified by three-fourths of the states. It was one of the great achievements of our Constitution that it ended legislative omnipotence here and placed all departments and agencies of government under one supreme law.

A third feature of our Government expressly designed to limit its powers was the division of authority into three coordinate branches none of which was to have supremacy over the others. This separation of powers with the checks and balances which each branch was given over the others was designed to prevent any branch, including the legislative, from infringing individual liberties safeguarded by the Constitution.

Finally, our Constitution was the first to provide a really independent judiciary. Moreover, as the Supreme Court held in *Marbury v. Madison,*[4] correctly I believe, this judiciary has the power to hold legislative enactments void that are repugnant to the Constitution and the Bill of Rights. In this country the judiciary was made independent because it has, I believe, the primary responsibility and duty of giving force and effect to constitutional liberties and limitations upon the executive and legislative branches. Judges in England were not always independent and they could not hold Parliamentary acts void. Consequently, English courts could not be counted on to protect the liberties of the people against invasion by the Parliament, as many unfortunate Englishmen found out, such as Sir Walter Raleigh, who was executed as the result of an unfair trial, and a lawyer named William Prynne, whose ears were first cut off by court order and who subsequently, by another court order, had his remaining ear stumps gouged out while he was on a pillory. Prynne's offenses were writing books and pamphlets.

All of the unique features of our Constitution show an underlying purpose to create a new kind of limited government. Central to all of the Framers of the Bill of Rights was the idea that since government, particularly the national government newly created, is a powerful institution, its officials—all of them—must be compelled to exercise their powers within strictly defined boundaries. As Madison told Congress, the Bill of Rights' limitations point "sometimes against the abuse of the Executive power, sometimes against the Legislative, and in some cases against the community itself; or, in other words, against the majority in favor of the minority."[5] Madison also explained that his proposed amendments were intended "to limit and qualify the powers of Government, by excepting out of the grant of power those cases in which the Government ought not to act, or to act only in a particular mode."[6] In the light of this purpose let us now turn to the language of the first ten amendments to consider whether their provisions were written as mere admonitions to Congress or as absolute commands, proceeding for convenience from the last to the first.

The last two Amendments, the Ninth and Tenth, are general in character, but both emphasize the limited nature of the Federal Government. Number Ten restricts federal power to what the Constitution delegates to the central government, reserving all other powers to the states or to the people. Number Nine attempts to make certain that enumeration of some rights must "not be construed to deny or disparage others retained by the people." The use of the words, "the people," in both these Amendments strongly emphasizes the desire of the Framers to protect individual liberty.

The Seventh Amendment states that "in Suits at common law, where the value in controversy shall exceed twenty dollars, the right of trial by jury shall be preserved. . . ." This language clearly requires that jury trials must be afforded in the type of cases the Amendment describes. The Amendment goes on in equally unequivocal words to command that "no fact tried by a jury, shall be otherwise re-examined in any Court of the United States, than according to the rules of the common law."

Amendments Five, Six, and Eight relate chiefly to the procedures that government must follow when bringing its powers to bear against any person with a view to depriving him of his life, liberty, or property.

The Eighth Amendment forbids "excessive bail," "excessive fines," or the infliction of "cruel and unusual punishments." This is one of the less precise provisions. The courts are required to determine the meaning of such general terms as "excessive" and "unusual." But surely that does not mean that admittedly "excessive bail," "excessive fines," or "cruel punishments" could be justified on the ground of a "competing" public interest in carrying out some generally granted power like that given to Congress to regulate commerce.

Amendment Six provides that in a criminal prosecution an accused shall have a "speedy and public trial, by an impartial jury of the State and district wherein the crime shall have been committed, which district shall have been previously ascertained by law, and to be informed of the nature and cause of the accusation; to be confronted with the witnesses against him; to have compulsory process for obtaining witnesses in his favor, and have the Assistance of Counsel for his defence." All of these requirements are cast in terms both definite and absolute. Trial by jury was also guaranteed in the original Constitution. The additions here, doubtless prompted by English trials of Americans away from their homes, are that a trial must be "speedy and public," "by an impartial jury," and in a district which "shall have been previously ascertained by law." If there is any one thing that is certain it is that the Framers intended both in the original Constitution and in the Sixth Amendment that persons charged with crime by the Federal Government have a right to be tried by jury. Suppose juries began acquitting people Congress thought should be convicted. Could Congress then provide some other form of trial, say by an administrative agency, or the military, where convictions could be more readily and certainly obtained, if it thought the safety of the nation so required? How about secret trials? By *partial* juries? Can it be that these are not absolute prohibitions?

The Sixth Amendment requires notice of the cause of an accusation, confrontation by witnesses, compulsory process, and assistance of counsel. The experience of centuries has demonstrated the value of these procedures to one on trial for crime. And this Amendment purports to guarantee them by clear language. But if there are no absolutes in the Bill of Rights, these guarantees too can be taken away by Congress on findings that a competing public interest requires that defendants be tried without notice, without witnesses, without confrontation, and without counsel.

The Fifth Amendment provides:

> No person shall be held to answer for a capital, or otherwise infamous crime, unless on a presentment of indictment of a Grand Jury, except in cases arising in the land or naval forces, or in the Militia, when in actual service in time of War or public danger; nor shall any person be subject for the same offence to be twice put in jeopardy of life or limb; nor shall be compelled in any criminal case to be a witness against himself, nor be deprived of life, liberty, or property without due process of law; nor shall private property be taken for public use, without just compensation.

Most of these Fifth Amendment prohibitions are both definite and unequivocal. There has been much controversy about the meaning of "due process of law." Whatever its meaning, however, there can be no doubt that it must be granted. Moreover, few doubt that it has an historical meaning which denies Government the right to take away life, liberty, or property without trials properly conducted according to the Constitution and laws validly made in accordance with it. This, at least, was the meaning of "due process of law" when used in Magna Charta and other old English Statutes where it was referred to as "the law of the land."

The Fourth Amendment provides:

> The right of the people to be secure in their persons, houses, papers, and effects, against unreasonable searches and seizures, shall not be violated, and no Warrants

> shall issue, but upon probable cause, supported by Oath of affirmation, and particularly describing the place to be searched, and the persons or things to be seized.

The use of the word "unreasonable" in this Amendment means, of course, that not *all* searches and seizures are prohibited. Only those which are *unreasonable* are unlawful. There may be much difference of opinion about whether a particular search or seizure is unreasonable and therefore forbidden by this Amendment. But if it *is* unreasonable, it is absolutely prohibited.

Likewise, the provision which forbids warrants for arrest, search, or seizure without "probable cause" is itself an absolute prohibition.

The Third Amendment provides that:

> No Soldier shall, in time of peace be quartered in any house, without the consent of the Owner, nor in time of war, but in a manner to be prescribed by law.

Americans had recently suffered from the quartering of British troops in their homes, and so this Amendment is written in language that apparently no one has ever thought could be violated on the basis of an overweighing public interest.

Amendment Two provides that:

> A well regulated Militia, being necessary to the security of a free State, the right of the people to keep and bear Arms, shall not be infringed.

Although the Supreme Court has held this Amendment to include only arms necessary to a well-regulated militia, as so construed, its prohibition is absolute.

This brings us to the First Amendment. It reads:

> Congress shall make no law respecting an establishment of religion, or prohibiting the free exercise thereof; or abridging the freedom of speech, or of the press; or the right of the people peaceably to assemble, and to petition the Government for a redress of grievances.

The phrase "Congress shall make no law" is composed of plain words, easily understood. The Framers knew this. The language used by Madison in his proposal was different, but no less emphatic and unequivocal. That proposal is worth reading:

> The civil rights of none shall be abridged on account of religious belief or worship, nor shall any national religion be established, nor shall the full and equal rights of conscience be in any manner, or on any pretext, infringed.

> The people shall not be deprived or abridged of their right to speak, to write, or to publish their sentiments; and the freedom of the press, as one of the great bulwarks of liberty, shall be inviolable.
>
> The people shall not be restrained from peaceably assembling and consulting for their common good; nor from applying to the Legislature by petitions, or remonstrances, for redress of their grievances.[7]

Neither as offered nor as adopted is the language of this Amendment anything less than absolute. Madison was emphatic about this. He told the Congress that under it "the right of freedom of speech is secured; the liberty of the press is expressly declared to be *beyond the reach of this Government.*"[8] Some years later Madison wrote that "it would seem scarcely possible to doubt that *no power whatever* over the press was supposed to be delegated by the Constitution, as it originally stood, and that the amendment was intended as a *positive and absolute reservation of it.*"[9] With reference to the positive nature of the First Amendment's command against infringement of religious liberty, Madison later said that "there is not a shadow of right in the general government to intermeddle with religion,"[10] and that "this subject is, for the honor of America, perfectly free and unshackled. The *government has no jurisdiction over it.*"[11]

To my way of thinking, at least, the history and language of the Constitution and the Bill of Rights, which I have discussed with you, make it plain that one of the primary purposes of the Constitution with its amendments was to withdraw from the Government all power to act in certain areas—whatever the scope of those areas may be. If I am right in this then there is, at least in those areas, no justification whatever for "balancing" a particular right against some expressly granted power of Congress. If the Constitution withdraws from Government all power over subject matter in an area, such as religion, speech, press, assembly, and petition, there is nothing over which authority may be exerted.

For my own part, I believe that our Constitution, with its absolute guarantees of individual rights, is the best hope for the aspirations of freedom which men share everywhere. I cannot agree with those who think of the Bill of Rights as an eighteenth-century straitjacket, unsuited for this age. It is old but not all old things are bad. The evils it guards against are not only old, they are with us now, they exist today. Almost any morning you open your daily paper you can see where some person somewhere in the world is on trial or has just been convicted of supposed disloyalty to a new group controlling the government which has set out to purge its suspected enemies and all those who had dared to be against its successful march to power. Nearly always you see that these political heretics are being tried by military tribunals or some other summary and sure method for disposition of the accused. Now and then we even see the convicted victims as they march to their execution.

Experience all over the world has demonstrated, I fear, that the distance between stable, orderly government and one that has been taken over by force is not so great as we have assumed. Our own free system to live and progress has to have intelligent citizens, citizens who cannot only think and speak and write to influence people, but citizens who are free to do that without fear of governmental censorship or reprisal.

The provisions of the Bill of Rights that safeguard fair legal procedures came about largely to protect the weak and the oppressed from punishment by the strong and the powerful who wanted to stifle the voices of discontent raised in protest against oppression and injustice in public affairs. Nothing that I have read in the Congressional debates on the Bill of Rights indicates that there was any belief that the First Amendment contained any qualifications. The only arguments that tended to look in this direction at all were those that said "that all paper barriers against the power of the community are too weak to be worthy of attention."[12] Suggestions were also made in and out of Congress that a Bill of Rights would be a futile gesture since there would be no way to enforce the safeguards for freedom it provided. Mr. Madison answered this argument in these words:

> If they [the Bill of Rights amendments] are incorporated into the Constitution, independent tribunals of justice will consider themselves in a peculiar manner the guardians of those rights; they will be an impenetrable bulwark against any assumption of power in the Legislative or Executive; they will be naturally led to resist every encroachment upon rights expressly stipulated for in the Constitution by the declaration of rights.[13]

I fail to see how courts can escape this sacred trust.

Notes

1. 32 U.S. (7 Pet.) 242, 249 (1833).
2. 332 U.S. 46, 71–72 (1947) (dis. op.)
3. T. Jefferson, *Writings*, Vol. 4, 506 (Washington ed., 1859).
4. 5 U.S. (1 Cranch) 137 (1803).
5. 1 *Annals of Cong.* 437 (1789).
6. Ibid.
7. 1 *Annals of Cong.* 434 (1789).
8. 1 *Annals of Cong.* 738 (1789) (emphases added in all quotations).
9. J. Madison, *Writings*, Vol. 6, 391 (Hunt ed., 1906).
10. J. Madison, *Writings*, Vol. 5, 176 (Hunt ed., 1904).
11. Ibid., at 132.
12. 1 *Annals of Cong.* 437 (1789).
13. 1 *Annals of Cong.* 439 (1789).

CHAPTER 32

Guardians of Our Liberties—State Courts No Less Than Federal

William J. Brennan Jr.
Justice, Supreme Court of the United States (1956–1990) and Justice, Supreme Court of New Jersey (1952–1956)

Over the past two decades, decisions of the Supreme Court of the United States have returned to the fundamental promises wrought by the blood of those who fought our War between the States, promises which were thereafter embodied in our Fourteenth Amendment—that the citizens of all our States are also and no less citizens of our United States, that this birthright guarantees our federal constitutional liberties against encroachment by governmental action at any level of our federal system, and that each of us is entitled to due process of law and the equal protection of the laws from our state governments no less than our national one. Although courts do not today substitute their personal economic beliefs for the judgments of our democratically elected Legislatures, Supreme Court decisions under the Fourteenth Amendment have significantly affected virtually every other area, civil and criminal, of state action. And while these decisions have been accompanied by the enforcement of federal rights by federal courts, they have significantly altered the work of state court judges as well. This is both necessary and desirable under our federal system—state courts no less than federal are and ought to be the guardians of our liberties.

The decisions of the Supreme Court enforcing the protections of the Fourteenth Amendment generally fall into one of three categories. The first concerns enforcement of the federal guarantee of equal protection of the laws. The best

---

Acknowledgment to Justice William J. Brennan Jr. for his address before the New Jersey State Bar Association, appearing in 15 The Judges' Journal *82 (1976).*

known of course are *Brown v. Board of Education,*[1] invalidating state laws requiring public schools to be racially segregated, and *Baker v. Carr,*[2] and its progeny,[3] which invalidated state laws diluting individual voting rights by legislative malapportionments. But perhaps even more the concern of state bench and bar, in terms of state court litigation, are decisions invalidating state legislative classifications that impermissibly impinge on the exercise of fundamental rights, such as the rights to vote,[4] and to travel interstate,[5] or to bear or beget a child,[6] and decisions that require exacting judicial scrutiny of classifications that operate to the peculiar disadvantage of politically powerless groups whose members have historically been subjected to purposeful discrimination—racial minorities[7] and aliens[8] are two examples.

The second category of decisions concern the Fourteenth Amendment's guarantee against the deprivation of life, liberty or property where that deprivation is without due process of law. The root requirement of due process is that, except for some extraordinary situations, an individual be given an opportunity for a hearing before he is deprived of any significant "liberty" or "property" interest. Our decisions enforcing the guarantee of the Due Process Clause have elaborated the essence of "liberty" and "property" in light of conditions existing in contemporary society. For example, "property" has come to embrace such crucial expectations as a driver's license[9] and the statutory entitlement to minimal economic support, in the form of welfare, of those who by accident or birth or circumstance find themselves without the means of subsistence.[10] The due process safeguard against arbitrary deprivation of these entitlements, as well as of more traditional forms of property, such as a workingman's wages[11] and his continued possession and use of goods purchased under conditional sales contracts[12] has been recognized as mandating prior notice and the opportunity to be heard. At the same time, conceptions of "liberty" have come to recognize the undeniable proposition that prisoners and parolees retain some vestiges of human dignity, so that prison regulations and parole procedures must provide some form of notice and hearing prior to confinement in solitary[13] or the revocation of parole.[14] Moreover, the concepts of liberty and property have combined in recognizing that under modern conditions tenured public employees may not have their reasonable expectation of continued employment,[15] and school children their right to a public education,[16] revoked without notice and opportunity to be heard.

I suppose, however, that it is mostly the third category of decisions by the United States Supreme Court during the last 20 years—enforcing the specific guarantees of the Bill of Rights against encroachment by state action—that has required the special consideration of state judges, particularly as those decisions affect the administration of the criminal justice system.

After his retirement, Chief Justice Earl Warren was asked what he regarded to be the decision during his tenure that would have the greatest consequence for all Americans. His choice was *Baker v. Carr,* because he believed that if each of us has an equal vote, we are equally armed with the indispensable means to make our views felt. I feel at least as good a case can be made that the series of decisions binding the States to almost all of the restraints of the Bill of Rights will be even more significant in preserving and furthering the ideals we have fashioned for our society. Before the Fourteenth Amendment was added to the Constitution, the Supreme Court held that the Bill of Rights did not restrict state, but only federal, action.[17] In the decades between 1868, when the Fourteenth Amendment was adopted, and 1897, the Court decided in case after case that the Fourteenth Amendment did not apply various specific restraints in the Bill of Rights to state action.[18] The breakthrough came in 1897 when prohibition against taking private property for public use without payment of just compensation was held embodied in the Fourteenth Amendment's proscription, "nor shall any state deprive any person of ... property, without due process of law."[19] But extension of the rest of the specific restraints was slow in coming. It was 1925 before it was suggested that perhaps the restraints of the First Amendment applied to state action.[20] Then in 1949 the Fourth Amendment's prohibition of unreasonable searches and seizures was extended,[21] but the extension was virtually meaningless because the States were left free to decide for themselves whether any effective means of enforcement of the guarantee was to be made available. It was not until 1961 that the Court applied the exclusionary rule to state proceedings.[22]

But the years from 1962 to 1969 witnessed the extension of nine of the specifics of the Bill of Rights, and these decisions have had a profound impact on American life, requiring the deep involvement of state courts in the application of federal law. The Eighth Amendment's prohibition of cruel and unusual punishment was applied to state action in 1962,[23] and is the guarantee under which the death penalty as then administered was struck down in 1972.[24] The provision of the Sixth Amendment that in all prosecutions the accused shall have the assistance of counsel was applied in 1963 and in consequence counsel must be provided in every courtroom of every State of this land to secure the rights of those accused of crime.[25] In 1964, the Fifth Amendment privilege against compulsory self-incrimination was extended.[26] And after decades of police coercion, by means ranging from torture to trickery, the privilege against self-incrimination became the basis of *Miranda v. Arizona*, requiring police to give warnings to a suspect before custodial interrogation.[27]

The year 1965 saw the extension of the Sixth Amendment right of an accused to be confronted by the witnesses against him;[28] in 1967 three more guarantees of the Sixth Amendment—the right to a speedy and public trial, the right to a trial by an impartial jury, and the right to have compulsory process for obtaining witnesses were extended.[29] In 1969 the double jeopardy clause of the Fifth Amendment was applied.[30] Moreover, the decisions barring state-required prayers in public schools,[31] limiting the availability of state libel laws to public officials and public figures,[32] and confirming that a right of association is implicitly protected,[33] are significant restraints upon state action that resulted from the extension of the specifics of the First Amendment.

These decisions over the past two decades gave full effect to the principle of *Boyd v. United States,*[34] the case Mr. Justice Brandeis hailed as "a case that will be remembered so long as civil liberty lives in the United States."[35] It is a matter of pride to all of us from New Jersey that *Boyd* was written by Mr. Justice Bradley who was appointed to the Supreme Court from our State. The *Boyd* principle stated by Mr. Justice Bradley was: "... constitutional provisions for the security of person and property should be liberally construed. It is the duty of courts to be watchful for the constitutional rights of the citizen, and against any stealthy encroachment thereon."[36]

The thread of this series of holding that the Fourteenth Amendment guarantees citizens the protections of the Bill of Rights in confrontations with state action reflects a conclusion—arrived at only after a long series of decisions grappling with the pros and cons of the question—that there exists in modern America the necessity for protecting all of us from arbitrary action by governments more powerful and pervasive than in our ancestors' time, and that the protections must be construed to preserve their fundamental policies, and thereby the maintenance of our constitutional structure of government for a free society.

For the genius of our Constitution resides not in any static meaning that it had in a world that is dead and gone, but in the adaptability of its great principles to cope with the problems of a developing America. A principle to be vital must be of wider application than the mischief that gave it birth. Constitutions are not ephemeral documents, designed to meet passing occasions. The future is their care, and therefore, in their application, our contemplation cannot be only of what has been but of what may be.

Of late, however, more and more state courts are construing state constitutional counterparts of provisions of the Bill of Rights as guaranteeing citizens of their States even more protection than the federal provisions, even those identically phrased. This is surely an important and highly significant development for our constitutional jurisprudence and for our concept of federalism. I suppose it was only natural that when during the 1960s our rights and liberties were in the process of becoming increasingly federalized, state courts saw no reason to consider what protections, if any, were secured by state constitutions. It isn't easy to pinpoint why state courts are beginning to emphasize the protections of their States' own Bill of Rights. It may not be wide of the mark, however, to suppose that these state courts discern in recent opinions of the United States Supreme Court, and disagree with, a pulling back from, or at least, a suspension for the time being of the enforcement of the *Boyd* principle in respect of application of the federal Bill of Rights and the restraints of the Due Process and Equal Protection Clauses of the Fourteenth Amendment. Under the Equal Protection Clause, for example, the Court has found permissible laws that accord lesser protection to over half of the members of our society due to their susceptibility to the medical condition of pregnancy.[37] The Court has found uncompelling the claims of those barred from judicial forums due to their inability to pay access fees.[38]

Under the Due Process Clause, it has found no liberty interest in the reputation of an individual—never-tried and never-convicted—who is publicly branded as a criminal by the police without benefit of notice, let alone hearing.[39] The Court has recently indicated that tenured public employees might not be entitled to any more process before deprivation of their employment than the Government sees fit to give them.[40] It has approved the termination of payments to disabled individuals completely dependent upon those payments prior to an oral hearing, a form of hearing statistically shown to result in a huge rate of reversals of preliminary administrative determinations.[41]

In the category of the specific guarantees of the Bill of Rights, the Court has found the First Amendment insufficiently flexible to guarantee access to essential public forums when in our evolving society those traditional forums are under private ownership in the form of suburban shopping centers.[42] It has found that the warrant requirement plainly appearing on the face of the Fourth Amendment does not require the police to obtain a warrant before arrest, however easy it might have been to get an arrest warrant.[43] It has declined to read the Fourth Amendment to prohibit searches of an individual by police officers following a stop for a traffic violation, although there exists no probable cause to believe the individual has committed any other legal infraction.[44] The Court has found permissible police searches grounded upon consent regardless of whether the consent was a knowing and intelligent one.[45] The Court has found that none of us has a legitimate expectation of privacy in the contents of our bank records, thus permitting governmental seizure of those records without our knowledge or consent.[46]

Moreover, the Court has held, contrary to *Boyd v. United States*, that we may not interpose the privilege against self-incrimination to bar Government attempts to obtain our personal papers, no matter how private the nature of their contents.[47] The Court has held that the privilege against self-incrimination is not violated when statements unconstitutionally obtained from an individual are used for purposes of impeaching his testimony,[48] or securing his indictment by a grand jury.[49]

The Sixth Amendment guarantee of assistance of counsel has been held not available to an accused in custody when shuffled through pre-indictment identification procedures, no matter how essential counsel might be to the avoidance of prejudice to his rights at later stages of the criminal process.[50] And in the face of our requirement of proof of guilt beyond a reasonable doubt, the Court has upheld the permissibility of less than unanimous jury verdicts of guilty.[51]

Also a series of decisions have shaped the doctrines of jurisdiction, justiciability, and remedy, so as increasingly to bar the federal courthouse door in the absence of showings probably impossible to make.[52] It is true of course that there has been an increasing amount of litigation of all types filling the calendars of virtually every state and federal court. But a solution that shuts the courthouse door in the face of the litigant with a legitimate claim for relief, particularly a claim of deprivation of a constitutional right, seems to be not only the wrong tool but also a dangerous tool for solving the problem. The victims of the use of that tool are most often the litigants most in need of judicial protection of their rights—the poor, the underprivileged, the deprived minorities. The very life blood of courts is popular confidence that they mete out even-handed justice, and any discrimination that denies these groups access to the courts for resolution of their meritorious claims unnecessarily risks loss of that confidence.

Some state decisions have indeed suggested a connection between these recent decisions of the United States Supreme Court and the state court's reliance on the state's Bill of Rights. For example, the California Supreme Court recently held that statements taken from suspects before first giving them *Miranda* warnings are inadmissible in California courts to impeach an accused who testifies in his own defense; and stated: "We declare that [the decision to the contrary of the U.S. Supreme Court] is not persuasive authority in any state prosecution in California.... We pause to reaffirm the independent nature of the California Constitution and our responsibility to separately define and protect the rights of California citizens despite conflicting decisions of the United States Supreme Court interpreting the federal Constitution."[53]

Other examples abound where state courts have independently considered the merits of constitutional arguments and declined to follow opinions of the United States Supreme Court they find unconvincing, even where the state and federal constitutions are similarly or identically phrased. As the Supreme Court of Hawaii has observed, "while this results in a divergence of meaning between words which are the same in both federal and state constitutions, the system of federalism envisaged by the United States Constitution tolerates such divergence where the result is greater protection of individual rights under state law than under federal law...."[54]

And of course state courts that rest their decisions wholly or even partly on state law need not apply federal principles of standing and justiciability that deny litigants access to the courts. Moreover, the state decisions not only cannot be overturned by, they indeed are not even reviewable by, the Supreme Court of the United States. We are utterly without jurisdiction to review such state decisions.[55]

Some state courts seem apparently even to be anticipating contrary rulings by the United States Supreme Court and are therefore resting decisions on state law grounds to avoid review. For example, the California Supreme Court held, as a matter of state constitutional law, that bank depositors have a sufficient expectation of privacy in their bank records to invalidate the voluntary disclosure of such records by a bank to the police without the knowledge or consent of the depositor;[56] thereafter the United States Supreme Court ruled that Federal law was to the contrary.[57]

This development puts to rest the notion that state constitutional provisions were adopted to mirror the federal Bill of Rights. The lesson of history is otherwise; indeed, the drafters of the federal Bill of Rights drew upon corresponding provisions in the various state constitutions. Prior to the adoption of the Federal Constitution, each of the rights eventually recognized in the federal Bill of Rights had previously been protected in one or more state constitutions.[58]

The essential point I am making, of course, is not that the United States Supreme Court is necessarily wrong in its interpretation of the Federal Constitution, or that ultimate constitutional truths invariably come prepackaged in the dissents, including my own, from decisions of the Court. It is simply that the decisions of the Court are not dispositive of questions regarding rights guaranteed by counterpart provisions of state law.

Notes

1. *Brown v. Board of Education*, 347 U.S. 483 (1954).
2. *Baker v. Carr*, 269 U.S. 186 (1962).
3. *Reynolds v. Sims*, 377 U.S. 533 (1964).
4. *Harper v. Va. State Board*, 383 U.S. 663 (1966).
5. *Shapiro v. Thompson*, 394 U.S. 618 (1969).
6. *Eisenstadt v. Baird*, 405 U.S. 438 (1972); *Griswold v. Connecticut*, 381 U.S. 479 (1965).
7. *Brown v. Board of Education*, 347 U.S. 483 (1954).
8. *Sugarman v. Dougall*, 413 U.S. 634 (1973).
9. *Bell v. Burston*, 402 U.S. 535 (1971).
10. *Goldberg v. Kelly*, 397 U.S. 254 (1970).
11. *Sniadach v. Family Finance Corp.*, 395 U.S. 337 (1969).
12. *Fuentes v. Shevin*, 407 U.S. 67 (1972).
13. *Wolf v. McDonnell*, 418 U.S. 539 (1974).
14. *Morrissey v. Brewer*, 408 U.S. 471 (1972).
15. *Perry v. Sinderman*, 408 U.S. 593 (1972).
16. *Goss v. Lopez*, 419 U.S. 565 (1975).
17. *Barron v. Baltimore*, 32 U.S. (7 Pet.) 243 (1833).
18. See *Walker v. Sauvinet*, 92 U.S. 90 (1875); *United States v. Cruikshank*, 92 U.S. 542, 552–556 (1875); *Hurtado v. California*, 110 U.S. 516 (1884); *Presser v. Illinois*, 116 U.S. 252, 263–268 (1886); *In re Kemmler*, 136 U.S. 436, 448, (1890); *McElvaine v. Brush*, 142 U.S. 155, 158–159 (1891); *O'Neil v. Vermont*, 144 U.S. 323, 332 (1892).
19. *Chicago B. & Q. R.R. v. Chicago*, 166 U.S. 226, 241 (1897).
20. *Gitlow v. New York*, 268 U.S. 652, 666 (1925); compare *Prudential Insurance Co. v. Cheek*, 259 U.S. 530, 543 (1922).

21. *Wolf v. Colorado*, 338 U.S. 25, 27–28 (1949).
22. *Mapp v. Ohio*, 367 U.S. 643 (1961).
23. *Robinson v. California*, 370 U.S. 660 (1962).
24. *Furman v. Georgia*, 408 U.S. 238 (1972).
25. *Gideon v. Wainwright*, 372 U.S. 335 (1963); *Argersinger v. Hamlin*, 407 U.S. 25 (1972).
26. *Mallory v. Hogan*, 378 U.S. 1 (1964).
27. *Miranda v. Arizona*, 384 U.S. 436 (1966).
28. *Pointer v. Texas*, 380 U.S. 400 (1965).
29. *Klopfer v. North Carolina*, 386 U.S. 213 (1967); *Parker v. Gladden*, 385 U.S. 363 (1966); *Washington v. Texas*, 388 U.S. 14 (1967).
30. *Benton v. Maryland*, 395 U.S. 784 (1969).
31. *School District of Abinton v. Schempp*, 374 U.S. 203 (1963).
32. *New York Times v. Sullivan*, 376 U.S. 254 (1964).
33. *NAACP v. Alabama*, 377 U.S. 288 (1964).
34. *Boyd v. United States*, 116 U.S. 616 (1886).
35. *Olmstead v. United States*, 277 U.S. 438, 474 (1928) (dis. op.).
36. *Boyd v. United States*, 116 U.S., at 635 (1886).
37. *Geduldig v. Aiello*, 417 U.S. 484 (1974).
38. *Ortwein v. Schwab*, 410 U.S. 656 (1973); *United States v. Kras*, 409 U.S. 434 (1973).
39. *Paul v. Davis*, 96 S. Ct. 1155 (1976).
40. *Arnett v. Kennedy*, 416 U.S. 134 (1974).
41. *Matthews v. Eldridge*, 424 U.S. 319 (1976).
42. *Hudgens v. NLRB*, 424 U.S. 507 (1976); *Lloyd Corp., Ltd. v. Tanner*, 407 U.S. 551 (1972).
43. *United States v. Watson*, 423 U.S. 411 (1976).
44. *United States v. Robinson*, 414 U.S. 218 (1973); *Gustafson v. Florida*, 414 U.S. 260 (1973).
45. *Schneckloth v. Bustamonte*, 412 U.S. 218 (1973); *United States v. Watson*, 423 U.S. 411 (1976).
46. *United States v. Miller*, 96 S. Ct. 1619 (1976).
47. *Fisher v. United States*, 96 S. Ct. 1569 (1976).
48. *Harris v. New York*, 401 U.S. 222 (1971).
49. *United States v. Calandra*, 414 U.S. 338 (1974).
50. *Kirby v. Illinois*, 406 U.S. 682 (1972).
51. *Apodaca v. Oregon*, 406 U.S. 404 (1972).
52. *Rizzo v. Goode*, 96 S. Ct. 598 (1976); *Warth v. Seldin*, 422 U.S. 490 (1975); *O'Shea v. Littleton*, 414 U.S. 488 (1974).
53. *People v. Disbrow*, 127 Cal. Rptr. 360, 545 P.2d 272 (1976).
54. *State v. Kaluna*, 520 P.2d 51, 58 n.6 (Hawaii 1974).
55. *Murdock v. City of Memphis*, 20 Wall. 590 (1875).
56. *Burrows v. Superior Court*, 13 Cal. 3d 238, 529 P.2d 590 (1974).
57. *United States v. Miller*, 96 S. Ct. 1619 (1976).
58. See generally W. Brennan, "The Bill of Rights and the States," in *The Great Rights*, ed. E. Cahn 71–72 (New York: Macmillan, 1963).

CHAPTER 33

First Things First

Rediscovering the States' Bills of Rights

Hans A. Linde

Justice, Oregon State Supreme Court (1977–1990)

STATE BILLS OF RIGHTS are first in two senses:first in time and first in logic.

History

It was not unheard of in 1776, long before the drafting of the Federal Constitution, for the revolutionaries of that day to declare in the charters of their new states that the liberty of the press should be inviolably preserved, or that warrants to search any place or to seize any person or property must be based on information under oath and describing the place or the person. Nor was it unusual in these charters to grant every criminal defendant a right to a speedy trial before an impartial jury, with the assistance of counsel, to confront and question the witnesses against him, not to be compelled to give evidence against himself, nor to be subjected to excessive bail or fines nor to cruel or unusual punishment.[1]

By 1783, 13 states, all but Rhode Island, had adopted written constitutions. The majority of them contained most of the catalogue of civil liberties included in Virginia's Declaration of Rights, and Maryland's, and Delaware's, and Pennsylvania's. But they were by no means identical.[2] That was no accident. During the months preceding independence, political leaders debated the case for having the Continental Congress prepare uniform constitutions for the states. They finally

Acknowledgment to Justice Hans A. Linde for excerpts from his lecture at the University of Baltimore School of Law (May 16, 1979), which appears in 9 University of Baltimore Law Review *379 (1980).*

rejected this idea in favor of calling upon each state to write a constitution satisfactory to itself.[3]

Far from being the model for the states, the Federal Bill of Rights was added to the Constitution to meet demands for the same guarantees against the new central government that people had secured against their own local officials. Moreover, the states that adopted new constitutions during the following decades took their bills of rights from the preexisting state constitutions rather than from the federal amendments. For example, Oregon's constitution in 1859 adopted Indiana's copy of Ohio's version of sources found in Delaware and elsewhere.

The Federal Bill of Rights did not supersede those of the states. It was not interposed between the citizen and his state. When the Fifth Amendment was invoked against the City of Baltimore in 1833, John Marshall replied that its adoption "could never have occurred to any human being, as a mode of doing that which might be effected by the state itself."[4] Only the Civil War made it clear that it might sometimes be necessary to use federal law as a mode of doing that which a state could but did not effect for itself—the protection of some of its citizens against those in control of its government.

It is the Fourteenth Amendment that has bound the states to observe the guarantees of the Federal Bill of Rights. I do not underestimate that crucial role of the Fourteenth Amendment. But the effect has gone beyond assuring that state officials respect the rights guaranteed by federal law. It has led many state courts and the lawyers who practice before them to ignore the state's law, enforcing only those personal rights guaranteed by federal law, or to assume that the state's own guarantees must reflect whatever the United States Supreme Court finds in their federal analogues.

We tend to forget how recently the application of the Federal Bill of Rights to the states developed. Throughout the nineteenth century and the first quarter of the twentieth, state courts decided questions of constitutional rights under their own state constitutions. In 1925, it was only a hypothesis that the states were bound by the First Amendment.[5] That was really settled only after 1937.[6] Fifth Amendment guarantees against compulsory self-incrimination and double jeopardy did not bind the states until 1964 and 1969, respectively.[7] I shall not go through the catalogue; most of the decisions binding the states to observe the procedures of the Fourth, Fifth, and Sixth amendments date from the same period.[8] Of course, the states had all these guarantees in their own laws long before the Federal Bill of Rights was applied to the states. State courts had been administering these laws, sometimes generously, more often not, for a century or more without awaiting an interpretation from the United States Supreme Court.

Historically, the states' commitment to individual rights came first. Restraints on the federal government were patterned upon the states' declarations of rights. Even in modern times the United States Supreme Court has sometimes looked to that original history to interpret a federal clause.[9] But today, most state courts look to interpretations of the Federal Bill of Rights for the meaning of their own state constitutions, in the rare cases when they consider them at all.

The Logic of Federalism

Just as rights under the state constitutions were first in time, they are first also in the logic of constitutional law. For lawyers, the point is quickly made. Whenever a person asserts a particular right, and a state court recognizes and protects that right under state law, then the state is not depriving the person of whatever federal claim he or she might otherwise assert. There is no federal question.

Every state supreme court, I suppose, has declared that it will not needlessly decide a case on a constitutional ground if other legal issues can dispose of the case. The identical principle applies when examining that part of the state's law which is in its own constitution. In my view, a state court should always consider its state constitution before the Federal Constitution. It owes its state the respect to consider the state constitutional question even when counsel does not raise it, which is most of the time. The same court probably would not let itself be pushed into striking down a state law before considering that law's proper interpretation. The principle is the same.

Let us avoid any misunderstanding. The United States Constitution is the supreme law of the land. Nothing in the state's law or constitution can diminish a federal right. But no state court needs or, in my view, ought to hold that the law of its state denies what the Federal Constitution demands, without at least discussing the guarantees provided in its own bill of rights. In fact, Justices of the Supreme Court frequently invite a state court to do just that, usually when those Justices disagree with the majority's decision of the federal issue presented. As Chief Justice Burger once observed, "for all we know, the state courts would find this statute invalid under the State Constitution, but no one on either side of the case thought to discuss this or exhibit any interest in the subject."[10] Justices Brennan and Marshall, disappointed at decisions that have reversed state courts when they protected a claim under the Fourteenth Amendment, have issued frequent reminders that the state courts could have reached the same decisions under the state constitution.[11]

Granted, a state court might often reach the opposite result under the state constitution and bend only to the external compulsion of the Fourteenth Amendment. A state constitution does not always protect whatever the Federal Constitution protects. But a state court should put things in their logical sequence and routinely examine its state law first, before reaching a federal issue.

Putting Principle into Practice

Let us examine what putting first things first means in practice, both for courts and for the practitioner.

When a state court deals with constitutional claims that do not currently occupy the *United States Reports*, the state court is quite accustomed to making its own analysis under the state constitution. Commonplace examples are issues of the condemnation of property for public use or alleged disparities of assessments for taxation. But when the issue arises in an area in which the Supreme Court has been active, lawyers generally stop citing the state's own law and decisions of the state court, and the court abandons reference to the state constitution. Such reference to the state constitution reappears only when counsel and the state court wish to extend a constitutional right beyond the decisions of the Supreme Court and to do so without facing possible reversal on *certiorari*. In other words, the normal and logical sequence is reversed:counsel and court first determine whether the state has violated the Federal Constitution, and only when it has done so do they reach a question of state law. That practice stands the Constitution on its head.

The tactic of using the state constitution only selectively is best illustrated by two famous California cases concerning equal protection. In *Serrano v. Priest,*[12] the California Supreme Court held that the amount spent on public schools could not depend on the different tax bases available to rich and to poor local school districts. The opinion was written in the terminology of federal equal protection doctrine, with only a passing reference to California's own article 1, section 21.[13] That section forbade laws granting to any citizen or class of citizens privileges or immunities which, upon the same terms, shall not equally belong to all citizens. This is a common provision which is older than the Fourteenth Amendment and independent of its context of race discrimination. Before the *Serrano* litigation was concluded, the United States Supreme Court rejected the same equal protection claim in *San Antonio Independent School District v. Rodriguez.*[14] Thereafter, the California court reaffirmed its original holding under the California clause.[15]

One might think that, having discovered the clause in the California Constitution prohibiting laws granting to any class of citizens privileges which are not equally open to all citizens on the same terms, the California court either would have found the clause relevant to Allan Bakke's attack on the preferential admissions system at the medical school in Davis,[16] or that the court would at least discuss why not.

Indeed, California amended its constitution in 1974 to provide expressly that the "rights guaranteed by this Constitution are not dependent on those guaranteed by the United States Constitution."[17] But that discussion of equality of privileges did not occur. In *Bakke v. Regents of the University of California,*[18] the California court studiously bypassed all preliminary issues of state law and placed its decision squarely on the Fourteenth Amendment, so as to invite Supreme Court review of this controversial issue. The court did not seem concerned about the implication that the law of California offered Mr. Bakke no protection for a right to which the court, rightly or wrongly, believed him to be entitled.[19]

From the lawyer's standpoint, the state's bill of rights may seem utterly irrelevant when the federal precedents are squarely in his favor. Nevertheless, it is a mistake to ignore the state guarantee. In the early 1970s, lawyers invariably took every civil liberties case to the federal district court. One very good lawyer did just that in *Tanner v. Lloyd Corp., Ltd.*[20] The plaintiffs in that case were denied the right to distribute anti-war leaflets in a large shopping center in Portland. On the basis of existing Supreme Court decisions, both the federal district court,[21] and the Court of Appeals for the Ninth Circuit[22] sustained the claim under the First Amendment; no one bothered with the Oregon Constitution. By the time the Supreme Court granted certiorari and reversed its prior direction,[23] it was of course too late.

I would guess that if the plaintiff from the outset had invoked the Oregon Constitution's free speech and assembly provisions, these provisions would have been interpreted consistently with the existing First Amendment precedents in the plaintiff's favor. After the reversal under the First Amendment, lawyers who had litigated a similar shopping center case in state court and had relied on the lower federal court's decision against the Lloyd Center tried belatedly to switch their argument to the Oregon Constitution, but they found that the Oregon court was reluctant to contradict the Supreme Court's *Lloyd Corp.* decision.[24] California, incidentally, has done so under its constitution.[25]

Many other cases show that what is sound in theory is also intensely practical. In recent years, state courts have often found themselves reversed by the Supreme Court when they decided in favor of some individual right on the basis of the United States Constitution.[26] An Alabama court, for instance, held that an employer could not be made to pay an employee while on jury duty.[27] The Pennsylvania Supreme Court held that a gross receipts tax on parking lots took the operator's property without due process.[28] The Idaho court thought that its unemployment benefit rules violated the equal protection clause.[29] These decisions indeed may not have been good Fourteenth Amendment law and deserved to be reversed. But I venture to say that in every case the court could have cited the state's own constitution for its holding. Some years ago, for example, in *Maryland Board of Pharmacy v. Save-A-Lot, Inc.,*[30] Judge Levine reaffirmed the doctrine that in Maryland due process requires statutes to have a substantial relation to some identified objective, notwithstanding what the Supreme Court might say. I have little enthusiasm for that doctrine,[31] but I am the first to say Maryland is entitled to it under its own constitution. Without the Maryland Constitution, the court might have found itself reversed, as the North Dakota court was when it thought it was following an old federal due process case that had escaped being expressly overruled in the 1940s.[32]

The lesson, I suggest, is that a claim under the state's own law must be more than a perfunctory afterthought. First things first. Indeed, when a court ties a state constitutional guarantee as a tail to the kite of the corresponding federal clause, it may simply find the state ground ignored on certiorari, as happened recently in *Delaware v. Prouse.*[33] But the habit that developed in the 1960s of making a federal case of every claim and looking for all law in Supreme Court opinions dies hard.

Notes

1. See, e.g., Md. Const., Decl. of Rights arts. 19, 20, 22, 23, 38.
2. F. Green, *Constitutional Development in the South Atlantic States, 1776–1860,* at 52–56 (Chapel Hill: University of North Carolina Press, 1930).
3. *Barron v. Mayor of Baltimore*, 32 U.S. 242 (1833).
4. See *Gitlow v. New York,* 268 U.S. 652 (1925); cf. *Pierce v. Society of Sisters,* 268 U.S. 510 (1925), First Amendment not used to invalidate Oregon statute which would effectively close religious primary schools.
5. See *Cantwell v. Connecticut*, 310 U.S. 296 (1940); *Thornhill v. Alabama,* 310 U.S. 88 (1940); *DeJonge v. Oregon,* 299 U.S. 353 (1937).
6. See *Benton v. Maryland,* 395 U.S. 784 (1969); *Mallory v. Hogan,* 378 U.S. 1 (1964).
7. E.g., *Duncan v. Louisiana,* 391 U.S. 145 (1968) (trial by jury); *Klopfer v. North Carolina,* 386 U.S. 213 (1967) (speedy trial); *Pointer v. Texas,* 380 U.S. 400 (1965) (right to confrontation); *Gideon v. Wainwright,* 372 U.S. 335 (1963) (right to counsel); *Mapp v. Ohio,* 367 U.S. 643 (1961) (the exclusionary rule).
8. See *Apodaca v. Oregon,* 406 U.S. 404 (1972); *Williams v. Florida,* 399 U.S. 78 (1970); *Duncan v. Louisiana,* 391 U.S. 145 (1968). An earlier, interesting example arising in Maryland was *In re Provoo,* 17 F.R.D. 183 (1955).
9. Justice Marshall has suggested that the United States Supreme Court refrain from reversing a state judgment in favor of a defendant relying on constitutional grounds "unless it is quite clear that the state court has resolved all applicable state law questions adversely to the defendant and that it feels compelled by its view of the federal constitutional issue to reverse the conviction at hand." *Oregon v. Haas,* 420 U.S. 714, 729 (1975) (dissenting opinion); see P. Galie and L. Galie, "State Constitutional Guarantees and Supreme Court Review: Justice Marshall's Proposal in *Oregon v. Haas,*" 82 *Dickinson Law Review* 273 (1978). I have stated elsewhere that lower federal courts also should inquire into state constitutional guarantees when plaintiffs attack state action on federal constitutional grounds. See Linde, "Book Review," 52 *Oregon Law Review* 325 (1973).

10. *Wisconsin v. Constantineau,* 400 U.S. 440 (1971) (Burger, C.J., dissenting).
11. E.g., *Idaho Dept. of Employment v. Smith,* 434 U.S. 100 (1977); *Michigan v. Mosley,* 423 U.S. 96 (1975); *Texas v. White,* 423 U.S. 67 (1975). See also *New Jersey v. Portash,* 440 U.S. 450 (1979).
12. 5 Cal.3d 584, 487 P.2d 1241, 96 Cal. Rptr. 601 (1971).
13. Cal. Const. art. I, §21 (current version at §7).
14. 411 U.S. 1 (1973).
15. *Serrano v. Priest* (*Serrano* II), 18 Cal.3d 728, 557 P.2d 929, 135 Cal. Rptr. 345 (1976), *cert.* denied, 432 U.S. 907 (1977).
16. *Bakke v. Regents of Univ. of Cal.,* 18 Cal.3d 34, 553 P.2d 1152, 132 Cal. Rptr. 680 (1977), *aff'd.* in part, *rev'd.* in part, 438 U.S. 265 (1978).
17. Cal. Const. art I, §24.
18. 18 Cal.3d 34, 553 P.2d 1152, 132 Cal. Rptr. 680 (1977), *aff'd.* in part, *rev'd.* in part, 438 U.S. 265 (1978).
19. Since this speech was delivered, the California Supreme Court has applied the state constitution rather than the federal equal protection clause as well as statutory law to hold that a public utility company unlawfully discriminated against employment of homosexuals. *Gay Law Students Ass'n. v. Pacific Telephone & Telegraph,* Cal.3d 458, 595 P.2d 592, 156 Cal. Rptr. 14 (1979).

    Other recent California decisions relying on state constitutional provisions include: *Van Atta v. Scott,* 27 Cal.3d 424, 613 P.2d 210, 166 Cal. Rptr. 149 (1980) (bail practices invalidated under state due process clause); *City of Santa Barbara v. Adamson,* 27 Cal.3d 123, 610 P.2d 436, 164 Cal. Rptr. 539 (1980) (ordinance prohibiting five or more unrelated persons from residing in single-family home violated state constitutional right of privacy); *San Francisco Labor Council v. Regents of Univ. of Cal.,* 26 Cal.3d 785, 608 P.2d 277, 163 Cal. Rptr. 460 (1980) (statute requiring university to pay prevailing wages in community violated state constitutional provision establishing independence of university); *People v. Rucker,* 26 Cal.3d 368, 605 P.2d 843, 162 Cal. Rptr. 13 (1980) (evidence of interviews between defendant and police violated state constitutional privilege against self-incrimination).
20. 308 F. Supp 128 (D. Or. 1970), *rev'd.,* 407 U.S. 551 (1972).
21. Ibid.
22. *Tanner v. Lloyd Corp., Ltd.,* 446 F.2d 545 (9th Cir. 1971), *rev'd.,* 407 U.S. 551 (1972).
23. *Lloyd Corp., Ltd. v. Tanner,* 407 U.S. 551 (1972), *rev'd.,* 446 F.2d 545 (9th Cir. 1971).
24. See *Lenrich Assocs. v. Heyda,* 264 Or. 122, 504 P.2d 112 (1972); 52 *Oregon Law Review* 338 (1973).
25. See *Robins v. Pruneyard Shopping Center,* 22 Cal.3d 899, 592 P.2d 341, (153 Cal. Rptr. 854 (1979), *aff'd.,* 48 U.S.L.W. 4650 (U.S. 1980).
26. The Supreme Court has reversed state supreme courts under these circumstances more than 20 times since the October 1972 term. The most recent decisions reaching this result include *Michigan v. DeFillippo,* 443 U.S. 31 (1979); *Fare v. Michael C.,* 442 U.S. 707 (1979); and *North Carolina v. Butler,* 441 U.S. 369 (1979).
27. *Gadsden Times Publishing Corp. v. Dean,* 49 Ala. App. 45, 268 So.2d 829, *cert.* denied, 289 Ala. 743, 268 So.2d 834 (1972), *rev'd.,* 412 U.S. 543 (1973).

28. *Alco Parking Corp. v. City of Pittsburgh,* 453 Pa. 245, 307 A.2d 851 (1973), *rev'd.,* 417 U.S. 369 (1974).
29. *Smith v. Idaho Dept. of Employment,* 98 Idaho 43, 557 P.2d 637 (1976), *rev'd.,* 434 U.S. 100 (1977).
30. 270 Md. 103, 311 A.2d 242 (1973).
31. See H. Linde, "Due Process of Lawmaking," 55 *Nebraska Law Review* 195 (1976).
32. See *North Dakota State Bd. of Pharmacy v. Snyder's Drug Stores, Inc.,* 414 U.S. 156 (1973).
33. 440 U.S. 648 (1979). Justice White's opinion states: "The [Delaware] court analyzed the various decisions interpreting the Federal Constitution, concluded that the Fourth Amendment foreclosed spot checks of automobiles, and summarily held that the state constitution was therefore also infringed.... Had state law not been mentioned at all, there would be no question about our jurisdiction, even though the state constitution might have provided an independent and adequate state ground.... The same result should follow here where the state constitutional holding depended upon the state court's view of the reach of the Fourth and Fourteenth amendments." Ibid., at 652–653. Justice White expanded this proposition: "Moreover, every case holding a search or seizure to be contrary to the state constitutional provision relies on cases interpreting the Fourth Amendment and simultaneously concludes that the search or seizure is contrary to that provision...." Ibid., at 652–653 n. 5. See also *New Jersey v. Portash,* 440 U.S. 450, 460–461 (1979) (Brennan, J., concurring).

CHAPTER 34

State Courts at the Dawn of a New Century

Common Law Courts Reading Statutes and Constitutions

Judith S. Kaye

Chief Judge, New York Court of Appeals (1993) and Associate Justice, New York Court of Appeals (1983–1993)

Overwhelmingly, our nation's legal disputes are centered in the state courts, which handle more than ninety-seven percent of the litigation—tens of millions of new filings each year compared to some 250,000 in the federal courts. Given these numbers, it is no surprise that the top courtroom dramas to flicker across the nation's television screens—the trials of Joel Steinberg, William Kennedy Smith, the Menendez brothers, Lorena Bobbitt, O.J. Simpson—have unfolded in state courts.

Not only the number but also the nature of state court cases has changed dramatically. As society has evolved in ways our grandparents could hardly have dreamed, so have our cases, which present an inexhaustible array of novel issues. Today's state court dockets comprise the battlefields of first resort in social revolutions of a distinctly modern vintage: whether frozen embryos are marital property to be distributed equitably upon divorce; whether it is a crime to assist a terminally ill patient in committing suicide; whether DNA evidence should be admitted to establish a defendant's guilt.

In addition, whole categories of cases affecting the day-to-day circumstances, indeed survival, of our citizens are largely if not exclusively adjudicated in the state

---

Acknowledgment to Chief Judge Judith S. Kaye for excerpts from her article in 70 New York University Law Review *1 (1995).*

courts. As societal reception centers, we confront daily the very crises—AIDS, homelessness, drugs, juvenile violence—that continue to frustrate so many others in and out of government....

As the courts both literally and figuratively closest to the people, it is beyond question that state courts continue to play a vital role in shaping the lives of our citizenry.... The common law is, of course, lawmaking and policymaking by judges. It is law derived not from authoritative texts such as constitutions and statutes, but from human wisdom collected case by case over countless generations to form a stable body of rules that not only determine immediate controversies but also guide future conduct. While it is durable, certain, and predictable at its core, the common law is not static. It proceeds and grows incrementally, in restrained and principled fashion, to fit into a changing society.

Policymaking under the common law is not, however, a freewheeling exercise. Cases are themselves limits; courts do not render advisory opinions but instead resolve live disputes on the facts and law before them. Appellate decisions, moreover, are the product of a system that requires the agreement of several judges, values stability and faithful adherence to precedent, and safeguards those values by the requirement of written opinions publicly explaining the results reached.

That state courts—not federal courts—are the keepers of the common law has long been American orthodoxy. Even in today's legal landscape, dominated by statutes, the common-law process remains the core element in state court decisionmaking.

Every day, for example, state courts delineate the limits of tort liability, thereby defining socially acceptable conduct:which members of the general public can recover against a utility for damages incurred during a New York City black-out; whether a victim of rape in an urban apartment building can recover against the landlord; whether the State is liable to a murdered student's family for failure to disclose a former inmate's extensive psychiatric history to the school; whether the Transit Authority is responsible when a young student waiting for a subway train is beaten to death. Not unlike other state tribunals, my court has set the standard of care owed to baseball spectators, baseball players, jockeys, firefighters, swimmers and divers, trespassers, and fetuses. Though the facts of each case are different and the answers vary, the court's function is always the same—to weigh and balance the relation of the parties, the nature of the risk, and of course the public interest. Time and again, state courts have openly and explicitly balanced considerations of social welfare and have fashioned new causes of action where common sense justice required, most recently in the area of "cancerphobia" and emotional distress suffered by persons exposed to the HIV virus. Conversely, state courts have refused to enlarge the boundaries of the common law by declining to recognize new torts....

Whole categories of what can best be described as "gateway" issues like standing, choice of law, and admissibility of evidence are decided every day by state courts as a matter of pure policy. Applying the common law, the New York Court of Appeals even decided the 1988 America's Cup match between New Zealand and San Diego.

Yet despite the continued vitality of the common law, it is clear that "common law judging" now takes place in a "world of statutes." In my court, like other state courts, the ratio of strictly common-law cases unquestionably has declined, and even in traditional common-law fields like torts, contracts, and property we often confront statutes that affect our decisionmaking. This ubiquitous web of statutes, combined with more political concerns about "judicial activism," may in fact have caused state judges to feel that our role as common-law judges, cautiously and creatively developing the law in ways appropriate to a changing society, has been circumscribed.

Increasingly, judicial opinions reflect the notion that, in the absence of a statute, courts should not make law. In 1889, the New York Court of Appeals held, as a matter of common law, that a defendant who poisoned his grandfather could not inherit under the grandfather's will, and the court did so even though no such exception existed in the probate statute. One hundred years later, we would more likely say—as we in fact did in refusing to recognize a tort of wrongful discharge and in refusing to expand "dram shop" liability—that "such a significant change in our law is best left to the Legislature." In spite of the anxiety surrounding the legitimacy of judicial lawmaking, I believe that the inherent, yet principled flexibility of the common law remains the defining feature of the state court judicial process today. As our former Chief Judge Benjamin Cardozo observed more than seventy years ago, though the "fissures in the common law are wider than the fissures in a statute," the resulting "gaps" must still "be filled, whether their size be great or small." In keeping with that sentiment, former Chief Judge Mikva more recently defined "judicial activism" as "the decisional process by which judges fill in the gaps that they perceive in a statute or the ambiguities that they find in a constitutional phrase." Given the inevitability of this process, he continued, "all judges are activists." Thus, "the 'judicial activism' … so criticized by today's conservatives (and yesterday's liberals) is really judicial 'naturalism'—judges doing what comes naturally—what most of them were taught to do."

Today, as in the past, in applying the law declared by others (whether a constitution or a statute) there is little doubt that state judges are frequently left to choose among competing policies—to fill the gaps—thereby narrowing or broadening the reach of the law. The choices state judges make are based on a consideration of the "social welfare" which Cardozo described as "public policy, the good of the collective body," which may mean "expediency or prudence" or "the standards of right conduct, which find expression in the mores of the community."

No one disputes our role—indeed our responsibility—to draw and redraw the bounds of socially tolerable conduct by explicitly adapting established principles to changing circumstances, not by simply picking a result out of a hat but by reference to our precedents and our perceptions of the common good. Few would complain that state court decisions defining the scope of foreseeability, for example, were an arrogation of power. One might disagree with particular policy choices we make, but no one questions our authority to make them. Yet when it comes to constitutional and statutory adjudication—where we engage in a similar process—some are loath to admit that there is any "freedom of choice" at all....

Let me illustrate what I mean by examining the social policy choices state courts necessarily make (whether we admit it or not). First, I will address the role state judges have in interpreting state constitutions, and then I will focus on state judges interpreting state statutes.

Common Law Courts Construing State Constitutions

No doubt in part attributable to his experience as a state court judge, nearly twenty years ago Justice Brennan issued his now famous wake-up call for state courts to "step into the breach" and resuscitate our state constitutions as the living documents they are. I still remember the excitement those stirring words generated. Many of us had grown so federalized, so accustomed to the Supreme Court of the United States as the fount of constitutional wisdom, that we barely remembered that our state even had a constitution.

No serious idea is without its critics, and the movement toward active state constitutional interpretation has certainly attracted its share. But it is now clear that the promise inherent in Justice Brennan's challenge has made giant steps toward fulfillment. Perhaps the most accurate assessment of state constitutionalism today is that it has emerged from the cauldrons of our nation's law reviews into the crucible of our state courts, regrettably (I trust not fatally) missing most of our nation's law schools....

Examples of recent cases where state courts have concluded that their own constitutions afford greater protection than the minimum floor provided by the federal Constitution include decisions from Louisiana, Kentucky, and Michigan holding that it is unconstitutional to medicate a condemned prisoner forcibly so that the prisoner can be executed, that a criminal statute prohibiting "deviate sexual intercourse with another person of the same sex" violates privacy and equal protection guarantees, and that a sentence of life without the possibility of parole for possession of cocaine is improper. In the area of free speech and assembly, the Texas Supreme Court recently held that its constitution was violated by a civil gag order, and the New Jersey Supreme Court, in a decision released just before Christmas, joined at least four other states in concluding that its state constitution guarantees the right of free speech in large, privately owned shopping malls.

Every one of these cases is distinguished by close, heated divisions unusual in the jurisprudence of those courts. Like the debate in the scholarly literature, these divisions reflect important differences about methodology—about when and how a state court should rely on its own constitution. They also reflect deep differences about the role of state constitutions in our judicial system.

These debates are not limited to the pages of law reports or law reviews but have extended to media campaigns and political action committees, one judicial candidate even calling for term limits for judges. Because so many elected state court judges do not have the shield of life tenure—another contrast with the federal system—they have been swept into the whirlwind of new age politics. The intensity of these campaigns has had its effects, with some perceiving the vibrancy of state constitutions as linked to more overtly political debates about specific results, for example, how expansively a court will interpret its citizens' state constitutional right to be free from unreasonable searches and seizures. It is well to remember that even the principle that the Supreme Court has the power to authoritatively interpret the Federal Constitution was forged against a backdrop of fierce political partisanship.

Apart from extraordinary divisiveness, what distinguishes these state constitutional decisions from federal constitutional decisions is that, while federal constitutional law is cabined by the text of the Constitution, state courts move seamlessly between the common law and state constitutional law, the shifting ground at times barely perceptible.

Indeed, the common law and state constitutional law often stand as alternative grounds for individual rights, as one of my colleagues wrote recently of New York libel law. In New Jersey, common-law principles of privacy and "fundamental fairness," as distinguished from the analogous constitutional guarantees of equal protection and due process, have been invoked in situations as factually diverse as endorsing a dying patient's right to refuse medical treatment and preventing unfair exclusion of members of the public from blackjack tables....

There is of course a "critical difference" between when courts make constitutional law and when they make common law. Outside the area of constitutional adjudication, state court decisions "are subject to overrule or alteration by ordinary statute. The court is standing in for the legislature, and if it has done so in a way the legislature does not approve, it can soon be corrected." But when a case is decided on constitutional grounds, the court solidifies the law in ways that may not be as susceptible to subsequent modification either by courts or by legislatures. Because of this crucial difference, use of the common law to define rights at times has been preferable in that it has allowed both courts and legislatures room to adapt principles to changed circumstances, for example in areas like the "right to die" and forcible medication of mental patients. Of course, that same flexibility is not an option for the federal courts, which must decide either that a constitutional right has been violated or that it has not—a distinction perhaps not fully appreciated by those accustomed to litigating "rights" issues in federal court.

In the area of "rights" adjudication, state courts plainly have a distinct advantage in that the common law allows them to shape evolving legal standards more cautiously. It is therefore important that they be explicit about whether and why they are deciding cases on common-law or constitutional grounds. The New Jersey Supreme Court did exactly that in its recent shopping mall case involving the right of free speech on private property. The court had earlier been reluctant to rest that right on constitutional grounds and had decided instead on what it called the "more satisfactory" common-law free speech grounds. Given the more than two decades of "experimentation" that elapsed since the court first addressed the scope of those rights, it transplanted what had previously been a common-law right to firmer constitutional ground.

Despite the controversy that has surrounded the movement toward active state constitutionalism, and given the inherent role of state courts under the common law and the clear similarities between deciding a common-law case and what is currently required, for example, by the constitutional guarantee of "due process," I think it beyond doubt that we are well embarked on what has been called a "larger interpretive enterprise of American constitutionalism." I am confident that courts will continue to consult their own constitutions to vindicate the rights of their citizens.

My primary concern, however, in this age of political "sound bites" and "spin control" is that state courts continue to do so without reluctance or apology. As Justice Brennan wrote: "Each age must seek its own way to the unstable balance of those qualities that make us human, and must contend anew with the questions of power and accountability with which the Constitution is concerned." Those words are as true of the state constitutions as they are of the federal Constitution, which lawyers and judges are sworn to uphold.

Common Law Courts Construing State Statutes

Vital though the common law still may be, I think it inarguable that it has been surpassed as the preeminent source of law it once was. Why? The primary reason, of course, is the "orgy of statute making" engaged in by legislatures not only at the federal but also at the state level. In the years since the Depression and the Second World War, "statutorification" of the law has continued unabated so that today, after a half-century of the "relentless annual ... grinding of more than fifty legislative machines," statutory interpretation is likely the principal task engaged in by state courts. The current set of New York statutes, like the full set of the United States Code, takes up an entire wall of shelving in my Chambers.

Perhaps in reaction to the proliferation of statutes, perhaps inspired by Judge (then Professor) Guido Calabresi's thought-provoking work *A Common Law for the Age of Statutes*, or perhaps nudged along by the lively and ongoing debate at the Supreme Court, in the last decade the subject of statutory interpretation has seized center-stage in scholarly journals. In the words of a foremost proponent, statutory interpretation, once Cinderella, "now dances in the ballroom." And as tends to happen in scholarly places, Cinderella speaks a whole new language of elusive polysyllabic labels: "new textualists," "dynamic statutory interpreters," "metademocrats."

Despite the outpouring of scholarly ink, analysis has focused almost entirely on how federal courts read federal statutes. Few, if any, of the recent commentators have considered whether the subject of statutory interpretation presents a different set of issues for state judges reading state statutes.

I submit that it does. And of the many reasons that come to mind, perhaps most important, as is evident in the area of state constitutional law, is the fact that state courts regularly, openly, and legitimately speak the language of the common law whereas federal courts do not. The federal courts, after all, may have jurisdiction over a dispute only because a federal statute exists.

Accepting the reality of today's statutory world and its concomitant obligations, however, does not oust state courts from their traditional role. Even in a world dominated by statutes, there remain clear, direct links with the common law. In the words of one recent commentator, we now live in a "world where common and statutory law are woven together in a complex fabric defining a wide range of rights and duties."

As one rather obvious sample of this modern-day fabric, state legislatures frequently endorse court decisions by codifying causes of action created and carefully crafted by state courts as a matter of common law. A prominent instance in the law of New York is the legislature's endorsement of the ground-breaking court decision some twenty years ago discarding as unfair the concept of contributory negligence and embracing instead the principle of comparative fault. The Tennessee Supreme Court, in a more recent decision adopting comparative fault, stated as follows: "We recognize that this action could be taken by our General Assembly. However, legislative inaction has never prevented judicial abolition of obsolete common law doctrines, especially those ... conceived in the judicial womb." By the same token, legislatures at times express their disagreement by "repealing" or "vetoing" other common-law doctrines.

Legislatures have this same "veto" power over judicial interpretations of statutes. Although some scholars have concluded that the incidence of legislative "overruling" of court interpretations is exaggerated, I find this sort of "re-interpretation" not an altogether infrequent occurrence....

No one can question the legislature's authority to correct or redirect a state court's interpretation of a statute. Indeed, on our court we especially strive for consensus in statutory interpretation cases as a matter of policy, knowing that the legislature always can, and will, step in if it feels we have gotten it wrong.

In addition, the state legislative/judicial relationship often takes the form of an open dialogue. Some years ago, for example, the New York Court of Appeals felt constrained by the language of the New York private placement adoption statute to uphold an "irrevocable consent" to adoption by a newborn infant's biological parents, though they argued that they had not been given fair notice of the legal consequences. Courts having previously expressed difficulty applying that statute, we ended that opinion by suggesting to our legislative colleagues—who sit directly across the street from us in Albany—that they reexamine the statute "in light of 13 years' experience, for it appears that the well-founded concerns that engendered the law are not yet dispelled." And indeed, the statute was amended the following year....

Even when interpreting statutes that have been passed, ascertaining the legislative intent is often no less difficult than drawing common-law or constitutional distinctions, requiring "a choice between uncertainties," surely an "ungainly judicial function." When the meaning of a statute is in dispute, there remains at the core the same common-law process of discerning and applying the purpose of the law. As one commentator noted, "courts have not only a law-finding function ... but [also] ... a law-making function that engrafts on the statute meaning appropriate to resolving the controversy." Indeed, "there is no sharp break of method in passing from 'common law,' old style, to the combinations of decisional and statutory law now familiar. Statutes, after all, need to be interpreted, filled in, related to the rest of the corpus."

I certainly do not mean to suggest that as judges we are not always mindful of the "legislature's authority, within constitutional limits, to formulate whatever law it chooses." Unless a statute in some way contravenes the state or federal constitution, we are obliged to follow it—and of course we do. In many instances the "plain meaning" of the statutory language dictates a clear result. But that is not always invariably so. Statutory interpretation is not a mechanical exercise.

At times the common-law method compels courts even to read a statute in a way that appears contrary to its "plain meaning." Only recently, for example, my court construed the words "currently dangerous" in a criminal statute governing whether a paranoid schizophrenic, found not responsible for attempted murder by reason of mental disease or defect, should remain confined in a secure mental hospital. Surely the word "currently" is clear enough:it means right now, at this moment. But, as the court wrote, to apply those words strictly "would lead to the absurd conclusion that a defendant in a straightjacket, surrounded by armed guards, is not currently dangerous under the statute." Instead, we applied concepts of "common-sense and substantial justice" to give the term "currently" what must have been its intended meaning:dangerous not at the moment of confinement and treatment, but foreseeably dangerous if confinement and treatment were not continued into the future. Indeed, had our courts interpreted the word "currently" in its most literal sense, we would have been less than faithful to the underlying legislative purpose—to protect society from potentially dangerous insanity acquitees.

The very fact that a controversy over statutory interpretation has found its way to a state's high court—quite possibly after several other trial and appellate judges have divided on the question—signals that discerning the statutory meaning may not be quite so simple. As our Chief Judge Charles Breitel noted, "the words men use are never absolutely certain in meaning; the limitations of finite man and the even greater limitations of his language see to that." Modern linguists speak of language's innate "structural ambiguity," its "opaque context," "categorical indeterminacy," and "shared understandings." And everyone is by now familiar with Karl Llewellyn's demonstration, almost a half-century ago, that two equally time-honored maxims of statutory construction often support the contrary positions of each party to a litigation....

I do not think one has to be a "metademocrat," a "public law theorist," or even (heaven forfend) a "dynamic statutory interpreter" to acknowledge that the "will of the legislature" is not always easy (or even possible) to discern when it comes to specific facts before a court. I would venture the guess that in nearly every statutory case that reaches a state's highest court, there exist at least two plausible interpretations, each in some way supported by the text.

My own firsthand experience, study, and good sense convince me that state judges construing statutes are more than pharmacists filling prescriptions written by the legislature:often they are involved as well in treating the ailment. And that task becomes considerably more difficult when the legislature's handwriting is hard to decipher.

At times, of course, the delegation of lawmaking authority from the legislature to the courts is explicit. New York's "poison pill" statute, for example, specifies that decisions by a corporation's board of directors "shall be subject to judicial review in an appropriate proceeding in which courts formulate or apply appropriate standards."

But most often the delegation is implicit. I think, for instance, of cases where our court has had to define statutory terms such as "extraordinary circumstances," "due diligence," "best interests of the child," and "prejudice." The court had to decide whether equitable "circumstances" or "conditions"—words I am quoting directly from a New York statute—existed to grant standing where a child's grandparents were seeking visitation over the parents' objection.

Let's be frank: issues like these that reach a state appeals court cannot be resolved simply by consulting a good dictionary or communing with the statutory text. Yet, as with common-law cases, no one could doubt our Authority—indeed our responsibility—to define these terms, and to fit each case within the body of the law, thereby necessarily fixing the range and direction of the statute and the course of future litigation. . . .

Given the enormous volume of state court litigation, the unending array of novel fact patterns pushing the law to progress, and the inability of legislatures to react immediately to the many changes in society, I think it clear that common-law courts interpreting statutes and filling the gaps have no choice but to "make law" in circumstances where neither the statutory text nor the "legislative will" provides a single clear answer. Indeed, it is my perception that state legislatures not only accept such judicial decisionmaking as entirely legitimate, but also expect that within defined boundaries courts will make such choices, which can of course then be embraced, enlarged, or entombed.

However much we might prefer in this age of anxiety about "legislating from the bench" and "judicial activism" for only our elected representatives to make all the sensitive decisions, so long as human language remains imprecise and the human capacity to predict the future limited, the cascade of cases that call upon judges to fill the gaps—and to do so by reference to social justice—will unquestionably continue. For state judges, schooled in the common law, to refuse to make the necessary policy choices when properly called upon to do so would result in a rigidity and paralysis that the common-law process was meant to prevent. . . .

Appendix A

Constitution of the United States, Article III

Section 1

The judicial Power of the United States shall be vested in one supreme Court, and in such inferior Courts as the Congress may from time to time ordain and establish. The Judges, both of the supreme and inferior Courts, shall hold their Offices during good Behaviour, and shall, at stated Times, receive for their Services a Compensation, which shall not be diminished during their Continuance in Office.

Section 2

The judicial Power shall extend to all Cases, in Law and Equity, arising under this Constitution, the Laws of the United States, and Treaties made, or which shall be made, under their Authority;—to all Cases affecting Ambassadors, other public Ministers and Consuls;—to all Cases of admiralty and maritime Jurisdiction;—to Controversies to which the United States shall be a Party;—to Controversies between two or more States;—between a State and Citizens of another State [altered by the Eleventh Amendment]—between Citizens of different States—between Citizens of the same State claiming Lands under Grants of different States, and between a State, or the Citizens thereof, and foreign States, Citizens or Subjects.

In all Cases affecting Ambassadors, other public Ministers and Consuls, and those in which a State shall be Party, the supreme Court shall have original Jurisdiction. In all the other Cases before mentioned, the supreme Court shall have appellate Jurisdiction, both as to Law and Fact, with such Exceptions, and under such Regulations as the Congress shall make.

The Trial of all Crimes, except in Cases of Impeachment, shall be by Jury; and such Trial shall be held in the State where the said Crimes shall have been committed; but when not committed within any State, the Trial shall be at such Place or Places as the Congress may by Law have directed.

Section 3
Treason against the United States, shall consist only in levying War against them, or in adhering to their Enemies, giving them Aid and Comfort. No Person shall be convicted of Treason unless on the Testimony of two Witnesses to the same overt Act, or on Confession in open Court.

The Congress shall have Power to declare the Punishment of Treason, but no Attainder of Treason shall work Corruption of Blood, or Forfeiture except during the Life of the Person attainted.

Appendix B

The Federalist No. 78

Alexander Hamilton (1788)

We proceed now to an examination of the judiciary department of the proposed government.

In unfolding the defects of the existing Confederation, the utility and necessity of a federal judicature have been clearly pointed out. It is the less necessary to recapitulate the considerations there urged, as the propriety of the institution in the abstract is not disputed; the only questions which have been raised being relative to the manner of constituting it, and to its extent. To these points, therefore, our observations shall be confined.

The manner of constituting it seems to embrace these several objects: 1st. The mode of appointing the judges. 2d. The tenure by which they are to hold their places. 3d. The partition of the judiciary authority between different courts, and their relations to each other.

First. As to the mode of appointing the judges; this is the same with that of appointing the officers of the Union in general, and has been so fully discussed in the two last numbers, that nothing can be said here which would not be useless repetition.

Second. As to the tenure by which the judges are to hold their places; this chiefly concerns their duration in office; the provisions for their support; the precautions for their responsibility.

According to the plan of the convention, all judges who may be appointed by the United States are to hold their offices *during good behavior;* which is conformable to the most approved of the State constitutions and among the rest, to that of this State. Its propriety having been drawn into question by the adversaries of that plan, is no light symptom of the rage for objection, which disorders their imaginations and judgments. The standard of good behavior for the continuance in office of the judicial magistracy, is certainly one of the most valuable of the modern improvements in the practice of government. In a monarchy it is an excellent barrier to the despotism of the prince; in a republic it is a no less excellent barrier to the encroachments and oppressions of the representative body. And it is the best expedient which can be devised in any government, to secure a steady, upright, and impartial administration of the laws.

Whoever attentively considers the different departments of power must perceive, that, in a government in which they are separated from each other, the judiciary, from the nature of its functions, will always be the least dangerous to the political rights of the Constitution; because it will be least in a capacity to annoy or injure them. The Executive not only dispenses the honors, but holds the sword of the community. The legislature not only commands the purse, but prescribes the rules by which the duties and rights of every citizen are to be regulated. The judiciary, on the contrary, has no influence over either the sword or the purse; no direction either of the strength or of the wealth of the society; and can take no active resolution whatever. It may truly be said to have neither FORCE nor WILL, but merely judgment; and must ultimately depend upon the aid of the executive arm even for the efficacy of its judgments.

This simple view of the matter suggests several important consequences. It proves incontestably, that the judiciary is beyond comparison the weakest of the three departments of power; that it can never attack with success either of the other two; and that all possible care is requisite to enable it to defend itself against their attacks. It equally proves, that though individual oppression may now and then proceed from the courts of justice, the general liberty of the people can never be endangered from that quarter; I mean so long as the judiciary remains truly distinct from both the legislature and the Executive. For I agree, that "there is no liberty, if the power of judging be not separated from the legislative and executive powers." And it proves, in the last place, that as liberty can have nothing to fear from the judiciary alone, but would have every thing to fear from its union with either of the other departments; that as all the effects of such a union must ensue from a dependence of the former on the latter, notwithstanding a nominal and apparent separation; that as, from the natural feebleness of the judiciary, it is in continual jeopardy of being overpowered, awed, or influenced by its co-ordinate branches; and that as nothing can contribute so much to its firmness and independence as permanency in office, this quality may therefore be justly regarded as an indispensable ingredient in its constitution, and, in a great measure, as the citadel of the public justice and the public security.

The complete independence of the courts of justice is peculiarly essential in a limited Constitution. By a limited Constitution, I understand one which contains certain specified exceptions to the legislative authority; such, for instance, as that it shall pass no bills of attainder, no *ex post facto* laws, and the like. Limitations of this kind can be preserved in practice no other way than through the medium of courts of justice, whose duty it must be to declare all acts contrary to the manifest tenor of the Constitution void. Without this, all the reservations of particular rights or privileges would amount to nothing.

Some perplexity respecting the rights of the courts to pronounce legislative acts void, because contrary to the Constitution, has arisen from an imagination that the doctrine would imply a superiority of the judiciary to the legislative power. It is urged that the authority which can declare the acts of another void, must necessarily be superior to the one whose acts may be declared void. As this doctrine is of great importance in all the American constitutions, a brief discussion of the ground on which it rests cannot be unacceptable.

There is no position which depends on clearer principles, than that every act of a delegated authority, contrary to the tenor of the commission under which it is exercised, is void. No legislative act, therefore, contrary to the Constitution, can be valid. To deny this, would be to affirm, that the deputy is greater than his principal; that the servant is above his master; that the representatives of the people are superior to the people themselves; that men acting by virtue of powers, may do not only what their powers do not authorize, but what they forbid.

If it be said that the legislative body are themselves the constitutional judges of their own powers, and that the construction they put upon them is conclusive upon the other departments, it may be answered, that this cannot be the natural presumption, where it is not to be collected from any particular provisions in the Constitution. It is not otherwise to be supposed, that the Constitution could intend to enable the representatives of the people to substitute their *will* to that of their constituents. It is far more rational to suppose, that the courts were designed to be an intermediate body between the people and the legislature, in order, among other things, to keep the latter within the limits assigned to their authority. The interpretation of the laws is the proper and peculiar province of the courts. A constitution is, in fact, and must be regarded by the judges, as a fundamental law. It therefore belongs to them to ascertain its meaning, as well as the meaning of any particular act proceeding from the legislative body. If there should happen to be an irreconcilable variance between the two, that which has the superior obligation and validity ought, of course, to be preferred; or, in other words, the Constitution ought to be preferred to the statute, the intention of the people to the intention of their agents.

Nor does this conclusion by any means suppose a superiority of the judicial to the legislative power. It only supposes that the power of the people is superior to both; and that where the will of the legislature, declared in its statutes, stands in opposition to that of the people, declared in the Constitution, the judges ought to be governed by the latter rather than the former. They ought to regulate their decisions by the fundamental laws, rather than by those which are not fundamental.

This exercise of judicial discretion, in determining between two contradictory laws, is exemplified in a familiar instance. It not uncommonly happens, that there are two statutes existing at one time, clashing in whole or in part with each other, and neither of them containing any repealing clause or expression. In such a case, it is the province of the courts to liquidate and fix their meaning and operation. So far as they can, by any fair construction, be reconciled to each other, reason and law conspire to dictate that this should be done; where this is impracticable, it becomes a matter of necessity to give effect to one, in exclusion of the other. The rule which has obtained in the courts for determining their relative validity is, that the last in order of time shall be preferred to the first. But this is a mere rule of construction, not derived from any positive law, but from the nature and reason of the thing. It is a rule not enjoined upon the courts by legislative provision, but adopted by themselves, as consonant to truth and propriety, for the direction of their conduct as interpreters of the law. They thought it reasonable, that between the interfering acts of an EQUAL authority, that which was the last indication of its will should have the preference.

But in regard to the interfering acts of a superior and subordinate authority, of an original and derivative power, the nature and reason of the thing indicate the converse of that rule as proper to be followed. They teach us that the prior act of a superior ought to be preferred to the subsequent act of an inferior and subordinate authority; and that accordingly, whenever a particular statute contravenes the Constitution, it will be the duty of the judicial tribunals to adhere to the latter and disregard the former.

It can be of no weight to say that the courts, on the pretense of a repugnancy, may substitute their own pleasure to the constitutional intentions of the legislature. This might as well happen in the case of two contradictory statutes; or it might as well happen in every adjudication upon any single statute. The courts must declare the sense of the law; and if they should be disposed to exercise WILL instead of JUDGMENT, the consequence would equally be the substitution of their pleasure to that of the legislative body. The observation, if it prove any thing, would prove that there ought to be no judges distinct from that body.

If, then, the courts of justice are to be considered as the bulwarks of a limited Constitution against legislative encroachments, this consideration will afford a strong argument for the permanent tenure of judicial offices, since nothing will contribute so much as this to that independent spirit in the judges which must be essential to the faithful performance of so arduous a duty.

This independence of the judges is equally requisite to guard the Constitution and the rights of individuals from the effects of those ill humors, which the arts of designing men, or the influence of particular conjunctures, sometimes disseminate among the people themselves, and which, though they speedily give place to better information, and more deliberate reflection, have a tendency, in the meantime, to occasion dangerous innovations in the government, and serious oppressions of the minor party in the community. Though I trust the friends of the proposed Constitution will never concur with its enemies, in questioning that fundamental principle of republican government, which admits the right of the people to alter or abolish the established Constitution, whenever they find it inconsistent with their happiness, yet it is not to be inferred from this principle, that the representatives of the people, whenever a momentary inclination happens to lay hold of a majority of their constituents, incompatible with the provisions in the existing Constitution, would, on that account, be justifiable in a violation of those provisions; or that the courts would be under a greater obligation to connive at infractions in this shape, than when they had proceeded wholly from the cabals of the representative body. Until the people have, by some solemn and authoritative act, annulled or changed the established form, it is binding upon themselves collectively, as well as individually; and no presumption, or even knowledge, of their sentiments, can warrant their representatives in a departure from it, prior to such an act. But it is easy to see, that it would require an uncommon portion of fortitude in the judges to do their duty as faithful guardians of the Constitution, where legislative invasions of it had been instigated by the major voice of the community.

But it is not with a view to infractions of the Constitution only, that the independence of the judges may be an essential safeguard against the effects of occasional ill humors in the society. These sometimes extend no farther than to the injury of the private rights of particular classes of citizens, by unjust and partial laws. Here also the firmness of the judicial magistracy is of vast importance in mitigating the severity and confining the operation of such laws. It not only serves to moderate the immediate mischiefs of those which may have been passed, but it operates as a check upon the legislative body in passing them; who, perceiving that obstacles to the success of iniquitous intention are to be expected from the scruples of the courts, are in a manner compelled, by the very motives of the injustice they mediate, to qualify their attempts. This is a circumstance calculated to have more influence upon the character of our governments, than but few may be aware of. The benefits of the integrity and moderation of the judiciary have already been felt in more States than one; and though they may have displeased those whose sinister expectations they may have disappointed, they must have commanded the esteem and applause of all the virtuous and disinterested. Considerate men, of every description, ought to prize whatever will tend to beget or fortify that temper in the courts: as no man can be sure that he may not be to-morrow the victim of a spirit of injustice, by which he may be a gainer to-day. And every man must now feel, that the inevitable tendency of such a spirit is to sap the foundations of public and private confidence, and to introduce in its stead universal distrust and distress.

That inflexible and uniform adherence to the rights of the Constitution, and of individuals, which we perceive to be indispensable in the courts of justice, can certainly not be expected from judges who hold their offices by a temporary commission. Periodical appointments, however regulated, or by whomsoever made, would, in some way or other, be fatal to their necessary independence. If the power of making them was committed either to the Executive or legislature, there would be danger of an improper complaisance to the branch which possessed it; if to both, there would be an unwillingness to hazard the displeasure of either; if to the people, or to persons chosen by them for the special purpose, there would be too great a disposition to consult popularity, to justify a reliance that nothing would be consulted but the Constitution and the laws.

There is yet a further and a weightier reason for the permanency of the judicial offices, which is deducible from the nature of the qualifications they require. It has been frequently remarked, with great propriety, that a voluminous code of laws is one of the inconveniences necessarily connected with the advantages of a free government. To avoid an arbitrary discretion in the courts, it is indispensable that they should be bound down by strict rules and precedents, which serve to define and point out their duty in every particular case that comes before them; and it will readily be conceived from the variety of controversies which grow out of the folly and wickedness of mankind, that the records of those precedents must unavoidably swell to a very considerable bulk, and must demand long and laborious study to acquire a competent knowledge of them. Hence it is, that there can be but few men in the society who will have sufficient skill in the laws to qualify them for the stations of judges. And making the proper deductions for the ordinary depravity of human nature, the number must be still smaller of those who unite the requisite integrity with the requisite knowledge. These considerations apprise us, that the government can have no great option between fit character; and that a temporary duration in office, which would naturally discourage such characters from quitting a lucrative line of practice to accept a seat on the bench, would have a tendency to throw the administration of justice into hands less able, and less well qualified, to conduct it with utility and dignity. In the present circumstances of this country, and in those in which it is likely to be for a long time to come, the disadvantages on this score would be greater than they may at first sight appear; but it must be confessed, that they are far inferior to those which present themselves under the other aspects of the subject.

Upon the whole, there can be no room to doubt that the convention acted wisely in copying from the models of those constitutions which have established good behavior as the tenure of their judicial offices, in point of duration; and that so far from being blamable on this account, their plan would have been inexcusably defective, if it had wanted this important feature of good government. The experience of Great Britain affords an illustrious comment on the excellence of the institution.

PUBLIUS

Appendix C

Selected Bibliography of Off-the-Bench Commentaries

Abrahamson, Shirley S. "Criminal Law and State Constitutions: The Emergence of State Constitutional Law," 63 *Texas Law Review* 1141 (1985).

______. "How Tootsie the Goldfish Is Teaching People to Think Like a Judge." *Judges' Journal* 12 (Spring 1982).

______. "Judging in the Quiet of the Storm." 24 *St. Mary's Law Journal* 965 (1993).

______. "Toward A Courtroom of One's Own: An Appellate Court Judge Looks at Gender Bias." 61 *University of Cincinnati Law Review* 1209 (1993).

______. "The Woman Has Robes: Four Questions." 14 *Golden Gate University Law Review* 489 (1984).

______. "State Constitutional Law, New Judicial Federalism, and the Rehnquist Court." 51 *Cleveland State Law Review* 339 (2004).

______. "Judicial Independence as a Campaign Platform: The Importance of Fair and Impartial Courts." 84 *Michigan Bar Journal* 30 (2005).

______. "The Old Order Changes." 8 *Journal of Appellate Practice & Procedure* 77 (2006).

______. "The Ballot and the Bench." 76 *New York University Law Review* 973 (2001).

______. "Thorny Issues and Slippery Slopes: Perspectives on Judicial Independence." 64 *Ohio State Law Journal* 3 (2003).

______. "The Appeal of Therapeutic Jurisprudence." 24 *Seattle University Law Review* 223 (2000).

Adams, Arlin M. "Judicial Restraint, The Best Medicine." 60 *Judicature* 179 (1976).

Alarcon, Arthur L. "Off-the-Bench Criticism of Supreme Court Decisions by Judges Fosters Disrespect for the Rule of Law and Politicizes Our System of Justice." 28 *Loyola of Los Angeles Law Review* 795 (1995).

______. "Political Appointments and Judicial Independence—An Unreasonable Expectation." 16 *Loyola of Los Angeles Law Review* 9 (1983).

Aldisert, Ruggero J. "The House of the Law." 19 *Loyola at Los Angeles Law Review* 755 (1986).

______. "The Nature of the Judicial Process: Revisited." 49 *University of Cincinnati Law Review* 1 (1980).

______. "Philosophy, Jurisprudence, and Jurisprudential Temperament of Federal Judges." 20 *Indiana Law Review* 453 (1987).

______. "Precedent: What It Is and What It Isn't; When Do We Kiss It and When Do We Kill It?" 17 *Pepperdine Law Review* 605 (1990).

______. "The Role of the Courts in Contemporary Society." 38 *University of Pittsburgh Law Review* 437 (1977).

______. "What Makes a Good Appellate Judge? Four Views." *Judges' Journal* 14 (Spring 1983).

Alito, Samuel Anthony, Jr. Panel Speaker at the Federalist Society's 2000 National Lawyers Convention: Presidential Oversight and the Administrative State, in 2 *Engage* 11 (Federalist Society, Washington, D.C., 2001).

______. "The Role of the Lawyer in the Criminal Justice System." 2 *Federalist Society Criminal Law News* 3 (1998).

______. "The First Amendment: Information, Publication and the Media." 1 *Seton Hall Constitutional Law Review* 327 (1991).

Arnold, Richard S., and Myron H. Bright. "Oral Argument? It May Be Crucial!" *American Bar Association Journal* 68 (September 1984).

Baldwin, Henry. *A General View of the Origin and Nature of the Constitution and Government of the United States.* Philadelphia: Clark, 1837.

Barak, Aharon. *The Judge in a Democracy.* Princeton: Princeton University Press, 2006.

Bazelon, David L. "The Dilemma of Criminal Responsibility." 72 *Kentucky Law Journal* 263 (1984).

______. "The Impact of the Courts on Public Administration." 52 *Indiana Law Journal* 101 (1976).

______. "The Morality of the Criminal Law." 49 *Southern California Law Review* 385 (1976).

______. "New Gods for Old: 'Efficient' Courts in a Democratic Society." 46 *New York University Law Review* 653 (1971).

______. "Racism, Classism, and the Juvenile Process." 53 *Judicature* 373 (1970).

______. "Risk and Public Policy: 'To Live and ... Become Bold'." *Beverly Hills Bar Association Journal* 261 (Fall 1980).

______. "Science and Uncertainty: A Jurist's View." 5 *Harvard Environmental Law Review* 209 (1981).

Beer, Peter. "On Behalf of Judicial Restraint." 15 *Trial* 37 (1979).

Black, Hugo. "The Bill of Rights." 35 *New York University Law Review* 865 (1960).

______. *A Constitutional Faith.* New York: Knopf, 1968.

______. "Justice Black and the Bill of Rights." CBS News Special, December 3, 1968.

______. "The Lawyer and Individual Freedom." 21 *Tennessee Law Review* 461 (1950).

______. "Mr. Justice Murphy." 48 *Michigan Law Review* 739 (1950).

______. "Mr. Justice Rutledge." 25 *Indiana Law Review* 541 (1950).

Blackmun, Harry A. "A Candid Talk with Justice Blackmun." *New York Times Magazine,* Sec. 6 (February 20, 1983).

______. "Interview on the Death Penalty." *Nightline,* ABC, November 18, 1993.

______. "A Justice Speaks Out: A Conversation with Harry A. Blackmun." CNN, December 4, 1982.

Bork, Robert H. "The Constitution, Original Intent, and Economic Rights." 23 *San Diego Law Review* 823 (1986).

______. "Styles in Constitutional Theory." 26 *South Texas Law Journal* 383 (1985).

______. *The Tempting of America: The Political Seduction of the Law.* New York: Free Press, 1990.

Bradley, Joseph P. "Office and Nature of Law as the Basis and Bond of Society." 41 *Legal Intelligencer* 396 (1884).

Brandeis, Louis D. *Letters of Louis D. Brandeis.* Edited by M.I. Urofsky and D. Levy. Albany: State University of New York Press, 1971.

______. *Miscellaneous Papers.* Edited by O. K. Fraenkel. New York: Viking Press, 1934.

______. *The Words of Justice Brandeis.* Edited by S. Goldman. New York: Schuman, 1953.

Brennan, William J., Jr. "The Bill of Rights and the States: The Revival of State Constitutions as Guardians of Individual Rights." 61 *New York University Law Review* 535 (1986).

______. "Constitutional Adjudication." *Notre Dame Lawyer* 559 (1965).

______. "Constitutional Adjudication and the Death Penalty: A View from the Court." 100 *Harvard Law Review* 313 (1986).

______. "Construing the Constitution." 19 *University of California-Davis Law Review* 2 (1985).

______. "In Defense of Dissents." 37 *Hastings Constitutional Law Review* 427 (1986).

______. "Inside View of the High Court." *New York Times Magazine* 35 (October 6, 1963).

______. "A Life on the Court: A Conversation with Justice Brennan." *The New York Times Magazine* 25 (October 5, 1986).

______. "The National Court of Appeals: Another Dissent." 40 *University of Chicago Law Review* 473 (1973).

______. "The Proposed New National Court of Appeals." 28 *Record of the Association of the Bar of New York City* 627 (1973).

______. "Reason, Passion, and 'The Progress of the Law'." 18 *Trial Lawyer Quarterly* 7 (1987).

______. "State Constitutions and the Protection of Individual Rights." 91 *Harvard Law Review* (1977).

______. "State Supreme Court Judge Versus United States Supreme Court Justice: A Change in Function and Perspective." 19 *University of Florida Law Review* 225 (1966).

______. "The Supreme Court and the Meiklejohn Interpretation of the First Amendment." 79 *Harvard Law Review* 1 (1965).

______. "A Tribute to Justice Thurgood Marshall." 105 *Harvard Law Review* 24 (1991).

Brewer, David. "The Federal Judiciary." 12 *Kansas State Bar Association Proceedings* 81 (1895).

______. "The Nation's Anchor." 57 *Alabama Law Review* 166 (1898).

______. "Organized Wealth and the Judiciary." *Chicago Legal News* (August 27, 1904).

______. "Protection of Private Property from Public Attack." 10 *Railway and Corporation Law Review* 281 (1891).

______. "The Supreme Court of the United States." 33 *Scribner's* 273 (1903).

______. "Two Periods in the History of the Supreme Court." 19 *Virginia State Bar Association Report* 113 (1906).
______. "The Work of the Supreme Court." *Law Notes* 167 (1898).
Breyer, Stephen G. *Active Liberty: Interpreting Our Democratic Constitution.* (New York: Knopf, 2005).
______. "Breaking the Vicious Circle: Toward Effective Risk Regulation." 74 *Boston University Law Review* 365 (1994).
______. "Changing Relationships Among European Constitutional Courts." 21 *Cardozo Law Review* 1045 (2000).
______. "Economics and Judging: An Afterword on Cooter and Wald." 50 *Law & Contemporary Problems* 245 (Autumn 1987).
______. Exchange with Justice Scalia on "Constitutional Relevance of Foreign Court Decisions," at American University Washington College of Law (January 13, 2005), transcript by Federal News Service, available at http://domino.american.edu/AU/media/mediarel.nsf/1D265343BD.
______. "Harry A. Blackmun: Principle and Compassion." 99 *Columbia Law Review* 1393 (1999).
______. "Judicial Review: A Practicing Judge's Perspective." 78 *Texas Law Review* 761 (2000).
______. Keynote Address. 97 *American Society for International Law Proceedings* 265 (2003).
______. "The Legal Profession and Public Service." 57 *New York University Annual Survey of American Law* 403 (2000).
______. "Liberty, Prosperity, and a Strong Judicial Institution." 61 *Law & Contemporary Problems* 21 (1998).
______. "On the Uses of Legislative History in Interpreting Statutes." 65 *Southern California Law Review* 845 (1992).
______. "Our Democratic Constitution." 77 *New York University Law Review* 245 (2002).
______. "Speech: Crimes Against Humanity, Nuremberg, 1946." 71 *New York University Law Review* 1161 (1996).
Brown, Henry B. "The Distribution of Property." 16 *American Bar Association Report* 213 (1893).
______. "The Judiciary." *Addresses on the Celebration of the One Hundredth Anniversary of the Laying of the Cornerstone of the Capitol of the United States* 78 (1896).
______. "Liberty of Press." 23 *New York State Bar Association Proceedings* 133 (1900).
Burger, Warren E. "Arbitration, Not Litigation." *Nation's Business* 52 (August 1982).
______. "Causes of Dissatisfaction with Criminal Justice." Seminar of Investigative and Enforcement Officials, Washington, D.C., 15 November 1967.
______. "The Doctrine of Judicial Review: Mr. Marshall, Mr. Jefferson, and Mr. Marbury." Presidential Address, Bentham Club, University College, London, England (1 February 1972).
______. "Some Further Reflections on the Problem of Adequacy of Trial Counsel." 49 *Fordham Law Review* 1 (1980).
______. "The Special Skills of Advocacy." 42 *Fordham Law Review* 227 (1973).

______. "Who Will Watch the Watchmen?" 14 *American University Law Review* 1 (1964).

Burger, Warren E., and Earl Warren. "Retired Chief Justice Warren Attacks, Chief Justice Burger Defends Freund Study Group's Composition and Proposal." 59 *American Bar Association Journal* 721 (1973).

Burton, Harold. "The Cornerstone of American Constitutional Law: The Extraordinary Case of *Marbury v. Madison.*" 36 *American Bar Association Journal* 805 (1950).

______. "The Dartmouth College Case: A Dramatization." 38 *American Bar Association Journal* 991 (1952).

______. "*Ex parte Milligan* and *Ex parte McCardle.*" 41 *American Bar Association Journal* 176 (1955).

______. "An Independent Judiciary: The Keystone of Our Freedom." 39 *American Bar Association Journal* 1067 (1953).

______. "John Marshall—the Man." 104 *University of Pennsylvania Law Review* 3 (1955).

______. "Judging Is Also Administration." Address, Section on Judicial Administration, ABA Convention, Cleveland, Ohio, 1947.

______. "Justice the Guardian of Liberty: John Marshall at the Trial of Aaron Burr." 37 *American Bar Association Journal* 735 (1951).

______. "Unsung Services of the Supreme Court of the United States." 24 *Fordham Law Review* 169 (1955).

Butler, Pierce. "Some Opportunities and Duties of Lawyers." 9 *American Bar Association Journal* 583 (1923).

Byrnes, James F. *All in One Lifetime.* New York: Harper, 1958.

______. "Preserver People's Rights." 16 *Vital Speeches* 450 (1952).

______. "Segregation." 50 *Vermont Bar Association Proceedings* 86 (1956).

Cameron, James Duke. "Federal Review, Finality of State Court Decisions, and a Proposal for a National Court of Appeals—A State Judge's Solution to a Continuing Problem." 3 *Brigham Young University Law Review* 545 (1981).

Calabresi, Guido. "The Current, Subtle—and Not so Subtle—Rejection of an Independent Judiciary." 4 *University of Pennsylvania Journal of Constitutional Law* 637 (2002).

______. "Federal and State Courts: Restoring a Workable Balance." 78 *New York University Law Review* 1293 (2003).

______. "An Introduction to Legal Thought: Four Approaches to Law and to the Allocation of Body Parts." 55 *Stanford Law Review* 2113 (2003).

Campbell, John. "Address." 6 *Alabama State Bar Association Proceedings* 75 (1884).

Cardozo, Benjamin N. *The Growth of the Law.* New Haven: Yale University Press, 1924.

______. *Law and Literature and Other Essays and Addresses.* New York: Harcourt Brace, 1931.

______. *The Nature of the Judicial Process.* New Haven: Yale University Press, 1921.

______. *Paradoxes of the Legal Science.* New York: Columbia University Press, 1928.

Clark, Charles E. "The Limits of Judicial Objectivity." 12 *American University Law Review* 1 (1963).

______. "A Plea for the Unprincipled Decision." 49 *Virginia Law Review* 660 (1963).

Clark, Tom C. "Constitutional Adjudication and the Supreme Court." 9 *Drake Law Review* 59 (1960).

______. "The Court and Its Functions." 34 *Alabama Law Review* 497 (1970).
______. "The Internal Operations of the United States Supreme Court." 43 *Journal of the American Judicature Society* 45 (1959).
______. "Introduction, Judicial Reform: A Symposium." 23 *University of Florida Law Review* 217 (1971).
______. "Random Thoughts on the Court's Interpretation of Individual Rights." 1 *Houston Law Review* 75 (1963).
______. "Reminiscences of an Attorney General Turned Associate Justice." 6 *Houston Law Review* 623 (1969).
______. "Some Thoughts on Supreme Court Practice." Address, 13 April 1959.
Clarke, John H. "History and the 1937 Court Proposal." 3 *Vital Speeches* 369 (1937).
______. "Methods of Work of the United States Supreme Court Judges." 9 *American Bar Association Journal* 80 (1923).
______. "Practice Before the Supreme Court." 8 *Virginia Law Review* 241 (1922).
Coffin, Frank M. *On Appeal: Courts, Lawyering, and Judging.* New York: Norton, 1994.
______. *The Ways of a Judge: Reflections from the Federal Appellate Bench.* Boston: Houghton Mifflin, 1980.
Cooley, Thomas. *A Treatise on Constitutional Limitations.* Boston: Little, Brown, 1868.
Crockett, George W., Jr. "A Black Judge Speaks." 53 *Judicature* 360 (1970).
Curtis, Benjamin. *Executive Power.* Boston: Little, Brown, 1862.
______. *Jurisdiction, Practice, and Peculiar Jurisprudence of the Courts of the United States.* Boston: Little, Brown, 1880.
Day, Jack Grant. "How Judges Think: Verification of the Judicial Hunch." *Journal of Contemporary Legal Studies* 73 (Spring 1988).
______. "Why Judges Must Make Law." 26 *Case Western Law Review* 563 (1976).
Day, William. "The Judicial Power of the Nation." 17 *Michigan Alumnus* 357 (1911).
Devitt, Edward J. "Ten Commandments for the New Judge." 65 *American Bar Association Journal* 574 (1979).
Douglas, William O. "The Bill of Rights Is Not Enough." 38 *New York University Law Review* 207 (1963).
______. "Chief Justice Stone." 46 *Columbia Law Review* 693 (1946).
______. "The Dissent: A Safeguard of Democracy." 32 *Journal of the American Judicature Society* 104 (1948).
______. "In Forma Pauperis Practice in the United States." 2 *New Hampshire Bar Journal* 5 (1959).
______. "The Lasting Influence of Brandeis." 19 *Temple Law Quarterly* 361 (1946).
______. "Mr. Justice Black." 65 *Yale Law Journal* 449 (1956).
______. "Mr. Justice Cardozo." 58 *Michigan Law Review* 549 (1960).
______. "Mr. Justice Douglas." CBS Reports, 6 September 1972.
______. "On Misconception of the Judicial Function and the Responsibility of the Bar." 59 *Columbia Law Review* 735 (1949).
______. "Procedural Safeguards in the Bill of Rights." 31 *Journal of the American Judicature Society* 166 (1948).
______. *The Right of the People.* Garden City: Doubleday, 1958.
______. "The Role of the Lawyer." 12 *Oklahoma Law Review* 1 (1959).

______. "Stare Decisis." 49 *Columbia Law Review* 735 (1949).

______. "The Supreme Court and Its Case Load." 45 *Cornell Law Quarterly* 401 (1960).

______. *We the Judges*. New York: Doubleday, 1956.

Easterbrook, Frank H. "Abstraction and Authority." 59 *University of Chicago Law Review* 349 (1992).

______. "The Crisis in Legal Theory and the Revival of Classical Jurisprudence: Stability and Reliability in Judicial Decisions." 73 *Cornell Law Review* 422 (1988).

______. "Substance and Due Process." 1982 *Supreme Court Review* 85 (Chicago: University of Chicago Press, 1982).

______. "Unitary Executive Interpretation: A Comment." 15 *Cardozo Law Review* 313 (1993).

______. "Levels of Generality in Constitutional Interpretation." 59 *Chicago Law Review* 349 (1992).

______. "Do Liberals and Conservatives Differ in Judicial Activism?" 73 *University of Colorado Law Review* 1401 (2002).

______. "Textualism and Democratic Legitimacy: Textualism and the Dead Hand." 66 *George Washington Law Review* 1119 (1998).

Edwards, Harry T. "A Judge's View on Justice, Bureaucracy, and Legal Method." 80 *Michigan Law Review* 259 (1981).

______. "The Judicial Function and the Elusive Goal of Principled Decision making." 1991 *Wisconsin Law Review* 837 (1991).

______. "Public Misperceptions Concerning the 'Politics' of Judging: Dispelling Some Myths About the D.C. Circuit." 56 *University of Colorado Law Review* 619 (1985).

______. "The Role of a Judge in Modern Society: Some Reflections on Current Practice in Federal Appellate Adjudication." 32 *Cleveland State Law Review* 385 (1983–1984).

Feinberg, Wilfred. "Constraining 'The Least Dangerous Branch': The Tradition of Attacks on Judicial Power." 59 *New York University Law Review* 252 (1984).

Field, Stephen J. "Farewell to the Supreme Court." 5 *American Law Review* 537 (1897).

______. "The Late Chief Justice Chase." 11 *Overland Monthly* 305 (1873).

______. "The Supreme Court of the United States." Centennial Celebration of the Organization of the Federal Judiciary, New York, N.Y., 134 U.S. 729 (1890).

Fortas, Abe. "Chief Justice Warren: The Enigma of Leadership." 84 *Yale Law Journal* 405 (1970).

Frank, Jerome. *Courts on Trial: Myth and Reality in American Justice*. Princeton: Princeton University Press, 1949.

______. *Law and the Modern Mind*. New York: Coward-McCann, 1930.

Frankel, Marvin E. "The Adversary Judge." 54 *Texas Law Review* 465 (1976).

______. "From Private Fights Toward Public Justice." 51 *New York University Law Review* 516 (1976).

______. *Partisan Justice*. New York: Hill and Wang, 1980.

______. "The Search for Truth: An Umpireal View." 123 *University of Pennsylvania Law Review* 1031 (1975).

Frankfurter, Felix. "The 'Administrative Side' of Chief Justice Hughes." 63 *Harvard Law Review* 1 (1949).

______. "Benjamin Nathan Cardozo." 22 *Dictionary of American Biography* 93 (1949).

______. "Chief Justices I Have Known." 39 *Virginia Law Review* 883 (1953).
______. *Felix Frankfurter on the Supreme Court: Extrajudicial Essays on the Court and the Constitution.* Edited by Philip B. Kurland. Cambridge: Belknap Press, 1970.
______. "Harlan Fiske Stone." *American Philosophical Society Yearbook* 334 (1946).
______. "The Job of a Supreme Court Justice." *New York Times Magazine* 14 (28 November 1954).
______. "John Marshall and the Judicial Function." 69 *Harvard Law Review* 217 (1955).
______. *Law and Politics: Occasional Papers of Felix Frankfurter 1913–1938.* Edited by Archibald MacLeish and E. F. Prichard Jr. New York: Harcourt Brace, 1939.
______. "'Moral Grandeur' of Justice Brandeis." *New York Times Magazine* 26 (11 November 1956).
______. "Mr. Justice Brandeis." 55 *Harvard Law Review* 181 (1941).
______. *Mr. Justice Holmes and the Supreme Court.* Cambridge: Belknap Press, 1961.
______. "Mr. Justice Jackson." 68 *Harvard Law Review* 937 (1955).
______. "Mr. Justice Roberts." 104 *University of Pennsylvania Law Review* 311 (1955).
______. *Of Law and Life and Other Things That Matter: Papers and Addresses of Felix Frankfurter 1956–1963.* Edited by Philip B. Kurland. Cambridge: Belknap Press, 1965.
______. *Of Law and Men: Papers and Addresses 1939–1956.* Edited by Philip Elman. New York: Harcourt Brace, 1956.
______. "Personal Ambitions of Judges: Should a Judge 'Think Beyond the Judicial'?" 34 *American Bar Association Journal* 656 (1948).
______. "Some Observations on the Nature of the Judicial Process of Supreme Court Litigation." 98 *American Philosophical Society Proceedings* 233 (1954).
______. "Some Reflections on the Reading of Statutes." 47 *Columbia Law Review* 527 (1947).
______. "The Supreme Court in the Mirror of the Justices." 105 *University of Pennsylvania Law Review* 781 (1957).
Frankfurter, Felix, and Harlan B. Phillips. *Felix Frankfurter Reminisces.* New York: Reynal, 1960.
Fried, Charles. "Scholars and Judges: Reason and Power." 23 *Harvard Journal of Law & Public Policy* 807 (2000).
Friendly, Henry J. "Averting the Flood by Lessening the Flow." 105 *Cornell Law Review* 634 (1957).
______. *Benchmarks.* Chicago: University of Chicago Press, 1967.
______. "The Courts and Social Policy: Substance and Procedure." 33 *University of Miami Law Review* 21 (1978).
______. "The Gap in Lawmaking—Judges Who Can't and Legislatures Who Won't." 63 *Columbia Law Review* 787 (1963).
______. "Indiscretion About Discretion." 31 *Emory Law Journal* 747 (1982).
______. "Some Kind of Hearing." 123 *University of Pennsylvania Law Review* 1267 (1975).
Fuller, Melville W. "Centennial of the Constitution of the United States." 21 *Chicago Legal News* 303 (1889).
Ginsburg, Douglas H., and Donald Falk. "The Court En Banc: 1981–1990." 59 *George Washington Law Review* 1008 (1991).

Ginsburg, Ruth Bader. "Constitutional Adjudication in the United States as a Means of Advancing the Equal Stature of Men and Women Under the Law." 26 *Hofstra Law Review* 263 (1997).

_____. "The Role of Dissenting Opinions." (October 21, 2007), available at www.supremecourtus.gov/publicinfo/speeches/sp_10-21-07.html.

_____. "'A Decent Respect to the Opinions of [Human]kind': The Value of a Comparative Perspective in Constitutional Adjudication." Address to the Constitutional Court of South Africa (February 7, 2006), available at www.supremecourtus.gov/publicinfo/speeches/sp_02-07b-06.html; also in 1 *Florida International University Law Review* 27 (2006).

_____. "*Brown v. Board of Education* in International Context." Address at Columbia University School of Law (October 21, 2004), available at www.supremecourtus.gov/public info/speeches/sp_10-25-04.html; also in 36 *Columbia Human Rights Law Review* 493 (2005).

_____. "Looking Beyond Our Borders: The Value of a Comparative Perspective in Constitutional Adjudication." 40 *Idaho Law Review* 1 (2003).

______. "From Benjamin to Brandeis to Breyer: Is There a Jewish Seat?" 41 *Brandeis Law Journal* 229 (2002).

______. "Remarks on Women's Progress at the Bar and on the Bench." 89 *Cornell Law Review* 801 (2004).

______. "Tribute to Chief Justice William Hubbs Rehnquist." 74 *George Washington Law Review* 869 (2006).

______. "Communicating and Commenting on the Court's Work." 83 *Georgetown Law Journal* 2119 (1995).

______. "Constitutional Adjudication in the United States as a Means of Advancing the Equal Stature of Men and Women under the Law." 26 *Hofstra Law Review* 263 (1997).

______. "Judicial Independence: The Situation of the U.S. Federal Judiciary." 85 *Nebraska Law Review* 1 (2006).

______. "Workways of the Supreme Court." 25 *Thomas Jefferson Law Review* 517 (2003).

______. "Informing the Public about the U.S. Supreme Court's Work." 29 *Loyola University of Chicago Law Journal* 275 (1998).

______. "Inviting Judicial Activism: A 'Liberal' or 'Conservative' Technique?" 15 *Georgia Law Review* 539 (1981).

______. "On the Interdependence of Law Schools and Law Courts." 83 *Virginia Law Review* 829 (1997).

______. "An Overview of Court Review for Constitutionality in the United States." 57 *Louisiana Law Review* 1019 (1997).

______. "The Progression of Women in the Law." 28 *Valparaiso University Law Review* 1161 (1994).

______. "Reflections on the Independence, Good Behavior and Workload of Federal Judges." 55 *University of Colorado Law Review* 1 (1983).

______. "Remarks on Judicial Independence." 20 *Hawaii Law Review* 603 (1998).

______. "Remarks on Women's Progress in the Legal Profession in the United States." 33 *Tulsa Law Journal* 13 (1997).

______. "Remarks on Writing Separately." 65 *Washington Law Review* 133 (1990).

______. "Some Thoughts on Autonomy and Equality in Relation to *Roe v. Wade*." 63 *North Carolina Law Review* 375 (1985).

______. "Speaking in a Judicial Voice." 67 *New York University Law Review* 1185 (1992).

______. "Styles of Collegial Judging: One Judge's Perspective." 39 *Federal Bar News and Journal* 199 (1992).

______. "Supreme Court Pronouncements on the Conduct of Lawyers." 1 *Journal of the Institute for the Study of Legal Ethics* 1 (1996).

Ginsburg, Ruth Bader, and Deborah Jones Merritt. "Affirmative Action: An International Human Rights Dialogue." 21 *Cardozo Law Review* 253 (1999).

Godbold, John C. "Twenty Pages and Twenty Minutes—Effective Advocacy on Appeal." 30 *Southwestern Law Journal* 801 (1976).

Goldberg, Arthur J. *The Defenses of Freedom: The Public Papers of Arthur J. Goldberg*. Edited by Daniel Patrick Moynihan. New York: Harper & Row, 1966.

______. *Equal Justice: The Warren Era of the Supreme Court*. Evanston: Northwestern University Press, 1971.

Graber, Susan P. "Looking at Feminist Legal Theory from the Bench." *The Advocate* (Northwestern School of Law, Lewis & Clark College) 35 (Summer 1992).

Gray, Horace. "An Address on the Life, Character, and Influence of Chief Justice Marshall." 14 *Virginia State Bar Association Report* 365 (1901).

Grodin, Joseph R. *In Pursuit of Justice: Reflections of a State Supreme Court Justice*. Berkeley: University of California Press, 1989.

Gunderson, Elmer. "Jurisprudential Character: The Typology of James David Barber in a Judicial Context." 13 *Southwestern University Law Review* 396 (1983).

Hand, Learned. *The Bill of Rights*. Cambridge: Harvard University Press, 1958.

______. "Chief Justice Stone's Conception of the Judicial Function." 46 *Columbia Law Review* 696 (1946).

______. "Mr. Justice Cardozo." 52 *Harvard Law Review* 361 (1939).

______. *The Spirit of Liberty: Papers and Addresses of Learned Hand*. New York: Knopf, 1952.

Harlan, John M. "The Courts in the American System of Government." 37 *Chicago Legal News* 271 (1905).

______. "Government Under the Constitution." *Law Notes* 206 (1908).

______. "James Wilson and the Formation of the Constitution." 34 *American Law Review* 481 (1900).

______. "The Supreme Court of the United States and Its Work." 30 *American Law Review* 900 (1896).

Harlan, John M. (the second). *The Evolution of a Judicial Philosophy: Selected Opinions and Papers of Justice John M. Harlan*. Edited by David L. Shapiro. Cambridge: Harvard University Press, 1969.

______. "A Glimpse of the Supreme Court at Work." 11 *University of Chicago Law School Record* 1 (1963).

______. "Manning the Dikes." 13 *Record of the New York City Bar Association* 541 (1958).

______. "Some Aspects of Handling a Case in the United States Supreme Court." Address, New York State Bar Association, N.Y., 1957.

______. "Some Aspects of the Judicial Process in the United States Supreme Court." 33 *Australian Law Journal* 108 (1959).

______. "What Part Does the Oral Argument Play in the Conduct of an Appeal?" Address, Judicial Conference, Asheville, N.C., 1955.

Hastie, William H. "Judicial Role and Judicial Image." 121 *University of Pennsylvania Law Review* 947 (1973).

Higginbotham, A. Leon, Jr. "The Priority of Human Rights in Court Reform." *Judges' Journal* 34 (Spring-Summer 1976).

Higginbotham, Patrick. "Bureaucracy—The Carcinoma of the Federal Judiciary." 31 *Alabama Law Review* 261 (1980).

Holmes, Oliver Wendell. *The Common Law.* Boston: Little, Brown, 1881.

______. *The Holmes–Laski Letters.* Edited by Mark De Wolfe Howe. Cambridge: Harvard University Press, 1953.

______. *The Holmes–Pollock Letters, 1874–1932.* Edited by Mark De Wolfe Howe. Cambridge: Harvard University Press, 1941.

______. *The Mind and Faith of Justice Holmes.* Edited by Max Lerner. Boston: Little, Brown, 1943.

Hornby, D. Brock. "The Business of the U.S. District Courts." 10 *Green Bag* 453–468 (2007).

Hufstedler, Shirley. "New Blocks for Old Pyramids: Reshaping the Judicial System." 44 *Southern California Law Review* 901 (1971).

Hughes, Charles Evans. *Addresses.* New York: Harper, 2d ed., 1916.

______. "An Imperishable Ideal of Liberty Under Law." 25 *Journal of the American Judicature Society* 99 (1941).

______. "Mr. Justice Holmes." 44 *Harvard Law Review* 677 (1932).

______. "Roger Brooke Taney." 17 *American Bar Association Journal* 785 (1931).

______. "The Social Thought of Mr. Justice Brandeis." In *Mr. Justice Brandeis.* Edited by Felix Frankfurter. New Haven: Yale University Press, 1932.

______. *The Supreme Court of the United States: Its Foundation, Methods, and Achievements—An Interpretation.* New York: Columbia University Press, 1928.

______. "War Powers Under the Constitution." Address, American Bar Association Meeting, 1917.

Hutcheson, Joseph C., Jr. "Judging as Administration, Administration as Judging." 21 *Texas Law Review* 1 (1942).

______. "The Judgment Intuitive: The Function of the 'Hunch' in Judicial Decision." 14 *Cornell Law Quarterly* 274 (1929).

Jackson, Robert H. "Advocacy Before the Supreme Court: Suggestions for Effective Case Presentations." 37 *American Bar Association Journal* 801 (1951).

______. "Decisional Law and *Stare Decisis.*" 30 *American Bar Association Journal* 334 (1945).

______. "The Meaning of Statutes: What Congress Says or What the Court Says." 34 *American Bar Association Journal* 535 (1948).

______. *The Struggle for Judicial Supremacy.* New York: Knopf, 1941.

______. *The Supreme Court in the American System of Government.* Cambridge: Harvard University Press, 1955.

______. "The Task of Maintaining Our Liberties: The Role of the Judiciary." 39 *American Bar Association Journal* 961 (1953).

Jay, John. *The Correspondence and Public Papers of John Jay.* New York: Putnam's, 1890–1893.

Johnson, Frank M., Jr. "In Defense of Judicial Activism." 28 *Emory Law Journal* 901 (1979).

______. "Judicial Activism Is a Duty—Not an Intrusion." *Judges' Journal* 4 (Fall 1977).

______. "The Role of the Judiciary with Respect to the Other Branches of Government." 11 *Georgia Law Review* 455 (1977).

Justice, William Wayne. "The New Awakening: Judicial Activism in a Conservative Age." 43 *Southwestern Law Journal* 657 (1989).

______. "Putting the Judge Back in Judging." 63 *University of Colorado Law Review* 441 (1992).

______. "A Relativistic Constitution." 52 *University of Colorado Law Review* 19 (1980).

______. "The Two Faces of Judicial Activism." 61 *George Washington Law Review* 1 (1992).

Kaufman, Irving R. "Chilling Judicial Independence." 88 *Yale Law Journal* 681 (1979).

______. "The Essence of Judicial Independence." 80 *Columbia Law Review* 671 (1980).

Kaye, Judith S. "The Human Dimension in Appellate Judging: A Brief Reflection on a Timeless Concern." 73 *Cornell Law Review* 1004 (1988).

______. "My 'Freshman Years' on the Court of Appeals." 70 *Judicature* 166 (1986).

______. "State Courts at the Dawn of a New Century: Common Law Courts Reading Statutes and Constitutions." 70 *New York University Law Review* 1 (1995).

______. "The Human Dimension in Appellate Judging: A Brief Reflection on a Timeless Concern." 73 *Cornell Law Review* 1004 (1988).

______. "Women Chiefs: Shaping the Third Branch." 36 *University of Toledo Law Review* 899 (2005).

Keith, Damon J. "Should Color-Blindness and Representativeness Be a Part of American Justice?" 26 *Howard Law Journal* 1 (1983).

Kennedy, Anthony M. "Q&A." *The Docket Sheet* 1 (Winter 1988).

______. "The Voice of Thurgood Marshall." 44 *Stanford Law Review* 1221 (1992).

______. "Tribute: William H. Rehnquist and Sandra Day O'Connor." 58 *Stanford Law Review* 1663 (2006).

Kirby, Michael. "International Law—The Impact on National Constitutions." 21 *American University International Law Review* 327 (2006).

Kozinski, Alex. "Conduct Unbecoming: *Closed Chambers:* The First Eyewitness Account of the Epic Struggles Inside the Supreme Court." 108 *Yale Law Journal* 835 (1999).

______. "Confessions of a Bad Apple." 100 *Yale Law Journal* 1707 (1991).

______. "Constitutional Federalism Reborn." 22 *Harvard Journal of Law & Public Policy* 91 (1998).

______. "The Dark Lessons of Utopia." 58 *University of Chicago Law Review* 575 (1991).

______. "Finding Justice in the Internet Dimension." 20 *Seattle University Law Review* 619 (1997).

______. "The Many Faces of Judicial Independence." 14 *Georgia State University Law Review* 861 (1998).

______. "My Pizza with Nino." 12 *Cardozo Law Review* 1583 (1991).

______. "What I Ate for Breakfast and Other Mysteries of Judicial Decision Making." 26 *Loyola of Los Angeles Law Review* 993 (1993).

Kozinski, Alex, and Eugene Volokh. "A Penumbra Too Far." 106 *Harvard Law Review* 1639 (1993).

Lay, Donald P. "The Federal Appeals Process: Whither We Goest? The Next Fifty Years," 15 *William Mitchell Law Review* 515 (1983).

L'Heureux-Dube, C. "The Importance of Dialogue: Globalization and the International Impact of the Rehnquist Court," 34 *Tulsa Law Journal* 15 (1998).

Leflar, Robert A. "Honest Judicial Opinions." 74 *Northwestern University Law Review* 721 (1979).

Leventhal, Harold. "Environmental Decisionmaking and the Role of the Courts." 122 *University of Pennsylvania Law Review* 509 (1974).

______. "A Modest Proposal for a Multi-Circuit Court of Appeals." 24 *American University Law Review* 881 (1975).

Linde, Hans A. "Elective Judges: Some Comparative Comments." 61 *Southern California Law Review* 1995 (1988).

______. "First Things First: Rediscovering the States' Bills of Rights." 9 *University of Baltimore Law Review* 379 (1980).

Lurton, Horace. "A Government of Law or a Government of Men?" 193 *North American Review* 9 (1911).

Markey, Howard T. "On the Cause and Treatment of Judicial Activism." *Federal Bar News* 296 (December 1982).

Marshall, John. Letter to the editor (under pseudonym "A Friend to the Union"). *Philadelphia Union* (18 April, 1 May 1819).

Marshall, Thurgood. "Group Action in the Pursuit of Justice." 44 *New York University Law Review* 661 (1969).

______. "Law and the Quest for Equality." 1 *Washington University Law Quarterly* 1 (1967).

______. "Recent Development, Supreme Court Summary Dispositions: Either Change the Rules or Stop Giving Short Shrift to Important Issues." 19 *Willamette Law Review* 313 (1983).

______. "Reflections on the Bicentennial of the United States Constitution." 101 *Harvard Law Review* 1 (1987).

______. "Remarks on the Death Penalty Made at the Judicial Conference of the Second Circuit." 86 *Columbia Law Review* 1 (1986).

Martin, Boyce F., Jr. "Gee Whiz., The Sky is Falling!" 106 *Michigan Law Review* 1 (2007).

Matthews, Stanley. "The Federal Judiciary." 2 *History of the Celebration of the One Hundredth Anniversary of the Promulgation of the Constitution of the United States.* Edited by Hampton L. Carson, 1889.

______. "The Judicial Power of the United States." Yale Law School, 26 June 1898.

McCree, Wade H., Jr. "Bureaucratic Justice: An Early Warning." 129 *University of Pennsylvania Law Review* 777 (1981).

McGowan, Carl. "Congress, Court, and Control of Delegated Power." 77 *Columbia Law Review* 1119 (1977).

______. "The View from an Inferior Court." 19 *San Diego Law Review* 659 (1983).

McMillan, James B. "Social Science and the District Court: The Observations of a Journeyman Trial Judge." 39 *Law and Contemporary Problems* 157 (1975).

Medina, Harold R. "The Judge and His God: 'We Are Not the Masters'." 38 *American Bar Association Journal* 661 (1952).

______. "Some Reflections on the Judicial Function: A Personal Viewpoint." 38 *American Bar Association Journal* 107 (1952).

______. "Some Reflections on the Judicial Function at the Appellate Level." 1961 *Washington University Law Quarterly* 148 (1961).

______. "The Trial Judge's Notes: A Study in Judicial Administration." 49 *Cornell Law Quarterly* 1 (1963).

Merritt, Gilbert S. "The Decision Making Process in Federal Courts of Appeals." 51 *Ohio State Law Journal* 1385 (1990).

Messitte, Peter J. "Citing Foreign Law in U.S. Courts: Is Our Sovereignty Really At Stake?" 35 *University of Baltimore Law Review* 171 (2005).

Mikva, Abner J. "Bringing the Behavioral Sciences to the Law: Tell It to the Judge or Talk to Your Legislator?" 8 *Behavioral Science and Law* 285 (1990).

______. "For Whom Judges Write." 61 *Southern California Law Review* 1357 (1988).

______. "The Role of Theorists in Constitutional Cases." 63 *University of Colorado Law Review* 451 (1992).

______. "Statutory Interpretation: Getting the Law to Be Less Common." 50 *Ohio State Law Journal* 979 (1989).

Miller, Samuel F. "Introduction to Constitutional Law." 4 *Scotland Law Review* 79 (1878).

______. "Judicial Reform." 6 *Western Jurist* 49 (1872).

______. *Lectures on the Constitution*. Washington, D.C.: Morrison, 1880.

______. "Legislation in This Country as It Affects the Administration of Justice." 2 *New York State Bar Association Proceedings* 31 (1879).

______. "The Study and Practice of Law in the United States." 48 *Legal Times* 171 (1870).

______. "The System of Trial by Jury." 21 *American Law Review* 859 (1887).

______. "The Use and Value of Authorities." 23 *American Law Review* 165 (1889).

______. "The Weight of Authorities." 10 *Virginia Law Journal* 582 (1886).

Miner, Roger J. "Advice and Consent in Theory and Practice." 41 *American University Law Review* 1075 (1992).

______. "Identifying, Protecting and Preserving Individual Rights: Traditional Federal Court Functions." 23 *Seton Hall Law Review* 821 (1993).

Mosk, Stanley. "The Common Law and the Judicial Decision-Making Process." 11 *Harvard Journal of Law and Public Policy* 35 (1988).

______. "Rediscovering the 10th Amendment." 20 *Judges' Journal* 16 (1981).

______. "Whither Thou Goest—The State Constitution and Election Returns." 7 *Whittier Law Review* 753 (1985).

Neely, Richard. *How Courts Govern America.* New Haven: Yale University Press, 1981.
______. *Why Courts Don't Work.* New York: McGraw Hill, 1983.
Newman, Jon O. "Between Legal Realism and Neutral Principles: The Legitimacy of Institutional Values." 72 *California Law Review* 200 (1984).
______. "Last Words of an Appellate Opinion." 70 *Brooklyn Law Review* 727 (2005).
______. "1,000 Judges—The Limit for an Effective Federal Judiciary," 76 *Judicature* 187 (1993).
______. "Restructuring Federal Jurisdiction: Proposals to Preserve the Federal Judicial System," 56 *University of Chicago Law Review* 761 (1989).
Oakes, James L. "The Proper Role of the Federal Courts in Enforcing the Bill of Rights." 54 *New York University Law Review* 911 (1979).
______. "Remarks on Justice Harlan as a Judicial Conservative." 36 *New York Law School Law Review* 3 (1991).
O'Connor, Sandra Day. "The History of the Women's Suffrage Movement." 49 *Vanderbilt Law Review* 657 (1996).
______. Keynote Address, 96 *American Society for International Law Proceedings* 348 (2002).
______. *The Lazy B.* (New York: Modern Library, 2005).
______. "Lessons from the Third Sovereign: Indian Tribal Courts." 33 *Tulsa Law Review* 1 (1997).
______. "The Life of the Law: Principles of Logic and Experience from the United States." 1996 *Wisconsin Law Review* 1.
______. *The Majesty of the Law.* (New York: Random House, 2003).
______. "Our Judicial Federalism." 35 *Case Western Reserve Law Review* 1 (1985).
______. "Portia's Progress." 66 *New York University Law Review* 1546 (1991).
______. "Thurgood Marshall: The Influence of a Raconteur." 44 *Stanford Law Review* 1217 (1992).
______. "Trends in the Relationship Between the Federal and State Courts from the Perspective of a State Court Judge." 22 *William & Mary Law Review* 801 (1981).
______. "A Tribute to Justice Lewis F. Powell, Jr." 101 *Harvard Law Review* 395 (1987).
Posner, Richard A. *Breaking the Deadlock: The 2000 Election, the Constitution, and the Courts.* (Princeton: Princeton University Press, 2001).
______. *Cardozo: A Study in Reputation.* Chicago: University of Chicago Press, 1990.
______. *Countering Terrorism: Blurred Focus, Halting Steps.* (Lanham, Md.: Rowman & Littlefield, 2007).
______. "Dworkin, Polemics, and the Clinton Impeachment Controversy." 94 *Northwestern University Law Review* 1023 (2000).
______. *The Federal Courts: Crisis and Reform.* Cambridge: Harvard University Press, 2d ed. 1996.
______. *Frontiers of Legal Theory.* (Cambridge: Harvard University Press, 2004).
______. *How Judges Think.* (Cambridge: Harvard University Press, 2008).
______. "The Institutional Dimension of Statutory and Constitutional Interpretation." 101 *Michigan Law Review* 952 (2003).
______. "Is the Ninth Circuit Too Large? A Statistical Study of Judicial Quality." 29 *Journal of Legal Studies* 711 (2000).

______. "Judicial Autonomy in a Political Environment." 38 *Arizona State Law Journal* 1 (2006).
______. *Not a Suicide Pact: The Constitution in a Time of National Emergency.* (New York: Oxford University Press, 2006.
______. *Overcoming Law.* Cambridge: Harvard University Press, 1995.
______. "Past-Dependency, Pragmatism, and Critique of History in Adjudication and Legal Scholarship." 67 *University of Chicago Law Review* 573 (2000).
______. *The Problematics of Moral and Legal Theory.* Cambridge: Belknap Press, 1999.
______. *The Problems of Jurisprudence.* Cambridge: Harvard University Press, 1990.
______. "The Role of the Judge in the Twenty-First Century." 86 *Boston University Law Review* 1049 (2006).
______. *Sex and Reason.* Cambridge: Harvard University Press, 1992.
Powell, Lewis F., Jr. "Are the Federal Courts Becoming Bureaucracies?" 68 *American Bar Association Journal* 1370 (1982).
______. "Carolene Products Revisited." 82 *Columbia Law Review* 1087 (1982).
______. "Constitutional Interpretation." An Interview. *Kenyon College Alumni Bulletin* 14 (Summer 1979).
______. "Myths and Misconceptions about the Supreme Court." 48 *New York University Law Review* 6 (1976).
______. "Of Politics and the Court." *Yearbook of the Supreme Court Historical Society* (1982).
______. "*Stare Decisis* and Judicial Restraint." 47 *Washington & Lee Law Review* 281 (1990).
______. "What the Justices Are Saying." 62 *American Bar Association Journal* 1454 (1976).
Re, Edward D. "The University Declaration of Human Rights and the Domestic Courts." 31 *Suffolk University Law Review* 585 (1998).
Reed, Stanley F. "The Living Law." Address, Columbia University Law School, 8 November 1958.
______. "Our Constitutional Philosophy: Concerning the Significance of Judicial Review in the Evolution of American Democracy." 21 *Kentucky State Bar Journal* 136 (1957).
______. "*Stare Decisis* and Constitutional Law." 35 *Pennsylvania Bar Association Quarterly* 131 (1938).
Rehnquist, William H. "The Adversary Society." 33 *University of Miami Law Review* 1 (1978).
______. *All the Laws But One: Civil Liberties in Wartime.* New York: Knopf, 1998.
______. "The Changing Role of the Supreme Court." 14 *Florida State University Law Review* 1 (1986).
______. "Civil Liberty and the Civil War: The Indianapolis Treason Trials." 72 *Indiana Law Journal* 927 (1997).
______. "Constitutional Law and Public Opinion." 20 *Suffolk University Law Review* 751 (1986).
______. "The Cult of the Robe." *Judges' Journal* 74 (Fall 1976).
______. "The First Amendment: Freedom, Philosophy, and the Law." 12 *Gonzaga Law Review* 1 (1976).
______. "Government by Cliche." 45 *Missouri Law Review* 379 (1980).

______. *Grand Inquests: The Historic Impeachments of Justice Samuel Chase and President Andrew Johnson.* New York: Morrow, 1992.

______. "The Impeachment Clause: A Wild Card in the Constitution." 85 *Northwestern University Law Review* 903 (1991).

______. "The Notion of a Living Constitution." 54 *Texas Law Review* 693 (1976).

______. "The Open and Closed Nature of the U.S. Supreme Court." *IPS Byliner* release (United States Information Service, October 1977).

______. "Oral Advocacy." 27 *South Texas Law Review* 289 (1986).

______. "The Partisan: A Talk With Justice Rehnquist." *New York Times Magazine* 28 (3 March 1985).

______. "Point, Counterpoint: The Evolution of American Political Philosophy." 34 *Vanderbilt Law Review* 249 (1981).

______. "Presidential Appointments to the Supreme Court." 2 *Constitutional Commentary* 319 (1985).

______. "Seen in a Glass Darkly: The Future of Federal Courts." 1993 *Wisconsin Law Review* 1 (1993).

______. "Sunshine in the Third Branch." 16 *Washburn Law Journal* 559 (1977).

______. "The Supreme Court: 'The First Hundred Years Were the Hardest'." 42 *University of Miami Law Review* 475 (1988).

______. *The Supreme Court: How It Was, How It Is.* New York: Morrow, 1987, 2001.

______. *Centennial Crisis: the Disputed Election of 1876.* New York: Knopf, 2004.

Reinhardt, Stephen. "The Anatomy of an Execution: Fairness vs. 'Process'." 74 *New York University Law Review* 313 (1999).

______. "Civil Rights and the New Federal Judiciary: The Retreat from Fairness." 14 *Harvard Journal of Law & Public Policy* 142 (1991).

______. "Judicial Speech and the Open Judiciary." 28 *Loyola of Los Angeles Law Review* 805 (1995).

______. "Legal & Political Perspectives on the Battle over Same-Sex Marriage," 16 *Stanford Law & Policy Review* 11 (2005).

______. "Riots, Racism, and the Courts." 23 *Golden Gate University Law Review* 1 (1993).

______. "The Role of Social Justice in Judging Cases," 1 *University of St. Thomas Law Journal* 18 (2003).

______. "Whose Federal Judiciary Is It Anyway?" 27 *Loyola of Los Angeles Law Review* 1 (1993).

Richey, Charles R. "A Federal Trial Judge's Reflections on the Preparation for and Trial of Civil Cases." 52 *Indiana Law Journal* 111 (1976).

Roberts, John G., Jr. "In Memoriam: William H. Rehnquist," 119 *Harvard Law Review* 1 (2005).

______. "Oral Advocacy and the Re-emergence of a Supreme Court Bar" 30 *Journal of Supreme Court History* 68 (2005).

______. "What Makes the D.C. Circuit Different? A Historical View," 92 *Virginia Law Review* 375 (2006).

Roberts, Owen J. "American Constitutional Government: The Blueprint and Structure." 29 *Boston University Law Review* 1 (1953).

______. *The Court and the Constitution.* Cambridge: Harvard University Press, 1951.

Rubin, Alvin B. "Doctrine in Decision-Making: Rationale or Rationalization." 1987 *Utah Law Review* 357 (1987).

______. "Does Law Matter? A Judge's Response to the Critical Legal Studies Movement." 37 *Journal of Legal Education* 307 (1987).

______. "Managing Problems in the Federal Courts: Curbing Bureaucratization and Reducing Other Tensions Between Justice and Efficiency." 55 *Notre Dame Lawyer* 648 (1980).

______. "Views from the Lower Court." 23 *UCLA Law Review* 448 (1976).

Rutledge, Wiley B. "The Appellate Brief." 28 *American Bar Association Journal* 251 (1942).

______. *A Declaration of Legal Faith.* Lawrence: University of Kansas Press, 1947.

Ryan, J. Brendan. "Different Voices, Different Choices? The Impact of More Women Lawyers and Judges on the Justice System." 74 *Judicature* 138 (1990).

Scalia, Antonin. "Assorted Canards of Contemporary Legal Analysis." 40 *Case Western Reserve Law Review* 581 (1990).

______. "Commentary," 40 *St. Louis University Law Journal* 1119 (1996).

______. "The Dissenting Opinion." *Journal of Supreme Court History* 33 (1994).

______. "Judicial Deference to Administrative Interpretations of Law." 1989 *Duke Law Journal* 511 (1989).

______. Keynote Address, 98 *American Society of International Law Proceedings* 305 (2004).

______. *A Matter of Interpretation: Federal Courts and the Law.* Princeton: Princeton University Press, 1997.

______. "Morality, Pragmatism and the Legal Order." 9 *Harvard Journal of Law & Public Policy* 123 (1986).

______. "Originalism: The Lesser Evil." 57 *University of Cincinnati Law Review* 849 (1989).

______. "The Rule of Law as a Law of Rules." 56 *University of Chicago Law Review* 1175 (1989).

Schaefer, Walter V. "The Appellate Court." 3 *University of Chicago Law School Record* 10 (1954).

______. "Precedent and Policy." 34 *University of Chicago Law Review* 3 (1966).

Schroeder, Mary M. "Compassion on Appeal." 22 *Arizona State Law Journal* 45 (1990).

Seitz, Collins J. "Collegiality and the Court of Appeals." 75 *Judicature* 26 (1991).

Sentelle, David B. "Judicial Discretion: Is One More of a Good Thing Too Much?" 88 *Michigan Law Review* 1828 (1990).

Silberman, Laurence H. "The American Bar Association and Judicial Nominations." 59 *George Washington Law Review* 1092 (1991).

Sneed, Joseph T. "The Art of Statutory Interpretation." 62 *Texas Law Review* 665 (1983).

______. "When Should the Lions Be on the Throne? Reflections on Judicial Supremacy." 21 *Arizona Law Review* 925 (1979).

Souter, David H. "In Memoriam: Will J. Brennan, Jr." 111 *Harvard Law Review* 1 (1997).

______. "A Tribute to Justice Harry A. Blackmun." 104 *Yale Law Journal* 5 (1994).

Starr, Kenneth W. "Observations About the Use of Legislative History." 1987 *Duke Law Journal* 371 (1987).

______. "Of Forests and Trees: Structuralism in the Interpretation of Statutes." 56 *George Washington Law Review* 703 (1988).

Stevens, John Paul. "The Bill of Rights: A Century of Progress." 59 *University of Chicago Law Review* 13 (1992).

______. "The Freedom of Speech." 102 *Yale Law Journal* 1293 (1993).

______. "How a Mundane Assignment Affected My Re-examination of Miranda." 14 *Chicago Bar Record* 34 (2000).

______. "A Judge's Use of History." 1989 *Wisconsin Law Review* 223 (1989).

______. "Judicial Predilections." 6 *Nevada Law Review* 1 (2005).

______. "Judicial Restraint." 22 *San Diego Law Review* 437 (1985).

______. "Learning on the Job." 74 *Fordham Law Review"* 1561 (2006).

______. "The Life Span of a Judge-Made Rule." 58 *New York University Law Review* 1 (1983).

______. "The Shakespeare Canon of Statutory Construction." 140 *University of Pennsylvania Law Review* 1371 (1992).

______. "Some Thoughts About a General Rule." 21 *Arizona Law Review* 599 (1979).

______. "The Third Branch of Liberty." 41 *University of Miami Law Review* 277 (1986).

______. "Two Questions About Justice." 2003 *University of Illinois Law Review* 821 (2003).

Stewart, Potter. "The Indigent Defendant and the Supreme Court of the United States." 58 *Legal Aid Review* 3 (1960).

______. "Or of the Press." 16 *Hastings Constitutional Law Quarterly* 631 (1975).

______. "Reflections on the Supreme Court." *Litigation* 8 (Spring 1982).

Stone, Harlan Fiske. "The Chief Justice." 27 *American Bar Association Journal* 407 (1941).

______. "The Constitution of the United States." Address, League of Republican Women of the District of Columbia, 1924.

______. "Dissenting Opinions Are Not Without Value." 26 *Journal of the American Judicature Society* 78 (1942).

______. "Fifty Years' Work of the United States Supreme Court," 14 *American Bar Association Journal* 428 (1928).

______. "Functions of the Circuit Conferences." 28 *American Bar Association Journal* 78 (1942).

______. *Law and Its Administration.* New York: Columbia University Press, 1915.

______. *Public Control of Business.* N.p.: Howell, Soskin, 1940.

Story, Joseph. *Commentaries on the Constitution of the United States.* Boston: Little, Brown, 1833.

______. "Life, Character, and Service of Chief Justice Marshall." In *Miscellaneous Writings of Joseph Story.* Boston: Little, Brown, 1852.

Strong, William. "The Needs of the Supreme Court." 132 *North American Review* 437 (1881).

______. "Relief for the Supreme Court." 151 *North American Review* 567 (1890).

Sutherland, George. *Constitutional Power and World Affairs.* New York: Columbia University Press, 1919.

______. "The Courts and the Constitution." Address, American Bar Association, 1912.

Taft, William H. "Adequate Machinery for Judicial Business." 7 *American Bar Association Journal* 453 (1921).

______. "Administration of Criminal Justice." 15 *Yale Law Journal* 631 (1905–1906).

______. *The Anti-Trust Act and the Supreme Court.* New York: Harper & Bros., 1914.

______. "Delays and Defects in the Enforcement of Laws in this Country." 183 *North American Review* 851 (1908).

______. "The Jurisdiction of the Supreme Court Under the Act of February 13, 1925." 35 *Yale Law Journal* 1 (1925).

______. *Liberty Under Law, an Interpretation of the Principles of Our Constitutional Government.* New Haven: Yale University Press, 1922.

______. "Possible and Needed Reforms in Administration of Justice in Federal Courts." 8 *American Bar Association Journal* 601 (1922).

______. *Present Day Problems.* New York: Dodd, Mead, 1908.

______. "Salmon P. Chase Memorial." 9 *American Bar Association Journal* 348 (1923).

Tamm, Edward A., and Paul C. Reardon. "Warren E. Burger and the Administration of Justice." 3 *Brigham Young University Law Review* 447 (1981).

Thomas, Clarence. "Civility and Public Discourse." 31 *New England Law Review* 515 (1997).

______. "Freedom: A Responsibility, Not a Right." 21 *Ohio Northern University Law Review* 5 (1994).

______. "Judging." 45 *Kansas Law Review* 1 (1996).

______. *My Grandfather's Son: A Memoir.* (New York: Harper, 2007).

______. "Personal Responsibility." 12 *Regent University Law Review* 317 (2000).

______. "A Return to Civility." 33 *Tulsa Law Review* 7 (1997).

Traynor, Roger J. "Badlands in an Appellate Judge's Realm of Reason." 7 *Utah Law Review* 157 (1960).

______. "The Limits of Judicial Creativity." 63 *Iowa Law Review* 1 (1977).

______. "No Magic Words Could Do It Justice." 49 *California Law Review* 615 (1961).

______. "Quo Vadis, Prospective Overruling: A Question of Judicial Responsibility." 28 *Hastings Law Journal* 533 (1977).

______. "Reasoning in a Circle of Law." 56 *Virginia Law Review* 739 (1970).

______. "La Rude Vita, la Dolce Giustizia; or Hard Cases Can Make Good Law." 29 *University of Chicago Law Review* 223 (1962).

______. "Transatlantic Reflections on Leeways and Limits of Appellate Courts." 1980 *Utah Law Review* 255 (1980).

Vanderbilt, Arthur T. *The Doctrine of the Separation of Powers and Its Present Day Significance.* Lincoln: University of Nebraska Press, 1963.

______. *Men and Measure in the Law.* New York: Knopf, 1949.

Vinson, Fred M. "The Business of Judicial Administration: Suggestions to the Conference of Chief Justices." 35 *American Bar Association Journal* 893 (1949).

______. "Our Enduring Constitution." *Washington & Lee Law Review* 1 (1949).

______. "Vinson Tells A.B.A. of the Supreme Court's Work; Opinion on Dissents." 20 *Journal of the Oklahoma Bar Association* 1269 (1949).

______. "The Work of the United States Supreme Court." 12 *Texas Bar Journal* 551 (1948).

Waite, Morrison, Jr. "The Supreme Court of the United States." 36 *Alabama Law Journal* 318 (1887).

Wald, Patricia M. "The Conscience of a Judge." 25 *Suffolk University Law Review* 619 (1991).

______. "Constitutional Conundrums." 61 *University of Colorado Law Review* 727 (1990).

______. "Limits on the Use of Economic Analysis in Judicial Decisionmaking." *Law & Contemporary Problems* 224 (Autumn 1987).

______. "The Problem with the Courts: Black-Robed Bureaucracy, or Collegiality Under Challenge?" 42 *Maryland Law Review* 766 (1983).

______. "The Role of Morality in Judging: A Woman Judge's Perspective." 4 *Law & Inequality Journal* 3 (1986).

______. "The Sizzling Sleeper: The Use of Legislative History in Construing Statutes in the 1988–89 Term of the United States Supreme Court." 39 *American University Law Review* 277 (1990).

______. "Some Real Life Observations About Judging." 26 *Indiana Law Journal* 171 (1992).

______. "Thoughts on Decisionmaking." 87 *West Virginia Law Review* 1 (1984).

Wallace, J. Clifford. "Interpreting the Constitution: The Case for Judicial Restraint." 71 *Judicature* 81 (1987).

______. "The Jurisprudence of Judicial Restraint: A Return to the Moorings." 50 *George Washington Law Review* 1 (1981).

______. "Resolving Judicial Corruption While Preserving Judicial Independence: Comparative Perspectives." 28 *California Western School of Law International Law Journal* 341 (1998).

Warren, Earl. "Chief Justice Marshall." 41 *American Bar Association Journal* 1008 (1955).

______. "Chief Justice Taney." 41 *American Bar Association Journal* 504 (1955).

______. "Chief Justice William Howard Taft." 67 *Yale Law Journal* 353 (1958).

______. "A Conversation with Earl Warren." WGBH-TV, Boston, 1972.

______. "Delay and Congestion in the Federal Courts." 42 *Journal of the American Judicature Society* 6 (1958).

______. "Fourteenth Amendment: Retrospective and Prospective." In *The Fourteenth Amendment.* Edited by Bernard Schwartz. New York: New York University Press, 1970.

______. *Hughes and the Court.* New York: Colgate University Press, 1962.

______. *The Memoirs of Earl Warren.* New York: Doubleday, 1977.

______. "Mr. Justice Brennan." 80 *Harvard Law Review* 1 (1966).

______. *The Public Papers of Chief Justice Earl Warren.* Edited by Henry Christman. New York: Simon & Schuster, 1959.

Weinstein, Jack B. "Limits on Judges' Learning, Speaking, and Acting." 20 *University of Dayton Law Review* 1 (1994).

______. "The Poor's Right to Equal Access to the Courts." 13 *Connecticut Law Review* 651 (1981).

White, Byron R. "Challenges for the U.S. Supreme Court and the Bar: Contemporary Reflections." 51 *Antitrust Law Journal* 275 (1982).

______. "The Role of Judicial Review." *Horizons* 52 (1970).

______. "The Work of the Supreme Court: A Nuts and Bolts Description." 54 *New York State Bar Journal* 346 (1982).

White, Edward D. "The Supreme Court of the United States." 7 *American Bar Association Journal* 341 (1921).

Whittaker, Charles E. "Judicial Discretion." Address, Illinois Division of the Federal Bar Association, Chicago, Ill., 1960.

Wilkey, Malcolm R. "Judicial Activism, Congressional Abdication, and the Need for Constitutional Reform." 8 *Harvard Journal of Law & Public Policy* 503 (1985).

Wilkinson, J. Harvie, III. "The Drawbacks of Growth in the Federal Judiciary." 43 *Emory Law Journal* 1147 (1994).

______. *"Gay Rights and American Constitutionalism: What's a Constitution For?" 56* Duke Law Journal *545 (2006).*

______. "Is There a Distinctive Conservative Jurisprudence?" 73 *University of Colorado Law Review* 1383 (2002).

______. *One Nation Indivisible: How Ethnic Separatism Threatens America.* New York: Addison-Wesley, 1997.

______. "Our Structural Constitution." 104 Columbia Law Review *1687 (2004).*

______. "The Powellian Virtues in a Polarized Age." 49 *Washington & Lee Law Review* 271 (1992).

______. "The Rehnquist Court and the Search for Equal Justice." 34 *Tulsa Law Journal* 41 (1998).

______. "The Rehnquist Court at Twilight: The Lures and Perils of Split-the-Difference Jurisprudence." 58 *Stanford Law Review* 1969 (2006).

______. "The Role of Reason in the Rule of Law." 56 *University of Chicago Law Review* 779 (1989).

______. "Why Conservative Jurisprudence is Compassionate." 89 *Virginia Law Review* 753 (2003).

Wilson, James. *The Works of James Wilson.* Chicago: Callaghan, 1896.

Winter, Ralph K., Jr. "The Equal Protection Clause: Its Framers' Intent and the Contemporary Mind." 9 *Harvard Journal of Law & Public Policy* 47 (1986).

Wisdom, John Minor. "Random Remarks on the Role of Social Sciences in the Judicial Decision-Making Process in School Desegregation Cases." 39 *Law and Contemporary Problems* 134 (1975).

Wright, J. Skelly. "Beyond Discretionary Justice." 81 *Yale Law Journal* 575 (1972).

______. "The Courts and the Rulemaking Process: The Limits of Judicial Review." 59 *Cornell Law Review* 375 (1974).

______. "Judicial Review and the Equal Protection Clause." 15 *Harvard Civil Liberties-Civil Rights Law Review* 1 (1980).

______. "The Judicial Right and the Rhetoric of Restraint: A Defense of Judicial Activism in an Age of Conservative Judges." 14 *Hastings Constitutional Law Quarterly* 487 (1987).

______. "Professor Bickel, the Scholarly Tradition, and the Supreme Court." 84 *Harvard Law Review* 769 (1971).

______. "The Role of the Supreme Court in a Democratic Society—Judicial Activism or Restraint?" 54 *Cornell Law Review* 1 (1968).

Wyzanski, Charles E., Jr. *Whereas—A Judge's Premises: Essays in Judgment, Ethics, and the Law.* Boston: Little, Brown, 1965.

Appendix D

Time Chart of Members of the Supreme Court of the United States

Name	*Appointed by President*	*Term of Office*
Chief Justices:		
Jay, John	Washington	1789–1795
Rutledge, John	Washington	1795
Ellsworth, Oliver	Washington	1796–1800
Marshall, John	Adams, J.	1801–1835
Taney, Roger B.	Jackson	1836–1864
Chase, Salmon P.	Lincoln	1864–1873
Waite, Morrison R.	Grant	1874–1888
Fuller, Melville W.	Cleveland	1888–1910
White, Edward D.	Taft	1910–1921
Taft, William Howard	Harding	1921–1930
Hughes, Charles Evans	Hoover	1930–1941
Stone, Harlan Fiske	Roosevelt, F.	1941–1946
Vinson, Frederick M.	Truman	1946–1953
Warren, Earl	Eisenhower	1953–1969
Burger, Warren E.	Nixon	1969–1986
Rehnquist, William H.	Reagan	1986–2005
Roberts, John G.	Bush, G. W.	2005–
Associate Justices:		
Wilson, James	Washington	1789–1798
Rutledge, John	Washington	1790–1791
Cushing, William	Washington	1790–1810
Blair, John	Washington	1790–1796
Iredell, James	Washington	1790–1799

Johnson, Thomas	Washington	1792–1793
Paterson, William	Washington	1793–1806
Chase, Samuel	Washington	1796–1811
Washington, Bushrod	Adams, J.	1799–1829
Moore, Alfred	Adams, J.	1800–1804
Johnson, William	Jefferson	1804–1834
Livingston, Henry B.	Jefferson	1807–1823
Todd, Thomas	Jefferson	1807–1826
Duvall, Gabriel	Madison	1811–1835
Story, Joseph	Madison	1812–1845
Thompson, Smith	Monroe	1823–1843
Trimble, Robert	Adams, J.Q.	1826–1828
McLean, John	Jackson	1830–1861
Baldwin, Henry	Jackson	1830–1844
Wayne, James M.	Jackson	1835–1867
Barbour, Philip P.	Jackson	1836–1841
Catron, John	Van Buren	1837–1865
McKinley, John	Van Buren	1838–1852
Daniel, Peter V.	Van Buren	1842–1860
Nelson, Samuel	Tyler	1845–1872
Woodbury, Levi	Polk	1845–1851
Grier, Robert C.	Polk	1846–1870
Curtis, Benjamin R.	Fillmore	1851–1857
Cambell, John A.	Pierce	1853–1861
Clifford, Nathan	Buchanan	1858–1881
Swayne, Noah H.	Lincoln	1862–1881
Miller, Samuel F.	Lincoln	1862–1890
Davis, David	Lincoln	1862–1877
Field, Stephen J.	Lincoln	1863–1897
Strong, William	Grant	1870–1880
Bradley, Joseph P.	Grant	1870–1892
Hunt, Ward	Grant	1873–1882
Harlan, John M.	Hayes	1877–1911
Woods, William B.	Hayes	1881–1887
Matthews, Stanley	Garfield	1881–1889
Gray, Horace	Arthur	1882–1902
Blatchford, Samuel	Arthur	1882–1893
Lamar, Lucius Q.	Cleveland	1888–1893
Brewer, David J.	Harrison, B.	1890–1910
Brown, Henry B.	Harrison, B.	1891–1906
Shiras, George, Jr.	Harrison, B.	1892–1903

Jackson, Howell E.	Harrison, B.	1893–1895
White, Edward D.	Cleveland	1894–1910
Peckham, Rufus W.	Cleveland	1896–1909
McKenna, Joseph	McKinley	1898–1925
Holmes, Oliver Wendell	Roosevelt, T.	1902–1932
Day, William R.	Roosevelt, T.	1903–1922
Moody, William H.	Roosevelt, T.	1906–1910
Lurton, Horace H.	Taft	1910–1914
Hughes, Charles Evans	Taft	1910–1916
Van Devanter, Willis	Taft	1911–1937
Lamar, Joseph R.	Taft	1911–1916
Pitney, Mahlon	Taft	1912–1922
McReynolds, James C.	Wilson	1914–1941
Brandeis, Louis D.	Wilson	1916–1939
Clarke, John H.	Wilson	1916–1922
Sutherland, George	Harding	1921–1938
Butler, Pierce	Harding	1923–1939
Sanford, Edward T.	Harding	1923–1930
Stone, Harlan Fiske	Coolidge	1925–1941
Roberts, Owen J.	Hoover	1930–1945
Cardozo, Benjamin N.	Hoover	1932–1938
Black, Hugo L.	Roosevelt, F.	1937–1971
Reed, Stanley F.	Roosevelt, F.	1938–1957
Frankfurter, Felix	Roosevelt, F.	1939–1962
Douglas, William O.	Roosevelt, F.	1939–1975
Murphy, Frank	Roosevelt, F.	1940–1949
Byrnes, James F.	Roosevelt, F.	1941–1942
Jackson, Robert H.	Roosevelt, F.	1941–1954
Rutledge, Wiley B.	Roosevelt, F.	1943–1949
Burton, Harold H.	Truman	1945–1958
Clark, Thomas C.	Truman	1949–1967
Minton, Sherman	Truman	1949–1956
Harlan, John Marshall	Eisenhower	1955–1971
Brennan, William J., Jr.	Eisenhower	1956–1990
Whittaker, Charles E.	Eisenhower	1957–1962
Stewart, Potter	Eisenhower	1958–1981
White, Byron R.	Kennedy	1962–1993
Goldberg, Arthur J.	Kennedy	1962–1965
Fortas, Abe	Johnson, L.	1965–1969
Marshall, Thurgood	Johnson, L.	1967–1991
Blackmun, Harry A.	Nixon	1970–1994

Powell, Lewis F., Jr.	Nixon	1972–1987
Rehnquist, William H.	Nixon	1972–1986
Stevens, John Paul	Ford	1975–
O'Connor, Sandra Day	Reagan	1981–2006
Scalia, Antonin	Reagan	1986–
Kennedy, Anthony M.	Reagan	1988–
Souter, David H.	Bush, G. H. W.	1990–
Thomas, Clarence	Bush, G. H. W	1991–
Ginsburg, Ruth Bader	Clinton	1993–
Breyer, Stephen G.	Clinton	1994–
Alito, Samuel	Bush, G. W.	2006–

NOTE: The acceptance of the appointment and commission by the appointee, as evidenced by the taking of the prescribed oaths, is here implied; otherwise the individual is not carried on this list of the members of the Court. Examples: Robert H. Harrison is not carried, as a letter from President Washington of February 9, 1790 states that Harrison declined to serve. Neither is Edwin M. Stanton, who died before he could take the necessary steps toward becoming a member of the Court. Chief Justice Rutledge is included because he took his oaths, presided over the August Term of 1795, and his name appears on two opinions of the Court for that term. This material was adapted from a chart prepared by the Marshal of the Supreme Court of the United States.

About the Editor

David M. O'Brien is the Leone Reaves and George W. Spicer Professor at the University of Virginia. Prior to teaching at the University of Virginia, he taught at the University of California, Santa Barbara, and the University of Puget Sound, where he was chairman of the Department of Politics. He served as a research associate in the Office of the Administrative Assistant to the Chief Justice and, in 1982–1983, as a judicial fellow at the Supreme Court. He has also been a visiting fellow at the Russell Sage Foundation (1981–1982); a Fulbright lecturer in constitutional studies at Oxford University, Oxford, England (1987–1988); a Fulbright researcher in Japan (1993–1994); held the Fulbright Chair for Senior Scholars at the University of Bologna in Italy (1999); and was a visiting professor at Florida International University (2002) and at the Institut d'Etudes Politique, Université Lumière-Lyon II in Lyon, France (2006).

Among his many books are *Storm Center: The Supreme Court in American Politics* (8th ed., 2008), which won the American Bar Association's Silver Gavel Award; *Constitutional Law and Politics*, 2 vols. (7th ed., 2008); *Animal Sacrifice and Religious Freedom:* Church of the Lukumi Babalu Aye v. City of Hialeah (2004); *To Dream of Dreams: Religious Freedom and Constitutional Politics in Postwar Japan* (1996); *Supreme Court Watch,* published annually since 1991; *Judicial Roulette* (1988); *What Process Is Due? Courts and Science Policy Disputes* (1987); *The Public's Right to Know: The First Amendment and the Supreme Court* (1981); and *Privacy, Law, and Public Policy* (1979). He has also coauthored *Courts and Judicial Policymaking* (2008) and *Abortion and American Politics* (1993), and has edited or coedited several books, including *The Lanahan Readings on Civil Rights and Civil Liberties* (2nd ed., 2004) and *Judicial Independence in the Age of Democracy: Critical Perspectives from Around the World* (2001).